Immigrants, and Slaves

Racial and Ethnic Groups in America

George Henderson
Thompson Olasiji

University Press of America, Inc.
Lanham • New York • London

Copyright© 1995 by
George Henderson
University Press of America,® Inc.
4720 Boston Way
Lanham, Maryland 20706

3 Henrietta Street
London, WC2E 8LU England

Library of Congress Cataloging-in-Publication Data

Henderson, George
Migrants, immigrants, and slaves : racial and ethnic groups in
America / George Henderson and Thompson Olasiji.
p.   cm.
Includes bibliographical references and index.
1. Ethnology--United States.   2. United States--Ethnic relations.
3. United States--Race relations.   I. Olasiji, Thompson Dale ,

II. Title.
0184.AlH458   1994

305.8 ' 00973--dc20   94-37968 CIP

ISBN 0-8191-9738-6 (pbk.: alk paper)

⊖™The paper used in this publication meets the minimum
requirements of American National Standard for Information
Sciences—Permanence of Paper for Printed Library Materials,
ANSI Z39.48–1984.

To the people whose ancestors
helped create the United States of America.

Contents

Illustrations

Preface

From the outset of colonialization, America was a haven for the persecuted, the ambitious, and the homeless peoples of the world. "The New Colossus," a poem by Emma Lazarus inscribed on a tablet in the pedestal of the Statue of Liberty, captures the essence of the United States of America. It promises freedom and justice for all. As the tired, poor, and huddled masses have come to this country and contributed to its development, it has become clear to astute observers that we are a nation of immigrants and ethnic minority groups.

Because of intermarriage, most Americans have multiple ethnic identities. Some persons of mixed lineage prefer to assume culturally nondescript identities. That is, they have become "white people" or "Americans" in order to somehow deflect from themselves any connection with their ancestors. The task of tracing families has become too taxing or too insignificant. Yet the reality of ethnicity is pervasive: immigrant patterns of community relationships and economic opportunities continue to revolve around one's ethnicity.

At some time in their history, all ethnic groups in the United States have been immigrants and the underclass. Also, at different times, all ethnic groups have been both the oppressed and the oppressors. Therefore the information presented in this book highlights the best and worst aspects of our human relationships. This is not done to fix blame or to demean groups. Instead, it is done to place the United States within a human relations context.

It is not unusual to uncover documentation of individuals oppressing members of other ethnic groups without really knowing who or what they are rejecting. When such oppression occurs, the oppressors almost always believe they are right. Yet, the socioeconomic rise and fall of ethnic groups is neither predestined nor irreversible. Without knowing the beliefs and achievements of other groups, people cannot know what they have in common with each other. Furthermore, it stands to reason that if they do not know the histories of other ethnic groups, they cannot fully appreciate their own group's cultural contributions.

During the early years of America, a rigid *culture curtain* kept religious and ethnic groups apart. The twentieth-century ecumenical movements did much to remove prejudices in the area of religion, but a culture curtain still blocks ethnic group members' visions, causing many people to cling to outmoded, unscientific definitions of race and ethnicity. This is not to suggest that religious problems such as anti-Semitism and anti-Catholicism are no longer problems. They are. However, ethnic minority groups are discriminated against on both counts: racial and religious.

Through diversity, America has grown strong as a nation. Although all segments of the population share certain common elements in life patterns and basic beliefs, there are significant differences in the attitudes, interests, goals, and dialects that characterize ethnic groups. Respect for cultural differences—and appreciation for similarities—are the essence of our nation's democratic principles.

In order to provide readers with an appreciation for various ethnic groups, we discuss immigration patterns and cite examples of cultural contributions made to America by more than fifty ethnic groups. We do not present an exhaustive accounting of the ethnic groups discussed. Instead, it is our intention to whet the readers' appetite for additional information. This book is written for introductory American history, ethnic studies, and sociology courses. For most readers, *Migrants, Immigrants, and Slaves* will be a cross-cultural awakening; for others, it will be a confirmation of what they already know about their own group's historical importance. For all readers, we want the book to be a worthwhile journey.

We have drawn materials from several areas in the humanities and the social sciences in order to give readers a balanced view of forces affecting American ethnic groups. Individuals who wish to specialize in a particular ethnic group can pursue advanced undergraduate and graduate courses in history, ethnic studies, and sociology.

Perhaps one day the United States will be one nation, with liberty and justice for all. Until then, this book is a reminder of how far Americans have come toward achieving that goal—and how much farther they must go. Reading about change is not enough. More people must become change agents dedicated to finishing the creation of a United States of America.

We are indebted to Mary Biddick, Mona Knight, Shirley Marshall, and Maria Wilson, whose typing and moral support moved the ideas from assorted pages to a cohesive manuscript.

George Henderson
Thompson Olasiji

Chapter 1

No Place Like Home

Ethnicity and race are important aspects of American life because the peoples of the United States have been drawn from all parts of the world. Consequently, it is a nation of diverse religious and political groups. In any analysis of ethnic groups, it is important to remember that all but a few Americans are descendants of immigrants. During the first great wave of immigration (1606 to 1640), most of the newcomers came from Great Britain, Ireland, Germany, and Scandinavia to found the colonies of Massachusetts, New Hampshire, Connecticut, Rhode Island, Virginia, Maryland, and New York. The second wave of immigrants (1660 to 1713) was spearheaded by people who came mainly from eastern and southern Europe. Except Georgia, all of the other thirteen colonies were founded during that period. The Atlantic Coast was divided into New France, New England, New Netherland, New Sweden, and New Spain. In 1655, Dutch settlers conquered New Sweden; English settlers took New Amsterdam (New York) from the Dutch in 1664. The remainder of seventeenth-century American history is dominated by the struggle between Great Britain and France for control of the New World.

In the Beginning

Contrary to popular belief, America was not an accident that happened to various ethnic groups. Instead, it was an executed plan by the many peoples who sought to become part of a new concept and a new country. The largest number of early settlers came from England. And they came for three basic reasons—economic opportunity, political participation, and religious freedom. Some of the immigrants came to escape jail, some to escape poverty, some to avoid persecution, and some to reform the "Indians" and build the Kingdom of God. Most of them came to seek greater autonomy. Each immigrant brought aspects of his or her native country's culture to the New World. But it would be a grave mistake to lump all of the immigrants from one country into a single type. They were as different as the towns and villages from which they came. Most of the early colonial immigrants, however, were primarily Protestants who adhered to seventeenth-century political values spawned by the Puritan Revolution and the eighteenth-century teachings of Adam Smith.

It is important to make a clear distinction between the terms *immigration*, *emigration*, *migration*, and *internal migration*. Immigration means the entry of people from other lands into a country deemed to be more promising. Emigration means the departure of people from their homeland to take up residence in a new dwelling place: entering a new country is immigration; departing from an old country is emigration. The permanent movement of people across national borders is defined as migration. Internal migration describes the movement of people within a specific nation, for example the Trail of Tears movement of American Indians in the 1800s.

The *push-pull hypothesis* proposes that people will voluntarily vacate old premises and seek new ones when conditions are no longer comfortable or tolerable, or when conditions in another country offer more favorable circumstances for an improved standard of living. According to Juan Gonzales (1990), immigration to America reveals both of the aforementioned push and pull factors. The push factors include economic conditions, political conditions, social conditions, overpopulation, and natural disasters. The most common natural disasters are floods, droughts, and earthquakes. Human-made disasters include such things as radiation contamination of about a thousand people near Erwin, Tennessee, on August 7, 1979.

Other push factors that influence people to emigrate are economic downtrends that cause widespread poverty, business failures that result in high unemployment, and the specter of runaway inflation. Political push factors include such unsettling events as rebellion, revolution, war, and seizure of the government—all of which reflect grave instability in a society. Social conditions that can prompt emigration center on lack of social harmony and religious persecution. Another push factor for people to leave their home country is the practice of arranged marriages. Young people often leave parental homes that deny them the decision of a mate choice. They sometimes seek freedom in other countries where such a constraint is not imposed (Seller, 1977). Overpopulation is another push factor that gives impetus to emigration.

Conversely, the pull factors include availability of jobs at higher pay scales, religious and political freedom, social stability, and respite from population pressures. Active recruitment of immigrants was also a positive factor in the early history of immigration in the United States. There were people, particularly shipowners, in America who very early recognized the economic value of immigrants. American shipowners would send abroad bulky cargoes of raw material. On the return trip finished products did not take up as much space, and the saved space was loaded with immigrants whose passage fees added to the profits of the ocean vessels. Railroad companies were also eager to facilitate immigration because cheap labor was needed to perform the arduous task of laying track—work that was seldom sought by native-born Americans. The states were zealous in their efforts to support immigration because increased population added to their representation in Congress. Additional people increased the value of land and brought new skills to the labor market which in turn swelled state coffers.

Of all the reasons cited, however, increased population in America was mainly the result of the continuous search for new labor sources. Initially, this void was filled by indentured servants from England. Later, it was filled by the creation of the slave trade, the Chinese ("coolie") trade, and, in more recent times, the recruitment of contract laborers from Mexico. An influx of millions of new workers serves two purposes: It creates an oversupply of labor and thus cheapens wages for the industrial complex. It further creates a large supply of consumers who purchase goods that become more scarce and expensive as greater numbers of people seek to buy them.

In the first half of the nineteenth century, the vast and fertile Mississippi Valley, Oregon, and the Southwest, including California and Texas, were added to the available land area. "American letters" extolling the virtues and vigor of the New World were like a seductive siren song to people who yearned for the golden opportunities and glory depicted by friends who had already made the leap of faith to the New World. The emigration to America took place in a way that made the English language and English institutions culturally dominant. Neither the early Germans nor the French Huguenots set up separate colonies. Instead, they mingled with the British newcomers and adopted their language and values. Wealthy immigrants imitated

British intellectual and cultural lifestyles.

Two main propelling forces were used to get British and other European immigrants across the seas to the New World. The first moving force was *chartered trading companies* that were organized primarily for profit. The most successful British trading companies were the London Company, the Plymouth Company, and the Massachusetts Bay Company. These companies were granted charters by kings to distribute land, coin money, operate mines, and defend their colonies. The London Company founded Virginia; the Plymouth Company and its successor, the Council for New England, founded settlements in Massachusetts, New Hampshire, and Maine. The most disadvantaged members of European societies were the ones most likely to participate in labor immigration. Surges of immigration arose spontaneously out of the sheer existence of worldwide economic inequalities (Portes & Rumbaut, 1990). But mass labor displacements do not occur exclusively through workers' comparison of economic situations. To the contrary, emigration requires an organized and concerted effort to direct people to particular countries.

The second prime mover of colonization was the *proprietary grant*. A proprietor was a man who belonged to the gentry or nobility. Each proprietor was given a tract of land in America the same way other people were given an estate at home. English law decreed that all land not otherwise held belonged to the king or royalty, and most of America came under the rule.

The journey to the New World was in itself a hardship. Passage was a financial drain on most immigrants' resources. Once aboard the ship the travelers had to endure weeks or months of deplorable living conditions. The ships were overcrowded and unsanitary, and diseases took heavy tolls. On some voyages, fewer than 10 percent of the original passengers arrived safely. Most passengers were treated like animals—they had too little food, inadequate space, and very limited medical care. The height between decks seldom exceeded five feet and sometimes the passengers slept two to three in a bunk, regardless of their gender or marital status. A typical passenger had an area of two feet by six feet below deck space to call his or her own. On stormy days passengers were confined below deck where natural light and adequate ventilation were usually nonexistent. Because of inadequate diet and insufficient food supplies, a large number of passengers starved to death.

The ocean crossing involved a startling reversal of old roles and a dramatic shift of attitudes. Qualities that had been respected in "good" people were not conducive to success on the transition voyage. Status, respect, obedience, and neighborliness were not valued by the masses that struggled for space on the high seas. Generally, people who put aside old courtesies, people who pushed and took care of themselves, were the ones who survived. Gradually, most immigrants acted as individuals—each for himself or herself (Handlin, 1973). One-third of the early immigrants were indentured servants, people who agreed to work in America for three to seven years to pay for their passage.

Initially, most ethnic groups established their own churches and social clubs and married within their own groups. In most instances, it was the second and subsequent generations that gradually adopted "American ways," which meant giving up ethnic isolation. Not all ethnic groups' experiences as immigrants were similar. As will be discussed in greater detail in later chapters, some groups suffered more than others. But *all* groups suffered.

The uniqueness of the United States is not the presence of its ethnic groups but the large number of ethnic groups that helped to create it. No other nation has been established with as many ethnic groups. Although the seventeenth-century immigrants were largely British Protestants, large waves of other ethnic groups also immigrated to the New World after the 1680s. A brief review of history reveals that English settlers were not the first to colonize America. Dutch, Spanish, and French explorers had claimed large portions of the New World long before the English settlers arrived. Mongolian ancestors of the people Columbus called *Indians* settled the country long before Europeans came.

The English settlers succeeded where their European predecessors had failed. They made the colonies economically profitable. Not even Charles II's restoration, which discouraged English citizens from leaving home, could stop emigration from England to America. Unlike Spanish and French monarchs who closely ruled their overseas colonies and required absolute allegiance to the Roman Catholic Church, England seldom interfered with its colonies except to regulate trade. During the early years of colonization, this illusion of complete freedom played an important role in encouraging various ethnic groups to settle in the English colonies.

From the beginning, immigrants were treated as distinct ethnic minority groups. By common definition, a minority group usually has a record of long-term discrimination which includes being segregated, avoided, and rejected by the empowered members of society. Acts of discrimination and accepted patterns of segregation against new immigrants usually are legalized by the governing bodies of the host country. In *Minorities in the New World: Six Case Studies*, Charles Wagley and Marvin Harris (1958) identified five key characteristics that determine minority group status: the group must have a history of unjust and unequal treatment; the group must have prominent physical or cultural characteristics that are recognizable; group membership must have been involuntary; some group members must have experienced in-group marriage; and the group must be aware of its minority status in relationship to the dominant majority. All American immigrant groups fulfill the requirements for minority group status.

Because of their many differences, very soon after their arrival in this country, new immigrants were the butt of negative treatment and prejudicial attitudes. This resulted in the development of erroneous stereotypes that assured their unequal treatment. The experience of Chinese immigrants in California is an example of such treatment. Shortly after the arrival of Chinese immigrants, disgruntled groups of unemployed white workers rioted in San Francisco and committed illegal acts, including violence, against the unwary Chinese. Reactionary legislatures joined in the vehemence and passed laws to prohibit the immigration of Chinese people. The Chinese Exclusion Act of 1882 was one of those laws. The symbol of the Statue of Liberty was tarnished in the eyes of hapless Chinese victims who were guilty only of trying to get work to provide their daily bread.

All societies that have subjugated immigrants have devised ways to emphasize ethnic-group differences rather than extol their similarities. Majority group leaders tend to embrace social philosophies that justify their bigoted actions. In some instances, they attempt to make certain that particular ethnic groups are treated as subhumans. For example, African slaves brought to America were bought and sold like bales of cotton or any other commodity. This is a glaring example of persecution by prejudice. Gunnar Myrdal (1944) referred to the process of discrimination against minorities on the basis of cultural differences as a pattern of *cumulative causation*, which connotes a vicious circle of prejudice and discrimination. Prejudicial attitudes lead to discrimination and discrimination in turn supports prejudicial attitudes. Thus, false prophecies of racial or ethnic group superiority and inferiority are fulfilled.

To make distinctions among people on the basis of their skin color, facial features, color and texture of hair, body build and body size, and gender differences is to condemn them on the basis of factors over which they usually have little or no control. When people immigrate to a country, it is most often a voluntary, conscious decision but their ethnicity is not voluntary. To the contrary, ethnicity is an accident of birth and a capricious criterion for either acceptance or rejection. Yet, in the final analysis, it is true that humankind has yet to achieve a state where accident of birth does not have profound consequences on one's life chances. The early immigrants, as well as those who have recently come to the United States, were very soon made aware of ethnic group impediments they faced in pursuit of the American dream. Joe Feagin (1984) proclaimed that imbalance of privileges in a society shapes what happens to a group in the cultural, marital, identificational, and other adaptive dimensions.

The Ominous Beginning

On June 21, 1608, the Reverend Robert Hunt held the first Protestant service in America. Those historic rites were performed in Jamestown, Virginia, under part of a ship's sail hung between the trees, with a pulpit made of a bar of wood, and worshipers seated on unhewn logs. In 1634, led by Lord Baltimore, the first Catholics to settle in the original thirteen colonies came to Maryland. In 1654, Jacob Barsimon, one of the first Jews to settle in America, arrived in New Amsterdam. Ironically, along with those settlers, who came in search of religious freedom, also came indentured servants and slaves. Thus began the contradictory social conditions of America: religious freedom and human bondage.

In the 1660s, the *mercantile theory* became dominant in Europe. It was based on the belief that the wealth of nations resided in their citizens and their production of goods. Therefore a country's loss of population meant a loss of wealth. The Royal African Slave Company was granted a monopoly from Charles II in 1662, and it imported slaves to the English colonies to lessen the drain of English citizens. Not all of the colonies wanted slaves as substitutes for white labor. William Penn, for example, did remarkably well recruiting white settlers. He printed hundreds of pamphlets in English, Dutch, French, and German describing the attractions of his new colony: abundant game and wood supplies, religious and political freedom, universal male suffrage, and no compulsory military service.

Although most of the early settlers came to America in search of religious, economic, and political freedom, they tried to deny similar freedoms to individuals of other persuasions. During the colonial period, at one time or another, the religious rights of every group—including Anglicans, Baptists, Catholics, Lutherans, Jews, Moravians, Presbyterians, Quakers, Deists, and atheists—were denied. That was the beginning of a pattern in which Americans would seek freedom *from* people instead of freedom to *be with people*. But soon it became clear to egalitarian-oriented settlers that the early Americans had to learn to live together in order to keep from dying separately. Survival on the frontier required cooperation rather than deadly confrontation. Only after concerned colony leaders warned that the act of denying religious and political freedom for some people actually threatened the precarious existence of all members in a colony did the state of America's human relations come into sharper public focus.

The gravest political threat was undoubtedly the increasing resentment and hostility between groups that was fueled by specific benefits for some people (jobs, social status, and so forth) at the expense of others. The result of such behavior was increased consciousness of ethnic group membership; increased divisiveness on the basis of race, religion, and national origin; and resentment by the underclass of the favored groups. The behavior of the colonists gave little clue that America would someday become the first nation in history to commit itself to the principles of democracy on a national scale. Yet a nation was indeed emerging that would dedicate itself to living the Old Testament message later inscribed on the Liberty Bell: "Proclaim liberty throughout all the land unto all the inhabitants thereof."

The majority of the early non-English immigrants were European Protestants who were compatible with English Protestants. The Scotch-Irish were the largest non-English group, and Germans were the second largest. The third largest group was comprised mainly of French Huguenots—Protestants evicted from France in 1685 when the revocation of the Edict of Nantes withdrew their right to worship in France. Dutch and Swedish people rounded out the early immigrants. That residents in the American colonies had preferences for certain ethnic groups was vividly seen in 1698, when South Carolina passed an act giving bounties to new residents but exempted Scotch-Irish and Roman Catholics from receiving the reward. Maryland temporarily suspended the importation of Scotch-Irish indentured servants, and Virginia prohibited the importation of more than twenty Scotch-Irish indentured servants at any one time. In 1729, Pennsylvania placed a 20-shilling duty on each imported servant. In all of the colonies, Indians and Africans were accorded the lowest social status.

From the beginning of nationhood it was evident that individual and group differences accentuated during the early years would plague the spirit, if not the letter, of the principles of the American Constitution. Women, Indians, and African Americans were denied political rights later made explicit in the Bill of Rights, and there were violent conflicts between religious and nationality groups. Churches and synagogues were burned; ethnic group individuals were beaten and sometimes killed; and certain ethnic groups were discriminated against merely because they were "different." There were numerous instances when "old" immigrants discriminated against new arrivals. For example, riots broke out against newcomer Irish in Boston, New York, and Philadelphia in 1864. Most of the "old timers" who participated in the riots ignored the fact that their parents were also immigrants. Out of this conflict came a new social ethos of cultural rejection.

America has always been the favorite place of refuge for political rebels and religious nonconformists. It has also been the foremost destination for socially and economically underprivileged citizens of Old World countries. Indeed, from its inception, to countless people, America has been symbolic of utopia and the Promised Land rolled into one vast landscape. Most eighteenth-century immigrant guidebooks distributed throughout European countries heaped praise on America as a place to begin a new life.

It was not until the nineteenth century that the exodus from Europe to America reached its peak. The American population grew from five million to fifty million between 1800 and 1880. People spread so rapidly across the land that by 1890 the federal government announced that the frontier was no more (Seller, 1977). Andrew Carnegie and John D. Rockefeller had launched their careers by 1880. And by then the United States was the world's largest producer of iron and steel. The Pittsburgh sky was cloudy with the smoke of industry at work.

Patterns of Immigration

The immigration patterns of the first half of the nineteenth century became clear as each successive wave of immigrants arrived. When they came to America, unskilled farmers and other immigrants moved from the seaboard as soon as possible in order to get land in areas behind the frontier. During the transition, the newly emerging towns and cities took on distinctive ethnic group characteristics. The frontier was settled by the end of the nineteenth century, and most European countries had a sizeable number of representatives in the newer states. (See Figure 1.1.) Once the frontier was settled, there was little land left in America "just for the taking." Because of this, new immigrants from eastern Europe, Asia, Latin America, and the Caribbean Islands were channeled into large cities where cheap, unskilled labor was needed. Consequently, cities such as Boston, Chicago, New York, and Philadelphia became home for most of the newest immigrants.

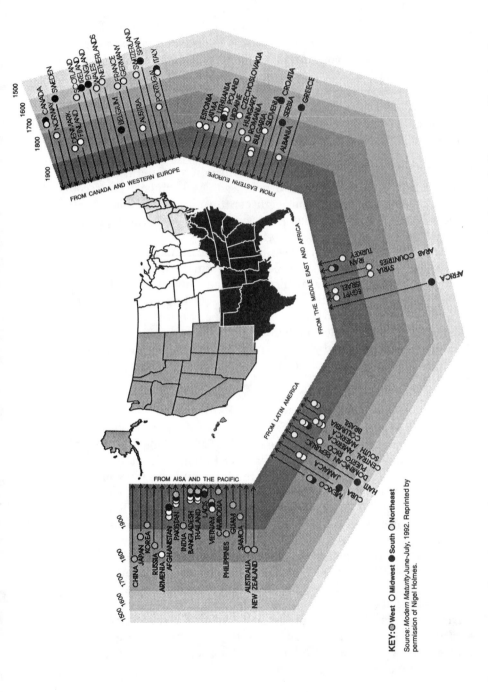

Figure 1.1. Post Indigenous Immigration to the Present United States Beginning with the Spanish Settlement of St. Augustine, Florida, in the 16th Century.

KEY: ◉ West ○ Midwest ● South ◎ Northeast

Source: *Modern Maturity* June–July, 1992. Reprinted by permission of Nigel Holmes.

As noted earlier, long before large numbers of Europeans came to America, small groups of ethnic peoples lived in isolated parts of the country. On the East Coast, English pioneers settled in Maryland; Dutch were in New York; and Swedes were in New Jersey. Quakers, Huguenots, English and French Catholics, Scotch-Irish Presbyterians, and Dutch Jews were prominent among the early New World immigrants. The last of those groups consisted of numerous German religious sects comprised of Mennonites, Amish, and Moravians. Also, famines and economic depressions drove thousands of Irish, Poles, Italians, Lithuanians, Latvians, Hungarians, Greeks, Russians, and other immigrants to America.

As the settlers spread from the original English colonies, they pushed the Indians farther west. A large number of Acadians (English who assisted French Canadians during the French and English conflict) fled from Canada to the Gulf Coast in 1755. After they settled in America, their Gulf Coast neighbors slurred the name *Acadian* to fit the colloquial pronunciation *Cajun*. Also during this period, English and Scotch-Irish were among the early settlers who moved westward from the Carolinas into Alabama, Mississippi, and Louisiana. In 1783, the peace treaty that ended the Revolutionary War was signed in Paris. The treaty called for a boundary line below the thirteen original states and above Florida and the Island of New Orleans, which was owned by Spain, and extended to the remainder of the territory west of the Mississippi which belonged to France. That territorial division lasted until New Orleans was ceded to the French by the Spanish in 1803. Also in 1803, President Thomas Jefferson bought Louisiana from France. With the Louisiana Purchase, which included a part of Florida, the United States incorporated a large mixture of French and Spanish people.

Prior to the Revolutionary War, a trickle of pioneers had forged their way westward beyond the Allegheny Mountains. After the war, the small trickle became a flood, especially when the Erie Canal was opened in 1825. Among the new immigrants were Scandinavians who settled in Wisconsin and Minnesota. They made this the dairy region of the United States. Danish coffeecake and Wisconsin cheese are illustrations of the impact those immigrants had on the United States. Relatedly, as Poles, Czechs, and Ukrainians settled in Chicago, Detroit, Gary, St. Louis, and other cities, they brought with them native foods such as *kielbasa* and *golobki*.

The first Western trails, known as traces, were made by Indians. And it was through treaties with Indians that white settlers were able to use the trails safely. The Oregon Trail, one of the most famous routes west, split into two forks in what is now Idaho: one fork went to Oregon and the other one went to California. The Mormon Trail closely paralleled the Oregon Trail until it diverged south to Salt Lake City. When the railroads came, more immigrants than ever before moved across the vast American landscape. Among this wave were the Ukrainians who planted a strain of wheat that survived the prairie climate.

President Thomas Jefferson sent Meriwether Lewis and William Clark to explore the Northwest in 1804 to see if a link by water existed between the Columbia River and Missouri River. A French trapper named Toussaint Charbonneau and his wife, Sacajawea, a Shoshone Indian, were hired to guide the expedition. Sacajawea served as the interpreter and Indian customs adviser. After the expedition, several of the men returned to the Missouri River area and established a trading company. Focal points for the trappers to meet, trade their catch, and celebrate were scattered along the rivers, mainly the Yellowstone, Wind, and Snake. Countless trappers would make their way to Jackson's Hole, Brown's Hole, Odene's Hole, and Pierre's Hole.

By 1860, large cattle ranches were established in Montana, Wyoming, and the Dakotas. The cattle were driven to the railhead in Independence, Missouri, and later to Dodge City, Kansas. Chinese and Mexican cooks were frequently employed by individuals who drove cattle to the railhead. Again using food as an example of how the United States became a mixture of immigrant contributions, we note that Mexican cooks took their cuisine north of the Rio Grande. *Tortillas, chili con carne, tamales*, and other Mexican foods ultimately made their way into American restaurants.

The first Europeans to establish permanent residences on the Pacific Coast were traders and sailors. At the end of the Mexican War, John Sutter and James Marshall formed a partnership to start a sawmill north of Sutter's Fort on the south fork of the American River in California. In 1848, after the mill was built, Marshall discovered bright brass-colored particles about the size of wheat grains. The grains turned out to be gold, and the discovery changed forever the demography of the Pacific Coast. When the news of gold spread throughout the United States, thousands of people rushed to the region to find their fortune. Gold was also discovered along the Sierra Nevada. In 1851, Count Agoston Haraszthy, a Hungarian, planted a grape vineyard in Sonoma County, California. As it turned out, fruit farms, not gold, became the major industry in California.

Unrestricted immigration ended after World War I. Only after the policy of restricted immigration was enacted did statisticians begin calculating the tremendous influx of immigrants during the period of unrestricted immigration. The data were mind-boggling: During the period of 1814 to 1914, 5.5 million immigrants came from Germany, 4.5 million from Italy, 4.5 million from Ireland, 4 million from Austria-Hungary, almost 4 million from Russia and Poland, 2 million from Scandinavia, and 500,000 from Great Britain.

Sojourners

Large numbers of immigrants came to America as sojourners—people who did not plan to settle permanently. Their motives differed greatly from ethnic peoples who were forced to sever ties with a home country. Most immigrants were sojourners—temporary residents in a strange land, who set out to earn a sizable amount of money and then return to their homeland. To accomplish their mission, they selected occupations that did not tie them to a territory for long assignments. Instead, they tended to select occupations that allowed them to be mobile and they worked jobs that were easily liquidated or transportable such as traders, peddlers, truck farmers, barbers, shoemakers, jewelers, restaurant owners, launderers, and tailors. Relatedly, sojourners were willing to endure short-term deprivation to achieve the long-term goal of returning to their homelands. Thus they worked excessively long hours and spent little money on consumption. They came to save money or to send some of it home, not to spend it.

Because they planned to return home, the sojourners had little motivation to develop intimate, lasting relationships with host country people. Ethnic and regional associations were maintained within enclaves that resisted marriage to non-ethnic group people, perpetuated residential self-segregation, established native language and cultural schools for children, encouraged distinctive religion and family institutions, and insulated enclave members against local politics except those that directly affected their group members. The communal solidarity of enclaves was characterized by common family, dialect, sect, and religion.

In some ethnic groups, family members staffed businesses. For example, Chinese family restaurants used unpaid family labor. If wage labor was needed, members of the extended family or regional associates were hired for wages lower than the market standard. Employees worked long hours for no income or minimum wages, and they were extremely loyal to the enterprise owners. In return, the workers became partners in the business or received assistance in starting their own businesses. Few sojourners in urban areas were members of labor guilds or unions. The net result was ethnic groups carving out niches for themselves in business and industry. For example, Jews were prominent in clothing manufacturing and retail outlets; Japanese in fruit and vegetable growing and wholesale; and Chinese in restaurants and laundries. This kind of industriousness often led to antagonism and conflict when sojourners competed with permanent residents. Competition between Japanese and white farmers was described in a report prepared for the California legislature of 1919:

> The working and living conditions of the Japanese farmer and farm laborer make successful competition by American farmers almost impossible. The Japanese farmers and every member in the family, physically able to do so, including the wife and little children, work in the field long hours, practically from daylight to dark, on Sunday and holidays, and, in the majority of cases, live in shacks or under conditions far below the standards required and desired by Americans . . . . American farmers cannot successfully compete with Japanese farmers if the Americans adhere to the American principles so universally approved in America, including clean and wholesome living quarters, reasonable working hours, the usual Sunday rest and holiday recreation and, above all, refraining from working the women and children in the fields. (State Board of Control of California, 1922, pp. 116–117)

Some sojourners earned enough money to return to their homeland as economic successes; most of them did not, however. The dream to return home was sometimes not feasible because of conditions that made the sojourners' return a situation of imminent danger—politically, economically, or religiously. Yet others returned to their homeland only to immigrate back to the United States where life was economically better for them. Those who remained in America kept love for their homeland alive by occasional visits and sending funds to family members. This kind of sojourner often became "the person who comes today and stays tomorrow. He is, so to speak, the potential wanderer: although he has not moved on, he has not quite overcome the freedom of coming and going" (Wolff, 1950, p. 408).

Consequences of Urbanization

By the end of the nineteenth century, rural immigrants could be divided into two groups: those who lived in the open country and those who lived in villages. Farmers who lived on and produced from the land made up the bulk of the open-country group. Also included in this category were nonfarming people—ministers, livestock truckers, creamery operators, and so forth—whose social and business associations were with farmers and village residents. Villagers provided the necessary business and service institutions for the surrounding farms. Even though some villages had small manufacturing plants, their major source of wealth could be traced to an interdependent relationship with the farming periphery. There were few completely independent communities.

Romantic conceptualizations assign different values to rural and urban communities. Some writers paint idyllic pictures of rural life. "Rural" conjured up the smell of meadows, herds of cattle, flocks of sheep, pigs, fields of crops, country stores, men in dirty overalls, and women in clean gingham housedresses. Farm families were the prototype of sturdy, independent people in a natural environment. Conversely, urban life was viewed as unnatural and indeed bad. Of course, there were critics of rural life too. For them, the city was the center of civilization: the epitome of progress and the good life. Unlike Jean-Jacques Rousseau who described rural people as "noble savages," critics of rural life labeled them "hicks" and "country bumpkins" who did not share in the richness of culture found in urban areas. The farmer therefore was viewed as a person of much brawn but little brain or cultural refinement. Somewhere between the two extremes is a more accurate picture of the rural and urban immigrants.

In terms of lifestyles, there was considerable similarity between urban and rural immigrants in the nineteenth and twentieth centuries. Both shared and were influenced by the products of urbanization. The extension of commercial farming based on profit, along with the introduction of improved machinery, greatly influenced the social organization of rural communities. The mechanization and commercialization of agriculture ended the separation of rural and urban cultures.

Before the introduction of rapid transportation and mass communication, along with other intrusions of urban culture into rural communities, many small towns and villages were isolated ethnic group enclaves very much like Washington Irving's Sleepy Hollow. Human contact for the most part was face-to-face. There was an overriding sense of independence on the one hand, and rural solidarity on the other. The range of interaction was restricted mostly to members of one's own ethnic group or other residents of the community. This resulted in community efforts to maintain the status quo and concurrently prejudice against outsiders, new ideas and practices. Contact with the outside world was slow coming but once established through newspapers, schools, and churches it altered forever the uniqueness of American ethnic groups in rural communities. But neither urbanization nor mechanization could completely eradicate poverty, a common condition in urban and rural communities.

In the nineteenth and twentieth centuries, the central cities and rural areas shared the distinction of having the highest proportions of males fourteen years and over in the labor force, and also the highest unemployment rates. Moving from the farm to the central city merely changed the location of unemployment. Although they usually migrated to urban communities in hopes of improving their economic condition, many rural people returned to their rural place of origin not because they had saved enough money to buy a small farm or send for family members but because they were broke.

In a strict sense, poverty was the same no matter where it was found. Rural and urban immigrants had many traits in common, including poor health and low levels of educational and occupational achievements. Upon closer analysis, rural poverty was different from urban poverty in two ways. Rural poverty was greater proportionately and it tended to be hidden because it was not near main thoroughfares. Whether urban or rural, poverty throughout history has been characterized by conditions of *not enough*—not enough money, food, adequate housing, health care facilities, or hope. Generally, when affluent people go without soap, hot water, lights, heat, food, and medicine, it is because they have no choice. Therein lies the major difference between the poor and the affluent. The poor are controlled by the economic system and the affluent control it. All of the ethnic groups described in this book have both kinds of immigrant ancestors.

Immigrants who lived in urban poverty were much more visible than the rural poor. Dilapidated buildings, garbage-strewn alleys, and rats were all too often the dominant characteristics of urban slums. These conditions tended to blur the memory of clean, well-kept buildings which also characterized urban poor neighborhoods. While it is difficult to change the negative image of the urban slum, it is almost impossible to erase the idyllic picture of rural poverty. Tourists riding through the countryside were likely to define the blight they saw as being "quaint" or "picturesque" or "Americana."

Migrant workers in American history are a composite of all poverty-stricken Americans. They are people of many ethnic groups. More important than their diverse cultures are their common conditions of poverty. For example, migrant workers moved through the citrus groves of Florida and California, stooped over the beans and tomatoes in Texas, picked cherries and blueberries in Michigan, hoed sugar beets in western Kansas, and crawled through the potato fields of Idaho and Maine. Life for them was seasonal: a day in one place, a week in another. They slept in dilapidated structures that almost always lacked adequate heat, refrigeration, and sanitary facilities. In addition, they walked and played on garbage strewn grounds infested with internal parasites, and they drank polluted water.

Because of clashing cultural patterns, the personal problems of rural people who migrated to cities often multiplied. Unlike established city residents who tended to be *object oriented*, the rural immigrants were largely *people oriented*. City dwellers were collectors of things but seldom people, while the newcomers from rural areas were constantly seeking out "home folks" to visit. For these and other reasons, the immigrants from rural areas found city dwellers to be cold, unconcerned neighbors. Nor could most rural people easily get caught up in the urban residents' preoccupation with getting consumer goods, amassing large sums of money, and being bound by demands for punctuality. To the contrary, many Third World people and Native Americans in particular were accustomed to scarcity, low income, and carefree visiting. None of these traits fit well into urban requirements for getting ahead.

Most of the rural immigrants were also *present oriented*. Survival was based upon perpetuating old, familiar ways of life—especially housekeeping practices, language and speech patterns, and health codes. There was a strong resistance to change. Along with the commitment to the status quo was passive resignation to unequal opportunities. Poverty and job discrimination, as an illustration, were not so much seen as bad but instead the way things were and would probably continue to be. Poverty became a vicious circle from which many immigrants were not able to extricate themselves. In summary, they learned to live today in the same manner their parents lived yesterday.

Rural immigrants tended to be *religion oriented*. They believed that whatever happened to them was God's will. Such a fatalistic view of life did not encourage them to become social climbers or scholars. For most immigrants from rural areas, "a little readin' and writin'" was sufficient. Also, too much money or sex implied that a person was in league with the devil. Consequently, they found urban patterns of adjustment too demanding and too immoral. The shift of populations from the farm to the city altered family members' relationships and activities. Instead of large, extended families that included many relatives, most urban families were isolated conjugal units, consisting only of husband, wife, and children. Other changes included the decline of male dominance and the rise in importance of women; an increase in mobility, resulting in social distance between family members and less emphasis on a family homestead; and the transfer of work from the home to the factory, accompanied by money wages and specialization of labor.

The urbanization of great numbers of people modified the way they were housed. The shift away from single-family dwelling units with their surrounding yards, gardens, and sometimes orchards or fields to smaller houses and yards to apartments in large buildings restricted the space for free movement for the entire family. In urban areas there was less space for privacy or for the development of hobbies— indoors or out. Other disruptive strains on family life included divorce, desertion, and cultural alienation. Gradually, the family relinquished most of its traditional economic production functions and became mainly a unit of economic consumption. And the socialization function was shared with the school. Thus the immigrants in the New World created a society that was new in appearance and substance. For example, the early history of American public education falls rather readily into two definite periods. The colonial period began in 1647 and, of course, ended in 1776 when the thirteen colonies declared themselves independent. The dominant motive for education during this period was religious.

The national period then followed for a century until the end of Reconstruction in 1876. This period of expansion, during which the country survived the supreme test of the Civil War, proved that the United States is one nation. The dominant motive for education was political and, impelled largely by this motive, political and education leaders established public school systems in all the states. The boundaries between periods became less distinct after 1876, and the motives for education became more complicated. Political and educational movements tended to become links in an endless chain rather than entirely new phenomena belonging to specific periods in history. The United States entered a period of rapid expansion in area, population, industrial and agricultural production, and influence in world affairs. The expansion was halted during the Great Depression of the 1930s but it was resumed during World War II and has been increasing in tempo ever since.

By the middle of the twentieth century, it was evident that America would probably never again be a predominantly rural nation. Today, as a result of a process that began in 1492, American villages are much like towns, towns shade into cities, and cities into metropolitan regions. Rural isolation and its concomitant social characteristics that were found in abundance at the beginning of the nineteenth century have all but disappeared. There are still semi-isolated rural communities (most of them marked by extreme poverty) but as a whole the urban and rural communities experienced by the early immigrants do not exist. Unfortunately, racial and ethnic bigotry has changed very little. Only the people have changed.

Anglocentric Views

At the time of the American Revolution, the American population was largely comprised of English Protestants who had absorbed a substantial number of German and Scotch-Irish settlers and a smaller number of French, Dutch, Swedes, Poles, Swiss, Irish, and other immigrants (Gordon, 1964). The colonies had a modest number of Catholics, and a smaller number of Jews. Excluding Quakers and Swedes, the colonists treated Native Americans with contempt and hostility, and engaged in wars that bordered on genocide. The natives were driven from the coastal plains in order to make way for a massive white movement to the West. Although Africans, most of whom were slaves, comprised one-fifth of the American population during the Revolution, they, similar to Indians, were not perceived by most white colonists as assimilable citizens.

The white peoples of the new nation had long since crossed Caucasian lines to create a conglomerate but culturally homogeneous society. In the words of Allan Nevins and Henry Steele Commager (1942): "People of different blood [*sic*]—English, Irish, German, Huguenot, Dutch, Swedish—mingled and intermarried with little thought of any difference" (p. 58). That was an overgeneralization, but English settlers and peoples from western and northern Europe had begun a process of cultural and ethnic assimilation that caused J. Hector St. John Crèvecoeur (1925) to incorrectly describe all Americans as being one nation melted into one ethnic group: American:

> He is either an European, or the descendant of an European, hence that strange mixture of blood, which you will find in no other country. I could point out to you a family whose grandfather was an Englishman, whose wife was Dutch, whose son married a French woman, and whose present four sons have now four wives of different nations. He is an American, who leaving behind him all his ancient prejudices and manners, receives new ones from the new mode of life he has embraced, the new government he obeys, and the new rank he holds. . . . Here individuals of all nations have melted into a new race of men, whose labors and posterity will one day cause great changes in the world. (pp. 54–55)

Non-Caucasian Americans were not included in Crèvecoeur's Eurocentric cultural pot.

During the 150 years immediately following the Revolution, large numbers of immigrants came to the United States from eastern European countries. They were the so-called "new immigrants." During the latter part of that period, slaves were emancipated, numerous Indian tribes were conquered and forced to relocate to reservations, and Asians began immigrating to the United States. The English language and English-oriented cultural patterns grew even more dominant. Relatedly, despite a proliferation of cultural diversity within the growing ethnic group enclaves, Anglo-conformity permeated the ideology attributed to the new nation. In turn, racist notions about Nordic and Aryan racial superiority gave rise to nativist political agendas and exclusionist immigration policies favoring western and northern European immigrants.

Non-English-speaking western Europeans and northern Europeans were also discriminated against. Benjamin Franklin expressed displeasure about the slowness of some immigrants, particularly Germans, to learn English, their tendency to live in enclaves, and the establishment of ethnic language newspapers (Davie, 1936). Such ethnic-oriented lifestyles prompted many Americanized people to believe, "If they don't like it here, they can go back where they came from." Yet this was too simplistic. On the one hand, immigrants were needed in America to help build a nation—to work the farms, dig the ore, build the railroads and canals, settle the prairies, and otherwise provide human resources. On the other hand, some of the immigrants were socially undesirable (paupers and criminals) and religiously undesirable (Catholics and Jews). Beginning in the 1890s, immigrants from eastern Europe and southern Europe were numerically dominant. This set the stage for racist statements that inferior, darker people threatened the purity of blond, blue-eyed Nordics or Aryans through miscegenation. From this point of view, intermixture was perceived as a deadly plague. If the immigrants from eastern and southern Europe could not effectively be stopped, the critics stated, then they should at least be properly assimilated and amalgamated:

> The southern and eastern Europeans are of a very different type from the northern Europeans who preceded them. Illiterate, docile, lacking in self-reliance and initiative, and not possessing the Anglo-Teutonic conceptions of law, order, and government, their coming has served to dilute tremendously our national stock, and to corrupt our civic life. . . . Our task is to break up these groups or settlements, to assimilate and amalgamate these people as a part of our American race, and to implant in their children, so far as can be done, the Anglo-Saxon conception of righteousness, law and order, and popular government, and to awaken in them a reverence for our democratic institutions and for those things in our national life which we as a people hold to be of abiding worth. (Cubberly, 1909, pp. 15–16)

This kind of ethnocentrism was the foundation upon which would be built a nation whose ideological gestalt would be greater than the individual ethnic groups that comprised it. And it would make difficult the assimilation of all peoples.

References

Crèvecoeur, J. H. S. J. (1925). *Letters from an American farmer*. New York: Albert & Charles Boni.

Cubberly, E. P. (1909). *Changing conceptions of education*. Boston: Houghton, Mifflin.

Davie, M. R. (1936). *World immigration*. New York: Macmillan.

Feagin, J. R. (1984). *Racial and ethnic relations*. Englewood Cliffs, NJ: Prentice Hall.

Gordon, M. (1964). *Assimilation in American life*. New York: Oxford University Press.

Gonzales, J. L., Jr. (1990). *Racial and ethnic groups in America*. Dubuque, IA: Kendall/Hunt.

Handlin, O. (1973). *The uprooted*, 2nd ed. Boston: Little, Brown.

Myrdal, G. (1944). *An American dilemma*. New York: Harper & Row.

Nevins, A., & Commager, H. S. (1942). *The heritage of America*. Boston: Little, Brown.

Portes, A., & Rumbaut, R. G. (1990). *Immigrant America*. Berkeley: University of California Press.

Seller, M. (1977). *To seek America: A history of ethnic life in the United States*. New York: Jerome S. Ozer.

State Board of Control of California. (1922). *California and the Oriental*. Sacramento: California Printing Office.

Wagley, C., & Harris, M. (1958). *Minorities in the new world: Six case studies*. New York: Columbia University Press.

Wolff, K. H. (1950). *The sociology of Georg Simmel*. Glencoe, IL: Free Press.

Chapter 2

Native Americans

About a thousand years ago the first Scandinavian settlers arrived on the Atlantic Coast of Canada. That Viking colony was decisively defeated by the native population. Five hundred years later, in 1492, Christopher Columbus and his three ships, lost in the Caribbean, accidentally made landfall on an island called *Guanahani* by the natives, but which he renamed *San Salvador*. It would be one hundred years more before the first permanent European settlers, some with African slaves in tow, set foot on what was to become Canada and the United States. "The settlers grafted their civilization onto the Native American roots and together they produced a hybrid civilization of unprecedented vigor" (Weatherford, 1991, p. 5).

The Land Before Columbus

The European conquest of the Western Hemisphere constituted one of the bleakest chapters of history. The whites came as the last contingent of many migrants to the New World. Conquistador armies, made up of restless veterans of European wars and other adventurers, plundered for gold, silver, pearls, and precious stones. Indian slaves were exchanged for monetary gain. They were used as miners and laborers in the treasure-producing areas of the New World, as cheap labor in Europe, and as objects for sale or barter in the burgeoning slave markets abroad (Axtell, 1981; Forsyth, 1957; Horgan, 1963). In a feeding frenzy of greed, manufactured goods were traded to the Indians by exploiters at a thousandfold profit, and the Indians paid the whites with furs and other valuable commodities which were in great demand in Europe and parts of Asia.

European explorers who "discovered" America were met by native populations who, it is speculated, had crossed the frozen Bering Strait. The true identity of the people Columbus called *los Indios*, the people of the Indies (or the Indians), is not known. However, it is likely they came from several origins (Morrison, 1942). Most historians believe that the Mongoloid ancestors of American Indians migrated from Asia more than twenty thousand years ago when the landmass between Asia and North America was frozen. This is plausible because the distance across the present Bering Strait is only about fifty miles. Thousands of people probably traveled to North America from the cold Asian land that had only sparse game for the subsistence of its large, rapidly growing population (Chiapelli, 1976; Gibson, 1980; Yenne, 1986). Theories of spontaneous generation, as an explanation for part of the Indian population, have been discounted by most historians because there is no anthropologic evidence to substantiate this.

By the time Columbus arrived in the New World, there were more than one million Indians living in what is now the continental United States, and they had explored almost all of the land. It is not known precisely how many different sovereign nations existed when the first contact with white explorers was made. A widely accepted approximation is that there were numerous language groups by the late 1600s. They were not one people; rather, they spoke different languages in several unrelated linguistic groups. Fifty or more groups are known to have become extinct as the result of disease, massacre by whites, absorption into other groups, or harsh conditions during the early phase of their contact with Europeans (Thernstrom, 1980).

The People Called "Indians"

The name each tribe took for itself almost always meant "the People" or "the Men." "Indian" was not a word in the vocabulary of the indigenous peoples. It is of interest to note that Native Americans once were divided into more than 600 tribes, which comprised more than two hundred language groups. For this reason, sign language was the medium through which the various language groups communicated. The first settlers of America were food gatherers and hunters. Very slowly, perhaps over a period of twenty thousand years, they spread southward and eastward until they occupied all of North, Central, and South America. In the course of this long migration, groups of indigenous people lost contact with each other. Because of this, cultural differentiation began to occur. It is estimated that by the time the Europeans arrived in America, the natives in North and South America spoke about two thousand different languages (Reich, 1989). A few of the native terms that enriched the English language include *iron horse* or *firewagon*, which means "train"; *little-wire speech*, which means "telephoning"; *deer of the water*, which means "fish"; and *thunder*, which means "his glance" (Bloomenfield, 1933, p. 455).

Different environmental conditions resulted in different Indian lifestyles. All tribes hunted, fished, and farmed but the terrain determined their major activities and the direction of their migration. Most Indians used the same weapons for hunting and for warfare, namely, bows and arrows or spears and clubs. Depending on the tribe, fish were caught with spears, traps, or nets. Hooks, poles, and drugs were made from tree bark or plants. Indian farmers used pointed sticks for digging, and also hoes made of wood, stone, bone, or shell. The main crops were corn, beans, and squash. In fact, Indians were the first people to grow corn. Other crops included avocados, cotton, peanuts, peppers, tobacco, and tomatoes.

The major divisions of Indians were sometimes classified according to cultural geographic areas. They include the Arctic home of the Eskimos and Aleuts and the Subarctic in which the coniferous forests and treeless tundra found in interior Canada and Alaska allowed people to live by hunting. New diseases and genocidal forays by settlers and miners had a substantial impact on those Indian groups (Feagin, 1984). Other cultural groups were the Northwest Pacific Coast people who were seafarers with a high sense of artistry, and the Eastern Forest Indians of the woodlands and open country in the eastern United States who were farmers and hunters. The Southeast was a land of confederacies and village people; and the Plateau, named for the plateaus of the Columbia River Basin, was home of the tribes that subsisted primarily on fish. Great Basin Indians lived in the area between the Rockies and the Sierra Nevada. Those who lived in this driest region of the United States had great difficulty subsisting there. Another cultural area was California, an area marked by great diversity of Indian types, speech, and cultures. Southwest Indians included the Pueblo, Navajo, and many other sedentary farming peoples. As seen in Figure 2.1, early North American natives can be divided into five broad cultural areas: (1) Eastern Forest, (2) Great Plains, (3) Southwest, (4) California Inter-Mountain, and (5) Northwest Coast (Brandon, 1933; Waldman, 1985; Yenne, 1986).

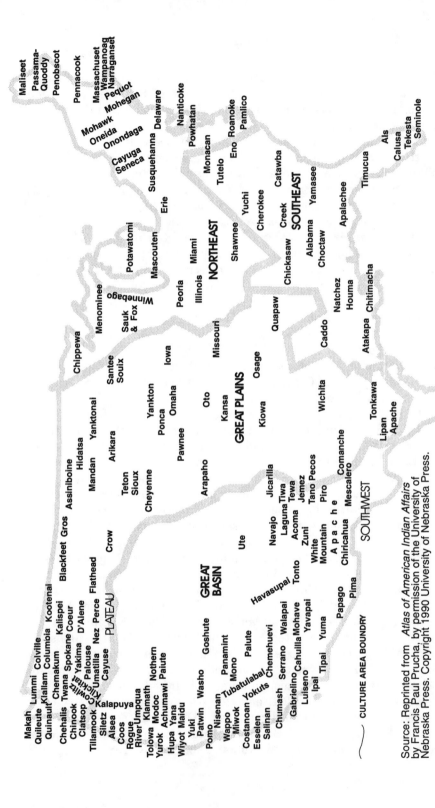

Source: Reprinted from *Atlas of American Indian Affairs* by Francis Paul Prucha, by permission of the University of Nebraska Press. Copyright 1990 University of Nebraska Press.

Figure 2.1. Tribal Locations

Eastern Forest Indians lived in all of what is now the United States east of the Great Plains. They were the first natives to feel the full brunt of the white European settlers' insatiable quest for land. From the moment white men first set foot on the North American continent, Indians were driven out of their territorial areas and forced to migrate before the onslaught of the settlers. Along with the loss of territory came the need to adjust to new environments or become extinct as tribes. Hundreds of tribes did not adjust. Two major cultural groups lived in the Eastern Forest: Southeastern farmers and Northeastern woods dwellers.

Southeastern farmers were once the most advanced natives in America. When white settlers arrived in the 1600s, however, they lived in a manner similar to other Indian tribes. The largest Southeastern tribes were the Cherokee, Chickasaw, Choctaw, Creek, Natchez, and Seminole. They lived in rectangular houses with plaster walls and thatched roofs. Some villages contained a council house. They also had a field where different forms of ball games were played. In most cases, in their games the players were not allowed to touch the ball with their hands. This was the origin of soccer. The rubber ball and the game of lacrosse—a goal game in which players use a long-handled stick that has a triangular head with a loose mesh pouch for catching and carrying the ball—were adopted by the settlers. The primary crops of this group were beans, corn, squash, and tobacco.

Northeastern woods dwellers consisted of the Delaware, Fox, Illinois, Iroquois, Menominee, Miami, Mohegan, Pequot, Potawatomi, Powhatan, Sauk, Shawnee, and Winnebago. They lived in the region between the Atlantic Ocean and the Mississippi River, from the Canadian border south to the Ohio River. Most of the tribes lived in round wigwams, but the Iroquois lived in rectangular, bark longhouses. Deer, wild birds, and rabbits were the major game they hunted.

Great Plains Indians lived in the region between the Mississippi River and the Rocky Mountains. The largest Plains tribes were the Arapaho, Arikara Blackfoot (the Piegan, the Bloods, and the Blackfoot proper), Caddo, Cheyenne, Comanche, Crow, Kiowa, Mandan, Osage, Pawnee, and Sioux. Some tribes were farmers, others were hunters. They were roaming tribes that lived mainly on buffalo and deer meat. Farming Plains Indians built permanent earth lodges which were partly underground and covered with logs and dirt. Their major crops were beans, corn, and squash. Roaming Indians built buffalo-hide tepees which could be easily assembled and dismantled, ideal for people who drifted from place to place.

Southwest Indians lived in what is now Arizona, New Mexico, and southern Utah. The Indian tribes in this region were the Apache, Hopi, Mohave, Navajo, Papago, Pima, Pueblo, Yuma, and Zuñi. Depending on the area they were in, Southwest Indians were villagers, farmers, or nomads. Villagers lived in multistoried houses made of adobe or clay. Farmers were more mobile than villagers and they lived in houses made of dirt and brush. Nomads were the most mobile of the three groups. They lived in a variety of structures, including earth lodges called hogans, brush huts, and tepees. Villagers and farmers survived by growing crops and gathering wild plants; nomads survived mainly by hunting. The arid climate of the Southwest has helped preserve a large number of ancient relics, and scanty vegetation and erosion have greatly favored archaeological exploration to document Indian cultures. The Spanish explorers entered the region in 1540, thus historical knowledge of the area spans more than four hundred years and is invaluable in reconstructing the tribulations and triumphs of native peoples as they left their marks upon the land.

California Inter-Mountain Indians lived in the region between the Sierra Nevada and the Rockies. The Maidu, Modoc, Paiute, Pomo, Southern Shoshones, and Western Ute were seed gatherers. They lived on nuts, roots, and seeds gathered as they roamed the dry areas of the region. Seed gatherers also hunted deer, antelope, and rabbits. Most of the tribes traveled regular routes and gathered each kind of seed in its own season. Their shelters consisted of a round or beehive frame of poles which were covered with grass or desert bushes and dirt. The Bannock, Flathead, Kutenai, Nez Percé, Northern Shoshones, and Colorado Ute were horsemen. They also gathered seeds, nuts, and roots but they hunted buffalo as well. Many of these tribes lived in tepees but most of them lived in grass or brush structures. At least two of the tribes, the Kutenai and the Nez Percé, fished in the northern rivers.

Northwest Coast Indians lived in the forest region along the Pacific Ocean, extending from northern California to southern Alaska (Drucker, 1963). These tribes consisted primarily of the Chinook, Hopi, and Klamath. They had the best climate for fish, game, roots, and berries. Consequently, they caught halibut, salmon, and other fish. The first attempt to exploit Indian fishing along the northern Pacific Coast originated with Hudson's Bay Company, which sought to market salted salmon in the 1830s. The company found an eager market in Hawaii but there were simply too few buyers to sustain a viable industry in commercial fishing in the Northwest. Northwest Coast Indians lived in rectangular wooden plank houses and hunted elk, deer, and whales (Boxberger, 1989; McFeat, 1989).

Even though not all Indians were the same, it was difficult for most white settlers to look at Indians and not view them as a homogeneous group of people. The natives who lived in the Great Basin of the southwestern United States illustrate this point. Great Basin Shoshones were divided into northern and western groups and both were mainly gatherers and hunters. There were abundant game animals in the north and this resulted in large northern Indian populations. But game was scarce in the west and this forced Western Shoshones to be almost exclusively gatherers who traveled great distances to find roots, fruits, and plants. Most settlers did not discern these differences, even though Western Shoshones were considerably smaller in number than Northern Shoshones and the northern tribes were more cooperative than the western tribes that scratched and eked out a meager existence. Most settlers saw only a single image: primitive savages to be used and abused for the settlers' comfort and gain.

To the south of Northern Shoshones were Paiutes. They too were hunters and gatherers. But Paiutes had learned how to irrigate wild crops by diverting small streams to them. Thus, while they were subjected to the same environmental conditions as their northern neighbors, Paiutes had larger and more stable populations. Such distinct differences in ways various tribes adjusted to their environments were consistently overlooked by most white settlers who could only see "red savages."

Sixteenth- and seventeenth-century European explorers were warlike and aggressive people who used long-range, oceangoing ships—armed with powerful cannons—to carry military men and materials around the world. No nation of North American Indians had the technological resources or knowledge, the level of organization, or the perception of the world required to resist the European advance. Relatedly, with few exceptions, the Europeans did not have the imagination or sensitivity to transcend the general view of the native peoples as barbarians, noble savages, or devil worshipers to be sacrificed so the settlers could implement their expansion of trade and increase power. Demand for furs rather than for territory brought the first significant contacts between Indians and whites in North America, turning tribes from agriculture and hunting to commercial trapping and commercial warfare.

Indian Removal

The land was holy to all the Indians. Their philosophy was to take only what they needed and neither sell nor despoil it. In a speech to territorial Governor Isaac Stevens, Chief Seálth, after whom Seattle is named, summarized with great eloquence the difference between the way Indians and the newcomers thought of the land:

> Every part of this soil is sacred in the estimation of my people. Every hillside, every valley, every plain and grove has been hallowed by some sad or happy event in days long vanished. The very dust upon which you now stand responds more lovingly to their footsteps than to yours, because it is rich with the blood of our ancestors and our bare feet are conscious of the sympathetic touch. (Turner, 1974, p. 253)

After the American Revolution, many white settlers were determined to win the battle for Indian land. To achieve this goal, they resorted to warfare, organized raids, and massacres. Eventually, they destroyed the ecological base of Indian survival, namely, their natural resources and their food supply (Cronon, 1983; Deloria, 1969). Various Indian nations fought valiantly against the white forces. After each war, Indians and white settlers signed treaties that usually were broken by whites who wanted, and got, Indian land. The treaties made in mid-seventeenth-century New England and Virginia colonies set precedent for subsequent ones. Simply stated, defeated Indian tribes were offered, and usually accepted, small parcels of land (reservations) as guaranteed homelands as compensation for the vast acres they relinquished. In return, they pledged themselves to be peaceful and allies with local white colonies in case of war with other Indian tribes or European foes. Encroachment of whites on Indian land was a continuous problem, particularly if game and valuable minerals, mainly gold and silver, were found there.

Taking their cue from the British government, the United States made Indian affairs a responsibility of the federal government. Article Three of the Constitution empowered Congress to "regulate commerce with foreign nations, and among the several states, and with the Indian tribes." At first the administration of Indian affairs was carried out through trading posts. The U.S. Army fought "hostile" Indians; peace negotiations and land sales, including establishing reservations, were within the purview of special treaty commissions appointed as needed. However, the concept of sovereignty over land was not abrogated when tribes were defeated—they had to be compensated for the land they relinquished. This concept was affirmed in the Northwest Ordinance of 1789 and extended in 1804 to cover tribes in the Louisiana Purchase.

After France ceased to be a power on the North American continent, several tribes formed alliances with the British against the Americans in the Revolution and the War of 1812. Only a few tribes allied themselves with the Americans. Consequently, when the Americans defeated the British, they also defeated large numbers of tribes. In defeat the tribes ceded land and were forced to live of reservations close to areas that would subsequently open up for white settlement. Eventually, there was no nearby place left to relocate Indians.

The War of 1812 between the British and the Americans divided Indian loyalties between the two nations. That division culminated in the Creek War, sometimes referred to as Andrew Jackson's war with the anti-American Creek which occurred at the end of the War of 1812. The war brought national prominence to Jackson and gained him the rank of major general in the regular army. The defeated Creeks made an involuntary migration to Spanish Florida where, in 1817, they and their Seminole allies were again defeated. This ended Spain's influence in the Southeast and resulted in the cession of Florida to the United States. Later, Jackson was elected president of the United States. After his inauguration in 1829, he encouraged the subordination of Native Americans. Indeed, he was a president critical of treaty-making, who even encouraged the states to defy U.S. Supreme Court decisions protecting Native American rights (Feagin, 1984).

In 1830, Congress passed the Indian Removal Act to empower President Jackson to initiate land exchanges with Indian nations. The act was aimed principally at relocating Indians off their land in Alabama, Florida, Georgia, North Carolina, Tennessee, and Mississippi. Some of the states had already prohibited tribal governments within their borders. The powerful Indian nations of the Creeks, Choctaws, Chickasaws, Seminoles, and Cherokees (called the Five Civilized Tribes) were the largest land losers. To complete the diminishment, they were bribed, tricked, and forced by whites to sign relocation treaties that led to extensive relocation to the Indian Territory (now called Oklahoma). In the winter of 1831, almost four thousand Choctaws began migration to their new homes in the western part of the Arkansas Territory. The winter was extremely severe and hundreds of barefoot and poorly clad Indians died in the sub-zero weather. The removal took several years, and before it was completed several hundred Choctaws died. Other tribes had similar losses. By some estimates, Cherokees lost four thousand of their sixteen thousand tribal members. Up to one-fourth of the Creeks and Chickasaws did not survive the relocation, later called the "Trail of Tears."

What at first glance appears to have been an equitable solution to dispossessing Indians of their land was a sham. For example, the Cherokees gave up 7 million acres of land for $4.5 million. The price paid across the continent averaged less than 10 cents an acre for land the government often sold to white land speculators for a minimum of $1.25 an acre. Also, the debt on each treaty was usually paid over a thirty-year period. Instead of instant payment, the federal government deposited in the U.S. Treasury to their credit monies owed the Indians. The government phased out the trading business as an Indian affair by 1824 and began to concentrate mainly on handling Indian land; the Bureau of Indian Affairs (BIA) was established in the Department of War. In 1849, the BIA was transferred to the newly established Department of Interior.

In the late nineteenth century, Theodore Roosevelt (1889) summarized the prevailing sentiment of whites who believed they were justified in removing Indians from their ancestral land: "This great continent would not have been kept as nothing but a game preserve for squalid savages" (p. 90). The desire for more land on the Great Plains resulted in white settlers, by law and outside the law, taking more Indian land. In 1871, Congress ended further treatymaking with the Indian tribes and declared that no Indian nation or tribe within the United States would be acknowledged or recognized as an independent nation, tribe, or power.

The history of white settlers in North America is tragically intertwined with that of Indians, as seen in the constant wars. From the beginning of European contacts with American natives, it was obvious that superior European organization and technology would lead to European domination of the Indians and their resources. Also, the extension of railroads gobbled up millions of acres of what was once land used by Indians. Buffalo were slaughtered by the thousands and the economy of the Plains tribes was destroyed. Settlers, miners, and the U.S. Army violated treaties with the Sioux and moved whites into the Dakota Territory. Controversy over the incursion escalated, and troops were sent in to force Sioux bands onto a smaller reservation, even though the bands were already on what the government had designated as "unceded Indian territory." Leading the military force was General George Custer. In 1876, the most widely known battle of the Plains struggle occurred at Little Bighorn, when Custer and the soldiers under his command were wiped out by a group of Sioux and allied tribes who had refused to settle on reservations.

The late nineteenth century was a period of numerous Indian-white confrontations and battles. Most notable were the Sand Creek and the Wounded Knee massacres. There were atrocities on both sides and, when the events were objectively analyzed, there were no winners. The entire American nation lost valuable human resources. The Indians lost thousands of lives and the use of millions of acres of land; their white opponents lost hundreds of lives and the respect of people who championed the cause of Indians. Helen Hunt Jackson, a friend of Emily Dickinson, did much to bring to the public's attention the plight of Native Americans. Of special note is Jackson's study of the U.S. government's mistreatment of Indians, *A Century of Dishonor* (1881).

Native Americans' protest against subordination has been the most sustained of any group in the history of North America. Several protest organizations had sprung up by the late nineteenth century. The Indian Rights Association, founded by Quakers, was one of the most important of them. Later, the American Indian Defense Association was formed to fight the attempts by Republican officials to establish executive order reservations not covered by treaty, which would be accessible to greedy whites who wished to extract minerals. Years later, the National Congress of American Indians (NCAI), the National Indian Youth Council (NIYC), and the American Indian Movement (AIM) were created in the twentieth century to champion Indian causes.

Indian Leaders

Indian removal programs became very ominous. From the time white men set foot on the North American continent, Indians were driven out of their territorial areas in instance after instance of involuntary migration. Indian resistance took the form of a series of wars with white settlers. Those wars resulted in an occasional Indian battle victory. Gradually, however, the Indians were pushed farther and farther into the wilderness. Each relocation brought new perils and problems to Indians as they were driven into more distant and hostile territories. As disastrous as the wars were, it was not the European weapons that claimed the highest Indian casualties. To the contrary, European diseases—measles, pneumonia, and tuberculosis—killed more Indians than all the wars combined. For example, approximately 60 percent of Northeastern Forest Indians died from European diseases during the first century of colonization.

The policies of the federal government toward American Indians can be separated into five distinct periods. They reflect shifting views of Indians specifically and the place of ethnic groups generally: (1) *separation*, during which the prime objective was to remove Indians from the land that whites desired and to draw boundaries between the two factions; (2) *coercive assimilation*, during which whites fought to replace Indian ways with their own ways and to help the Indians become self-sufficient farmers and artisans under conditions dictated by whites; (3) *tribal restoration,* Phase I, during which whites did an about-face and encouraged Indians to maintain their corporate tribal existence if they chose to do so; (4) *termination,* during which the objective was to break off all relationships of protection and assistance with the federal government; and (5) *tribal restoration,* Phase II, during which tribal corporate adaptation to American society was again encouraged and cultural choice was reaffirmed (Thernstrom, 1980).

It is ironic that without the help of Indians, it is unlikely the early white settlers would have survived. Relatedly, without outstanding Indian leaders, it is likely that all but a handful of tribes would have perished. First, the tribes had to pit their crude weapons against European guns. Next, they had to survive defeats by white soldiers. Finally, they had to adjust to new environments and accept cultural modifications but maintain their tribal identities. The following list is a sample of Indians who played important roles in various periods of American history.

Black Hawk, a chief of the Sauk Indians, refused to accept the treaty that gave the United States Sauk and Fox lands east of the Mississippi River. During the War of 1812, Black Hawk and his warriors fought on the side of the British.

Joseph Brant, a Mohawk chief and devout Christian, commanded the Iroquois tribe that fought on the side of the British in the American Revolutionary War. He was a colonel in the British army. Prior to the war, he translated the Episcopal prayer book and part of the New Testament into Mohawk. After the war, he moved to Canada and continued his missionary work.

Cochise was a member of the Chiricahua Apache of southern Arizona. He led an unsuccessful attacking force of more than one hundred warriors against Fort Buchanan in 1861. In late 1872 Thomas Jeffords, superintendent of mail between Fort Bowie and Tucson, rode into the encampment of Cochise to arrange safety for the mail. A lifetime friendship was formed. Subsequently, Jeffords took Otis Howard, special Indian commissioner, into the encampment of Cochise and a treaty was made whereby the Chiricahua Apache would be placed on a reservation to their liking. From that time until his death, Cochise remained friendly with white Americans.

Crazy Horse, a chief of the Oglala Sioux, was a principal leader in the Sioux War of 1876. His forces defeated General George Cook in the Battle of the Rosebud in Wyoming. Eight days later the Sioux joined with other tribes to defeat General George Custer in the battle near the Little Bighorn.

Geronimo was an Apache Indian chief and medicine man. When the federal government decided in 1876, because of his Mexican raids, to remove Geronimo to the White Mountain Reservation in Arizona, he fled to the Sierra Madre in Mexico, where earlier some Mexicans had massacred his whole family. General Nelson Miles captured Geronimo and his followers in 1886. They were deported as prisoners of war, first to Florida, then to Alabama, and finally to Fort Sill, Oklahoma, where Geronimo died on February 17, 1909.

Chief Joseph, a Nez Percé, led his tribe over more than 1,000 miles in retreat from the United States. They successfully retreated through Montana, Idaho, and Washington but were captured 50 miles from the Canadian border.

Massasoit, a chief of the Wampanóag, made a treaty in 1621 with John Carver, governor of the colony of Plymouth. The treaty stated that the Wampanóag would not harm Pilgrims so long as Massasoit lived. In return the Pilgrims agreed to protect the Indians and their rights. That treaty was never broken.

Osceola, a Seminole chief, resisted attempts by the U.S. government to force his tribe to move to the Indian territory west of the Mississippi. The Seminoles hid in the Florida Everglades from 1835 to 1842. The Seven Years War cost the United States fifteen hundred lives and $20 million. At the end, a large number of the Seminoles were left alone in the Florida Everglades.

Pontiac, a Chippewa chief, was the leader of the United Tribes of Chippewa, Potawatomi, and Ottawa. He was one of the best organizers of his period. Pontiac fought with the French against the English in the French and Indian War of 1757.

Sacajawea, a female Shoshone, was a guide and interpreter for the Lewis and Clark expeditions to the Pacific Ocean in 1804 and 1805. She joined the expedition at a Mandan village near modern Bismark, North Dakota, in 1804, and she led the expedition across North Dakota through Montana to the tribe of her brother, Cameahwait. She then accompanied the explorers to the Pacific Coast and back again. In the winter of 1805, along the way, she had a healthy baby. A mountain peak, a mountain pass, and a river were named for her (Weatherford, 1991).

Samoset, a chief of the Pequot, was a friend of the Pilgrims. He introduced the leaders of the colony to Massasoit. In 1625, Samoset transferred 12,000 acres of land to John Brown. That was the first deed of Indian land to English settlers.

Sequoyah, a Cherokee chief and scholar, invented an alphabet that enabled him to record the Cherokee language. He wrote Cherokee newspapers and books. He went to Washington, D.C., in 1828 as a representative of the Western tribes.

Sitting Bull, a chief of the Hunkpapa Teton Sioux, is best known for his leadership role in defeating General Custer at Little Bighorn on June 25, 1876.

Skikellamy, an Oneida chief, represented the Iroquois confederacy to the colonial government of Pennsylvania. He attended most of the treaty meetings between the Indians and white settlers in his territory.

Squanto, a member of the Pawtuxet tribe, helped the Pilgrim settlers of Massachusetts. He acted as their interpreter during the Treaty of Plymouth. More than any other person, Squanto taught the white settlers how to plant corn and where to fish. He was captured by an English slave trader named Thomas Hunt, who sold him in the Spanish port of Malaga. Subsequently, Squanto escaped and worked his way back to the village of Pautuxet, but it was deserted from the devastation of slave raids and epidemics (Forbes, 1988).

Tammany, a chief of the Lenni-Lenape (Delaware), is said to have greeted William Penn when he arrived on October 27, 1682, to found the colony of Pennsylvania. He helped the European colonists to survive in the North American environment for which their European cities did not prepare them. Some writers claim Chief Tammany built his primary wigwam in New Jersey on the site where Princeton University was built later (Myers, 1917).

Tecumseh, a Shawnee chief, united the eastern American Indian tribes after the American Revolutionary War. Along with his brother, Shawnee Prophet, Tecumseh did much to cause Indian tribes to maintain their traditional ways of living. He was a great athlete, hunter, and leader. He was helpful, honest, thrifty, and imbued with a religion that did not place emphasis in books, or creeds. Instead, he was a practicing model of manhood (Rosenthal, 1984). (Ernest Thompson Seton derived the *Boy Scout Handbook* from the principles attributed to Tecumseh.) Tecumseh conceived a unity among all the tribes of the North and the South. He urged the tribes in the Northwest Territory to hold onto their land, to cease selling it, and to resist all pressures to the contrary.

Uncas, a chief of the Mohegan, joined the English in the war against the Pequot in 1637. Although he helped the English, Uncas opposed teaching Christianity to his tribe.

Washakie, a chief of the Eastern Shoshone, aided white settlers who traveled the Oregon Trail. He also sent Indian scouts to help General George Crook in his battle with the Sioux in the 1870s.

Wovoka, a Paiute, founded the ghost dance religion of the Western

American Indians. In 1899, he dreamed that he was lifted to the sky and the Great Spirit talked to him. The Great Spirit taught him new songs and a new dance and told him to teach other Indians to stop fighting and live a good life. The prophet claimed that when his followers did the prescribed dance, accompanied by chants, it would cause the disappearance of the white settlers, bring back dead Indian heroes, and restore the old ways of life on the Plains. Also, no one would ever grow old, go hungry, or be sick, and the buffalo would come back to life. The fear of that religion frightened white settlers into the massacre at Wounded Knee, South Dakota, which became a burning symbol for both Indians and whites.

The complete list of all the great Indian leaders would comprise several volumes. Countless Indian leaders were subjected to contradictory demands of white settlers, who demanded total Indian assimilation into white cultures or total segregation. Because there was no middle ground for the Indians, most tribal chiefs found their roles quite tenuous. They were often chided by their own people for being too conciliatory toward whites; they were blamed by whites for being too militant. Gradually, old Indian customs gave way to new ones. This was also true for native religions, as white missionaries forced Christianity on countless Indians. However, in fairness it should be noted that faith in many of the traditional religious beliefs was lost long before Christianity was adopted. The chiefs showed great courage in trying to keep their tribes together as well as endeavoring to keep their tribal lands.

White settlers tended to define stereotypically all Indians (except the Pueblo) as nomadic persons who did not settle in permanent areas. That definition made it easier for colonists to steal or ravage Indian land. Not all whites agreed with the harsh treatment of Indians. Unfortunately, the latter group of whites was too few in numbers and too powerless to prevent the seizure of Indian land or to stop the decimation of Indian populations or to curb the loss of traditional native cultures. The remarkable fact is not that most Indian leaders failed in their efforts to prevent tribal losses. To the contrary, it is remarkable that so many of them succeeded in any measure against such insurmountable odds (Deloria, 1969; Wax & Buchanan, 1975).

Contributions

The foremost contributions of Indians to the development of the United States evolve around the survival of the white settlers. From the very beginning, the colonist had to borrow native know-how and indigenous cultural materials in order to survive (Axtell, 1981; Lauber, 1913; Lowes, 1986). From the end of the sixteenth century until the middle of the twentieth century, white contacts with Native Americans produced a considerable amount of cultural experimentation and diffusion of ideas and cultural items. The natives borrowed guns, household utensils, textiles, and tools. The exchange was two ways. Whites borrowed from Native Americans too. After all, the Indians had already learned how to survive in the New World. They had found the easiest trails through the forests, over the mountains, and across rivers and lakes. They had discovered most of the edible foods available and located useful and valuable mineral deposits. There was no typical Indian lifestyle or single Indian mode of survival, however.

One of the first needs of the colonists was to find or build suitable shelter. This they learned from the Indians who built many kinds of homes because they lived in a variety of climates and had dissimilar building materials. Thus, both Indian and white settler housing varied from dome-shaped wigwams to rectangular log houses, to the brush and matting wigwams, to hogans (logs covered with mud). As a temporary structure, the wigwam proved to be the most popular with the colonists. It was inexpensive and very easily and quickly constructed.

Food was the most important permanent contribution Indians made to White American culture. Prior to Columbus's voyage in 1492, Europeans were ignorant of avocados, chocolate, maple sugar, peanuts, peppers, pineapples, squash, tomatoes, and vanilla. In 1609, two Powhatan prisoners, Kemps and Tassore, taught the Jamestown colonists how to plant their first corn as well as how to gather and use American fruit. It was Squanto, however, who intervened to save the Pilgrims who landed on Cape Cod from starvation. He showed them how to set corn, dress it, and tend it. From him, they learned how to plant four to five seeds in hills about six feet apart rather than spread seed carelessly over a plowed field. Then they learned to plant beans beside the stalks of mature corn to give the vines support to climb. Later, when the corn crop was harvested, they learned to plant pumpkin and squash between the hills. Cornbreads, puddings, grits, hominy, tapioca, succotash, and popcorn were Indian dishes that have become part of American culture. So too have sassafras, ginseng, and clambakes. Other food additions include fish and game prepared by Indian methods of spitting the food and baking or smoking it.

Indians taught the settlers how to gather pecans, hickory nuts, pine nuts, acorns, and walnuts as well as wild fruits such as pawpaw and maypop. They also introduced them to the uses of sassafras and cranberries. Europeans were acquainted with honey but they had no experience with maple syrup and its by-products. Indians acquainted the settlers with the potential of this commodity and it quickly became an integral part of the colonial economy and cuisine. Whether catching fish or hunting game, the colonists imitated Indians. They learned to imitate bird and animal calls, set snare and dead fall traps, and to shoot the bow and arrow. In addition to calls and whistles, Indians taught hunters how to manufacture decoys to lure animals and birds. Like some Indians, many white hunters wore the skins of the animals they hunted as a disguise (Stewart, 1977; Weatherford, 1991). Indians used a variety of traps; the most common consisted of snares and dead falls. Also, they taught settlers how to tan skins with the fat and brains of animals; how to ferret out hibernating bears; how to preserve fresh game by smoking it, drying it in the sun, or packing it with snow; and how to use snowshoes and the toboggan.

The speed and accuracy of Indian hunters is well known but their genius actually lay in intimate knowledge of animal habits. One method they used was to imitate the calls of birds and animals. In order to reproduce sounds the human voice could not make, hunters constructed whistles of wood, clay, antler, and bone to summon prey by imitating distress or courtship calls (Weatherford, 1991). Indian fishermen made wooden lures in the form of small fish or used willow wood that could be pulled through the water in such a way that they reproduced the characteristic motions and ripples of a wounded fish and in this way were able to attract larger prey (Stewart, 1977).

Clothing styles changed dramatically for European settlers. Indian moccasins were better suited for the frontier than hard-heeled cobbled shoes. Brightly colored European clothes were exchanged for duller shades of brown and green to help woodsmen become more successful in stalking or avoiding wild animals or enemies. The box-skin hunting shirt worn by colonists, especially Virginians, was borrowed from Indians.

European settlers also learned to imitate the Indian health care regimen. They learned to sleep in the woods with their feet turned toward the fire. When sick, they often resorted to a variety of Indian cures. More than 150 drugs listed in the *Pharmacopeia of the United States* were discovered and used by North American Indians. (Bieder, 1986). Indeed, it was commonplace for colonial physicians to seek the assistance of Indian medicine persons, or shamans, to become acquainted with their herbal remedies. For example, quinine and herbs borrowed from the Indians became important medicine to bolster the health of white settlers.

American child-rearing practices and attitudes toward conservation owe much to Indian tradition. Child rearing in Europe was generally harsh and little thought was given to preserving the environment. But most tribes never physically punished their children. And they taught children to take only what was needed from the environment. It was considered in bad taste for Indians to spoil and destroy either the children or the environment.

As noted earlier, the American language owes much to Native Americans. Thousands of Indian words have become part of the American vocabulary, including *chipmunk, moose, raccoon, skunk, squash, woodchuck, hominy, succotash, hickory, Massachusetts, Mississippi,* and *Wisconsin.* Other words derived from vocabularies of Indians include *hammock, kayak, parka,* and *poncho.* And common terms derived from Indians include warpath, war paint, bury the hatchet, paleface, peace pipe, medicine man, and big chief.

Out of their struggles, even for identification, emerged modern-day Native Americans such as Jim Thorpe, who won the decathlon and pentathlon in the 1912 Olympic Games; N. Scott Momaday, the first Native American to win a Pulitzer Prize. Will Rogers, an actor and satirist of politicians, was internationally renowned. All successful Native Americans left their shining marks on the "pride" pages of American history. American Indian contributions to the nation's heritage are indeed enormous. This includes Ira Hayes, winner of the Congressional Medal of Honor during World War II; five ballerinas— Moscelyn Larkin, Maria Tallchief, Marjorie Tallchief, Rosella Hightower, and Yvonne Chouteau. Additionally, there is Simeon Simon, aide-de-camp to General George Washington; Oral Roberts, evangelist; Louis Ballard, noted American composer; Buffy Saint-Marie, noted Cree singer of Indian songs. Others of note include Willard Stone, sculptor; Jerome Tiger, internationally known painter; Louisa Kayes (Dat-So-La-Lee), one of the most famous basketmakers of modern times; Pablita Velarde, known as the most famous Native American woman painter; and Ina Souez (Rains), a Cherokee who won acclaim as an operatic soprano and musical comedy. Wilma Mankiller was the first female chief of the Cherokee Nation of Oklahoma.

References

Axtell, J. (1981). *The European and the Indian.* Oxford: Oxford University Press.

Bieder, R. E. (1986). *Science encounters the Indian, 1820–1880.* Norman: University of Oklahoma Press.

Bloomenfield, L. (1933). *Language*. New York: Holt.

Boxberger, D. L. (1989). *To fish in common: The ethnology of Lummi Indian salmon fishing*. Lincoln: University of Nebraska Press.

Brandon, W. (1933). *Indians*. New York: Holt.

Ceram, C. W. (1971). *The first American*. New York: New American Library.

Chiapelli, F. (Ed.). (1976). *First images of America: The impact of the New World on the old*. 2 vols. Berkeley: University of California Press.

Cronon, W. (1983). *Changes in the land: Indians, colonists and the ecology of New England*. New York: Hill & Wang.

Deloria, V., Jr. (1969). *Custer died for your sins: An Indian manifesto*. New York: Avon.

Drucker, P. (1963). *Indians of the Northwest Coast*. Garden City, NY: Natural History Press.

Feagin, J. R. (1984). *Racial and ethnic relations*. Englewood Cliffs, NJ: Prentice Hall.

Forbes, J. D. (1988). *Black Africans and Native Americans*. Oxford: Basil Blackwell.

Forsyth, T. (1957). The French, British and Spanish methods of treating Indians. *Ethnohistory, 4* (2), 335–368.

Gibson, A. M. (1980). *The American Indian: Prehistory to present*. Lexington, MA: Heath.

Horgan, P. (1963). *Conquistadors in North American history*. Greenwich, CT: Fawcett.

Jackson, H. H. (1881). *A century of dishonor*. London: Faber & Faber.

Lauber, A. W. (1913). *Indian slavery in colonial times*. Williamstown, MA: Corner House.

Lowes, W. (1986). *Indian giver: A legacy of North American native peoples*. British Columbia: Theytus Books.

McFeat, T. (Ed.). (1989). *Indians of the North Pacific Coast*. Seattle: University of Washington Press.

Morrison, S. E. (1942). *Admiral of the sea: A life of Christopher Columbus*. Boston: Little, Brown.

Myers, G. (1917). *The history of Tammany Hall*, 2nd ed. New York: Bomi & Liveright.

Reich, J. R. (1989). *Colonial America*. Englewood Cliffs, NJ: Prentice-Hall.

Roosevelt, T. (1889). *The winning of the West, 1858–1919*. New York: Putnam.

Rosenthal, M. (1984). *The character factory: Baden-Powell and the origins of the boy scout movement*. New York: Pantheon.

Stewart, H. (1977). *Indian fishing*. Seattle: University of Washington Press.

Thernstrom, S. (Ed.). (1980). *Harvard encyclopedia of American ethnic groups*. Cambridge: Harvard University Press.

Turner, F. W. II. (Ed.). (1974). *The portable North American reader*. New York: Viking.

Waldman, C. (1985). *Atlas of the North American Indian*. New York: Facts on File.

Wax, M. L., & Buchanan, R. L. (1975). *Indian Americans: Unity and diversity*. Englewood Cliffs, NJ: Prentice-Hall.

Weatherford, J. (1991). *Native roots: How the Indians enriched America*. New York: Crown.

Yenne, B. (1986). *The encyclopedia of North American Indian tribes*. New York: Crown.

The Trail of Tears
by Grant Foreman

The last party conducted by George Hicks did not start until November 4 [1838]. Hicks sorrowfully reported that day to Chief Ross: *"We are now about to take our final leave and kind farewell to our native land, the country that the great spirit gave our Fathers; we are on the eve of leaving that country that gave us birth . . . it is with sorrow that we are forced by the authority of the white man to quit the scenes of our childhood . . . we bid a final farewell to it and all we hold dear. From the little trial we have made in a start to move, we know that it is a laborious undertaking, but with firm resolution we think we will be able to accomplish it, if the white citizens will permit us. But since we have been on our march many of us have been stopped and our horses taken from our Teams for the payment of unjust & past Demands: Yet the Government says we must go, and its citizens say you must pay me, and if the debtor has not the means, the property of his next friend is levied on and yet the Government has not given us our spoliation [compensation] as promised; our property has been stolen and robbed from us by white men and no means given us to pay our debts. [The Government officers will not protect us, our property is] robbed of us in open Day light and in open view of hundreds, and why are they so bold; they know that we are in a defenseless situation.*

A sympathetic traveler who met them on the road describes the appearance of these unhappy people:

" . . . On Tuesday evening we fell in with a detachment of the poor Cherokee Indians . . . about eleven hundred Indians—sixty waggons— six hundred horses, and perhaps forty pairs of oxen. We found them in the forest camped for the night by the road side . . . under a severe fall of rain accompanied by heavy wind. With their canvas for a shield from the inclemency of the weather, and the cold wet ground for a resting place, after the fatigue of the day, they spent the night . . . many of the aged Indians were suffering extremely from the fatigue of the journey, and the ill health consequent upon it . . . several were then quite ill, and one aged man we were informed was then in the last struggles of death.

" . . . About ten officers and overseers in each detachment whose business it was to provide supplies for the journey, and attend to the general wants of the company . . . We met several detachments in the southern part of Kentucky on the 4th, 5th, and 6th of December . . . . The last detachment which we passed on the 7th embraced rising

two thousand Indians with horses and mules in proportion. The forward part of the train we found just pitching their tents for the night, and notwithstanding some thirty or forty waggons were already stationed, we found the road literally filled with the procession for about three miles in length. the sick and feeble were carried in waggons— about as comfortable for traveling as New England ox cart with a covering over it—a great many ride on horseback and multitudes go on foot—even aged females, apparently nearly ready to drop into the grave, were traveling with heavy burdens attached to the back—on the sometimes frozen ground, and sometimes muddy streets, with no covering for the feet except what nature had given them. We were some hours making our way through the crowd, which we felt fortunate to find ourselves freed from the crowd without leaving any part of our carriage. We learned from the inhabitants on the road where the Indians passed, that they buried fourteen or fifteen at every stopping place, and they make a journey of ten miles per day only on an average. One fact which to my own mind seemed a lesson indeed to the American nation is, that they will not travel on the Sabbath—a campmeeting in truth. One aged Indian who was commander of the friendly Creeks and Seminoles in a very important engagement in the company with General Jackson, was accosted on arriving in a little village in Kentucky by an aged man residing there, and who was one of Jackson's men in the engagement referred to, and asking him if he (the Indian) recollected him? The aged Chieftain looked him in the face and recognized him, and with a down-cast look and heavy sigh, referring to the engagement, he said 'Ah! my life and the lives of my people were then at stake for you and your country. I then thought Jackson my best friend. But ah! Jackson no serve me right. Your country no do me justice now!'

"*The Indians as a whole carry in their countenances every thing but the appearance of happiness. Some carry a downcast dejected look bordering upon the appearance of despair; others a wild frantic appearance as if about to burst the chains of nature and pounce like a tiger upon their enemies . . . Most of them seemed intelligent and refined. Mr. Bushyhead, son of an aged man of the same name, is a very intelligent and interesting Baptist clergyman. Several missionaries were accompanying them to their destination. Some of the Cherokees are wealthy and travel in style. One lady passed on in her hack in company with her husband, apparently with as much refinement and equipage as any of the mothers of New England; and she was a mother too and her youngest child about three years old was sick in her arms, and all she could do was to make it comfortable as circumstances would permit . . . she could only carry her dying child in her arms a*

*few miles farther, and then she must stop in a stranger-land and con-
sign her much loved babe to the cold ground, and that too without
pomp or ceremony, and pass on with the multitude . . .*

" *. . . When I past the last detachment of those suffering exiles and
thought that my native countrymen had thus expelled them from their
native soil and their much loved homes, and that too in this inclement
season of the year in all their suffering, I turned from the sight with
feelings which language cannot express and 'wept like childhood then.'
I felt that I would not encounter the secret silent prayer of one of these
sufferers armed with the energy that faith and hope would give it (if
there be a God who avenges the wrongs of the injured) for all the lands
of Georgia! . . . When I read in the President's Message that he was
happy to inform the Senate that the Cherokees were peaceably and
without reluctance removed—and remember that it was on the third
day of December when not one of the detachments had reached their
destination; and that a large majority had not made even half their
journey when he made that declaration, I thought I wished the
President could have been there that very day in Kentucky with myself,
and have seen the comfort and the willingness with which the
Cherokees were making their journey. But I forbear, full well I know
that many prayers have gone up to the King of Heaven from Maine in
behalf of the poor Cherokees."*

The Ohio river was crossed at a ferry near the mouth of the
Cumberland, and the army passed on through southern Illinois until
it reached the Mississippi river opposite Cape Girardeau, Missouri.
The drought having delayed the start so long, it was winter when the
emigrants reached that great river. *"In talking with old men and
women at Tahlequah, the author found that the lapse of over half a
century had not sufficed to wipe out the memory of the miseries of that
halt beside the frozen river, with hundreds of sick and dying penned
up in wagons or stretched upon the ground, with only a blanket over-
head to keep out the January blast. The crossing was made at last in
two divisions, at Cape Girardeau and at Green's ferry, a short distance below, whence the march was on through Missouri to Indian territory, the later detachments making a northerly circuit by
Springfield, because those who had gone before had killed off all the
game along the direct route."*

Nineteen hundred of these Indians passed through Jackson,
Missouri, early in December. "Some of them have considerable
wealth, and make a very respectable appearance; but most of them
are poor and exceedingly dissipated." Another detachment passed
near Batesville, Arkansas, December 15. Of this party John Benge
was conductor, George Lowery assistant, Dr. W. P. Rawles of

Gallatin, Tennessee, surgeon and physician, and William Shorey Coodey, contractor. Many of them came through the town to get their carriages repaired, have their horses shod and for other reasons. "They left Gunter's Landing on Tennessee River 35 miles above Huntsville, Alabama, October 10, since which time, owing to their exposure to the inclemency of the weather, and many of them being destitute of shoes and other necessary articles of clothing, about 50 of them have died." Twelve hundred Cherokee emigrants passed through Smithville, Lawrence County, Arkansas on December 12, *"many of whom appeared very respectable. The whole company appear to be well clothed, and comfortably fixed for travelling. I am informed that they are very peaceable, and commit not depredations upon any property in the country through which they pass. They have upwards of one hundred wagons employed in transporting them; their horses are the finest I have ever seen in such a collection. The company consumes about one hundred and fifty bushels of corn per day. It is stated that they have the measles and whooping cough among them and there is an average of four deaths per day."*

Evan Jones, with his party at Little Prairie, Missouri, wrote, December 30: . . . *"We have now been on our road to Arkansas seventy-five days, and have traveled five hundred and twenty-nine miles. We are still nearly three hundred miles short of our destination . . . It has been exceedingly cold . . . those thinly clad very uncomfortable . . . we have, since the cold set in so severely, sent on a company every morning, to make fires along the road, at short intervals. This . . . a great alleviation to the sufferings of the people. At the Mississippi river, we were stopped from crossing, by the ice running so that boats could not pass, for several days. Here Br. Bushyhead's detachment came up with us, and before our detachment was all over, Rev. Stephen Foreman's detachment came up, and encamped along side us. I am sorry to say that both their detachments have not been able to cross. I am afraid that with all the care that can be exercised with the various detachments, there will be an immense amount of suffering, and loss of life attending the removal. Great numbers of the old, the young, and the infirm will inevitably be sacrificed. And the fact that the removal is effected by coercion, makes it the more galling to the feelings of the survivors."*

Rev. Jesse Bushyhead wrote from Park Hill, March 19, that his party which departed October 5, was detained by the ice in the Mississippi river for a month, and that there were eighty-two deaths among them while on the road; they reached their destination on February 23 and he expected all the other parties would be in within a week or two. Several hundred of the emigrants in Jones's and

Bushyhead's parties were members of their church, the Baptist; "thus enabling them to continue, amidst all the toils and sufferings of the journey, their accustomed religious services."

At last their destination was reached. It was now March, 1839, the journey having occupied nearly six months of the hardest part of the year. Some of those whom sickness had prevented from emigrating by land with the main body of emigrants, were in a party of 228 Cherokee aboard the steamboat *Victoria*, which arrived at Little Rock about February 1, 1839. Among them were Chief John Ross and his family who had more cause to mourn than many at their enforced removal which was in part responsible for the death of Mrs. Ross as the boat landed at Little Rock; she was buried in the little cemetery at this village.

On the march there were many deaths, a few desertions and accessions and occasional exchanges from one party to another where some by sickness were obliged to drop out on the way and join those coming after; so that an accurate statement of the number removed and of those who perished on the way became impossible. But the following particulars concerning the movements of the emigrants are available:

Elijah Hick's party increased by accessions to 858, and traveling with forty-three wagons and 430 horses, arrived in their new home January 4, 1839, the first party to reach their destination, reduced then to 744; of the missing, thirty-four were accounted for by death, but they were offset by five births on the way. The next company to arrive three days later was that which started in charge of Hair Conrad, numbering 858, and ended the journey 654 in number commanded by Lieutenant Deas. Three days after these John Benge arrived in his new home in charge of a party of 1,103 remaining of a total of 1,200 who began the journey. Daniel Colton arrived January 16 with 651 emigrants.

A company of 1,033 Cherokee from the Valley Towns of East Tennessee in charge of the Rev. Evan Jones arrived February 2; these were all that remained of the original party numbering 1,250, headed by Situakee, who traveled with sixty-two wagons and 560 horses. There were seventy-one deaths and five births among them. The people of this party were strongly religious and maintained their church organization and services on the road with the inspiration of their Baptist conductor. Next behind them was the party headed by Rev. Jesse Bushyhead, a Cherokee Baptist minister who interpreted for Mr. Jones. His people numbered at the beginning 950, but he lost thirty-eight by death and after accounting for six births, he delivered 898 in their new home February 23.

Rev. Stephen Foreman, also a Cherokee preacher, who had been educated at Union and Princeton theological seminaries brought the next party of emigrants made up largely of Cherokee Indians of religious attachments who arrived February 27; they began their journey in charge of Capt. Old Field 983 in number, but there were fifty-seven deaths and nineteen births on the road and after accounting for a few desertions and accessions they numbered 921 on their arrival in the West. The party of Choowalooka began their journey numbering 1,150 but on arrival at their new home in the West March first there were but 970 of them. Mose Daniel's party originally numbering 1,035 suffered forty-eight deaths on the march, but there were six births, and Captain Stevenson, the certifying agent, receipted for only 924 in their new home March 2. James Brown's contingent of 859 was reduced to 717 when it reached their destination March 5, by thirty-four deaths and other causes. George Hicks reported to Captain Stevenson, March 14, 1039 of his original enrollment of 1,118.

John Drew delivered a small party of 219 emigrants in their new home on March 18 of 231 who started with him. Richard Taylor began his journey in charge of 1,029 emigrants and after fifty-five deaths and fifteen births in the party he brought 944 survivors to their new home March 24. Peter Hilderbrand's caravan of 1,776 emigrants extended for several miles along the highway. Eight-eight wagons contained the young children, the sick, aged and decrepit, and the personal effects of the emigrants. There were 881 horses in the equipment of the party, some of which were employed with the oxen in pulling the wagons; the remainder were used as riding horses for women and girls many of whom bore infants on their backs. Men, boys, and able bodied women and girls walked along in company with the wagons and horses containing members of their families and their property. Only 1,312 of this party were delivered to the agent in the West. March 25, the difference, 464, being accountable probably to diversion of some of them to another party and not altogether to deaths.*

---

*These figures were turned in by the conductors of the parties; there was much disagreement on the subject. John Ross claimed a total of 13,149 removed under his supervision. Captain Stevenson, who receipted for the Indians on their arrival, reported 11,504; and Captain Page, the disbursing officer, said there were 11,702. All told, about 4,000 died during the course of capture and detention in temporary stockades, and the removal itself.

Chapter 3

British and Irish

The first American immigrants were more than riffraff run out of their native lands. Instead, they were men, women, and children who represented many social classes and diverse lifestyles (Bridenbaugh, 1971; Gonzales, 1990; Handlin & Handlin, 1986). The largest number of early settlers came from the British Isles. Those frontier tamers brought with them the basic foundation for building a United States of America (Hutchinson, 1956). No nation contributed more than Great Britain to the early cultural development of America. The English, Scots, Welsh, and Irish greatly influenced America's language, form of government, common law, and concept of religious freedom (Larabee, 1972; Reich, 1989). Other countries were represented, too. As immigrants from other countries interacted with the British, the content and process of frontier living changed to reflect a unique form of cultural diversity (Simmons, 1976; Thernstrom, 1980).

English

Economic factors played a major role in the decision of English citizens to emigrate to unknown places. Many of the large estates in England during the early part of the sixteenth century supported tenant farmers who lived off the land in return for their labor in the fields. However, English landowners found that the wool market

offered them even larger profits than basic agriculture. They therefore turned their manors into sheep farms, enclosing the land, thus
forcing the tenants to seek their livelihood elsewhere. At the same
time, small landowners, unable to turn their property into successful
sheep farms, found themselves ruined by economic inflation which
swept over Western Europe during the sixteenth century as gold and
silver from the New World poured in. When escalating taxes became
an additional burden for small landowners, many of them decided to
sell their land in order to buy some of the vast amount of acreage
offered at low prices in the New World. Furthermore, the younger
sons of many families, denied land by the law of primogeniture,
looked across the ocean to a new life (Reich, 1989).

A second cause of the immigration to America lay in the religious
quarrels which began to afflict England after King Henry VIII broke
with the Roman Catholic Church in 1534. Elizabeth I, Henry's daughter, sought to steer a middle course in religion by giving official sanc-
tion to the Anglican Church, the faith which her father had established. This policy satisfied some but not all of her subjects. Roman
Catholics were often persecuted and denied their civil and political
rights under Elizabeth's rule. At the same time, the Puritans were
offended by many of the rituals and symbolism of the Anglican
Church, for they saw little difference between the official faith and
Roman Catholicism.

Elizabeth's successor, James I, forced clergy who favored the
Puritan cause out of their pulpits. He also enforced statutes against
Christians who would not attend Anglican services. Another group of
Christians, the Separatists, held that the Anglican Church was
beyond reforming and thus they advocated the establishment of independent religious bodies. Finally, a dissident named George Fox
emerged around 1650 to assert that churches, dogma, and ceremony
had no place in worship. His followers, the Quakers, refused to serve
in the army. King James dealt harshly with all religious dissenters,
but most brutally with Quakers. The religiously disaffected had good
reason to seek a new life in other countries. At the same time, as the
mercantile theory became dominant, the English government encouraged the formation of colonies in the New World.

The rationale for overseas development was twofold: the colonies
would become suppliers of raw materials for the mother country, and
they would become consumers of excess manufactured products.
Commerce generated by the establishment of overseas possessions
enriched England in many different ways, among which were stimu-
lation of home industries such as shipbuilding. This raised revenues
from goods sent to and from the colonies. Indeed, the creation of the

new colonies gave rise to entrepreneurs in England who wished to invest their capital in profitable ventures. It was they who financed many of the voyages to the New World with an eye to the great returns which a successful colony might generate. Large numbers of private investors fought for the right to send out groups of immigrants to new lands. The English Crown found that granting charters to new companies formed by investors in the New World was a lucrative business (Handlin & Handlin, 1986).

Contributions

Gradually, even before the Revolution, American ties to the mother country began to weaken. For this reason, several groups in America organized with the intent of promoting Anglo-American relations and preserving English customs and traditions. Some of those organizations were the General Society of Mayflower Descendants, the Ark and Dove, the Colonial Dames of America, and the Hereditary Descendants of Colonial Governors. But neither those nor similar organizations could keep the new country from taking on its own identity. Nevertheless, England remained the mother country for many Americans, and her influence on so many major areas of the country remains predominant. First, the two nations are united by a common language, a language made incomparably rich by the great novelists, playwrights, and poets of England. Even today, with the emphasis on bilingual education, the most pressing insistence on newly arrived immigrants is that they learn the English language. Language is the primary step to assimilation, and in most cases an immigrant will always feel like a stranger until he or she has mastered at least the rudiments of the primary tongue.

Second, English religious traditions were without a doubt the most salient factors in American religious life. Non-British Protestantism, as well as the Catholic and Jewish faiths, have been particularly influenced by the Anglo-Saxon culture. Among leading Christian churches in America, the Episcopal, Congregational, Methodist, Presbyterian, and Baptist denominations have English roots. Equally important are the American work ethic and the philosophy of capitalism that were shaped to a large degree by Britain's strong Puritan heritage. The early settlers on the New England Coast believed earnestly that work was a strong defense against the temptation to sin offered by Satan (Feagin, 1984).

Third, American higher education has been molded by Anglo-Saxon influences. Harvard, the first, and still the most influential university in America, was founded in 1636 with a gift of a library and 780 pounds from John Harvard, an immigrant Puritan minister. After the court of the Massachusetts Bay Colony had voted a small endowment toward the establishment of a "schoale" or "colledge," Yale, was founded in 1701 by leading citizens of New Haven, Connecticut, as the third oldest institution of higher learning in North America. Seven other universities were established in various communities before the Revolution, all of them are still in existence. The curriculum and pedagogical methods of each were taken directly from the great universities of England, particularly Oxford and Cambridge. The American public school system has been the primary instrument for perpetuating Anglo-Saxon values and culture.

Fourth, the United States is the heir to both the English system of common law, dating from the mid-twelfth-century reign of King Henry II, and the English political structure. Morrison (1965) points out that the Puritan institutions of New England provided the model for later political and legal developments in America. Not very long after the first permanent English settlements were made on this continent, the English monarchs established representative assemblies in the new colonies. The principle enshrined in the Magna Carta proclaiming that not even the ruler is above the law is still exalted in the United States.

Of the fifty-six signers of the Declaration of Independence, eight were not born in America. Those eight were born in the British Isles, and they emigrated to America: Button Gwinnett and Robert Morris (England); Francis Lewis (Wales); James Smith, George Taylor, and Matthew Thornton (Ireland); and James Wilson and John Witherspoon (Scotland). To further gauge the pervasive influence of the English ethnic strain, one has only to trace the ancestry of American presidents. Of the forty-two presidents from George Washington to Bill Clinton, more than 60 percent have been of English origin. All but five have had English, Welsh, Irish, Scotch-Irish, or Scottish origins. The five who lacked such a background have all been of Northern European background—Dutch or German-Swiss. A very large number of leaders in finance and industry in the latter part of the nineteenth century and the early twentieth century were the so-called "robber barons," of English and Scottish ancestry (Josephson, 1962). They were stalwart believers in the Puritan ethic, and they exercised an enormous influence, both for good and for ill, over the American economic and political systems. People of Anglo-Saxon stock have achieved impressive accomplishments in many other fields. Some writers have observed that the Anglo-Saxon Protestant domination of American life has declined within the past three decades. Even so, there is little doubt that U.S. citizens of

English ancestry still wield enormous power in America, both politically and economically.

Welsh

If asked, the Welsh make it quite plain that they are not English. Most of the present-day Welsh are descendants of the tribes Julius Caesar struggled with in his invasion of Britain in 54 B.C. The Welsh have a distinctive language of their own. It can be traced back to a common Celtic tongue, Breton, spoken by those fierce warriors who often fought Caesar to a standstill (the language is still spoken by many people today in Wales). Further, the Welsh people resisted the English kings down to the time of the defeat of Owen Glendower by Henry IV in 1415. They had been good Roman Catholics during the time of Henry VIII, following his lead in withdrawing from the authority of Rome. In the latter part of the sixteenth century, the doctrines of Baptists, Presbyterians, Quakers, and Congregationalists penetrated Wales. The dissenters from the Church of England suffered persecution for nearly a century. Further persecution of religious dissenters came with the restoration of the Stuarts to the throne of England in 1660. Consequently, most Quakers and many Baptists and Presbyterians left Wales to seek religious freedom in the New World (Hartmann, 1967).

Welsh Quaker and Baptist immigrants founded group settlements in America. John Myles, the "father of the Welsh Baptist movement," set sail with his flock to America in 1663, and they settled at Rehoboth in Plymouth Colony. However, it was not long before the little group brought down the wrath of the orthodox churches upon them. The Welsh then moved their meeting place to the township of Barrington and later to where it now stands—about 10 miles from Providence, Rhode Island. Shortly thereafter, the General Court of Plymouth bestowed upon them a fairly sizable grant of land called "Swansea" in honor of the largest town in the area of Wales from which they had come. Myles died in 1683, but by 1700 four more Baptist churches had been founded. The Welsh settlement did well and most of the families became successful farmers.

The second, and much larger, Welsh settlement in America was established by Quakers who were also fleeing from religious persecution in England. About the same time that William Penn had negotiated his vast grant of land from Charles II, Welsh Quakers got from Penn a tract of 40,000 acres that was set aside by mutual agreement as a separate barony so that the Welsh might preserve their language and institutions. The barony was situated on the west side of the

Schuylkill River to the northwest of Philadelphia. Penn gave them the right of self-government in the bargain. The first group of Welsh Quaker immigrants in Pennsylvania arrived in 1682. Between 1682 and 1700, the Welsh were the largest body of immigrants settling in Pennsylvania. Most of them were of the gentry or yeoman farm classes, and a large number were quite prosperous (Hartmann, 1967).

Although Penn denied the Welsh the right to civil authority and a regular township government, they did little more than protest strongly to him. While they could not govern themselves separately from the rest of the Pennsylvania inhabitants, they could still maintain their own institutions and language without fear of repression. A second group of Welsh Quakers arrived in Philadelphia in 1698. They were joined by people of other faiths, particularly Anglicans and Welsh Baptists. The immigrants founded seven churches in Pennsylvania as well as five in New Jersey. The Welsh Anglican immigrants were equally busy; they founded six churches in the Philadelphia area. In 1701, Penn granted 30,000 acres in the Great Valley of Delaware to three Welshmen—David Evans, William Davies, and William Willis. It was not long before most of the grant land was filled with Welsh immigrants from Pennsylvania and Wales.

The Welsh were also able to found two colonies in the Deep South: a small one near the Black River and Burgaw Creek in North Carolina in the 1730s and a much larger one along the Peedee River in South Carolina. Not much is known about the North Carolina settlement. The South Carolina settlement consisted at first of 173,000 acres granted to the Welsh in 1737 by the South Carolina Assembly. Within a decade, nearly all the South Carolina land, which had been extended, was taken by Welsh immigrants, mostly Baptists from Delaware, Pennsylvania, and Wales. The area became exclusively Welsh and the land was turned into a prosperous plantation settlement by 1776. African slaves were brought into the colony very early in its existence, and it was the only Welsh settlement in America where slavery was firmly established.

Welsh immigration to America continued during the nineteenth century but for reasons different from those that impelled the earlier immigrants in the seventeenth and eighteenth centuries. In the first two decades of the nineteenth century, most of the Welsh immigrants were farmers. The landlords and country gentry in Wales owned nearly all the land and they rented most of it to tenants on lease arrangements. According to Welsh tradition, when the father died, either the oldest or youngest son inherited the farm or the father's rights as a tenant. Welsh farm families were usually large and many of the sons had to work as farm laborers or leave the area where they had grown up. In addition, between 1798 and 1802, bad harvests undercut what small livelihood many Welsh farmers could eke out of the land. Little wonder that when they heard of good cheap land across the ocean, many Welsh farmers took advantage of it. Before 1812, five new Welsh farm settlements had been established in America—one in Pennsylvania, one in New York, and three in Ohio.

In the late 1830s, the vast iron and coal areas of Pennsylvania and Ohio were exploited for the first time, and there was a great need for workers experienced in such an environment. Welsh miners and steel workers soon began to leave Wales for America to take jobs in their respective industrial fields. Many of them even went to California to search for gold, although relatively few became wealthy. After the Civil War, numerous Welsh journeyed to Colorado to work in the coal mines there. Also, Welsh iron workers immigrated to Pittsburgh and soon became one of the most numerous immigrant groups in the city. In fact, the Welsh were the main immigrant group among iron workers in the 1850s in the United States (Golab, 1977). In 1843, the bituminous mines in Ohio attracted many Welsh immigrants. After the Civil War, experienced Welsh miners were in great demand in Mercer and Lawrence counties in Pennsylvania; bituminous coal attracted Welsh immigrants to West Virginia, Maryland, Tennessee, Iowa, Missouri, and Colorado. Welsh miners and steel workers became specialized pioneers in the development of the coal and steel industries in the United States. A substantial number of them rose to supervisory jobs within various American companies engaged in those enterprises. By the time of the Civil War, both the coal and steel industries in Scranton, Pennsylvania, had the largest Welsh immigration population of any city in America.

Contributions

Edward Roberts and Robert Wharton were early mayors of Philadelphia during the colonial period. Thomas Wynne, a noted physician, settled in Philadelphia, and attended William Penn on his first voyage to America. Nicholas Easton and his son, John, were both governors of Rhode Island during the colonial period. John Evans was governor of colonial Pennsylvania, as was Thomas Lloyd. Lewis Morris served as governor of New Jersey during the colonial period and later was chief justice of the New York Supreme Court. His son, Robert Hunter Morris, was governor of Pennsylvania and chief justice of the New Jersey Supreme Court. Gouverneur Morris, a grandson of Lewis and a signer of the Declaration of Independence, was an active member of the Continental Congress and of the Constitutional

Convention. He was a U.S. senator in 1800 and later served as chairman of the Erie Canal Commission. His half brother, Francis Lewis, was a signer of the Declaration of Independence. Another half brother, Robert Morris, was chief justice of the New York Supreme Court.

Thomas Jefferson—author of the Declaration of Independence, founder of the University of Virginia, governor of Virginia, and secretary of state—was the third president of the United States. Robert Morris, born in Liverpool of Welsh parents, was a financier of the American Revolution who arranged for purchase of supplies for Washington's army. He was also a signer of the Declaration of Independence and a U.S. senator from Pennsylvania. Lewis Evans, America's greatest geographer in the colonial period, made the finest maps of the middle colonies. Benjamin Griffith was the first historian of Baptists. Morgan Edwards founded Brown University. Thomas Cadwallader, a surgeon in colonial America, was the first colonial doctor to inoculate against smallpox in the colonies. His son, John, was a general in the Revolutionary War. John Morgan was physician-in-chief of the Revolutionary Army. John Jones was the author of the first American surgical textbook. Elihu Yale was the chief early benefactor of the college that became Yale University. William Floyd, a descendant of early seventeenth-century Welsh immigrants, was a signer of the Declaration of Independence. Button Gwinnett, born in England and the son of Welsh parents, was a governor of Georgia and a general in the Revolutionary Army as well as a signer of the Declaration of Independence.

The Reverend David Jones, a Baptist minister and son of Welsh immigrants, became perhaps the most famous chaplain during the Revolution. David Thomas, "the iron-master of America," perfected a technique that allowed anthracite coal to be used as a smelting fuel. Evan Stephens, a Welsh immigrant who guided the Mormon Tabernacle Choir to becoming one of the greatest American choral groups, was one of America's foremost composers of religious music. Frank Lloyd Wright, grandson of Welsh immigrants, was one of America's greatest architects. And Joseph Parry was one of the finest composers in both the United States and Wales.

Scotch-Irish

Many historians differentiate between Scotch-Irish and the Scottish immigrants in America, although the term "Scotch-Irish" was not used in the United States until the 1830s and the 1840s and is still not used anywhere else. The Scotch-Irish in American history are those Scots from the Lowlands of Scotland, two hundred thousand of whom were moved by the English to Ulster (now Northern Ireland) in the seventeenth century as a buffer against native Irish Catholics. After conquering Ireland, the English government wanted a loyal population settled there. When Irish Catholics immigrated to the United States in large numbers in the early decades of the nineteenth century, Irish Protestants of Scottish descent used the term "Scotch-Irish" to differentiate themselves from the "other Irish" (Daniels, 1990, p. 79). More than a hundred thousand of them came to America before 1760.

There were numerous reasons for the Scotch-Irish immigration to America. As Protestants, they shunned the native Irish Catholics, who in turn shunned them. However, as dissenters, they had to pay tithes to the Anglican Church, and they were denied full civil rights. Parliament passed the Wool Act in 1699 which forbade the export of finished products that might be competition with English products. Also, English landlords raised rents severalfold on the land so that even subsistence was difficult. As if economic hardships imposed by the English on them were not enough, famine sometimes stalked the land and prices rose capriciously on the necessities of life. At the same time, the Scotch-Irish had good reason to believe that they were at the mercy of uncaring masters. In 1704 the Test Act was passed in England, taking away non-Anglicans' right to vote and hold all but the most unimportant political positions (Reich, 1989).

Many of the immigrants from Protestant Ireland first settled on the New England frontiers. Although both the Scotch-Irish and the New England Congregationalists were Calvinists in their religious doctrines, the Congregationalists did not welcome Presbyterians. As so often is the case in the history of religious dissenters, many of those who desired freedom for themselves were not willing to grant the same freedom to others. Feeling unwanted in Massachusetts, some of the Scotch-Irish migrated to New York and New Jersey. Most of them, however, went to Pennsylvania. Many of the subsequent settlers from Ireland chose that colony also. To a great extent, however, they did so because the port of Philadelphia was the common port of arrival (Westerkamp, 1988). In fact, the first presbytery in the North American colonies was the Presbytery of Philadelphia, established in 1706.

Soon after settling in Pennsylvania, large numbers of Scotch-Irish branched out into the interior of the southern colonies, down Virginia's Shenandoah Valley. Augusta, the birthplace of Woodrow Wilson, was the most heavily Scotch-Irish county in the United States. In the 1740s, Scotch-Irish migrated into the North Carolina Piedmont and by the 1760s they were in South Carolina. Some of those settlers were fresh immigrants who had landed in Philadelphia, but many were second-generation younger sons of earlier immigrants. By 1776, the interior of North Carolina contained about sixty thousand settlers and South Carolina had about eighty thousand, with the Scotch-Irish being the majority. The flood of Scotch-Irish immigrants entering the colonies can be gauged by the fact that between 1760 and 1775, more than fifty-five thousand of them passed through colonial ports (Bailyn, 1986). Because Scotch-Irish were often noted for their aggressiveness and sometimes even downright truculence, some colonial officials deliberately settled them on the frontier as a buffer against the French and Indians.

Contributions

Since their first migration to America, Scotch-Irish immigrants have contributed significantly to the country's enrichment. Among distinguished Scotch Americans have been the following.

A large number of the Scotch-Irish immigrants came to the colonies as indentured servants before the Revolution. Like other immigrants, they were often packed into boats like cattle for the dangerous transatlantic crossing. Many of them were excellent craftsmen, often in linen manufacturing. Large numbers of them were also highly literate for their time. Wherever they settled, Scotch-Irish founded new churches and established additional presbyterys. Because these were new religious establishments, the church had to train young men as ministers and church administrators. To help do this, William Tennent, a graduate of the University of Edinburgh, built Log College in 1728 near Philadelphia, and it produced several distinguished Presbyterian ministers and theologians, many of whom became leaders of the religious movement called the "Great Awakening" (Reich, 1989). Scotch-Irish Americans established Hampden-Sydney (1776) in Virginia and Dickinson College (1783) in Pennsylvania; while Scots founded the College of New Jersey (later renamed Princeton) in 1736.

The Reverend Francis Alison, professor of moral philosophy at the College of Philadelphia, was perhaps the greatest classical scholar of colonial America. Charles Thompson was secretary to the Continental Congress. Thomas McKean was president of the Continental Congress, a signer of the Declaration of Independence, and chief justice and governor of Pennsylvania. James Smith, a lawyer, was a signer of the Declaration of Independence and member of the Continental Congress. George Read was a member of the Continental Congress, a signer of the Declaration of Independence, and a delegate to the Constitutional Convention. He was instrumental in convincing

Delaware voters to ratify the Constitution. Later, he was a senator from Delaware and chief justice of the Delaware Supreme Court.

John C. Calhoun was U.S. secretary of war, vice president of the United States, and a U.S. senator from South Carolina. Thomas "Stonewall" Jackson was one of the leading Confederate generals in the Civil War. William H. McGuffey was an educator and the compiler of McGuffey's Readers, the most widely used books in American schools in the nineteenth century. Edward A. MacDowell was a pianist and composer. Cyrus H. McCormick invented a reaping machine that revolutionized American farming. James Clark McReynolds was a U.S. attorney general and associate justice of the U.S. Supreme Court. American presidents of Scotch-Irish descent, fully or partially, have been: Andrew Jackson, James Polk, James Buchanan, Ulysses Grant, Chester Arthur, William McKinley, Woodrow Wilson, Harry Truman, and Richard Nixon.

Scots

Most historians refer to these immigrants as "Scots," as opposed to the "Scotch-Irish," who were partly Teutonic in origin. They came to America from the Highlands of Scotland. They were Celtic in origin, spoke Gaelic, and came to Scotland from Ireland, perhaps as early as A.D. 500. Although most Scots did not choose to emigrate from Scotland before 1730 many did so as a result of involuntary pressure by the English government. Each of the three times Oliver Cromwell's armies vanquished Scottish forces, he sent hundreds of Scottish prisoners-of-war to the New World, and so did governments after revolts by the Scottish people (Landsman, 1985).

There was considerably more voluntary immigration after 1730, when many Scots came as indentured servants. Between 1763 and 1775, about twenty-five thousand Highland Scots came to America. There were many reasons for the immigration to America before the Revolution. Just as in Ireland, rents were rising sharply in order to satisfy greedy landlords, most of whom were not Scots. Local industries were failing at a rapid rate because of English trade laws. At the same time, the landlords were busily enclosing their lands, which meant commercialization of agriculture and the eviction of tenants. A pronounced rise in the population after 1700 meant that overcrowding was making it very difficult for farm laborers to subsist (Bailyn, 1986).

Furthermore, the old social system was breaking up. The harsh laws imposed by the English on the Scots after the rebellion of 1745 effectively destroyed the relationship which had existed between the once-powerful lairds and the lowest cottagers. The English laws did away with private jurisdictions, banished the rebellious Highland lairds, and gave their lands to Lowland gentry, forbade the traditional dress, and made illegal all weapons that were privately owned. Thus, the centuries-old clan system was swiftly taken apart. There was a high price to be paid, however, for those conditions accelerated the emigration of some of the most skilled Scottish workers to the New World. Many of the merchants and traders in American cities were Scots, as were large numbers of professionals in various skills. No doubt, some Englishmen realized the mistakes of harsh laws when of the fifty-six members of the Continental Congress who adopted the Declaration of Independence at least eleven were of Scottish birth or ancestry.

Thousands of Scots immigrated to North Carolina, which granted them a ten-year tax exemption; and others built settlements in the Mohawk Valley of New York and on Prince Edward Island in Canada (Reich, 1989). An interesting enterprise was pursued in East Jersey, when the earliest groups of Scots from the northeast of Scotland settled in the middle colonies (Landsman, 1985). Scottish proprietors established a colony of Scots in East Jersey, which largely perpetuated rural Scotland lifestyles. The East Jersey settlement was Quaker or Episcopal-sponsored. The leader among the proprietors was Robert Barclay, a Northeastern Scottish laird Quaker.

The first Scottish immigrants to the East Jersey area consisted of about seven hundred Scots, about half of them indentured servants. It is significant that at least 40 percent of the early settlers came in family units, and a majority of them brought relatives with them. More than 20 percent of the population of central New Jersey in 1750 were of Scottish descent, a somewhat larger portion than found in other areas of the middle colonies. The Scots brought new commercial networks into central New Jersey, improved agricultural methods on the estates, and built mines, mills, and other industries. The proprietors of the estates imported servants and other settlers from Scotland and Ulster.

Contributions

James Wilson was a lawyer, a member of the Continental Congress, a signer of the Declaration of Independence, a delegate to the Constitutional Convention, an associate justice of the U.S. Supreme Court, and the first professor of law at the University of Pennsylvania. John Witherspoon was a signer of the Declaration of Independence (the only clergyman to sign it), president of the College of New Jersey (later Princeton), and one of the leaders in the Presbyterian Church. James Craik was organizer of the United States Army's medical service, and John Paul Jones, naval hero of the Revolutionary War, was the founder of the United States Navy.

Charles Nisbet was the first president of Dickinson College. James Gordon Bennett founded the *New York Daily Herald*. Alexander Wilson was author of the first great work in American bird study, *American Ornithology* (1808–1814). Andrew Carnegie, founder of Carnegie Steel (later United States Steel), gave away hundreds of millions of dollars for educational and other purposes in the United States and Scotland. In addition, he helped establish scores of American public libraries. James Monroe was the fifth president of the United States and promulgator of the Monroe Doctrine. Rutherford B. Hayes was the nineteenth president of the United States and governor of Ohio. At least fifteen of the fifty justices of the U.S. Supreme Court from 1789 to 1882 were of Scottish descent.

Irish

One of the most fateful days for the Irish people occurred when Pope Adrian IV bestowed Ireland on the English King Henry II. After the break with Rome in 1534, Henry VIII began the oppression of the Irish. He made the Irish ruling class dependent on the crown through the "surrender and re-grant" of land. Irish Catholic titleholders lost their titles to land, and the crown, through its intermediaries, redistributed it to Protestants. This procedure of disinvestment ignored the Irish custom of land tenure and made land heritable, rather than tenable for life only. This effectively replaced disloyal Irish with loyal English. It also provided a way for Henry to relieve England's increasing population pressures by encouraging migration to Ireland. Not all Irish were Catholics, however. The Irish society consisted of Anglicans (the politically dominant group), Protestant dissenters (mainly Scots), and Roman Catholics (the great majority of the population).

Protesting the land settlements, Tudor noblemen rebelled in 1590. They were defeated in 1603 and Gaelic Ireland was subsequently destroyed. Loyal Protestant nobles, gentry, and other officials were allocated forfeited dissenter noblemen's land. Equally devastating to Ireland was the resettlement of two thousand British families in six planted counties. Additional forfeitures followed the Irish insurrection of 1641. Between 1649 and 1652 Oliver Cromwell, "Lord Protector" of Great Britain, crushed Irish Catholic resistance to English rule. In that war, more than half the Irish people (about

750,000) were exterminated. Parliament declared that all land possessed by Irish Catholics was to be taken away and given to English loyalists, and the Irish could stay as renters or servants of the English. After Cromwell defeated the Irish, Protestants comprised ten percent of the population but owned 95 percent of the land; Irish Catholics, about 90 percent of the population, owned 5 percent of the land (Beckert, 1958; Gonzales, 1990).

Under the penal laws passed by Parliament during the eighteenth century, Catholics could not acquire land from Protestants unless they renounced Catholicism and converted to Protestantism. Nor could they lease land for more than thirty-one years; and they were ordered to divide the land among all descendants when a family head died, even though the Protestant landowners were allowed to practice primogeniture. Further, all priests had to pledge allegiance to the English or face dire punishment. The English banished all bishops from Ireland in 1719 and decreed that Irish Catholics could not vote for members of Parliament, could not place their children in public schools, could not have schools of their own, could not practice law, and could not serve in the military (Greeley, 1972). In addition, Irish Catholics were forced to pay higher rent. Also, Irish Catholics were forced to give free labor on public work projects and tithe to the district's Protestant churches.

Toward the end of the seventeenth century, a steady number of Irish indentured servants and convicted criminals came to North America (McCaffrey, 1976). Many of the immigrants came from Dublin, where large numbers of the Irish could find neither work nor lease land (Miller, 1985). South Carolina, Maryland, and Virginia passed laws to stop or reduce the importation of Irish immigrants.

The New World environment took its toll. In 1671, four-fifths of the indentured servants perished not long after they arrived—from disease, climate, or overwork. In all probability, the Irish were less hardy than the English immigrants in withstanding fatal illnesses. In addition, there was a great deal of abuse of Irish Catholic servants by their masters, especially in eighteenth-century Maryland where the plantation owners were particularly harsh on them. Most of the Irish Catholic servants did not become yeomen farmers when they received their freedom. Instead, they lived short, oppressed lives in colonial America.

Not all Irish Catholics lived such unfortunate lives. For example, Charles Carroll immigrated to Maryland in 1681 after the English took his estates in Ireland. Nearly a century later, Charles Carroll, one of his descendants, was a signer of the Declaration of Independence—the only Catholic to put his name to the document.

However all the Irish Catholics in America supported the Revolution. Quite plainly, they had no reason to be loyal to England. Nevertheless, during the eighteenth century, sporadic attacks on Irish Catholics took place in the colonies. In the 1790s, there were fierce assaults on Irish Catholics in Maryland and in other states of the new republic (Feagin, 1984).

Although the Bill of Rights had been enshrined in the Constitution, New York did not revoke its anti-Catholic laws until 1806; Connecticut did not do so until 1818, and Massachusetts waited until 1833 to take its discriminatory laws regarding Catholics off the books. Such discrimination seems particularly sad in view of the fact that, before 1820, at least three thousand Irish laborers helped dig the Erie Canal. From that time until long after the Civil War, Irish workers dug canals, built railways, and furnished many American cities with streets, sewers, waterworks, and other necessities of civilized life.

Contributions

Large numbers of Irish Americans have enriched the United States with their varied talents. William R. Grace, founder of the William R. Grace and Company shipping line was the first Roman Catholic mayor of New York City. William Randolph Hearst was an editor, publisher, and political leader. Joseph Patrick Kennedy was a highly successful businessman. He was also the first chairman of the Securities and Exchange Commission, as well as ambassador to Great Britain from 1937 to 1940. His four sons devoted their lives to their country: Joseph Kennedy Jr. was killed in an airplane explosion while flying a dangerous mission in World War II; John Kennedy was a U.S. senator from Massachusetts and the thirty-fifth president of the United States. He was the first Roman Catholic to hold that high office. Robert Kennedy was attorney general of the United States, a U.S. senator from New York, and a martyred presidential candidate killed in 1968. Edward Kennedy has achieved recognition as a U.S. senator from Massachusetts.

Harry "Bing" Crosby was a popular singer and movie star. Grace Kelly, one of the world's most admired movie actresses, was Princess of Monaco. John McCormack was one of the greatest tenors in history and a movie star. Although born in Dublin, McCormack became an American citizen in 1917. Spencer Tracy was a renowned movie actor and winner of two Oscars. Father Edward Flanagan founded Boys Town, U.S.A., a refuge for boys of all religions and races. William Buckley is an editor, writer, novelist, and a leading conservative theorist. Margaret Mitchell was the author of *Gone with the Wind*, one of the most popular American novels. F. Scott Fitzgerald and Flannery O'Connor were two of the finest writers the United States has produced; he wrote about upper-class life and she wrote about the rural South with considerable insight. Eugene O'Neill is the only American playwright to win four Pulitzer Prizes for his works, and the first American playwright to win a Nobel Prize for literature (1936).

William Donovan was a soldier, politician, and founder of the Office of Strategic Services (OSS), the forerunner of the Central Intelligence Agency (CIA). Philip Sheridan was a leading Civil War general in the Union Army. He became commander-in-chief of the U.S. Army in 1884. William Brennan was a distinguished U.S. Supreme Court justice. Eugene McCarthy, a renowned poet and professor of political science, was a U.S. senator from Minnesota; he ran as an independent presidential candidate in 1976. Daniel Patrick Moynihan was a professor at Harvard University and Massachusetts Institute of Technology, U.S. ambassador to India, ambassador to the United Kingdom, and currently, a U.S. senator from New York.

Thomas "Tip" O'Neill was a U.S. representative to Congress from Massachusetts and speaker of the House of Representatives. Alfred E. Smith was governor of New York and an unsuccessful candidate for the presidency in 1928. John Carroll, America's first Catholic bishop, was archbishop of Baltimore and one of the founders of Georgetown University, the nation's oldest Catholic institution of higher learning. James Gibbons, archbishop of Baltimore and a Roman Catholic cardinal, was a liberal churchman who defended organized labor both in the United States and at the Vatican. John McCloskey was the first American Roman Catholic cardinal and the first president of St. John's College (now Fordham University), as well as the archbishop of New York. He supervised the completion of St. Patrick's Cathedral and dedicated it in 1879.

References

Bailyn, B. (1986). *Voyagers to the West: A passage in the peopling of America on the eve of the Revolution*. New York: Knopf.

Beckert, J. C. (1958). *A short history of Ireland*. London: Oxford University Press.

Bridenbaugh, C. (1971). *Myths and realities: Societies of the colonial South*. New York: Atheneum.

Daniels, R. (1990). *Coming to America: A history of immigration and ethnicity in American life*. New York: Harper-Collins.

Feagin, J. R. (1984). *Racial and ethnic relations*, 2nd ed. Englewood Cliffs, NJ: Prentice-Hall.

Golab, C. (1977). *Immigrant destinations*, Philadelphia: Temple University Press.

Gonzales, J. L., Jr. (1990). *Racial and ethnic groups in America*. Dubuque, IA: Kendall/Hunt.

Greeley, A. M. (1972). *That most distressful nation*. Chicago: Quadrangle Books.

Handlin, O., & Handlin, L. (1986). *Liberty in America: 1600 to the present: Volume I: Liberty and power: 1600–1760*. New York: Harper & Row.

Hartmann, E. G. (1967). *Americans from Wales*. Boston: Christopher.

Hutchinson, E. P. (1956). *Immigrants and their children, 1850–1950*. New York: Russell & Russell.

Josephson, M. (1962). *The robber barons: The great American capitalists: 1861–1901*. New York: Harcourt Brace Harvest.

Larabee, B. W. (1972). *America's nation-time: 1607–1789*. New York: W. W. Norton.

Landsman, N. C. (1985). *Scotland and its first American colony, 1683–1765*. Princeton: Princeton University Press.

McCaffrey, L. J. (1976). *The Irish diaspora in America*, Bloomington: Indiana University Press.

Miller, K. A. (1985). *Emigrants and exiles: Ireland and the Irish exodus to North America*. New York: Oxford University Press.

Morrison, S. E. (1965). *The Oxford history of the American people*. New York: Oxford University Press.

Reich, J. R. (1989). *Colonial America*. Englewood Cliffs, NJ: Prentice Hall.

Thernstrom, S. (Ed.). (1980). *Harvard encyclopedia of American ethnic groups*. Cambridge: Harvard University Press.

Westerkamp, M. J. (1988). *Triumph of the laity: Scots-Irish piety and the great awakening, 1625–1760*. New York: Oxford University Press.

Pride and Poverty: An Irish Integrity
by William Alfred

My great-grandmother, Anna Maria, lived in a "city house," in the part of Brooklyn between Red Hook and Brooklyn Heights then called the Point, but recently rechristened Cobble Hill by real-estate agents. City houses were houses which fell to the borough by foreclosure for nonpayment of taxes, and which were rented out at nominal rents as a form of patronage. At this point, I must in honesty say investigable fact leaves off and legend begins. Born though I was in 1922, I am a child of the nineteenth century, for it was Anna Maria who raised me until I was four years old, that is, took care of me while my parents were out working. It is mostly her memories I propose to retell. But memories make uncertain evidence. Moreover, in many cases, I cannot rightly say where her memories leave off and my embroidering of them begins.

Anna Maria was the name I was conditioned to call her. I avoid "taught" advisedly. You learned what you were not to say to her as you learned not to lay hands on the ruby-red, cylindrical kerosene stoves scattered through that house of hers, which, now as I look back on it, she deliberately allowed to fall the ruin. She never struck but with her tongue, but when she did, you winced. When the quarter-a-week insurance man, with whom she played an endless game of hide-and seek, once flushed her out, she called him a pimp. And once in a spasm of reflex chauvinism, she called Queen Victoria, whom she rather admired, "a goddamned old water dog."

If I am a child of the nineteenth century, Anna Maria Gavin Egan was a child of the late eighteenth. She, too, was raised by an old woman, her grandmother. With little or no education, she spoke and acted in the quirkily formal manner of a character in a Sterne novel. Her women friends she called by their last names, as they did her. Perhaps her exacting that we call her by her first name was her way of admitting the children of her blood (the kind of phrase she'd have used) to deeper intimacy.

She was born in Castlebar, Mayo, sometime between 1845 and 1850. She never knew her true age. Perhaps her birth was unregistered; perhaps the records were destroyed during the bad years. She was born sickly; and her mother separated her from her twin brother and sent her as in infant to the seashore, where her grandmother raised her until she "grew into her strength." One of her brothers became a Fenian and was forced to emigrate to the states. After his emigration, it was impossible to make a go of the small bakeshop her mother ran. British soldiers harried the shop and dwelling with nuisance raids, bayoneting the flour bags and even the featherbeds in mock searches for the absent brother. In 1866 or 1867, she and her mother made the "eight weeks" voyage in a "sailing vessel" which brought her to New York.

Of Ireland she rarely spoke, save to recall that she was often hungry there and that for her main meal she often ate cress out of the brooks on oaten bread with a bit of lard. Although she always used to say she had no desire to return to Ireland to live, she lived out of a trunk to her dying day, and taught her children to do the same. I myself, till well on in my twenties, felt that Ireland, which I had never seen, was my true country. When, over eighty, she died in the early thirties, it did not seem strange six months afterward to receive a clipping from an Irish newspaper, which read: "Died in Exile: Anna Maria Gavin Egan."

Of her first years here, she never tired of speaking. She and her mother landed at Castle Garden and walked up Broadway to City Hall, with bundles of clothes and pots and featherbeds in their arms. The singing of the then exposed telegraph wires frightened them, as did the bustle of the people in the streets. They lost their fear when they met an Irish policeman who directed them to a rooming house on Baxter Street.

It must have been spring or summer when they arrived. The windows were open; and she was wakened often in the night by the sound of drunken voices singing:

We'll hang Jefferson Davis
On a sour apple tree.

Her training as a "manty-maker" (mantuamaker, in other words, dressmaker) gave her an advantage over other girls of her age. She got a job fast. No woman would wear black satin, she remembered, because Mrs. Surratt, the lady in whose rooming house the murder of Lincoln had been plotted, was hanged in a dress of that material. On her way from work the first year, she nightly passed a house in whose tall, lit first floor windows sat the most beautiful women she had ever seen, dressed to the nines, their hair as trimly curled, their faces painted fresh as new French china dolls. After weeks of gawking, she built up the courage to hazard a smile. "Come up here, you blond bitch," one of the women called to her, "and we'll wipe that smile off your face." Years after she was married, she was finally reunited with her brother, who had gone West in a vain quest for a fortune and returned without even the wife he had married in California. "What happened to her?" Anna Maria asked. "She ran off with another fellow," he answered. "Why?" said she. "Because," said he, "I've but a little bit of a thing."

The raciness of these stories, which she told me when I was eight, would make her seen atypical. But all of her women friends, even the pious ones, were as free-spoken. There was not a Mother Machree among them. Free-spoken though she was about human matters, Anna Maria was a sphinx of reserve when it came to religion. She never went to mass, although she prayed the rosary nightly. Nor would she ever allow a priest in her house. Visiting priests, she said, brought bad luck. Why, she would not say, for it also was unlucky "to talk against the cloth."

The city house she rented for eighteen dollars a month was an abandoned mansion, let to her because my dead great-grandfather had "done favors at the Hall" to someone dead even longer than he. Churchill's mother was born five minutes' walk from it. The Protestants, for it was what she called native-born Americans, moved out as the immigrants moved in. The first wave immigrants must have been German and Scandinavian: there were still a few families of them left in my day. Then from the backyard tenement houses on the other side of Court Street in Brooklyn, the Irish began to move in. They were succeeded by the Italians, with whom they lived in uncertain amity.

Her house was a narrow brownstone, two windows to every floor except the ground, where the place of one window was taken by a double door of solid walnut plated with layers of dust-pocked cheap black enamel. Its shallow stoop, with ornate, Gothic-arched wrought-iron railings eaten away by rust, was fronted by a long area (pronounced "airy"). A path of slate slabs led up to the stoop past an unkempt grass plot surrounded by overgrown privet hedges. Under the stoop was the blocked up front entrance to the basement kitchen. And to the side of that, the cellar door, which boys would try to steal every election eve to feed the bonfire up on Union Street.

A stationery store had nibbled into the basement of the brownstone on the corner of Clinton Street. It dealt in penny wares, lousy-heads (nonpareils), twisted wires with red and white propellers on them, seasons of decalcomania stamps, and sweet wax buckteeth and marbles. It was run by the Wechslers, the only Jews in the neighborhood. They were beloved by Irish and Italians alike, because of their kindness to children, and because they had the only phone on the block, and would walk the block's length to call a person to it.

Little Siberia, my mother called the house. Its center was the volcano of a coal stove in the basement kitchen. No comfort was to be won of a winter's night more than eighteen inches from it; and the butter had to be set on the mantel over it to prevent having to split it with a cleaver. Little Siberia—the full sense of being an alien and poor was also in the phrase.

In earlier years the two top floors were let out to aging Irish spinsters. But in the late twenties, there were only two left, a bedridden saint of seventy and her sister, both living on Old Age. All the other rooms were shut off. The house itself has always stood in my mind as a convenient symbol of what happened to the first two generations of my mother's family under the impact of immigration, each closed room standing for failed or refused chances.

In her late twenties, Anna Maria married a widower years her senior, who died long before I was born. His first wife had been a Sheridan, a distinction which the family rejoiced in as being theirs by osmosis. Whether he had children by that marriage, I do not know. I suspect not, because the legend that was made of him pictures him as lavishing more love on a scapegrace niece than on any of his children by Anna Maria. He comes down to me as a silent man in a tasseled smoking cap, who slept apart from his wife in the front room of the basement, and who, when his niece would scratch at the basement door at three in the morning, legless (drunk) and scared to go home, would relinquish his bed to her, bundling himself in his overcoat to keep fitful watch over her from a creaking rocker in the stoveless room.

Anna Maria seems to have been as much her own woman in the 1880s as she was in the 1920s and 1930s. From time to time she would disappear from the house for days at a time. On one of these occasions, my great-grandfather was asked "Where's Egan?" "I don't know," he answered, "I think she ran away with a soldier." That was the nearest anyone came to solving the mystery.

The Dad, as his children called him, was a junkman, a canny one, with party and institutional connections that let him on the ground floor of any major demolition. He could read or write nothing but numbers; but those he must have been able to manage with profitable shrewdness. Poverty did not empty the table or close the doors of the house until after his death.

Anna Maria had four children by him: my grandmother, Agnes, her twin, Martin, William, and Gertrude. Since Martin was a frail baby, Anna Maria gave Agnes to her mother to raise, thereby repeating the pattern of her own rearing. When my grandmother Agnes was in her early teens, Anna Maria took her to Ireland where she met her cousin, Stanislaus Bunyan, who as thoroughly loathed her at first sight as she did him. When he later emigrated to America with his sister, Katherine, he stayed with Anna Maria, fell in love with Agnes, and married her. She was eighteen at the time; he twenty-seven.

Impatient, dangerously temperamental, my grandfather earned his living by sketching for newspapers and by taking roles in the second and third-string Frohman road companies. He was said to have drawn for *World* and *Puck*, and to have played the lead in *Dr. Jekyll and Mr. Hyde*. In those simpler days the transformation from Jekyll to Hyde was achieved by a foaming tumbler of Seidlitz powder and a fast fall into a wooden armchair with an open tin of green greasepaint nailed upside down under one broad arm. The sizzling glass once drunk, Jekyll would writhe in the chair, dig his hand to the wrist in the greasepaint, pass the hand over his face as if to wipe away the cold sweat, then shoot up again toward the footlights, green as a beached corpse. Men in the audience gulped; women thudded to the floor.

My grandfather's life was hard, his habits wild; and he shaped his wife in his image. "He had her dancing day and night; and she'd sew sleighbells in the hems of her skirts so the men would be looking at her ankles." Six months after she bore my mother, early in her twentieth year, she died of "congestion of the lungs," a euphemism for tuberculosis, which then was considered stark and certain evidence of a shameless life.

Chapter 4

Other Western, Central, and Northern Europeans

Early in the history of its settlement, America received a substantial number of immigrants from western and northern Europe (Reich, 1989). In 1624, the Dutch West India Company established a trading post on the Hudson River. The Swedish West India Company transported Swedes and Finns to areas along the Delaware River in 1638. New Netherland annexed New Sweden in 1655. Thousands of French Protestants began immigrating to America in 1685 when Louis XIV revoked the Edict of Nantes, a decree by which Henry IV had granted religious toleration and other privileges to the Huguenots in 1598. These and other migratory movements made colonial America a cross-section of Europe by the time of the American Revolution (Handlin & Handlin, 1986). More immigration took place during the 150 years after the Napoleonic Wars in Europe than during any other period in world history.

Great Waves of Immigrants

Beginning in the late 1840s, as successive frontiers were settled, wave after wave of European immigrants came to America, most of them moving westward (Bailyn, 1986; Barton, 1975; Butler, 1983;

ARRIVAL TIDE

U. S. Immigration in the 20th Century

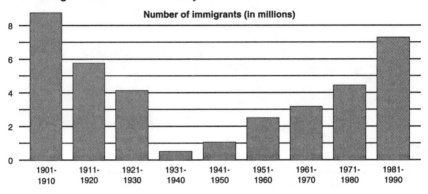

**Countries with the Most People
Immigrating to the USA, 1820-1990**

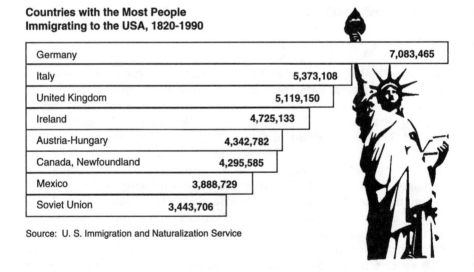

Country	Number
Germany	7,083,465
Italy	5,373,108
United Kingdom	5,119,150
Ireland	4,725,133
Austria-Hungary	4,342,782
Canada, Newfoundland	4,295,585
Mexico	3,888,729
Soviet Union	3,443,706

Source: U. S. Immigration and Naturalization Service

Figure 4.1. U.S. Immigration in the 20th Century

Cuddy, 1982). This immigration began with the Industrial Revolution, which forced Europeans out of rural areas into the cities. Along with various agricultural calamities (Taylor, 1971), between 1750 and 1850, transportation greatly improved, religious persecutions increased, and the population of Europe doubled. All of these factors were major motivational causes for emigration. The final impetus to population shifts was the relaxed immigration policies in many European countries (Gonzales, 1990). The first major wave of Europeans came to America between 1847 and 1856, a time when the frontier extended to the Mississippi Valley and the states on both sides of the central Mississippi region. During that decade, more than three million people immigrated to America, twice the number that had immigrated during the previous seventy years. Most of the new immigrants came from Great Britain, Ireland, and Germany. (See Figure 4.1.)

Even in economically good times, there was a substantial Irish immigration to America, but it increased significantly when potato crops rotted in the ground and famine struck in 1845 and 1846. This greatly accelerated the migratory process. In fact, Irish immigrants accounted for more than half of the inhabitants of New York, Pennsylvania, and Massachusetts in the 1860s. New York City alone had more Irish residents than any other city in the world. Within that period, Irish residents were becoming America's major slum dwellers. Low social status, housing segregation, and job discrimination that characterized Irish Americans in the nineteenth century have been equaled only by similar conditions suffered by African Americans. The "paddies," as the Irish were called, were a mobile group of individuals who filled a disproportionate number of unskilled labor jobs.

Conditions in Germany were not quite as bad as those in Ireland, but they were sufficiently negative to spark a major exodus. Foremost in triggering the German emigration were high rents, escalating prices, crop failures, and the changeover to an industrial economy. Other conditions that impelled emigration from Germany to America in the 1860s and 1870s included low wages, economic depressions, and a high military conscription rate. Between 1816 and 1914, about 5.5 million Germans came to the United States (Moltmann, 1985, p. 14). German immigrants were even more numerous than Irish. Many of the Germans were "Forty-Eighters," people who fled to America in 1848 after an unsuccessful revolution to overthrow various state governments. Most German immigrants, however, were not revolutionists. Instead, they were people looking for better working and living conditions—there were more than 1.5 million of them living in America by 1860 (Thernstrom, 1980). They usually arrived with sufficient funds to allow them to immediately continue inland if they desired to live outside the port city. Except for those who stayed in New York City, most German immigrants proceeded to the states in the upper Mississippi Valley, mainly Illinois, Missouri, Ohio, and Wisconsin. The largest concentration of Germans was in the cities of New York, Cincinnati, Louisville, Chicago, and Milwaukee. New York City had more Germans in the nineteenth century than any other cities in the world except Berlin and Vienna.

After Irish and German immigrants, Scandinavians were the largest northwestern European immigrant group. Famine and world upheaval also played major roles in their emigration. In Sweden and Norway, as in Ireland and Germany, religion and politics were added factors. Religious and political dissenters were persecuted. Furthermore, military conscription and the lack of universal suffrage displeased many Swedes and Norwegians. Added to these factors were the glowing letters that immigrants in America sent to their relatives and friends in Europe. These communications did much to give the United States the aura of a Promised Land.

Several small Scandinavian colonies arose in America before the nineteenth century, but it was not until the late 1800s that Scandinavian immigration began in large numbers. By 1850, nearly eighty thousand Norwegians, Swedes, Finns, and Danes were living in America. Of that group, Norwegians comprised more than half. The second major wave of European immigrants came between 1865 and 1873, and a large number of Scandinavians were in that group too. By then the frontier had moved to the upper Mississippi Valley. Illinois, Iowa, Minnesota, and Wisconsin became predominantly Scandinavian. The largest Scandinavian colonies sprang up in the northern part of Illinois, with Chicago serving as the distribution center for immigrants traveling to other areas of the West.

Although a substantial number of them were nonrevolutionist paupers, criminals, and orphans, French immigrants of the 1850s consisted largely of refugee revolutionists. It is important to note that during this period, French etiquette had begun to supplant English etiquette; French chefs and dancing masters added a new look to high society in America. Swiss, Dutch, and Belgians rounded out the major groups of "old immigrants." Religious dissenters from Holland founded colonies in Michigan, Iowa, and Wisconsin in the 1840s; Belgians established settlements along the lakes of Wisconsin, and Swiss immigrants settled in the hills.

The third major wave of immigrants came between 1880 and 1893, when more than seven million people emigrated from Europe to America. That was the last great group of western and northern

European immigrants and they consisted largely of English, Irish, Scots, Germans, and Scandinavians. This was also the beginning of the immigration of eastern European ethnic groups that would soon flood the nation. The frontier had been pushed to the Plains states of Colorado, Kansas, Nebraska, North Dakota, and South Dakota. The fourth major wave of immigration occurred between 1900 and 1914 as more than thirteen million people came to the United States. Most of them emigrated from the Russian Empire, the Austro-Hungarian Empire, and Italy. Unlike the earlier immigrants, the majority of this group settled in the eastern parts of the United States where industrial cities needed cheap labor.

European immigrants arrived on a variety of steamship lines, most of them having been actively sought as passengers, but very few of the immigrants traveled in comfort. Prior to the 1850s, the immigrant voyages were similar to those of the early colonists. The journeys across the Atlantic usually lasted forty to forty-five days, although some of them took four to six months. While the advent of steamships in the nineteenth century cut the travel time in half, passenger living conditions changed very little until the twentieth century. Many of the ships had been built to haul cargo instead of people, and their living conditions were deplorable. Inadequate space, poor ventilation, unsanitary and insufficient food, too little water, filth, and stench were typical of most ships. Such conditions led to dysentery, lice, typhoid fever, and cholera. On many trips, crew members physically and sexually assaulted the passengers. Upon reflection, there was a striking similarity between the conditions of European steerage passengers and those of seventeenth-century African slaves.

Because most of the immigrants landed in New York, the state of New York established the State Board of Commissioners in 1847 to board and inspect incoming ships, to quarantine immigrants who had communicable diseases, to manage an immigrant hospital, and to collect vital statistics. In 1855, the commissioners established Castle Garden, a reception center through which millions of immigrants who disembarked in New York passed. All of the arriving immigrants had to bathe with soap and water, and those who could afford it would then purchase on-site groceries and prepare meals. Individuals who did not have communicable diseases were encouraged to leave Castle Garden within a few hours after their arrival, but they could opt to sleep overnight in the galleries. Castle Garden was the main immigrant depot in the United States from 1855 until 1890, when the federal government took charge of immigration and Ellis Island replaced it.

Cultural Enclaves

During the early eighteenth century, most European ethnic groups in America maintained their own native identities (Gonzales, 1990). For example, Germans lived in cultural enclaves, where they built large homes, large barns, and well-kept farms. Swedish settlers built log cabins, cleared trees for farmland, fertilized their fields with ashes, and established Swedish Lutheran churches. Dutch immigrants built steep-roofed wooden houses and created thriving communities where Dutch Reformed churches and parochial schools perpetuated the mother language. No immigrant group, however, was able to permanently maintain a separate identity.

The German culture centered on language, religion, and agrarian folkways. The early German immigrants believed in an omnipotent God, rigidly controlled social behavior, and an ordered community life. Their churches promoted German culture, and German language was believed to be the best vehicle for expressing themselves spiritually. German children attended Lutheran, Reformed, and Pietist church schools to learn biblical truth, reading, writing, and arithmetic. Great emphasis was placed on having large families with grown children living near their parents. Family roots, stability, and productivity were central German values. Even so, the German-speaking immigrants were not homogeneous. Of all the immigrants, they were the most heterogeneous, for there were linguistic, ideological, and regional differences among them. Thus, while they spoke German dialects, there were distinct differences between immigrants from various parts of Germany. The most profound differences were religious. Loyalty was sharply split among Protestants, Catholics, and Pietists.

German-American Catholicism was deeply rooted in Benedictine monastic conservatism. It was not shaped by devotional fads; instead, the emphasis was on decorum, dignity, and the inner meaning of the official liturgy. The focus on the intellectual aspect of Catholicism was an extension of Old World German traditions that also valued industry, thoroughness, and orderliness. German-American Catholics established their own parishes, schools, monasteries, newspapers, publishing houses, and societies. The first German-American Catholic newspaper, *Der Wahrheitsfreund*, was published in 1835. The early immigrants were extremely nationalistic people who lived in semi-isolated enclaves away from mainstream American Catholics, particularly Irish Americans whom they viewed as being arrogant, overbearing, and culturally inferior. During World War I, when a public backlash against Teutonic things and people swept America, German-American nationalism began to wane. By World War II, German-American Catholicism was integrated into the American Catholic Church.

Basic to Scandinavian immigrants were the values of honesty and reliability. It was a dishonor to work at less than one's full ability or to fail to finish a job satisfactorily and on time. Consequently, Scandinavian workers, like German workers, were considered highly reliable and desirable by employers. Scandinavian immigrants were also deeply religious people. Bible and sermon reading, family prayer, and hymn singing were part of the family routine. The Lutheran Church was an important part of Scandinavian cultures, but it was also a divisive force. Subcultures within Scandinavian ethnic groups disagreed over proper religious doctrine and worship. For example, Norwegians were more concerned than Danes and Swedes with preserving Old World traditions. For that reason, Norwegians had fewer marriages outside their ethnic group. When the early Norwegian immigrants married people from other ethnic groups, they tended to marry other Scandinavians, primarily Swedes.

As a whole, French immigrants to the United States showed little propensity to establish lasting cultural enclaves. Geographically, they tended not to settle where other French were living. The notable exception to this pattern was New Orleans in the 1850s and 1860s and California in the 1870s, where the French did much to shape the indigenous cultures. French Huguenots introduced elements of Mediterranean culture into what at the time were very staid Protestant American lifestyles. Huguenot homes were decorated with fine French furniture, carpets, and mirrors, and French tables were set with lavish silverware. Wherever they settled, French immigrants altered the local cuisine by introducing buns, okra, tomatoes, artichokes, and yeast to American cooks. Also, French fashions, hairdressers, and shops added to the nation's cultural ambience. In many ways, Frenchness was to affluent Americans a highly esteemed foreign culture identity.

Germans

With the exception of English immigrants, German immigrants assimilated in the United States more easily and more successfully than any other immigrant groups (Coppa & Curran, 1976, Wokeck, 1985). More than seven million Germans came to America in a span of 400 years (Moltmann, 1985). Norse sagas tell us that a sailor on Leif Ericson's voyage to the northern coasts of America was a German named Tyrker. Of perhaps greater interest is the fact that in 1507 a German cartographer named Martin Waldseemueller completed a map of the world and wrote *America* on it to honor Amerigo Vespucci. In the 1560s, several Germans were with the French Huguenots who tried to settle in what is now South Carolina. In 1607, Captain John Smith brought with him to Jamestown three German carpenters, who later built a house for Powhatan, the father of Pocahontas. Peter Minuit (Minnewit in German) was another German of importance in American history. He was hired by the Dutch as the director of New Netherland (O'Connor, 1968). Later, Minuit founded the colony of New Sweden, and three Germans—Peter Ridder, John Printz, and Heinrich von Elswick—governed it. However, these were individual efforts and did not reflect a mass German settlement movement.

In the seventeenth century, Philadelphia was the principal port of disembarkation for German immigrants. The first large group of Germans, thirteen Quaker and Mennonite families from Krefeld, came to America on the *Concord* in 1683, with Francis Pastorius, their leader. They built a settlement on 43,000 acres of land a few miles north of Philadelphia, which today is called Germantown. Pastorius, a lawyer, attended five universities and later became Germantown's first mayor. He started America's first night school to teach English to immigrants, and he printed Pennsylvania's first schoolbook. It is significant that Germantown drew up and presented to a magistrate the first public protest against slavery (Rippley, 1976). At this period, Hollanders and Germans in the New World were called *Dutch*, since the word Dutch bears great similarity to the German *Deutsch*.

German newcomers to America spread from Germantown throughout the colonies. The history of German settlements in America is the history of an astounding mass movement of people. The first large wave of German immigrants started around 1710. In the following decade, more than three thousand Germans settled in New York. The majority of the immigrants settled along the Mohawk and Schoharie Rivers. For the most part, the relationship between the Germans and the Indians was harmonious. In fact, many German fathers began the custom of sending their sons to reside with the Mohawks for a number of years in order that they might learn the Mohawk language and ways of living and thinking. The English governor became so uneasy over the friendship between the Germans and the Mohawks that he discouraged it. Germans also had difficulties with the Dutch, with whom they disagreed over the vast areas of land which the latter group had taken for themselves (O'Connor, 1968). Conflict between Germans and other whites became so severe that many of the

Germans in the Mohawk Valley moved south to Pennsylvania.

As the Germans moved south, they established settlements that were usually successful (Rippley, 1976). German immigrants were among the most productive and innovative of the immigrants in America (Brancaforte, 1989; Hamerow, 1989; Harris, 1989). A German farmer in New Jersey introduced a new and superior variety of wheat; Germans in Maryland developed grain reproduction in a colony that had almost totally depended on tobacco; German farmers were the first to cultivate asparagus and cauliflower; German gunsmiths in Lancaster, Pennsylvania, conceived the *greasepad* method of loading a rifle, and the result was the Kentucky rifle; Germans adapted the German peasant wagon into the Conestoga wagon, a great boon to people who would later settle the West. Germans also brought the German barn and the iron stove to America. Nearly all of the early eighteenth century German immigrants retained their native languages and customs, even when living among non-Germans (Trommler & McVeigh, 1985; Wakeck, 1985; Nadel, 1990). Largely because of those immigrants, the Christmas tree, the frankfurter, and beer became a part of American lives. Perhaps the basic reason for retaining their customs was the fact that in the eighteenth century whole German communities came to America, and their members were bound together by a new religious doctrine which had been forbidden in their native lands. The list of Germans who contributed to American culture is too long to publish in one volume, and certainly it is too long to cite more than only a sample in this chapter.

Contributions

There have been many illustrious German musicians. Among symphony conductors were Leopold and Walter Damrosch. Carl Bergmann was conductor of the New York Philharmonic Symphony Orchestra in 1855, as was Bruno Walter nearly a century later. Theodore Thomas and Frederick Stock were conductors of the Chicago Symphony Orchestra earlier in this century; William Gericke and George Henschel were the first conductors of the Boston Symphony. Fritz Busch conducted several American orchestras before and after World War II. Among composers from Germany, Paul Hindemith, Kurt Weill, and Lukas Foss stand out. Great pianists who have enriched American music through their teaching and playing include Rudolf Serkin and Artur Schnabel. Carl Flesch and Adolf Busch, violinists, shared their art with audiences and students over many years in the United States. Lotte Lehmann, Frieda Hempel, and Herbert Janssen sang with the Metropolitan Opera Company. A number of fine German painters immigrated to the United States, including Emanuel Leutze, Albert Bierstadt, and Karl Ferdinand Wimar.

Architects Walter Gropius, Ludwig Mies van der Rohe, and Albert Kahn were responsible for many great works and were also noted as great teachers. Outstanding German-American engineers include Charles Steinmetz, George Westinghouse, and John Augustus Roebling (builder of the Brooklyn Bridge). Albert Einstein and Albert Michelson were renowned scientists. American businessmen of German ancestry include John D. Rockefeller and department store tycoon John Wanamaker; optical instrument developers John, Edward, Henry, and Louis Bausch; piano manufacturers Henry Steinway and Valentine Knabe; Frederick Weyerhaeuser; beer manufacturer Augustus Busch; food products distributor Henry John Heinz; automobile makers Clement and John Studebaker and Walter Chrysler.

Well-known German-American writers include Thomas Mann and Paul Tilich, a theologian. Othmar Morgenthaler invented the linotype machine, and Wernher von Braun was the "father of the American space program." Francis Leeber became known as the "father of political science in America," and Charles Follen was the first professor of German at Harvard University.

The outstanding German-American politician of the nineteenth century was Carl Schurz, a leader of the uprising against tyranny in Germany in 1848. He immigrated to the United States in 1852. A Union general in the Civil War, Schurz was later U.S. senator from Missouri and secretary of the interior under President Rutherford B. Hayes. He was one of the pioneers in civil service reform. His wife, Margarethe, started the first kindergarten in the United States in 1856. Henry Morgenthau was U.S. ambassador to Turkey and to Mexico, as well as a noted financial expert. His son, Henry Jr., became secretary of the treasury under President Franklin D. Roosevelt. Henry Kissinger was secretary of state under presidents Richard Nixon and Gerald Ford. Dwight D. Eisenhower was commander of Allied Forces in Europe during World War II, and he was the thirty-fourth U.S. president.

Swedes

The first significant group of Swedes to immigrate to America arrived in 1638 and founded New Sweden at the mouth of the Delaware River. Shortly thereafter Swedes established Fort Cristina at the place where the present city of Wilmington, Delaware, lies.

However, the colony contained no more than five hundred inhabitants at any time, and it lasted only seventeen years. In 1655, the Dutch seized the colony, and the English absorbed the Dutch in 1664. By then the Swedes had made a major contribution to American life: they built the first log cabins in the New World. Unlike most settlers, they bought land from the Indians, and they were the first white people to settle northern Delaware, southeastern Pennsylvania, and western New Jersey. The Swedes—along with Dutch, Germans, and Finns—established a few small settlements which attracted stragglers from other ethnic groups. When William Penn arrived late in 1682, he traveled up the Delaware River to the Swedish settlement of Upland, which he christened Chester. Penn was able to approach the Indians with little difficulty because of the good will the Swedes had already fostered among them. From the onset, Swedish settlers treated Indians as equals and as the "rightful lords of the country."

Relatively few Swedes immigrated to America until the 1840s, when three groups of them led by political idealists, young intellectuals, and religious dissenters arrived (Stephenson, 1932). The first group, led by Gustaf Unonius, settled in New Uppsala at Pine Lark, Wisconsin, in 1841. Unonius was a University of Uppsala student who wanted to establish a socialist commune in the New World. During the first four years, New Uppsala attracted several former university students, merchants, and military officers. Unfortunately, too few farmers joined the settlement. The land was hard to cultivate, and most of the settlers were inadequately prepared to farm it. A series of squabbles and failed crops caused the residents to split up and move to other areas. Only six Swedish families were still in the settlement by 1850. Unonius became an Episcopal priest and returned to Sweden in 1858. In 1862, he published a book entitled *A Pioneer in Northwest America, 1841–1858*, which became one of Sweden's classical pieces of immigrant literature. However, it was the idealized descriptions of America that Unonius wrote to newspapers during his American adventure that stimulated more Swedes to immigrate to the New World.

Inspired by Unonius's letters, a second group of Swedes, led by Thure Ludvig Kumlien, arrived in America in 1843. They settled in Wisconsin along Kushkonong Lake. Kumlien was a graduate of the University of Uppsala, where he studied botany with Elias Fries. Unlike Unonius, he was well qualified to lead a group of settlers into the wilderness and the immigrants in his group fared quite well. As a result of his work with ferns, mosses, insects, and birds, Kumlien became one of America's leading frontier naturalists. His collections are stored in a museum in Sweden, the British Museum of London, and the Smithsonian Institution in Washington, D.C.

In the 1840s, major discontent was taking shape in Sweden—discontent which would bring the first wave of Swedish immigrants to America in the nineteenth century. For centuries, the Lutheran Church in Sweden had enjoyed power as the state church. People who dissented from the church faced fines, prison, or exile. Church and state were so tightly bound together that to oppose one was to oppose the other. Yet some Swedes were beginning to ask whether the king really ruled by the grace of God (Stephenson, 1932, p. 134). The United States became an ideal place to those in Sweden who were fighting for religious liberty. At the same time, many people in Sweden were becoming increasingly unhappy with the problems of alcoholism and immorality in general among the youth. Those who had gone to America in the early 1840s observed the moral standards in the new land to be much stricter than those in Sweden.

In 1845, Erik Jansson was charged with heresy in Sweden, but he escaped to America rather than face trial. In 1846, twelve hundred of his flock joined him and together they founded the Christian communal colony of Bishop Hill in northwestern Illinois. Many of the Janssonists wrote letters to their family and friends in Sweden describing the new land with high praise, thus stimulating thousands more to think of emigrating. Some of the immigrants at Bishop Hill left to form their own settlements (Barton, 1975). The Janssonists believed that they could immediately live sinless lives without adhering to the writings of Martin Luther whose books they burned. The first winter was harsh for the Bishop Hill residents who lived in dugouts built into sides of ravines. The following spring, they built houses and started many industries such as textiles, wagon making, furniture making, and milling. The colony was organized as a collective, and for a short while it prospered. Jansson was killed by a vengeful husband in 1850, and the colony broke apart. Even so it was a powerful force in bringing additional Swedish immigrants to America.

Another, even more important factor was at work in Sweden to hasten immigration to America: a rapidly growing population made it extremely difficult for Swedish families to eke out a living. Sweden's population doubled from 1750 to 1850, and it grew another 50 percent by 1900. At the same time, a system of partial inheritance resulted in more children having less land to farm (Daniels, 1990, p. 168). The population growth was particularly severe because only about 10 percent of Sweden was arable land. In the 1850s, Sweden had not developed enough industry to absorb the people who fled from the farms to the cities. Many of the rural dwellers were reduced to the most menial jobs and unpleasant lives (Taylor, 1971). In addition, many of the young men deeply resented having to serve in the military, and they sought refuge elsewhere. High taxes, a social system that discriminated politically and economically against those who were not of the highest class, and continuing resentment of the pressure by the state church for religious conformity stimulated thousands of Swedes to emigrate. Rural dwellers in particular had little hope of ever owning their own land or even of being able to call a rented dwelling their own. Large numbers of the young people no longer saw Sweden as a land of promise (Scott, 1988). It is understandable then that by the middle of the 1850s agents of the Illinois Central Railroad found fertile ground for immigrant recruitment in Sweden (Barton, 1975). In the 1850s, thirty thousand Swedes immigrated to America.

When the United States passed the Homestead Act in 1862, Swedish immigration to America increased in the 1860s. In the same decade, a large crop failure, a monetary crisis, and local famines in Sweden acted as further spurs to mass departures. During the 1870s, the depression in the United States discouraged Swedes from immigrating. In the 1880s, low prices for Swedish farm products and further population pressure in Sweden renewed the outpouring of immigrants to America. Between 1851 and 1923, over one million Swedes left their homeland for the United States. One fact alone testifies to the large number who came to the United States: by 1900, Chicago had become the second largest Swedish city in the world; it had one hundred fifty thousand Swedes. Other Swedes settled in Minneapolis, New York, Worcester (Massachusetts), Seattle, and Spokane.

Contributions

In the fields of the sciences and invention, a large number of Swedish Americans have contributed to American life. Chester Carlson developed the photocopy process in the 1930s. John Ericsson built an ironclad ship, *Monitor*, for the Union during the Civil War. Carl Anderson won a Nobel Prize in physics in 1936; Glenn Seaborg won a Nobel Prize in chemistry in 1951. Carl Axel Roberts Lundin was one of the first leading opticians in America. Hans Christopher Christiansen built the first water pumping station for municipal use.

Leading Swedish-American businessmen have included G. Eric Wickman, founder of the Greyhound Bus Company; Charles Walgreen, founder of the Walgreen Drugstores; and Vincent Bendix, who established a number of Bendix manufacturing companies. Aksel Josephson was America's foremost bibliographer and an expert on library techniques. One of America's greatest poets was Carl

Sandburg; Joe Hill (Joel Hagglund) was probably America's greatest labor poet. Nelson Algren, Greta Garbo, and Gloria Swanson (Josephine Svensson) distinguished themselves in the movie industry.

Several Swedish Americans have stood out in politics. John Lind, a Swedish-born lawyer, became the first Swedish-American in Congress in 1886 and the first Swedish governor of Minnesota in 1898. The first Swedish American U.S. senator was Magnus Johnson. Charles A. Lindbergh Sr. was a noted congressman for a number of years, and his son, Charles A. Lindbergh Jr. was one of the most celebrated of all Americans for his flight over the Atlantic in 1927 as well as for his many contributions to American aviation. Swedish immigrants contributed to American higher education by establishing Augustana College and Seminary (1860) in Rock Island, Illinois; Gustavus Adolphus College (1862) in St. Peter, Minnesota; Bethany College (1881) in Lindsborg, Kansas; and Upsala College (1893) in East Orange, New Jersey.

Norwegians

Norwegians first traveled to the New World in A.D. 876 when Gunnbjorn discovered Greenland. Eric the Red, a Viking, settled there about 986. In the year 1000, Eric's son, Leif Ericson, sailed to the North American continent. Ericson's voyage took him from Greenland to what is now New England. In the early eleventh century, approximately one hundred sixty explorers, mainly Norwegians, founded a settlement that is now part of Massachusetts. It is also believed by some historians that Norwegian expeditions to the Saint Lawrence River and the Great Lakes traveled as far inland as what is now Minnesota (Gjerde, 1985).

In modern times an initial group of fifty-two Norwegians left Stavanger, Norway, in 1825 on the sloop *Restoration*. All of the passengers and crew were immigrants. Some of the travelers were self-professed Quakers. Shortly after the vessel landed, the others admitted to being Quakers. It was difficult to be a Quaker in Norway at that time. Unlike the members of the Lutheran State Church, Quakers did not accept the Lutheran rituals of baptism, marriage, and burial. But no amount of harassment altered the beliefs of the Quakers who fled to America in search of a place to practice their religion freely (Bjork, 1976; Wefald, 1971). They settled in Kendall Township, New York. The next large group of Norwegians did not come to America until 1836, and they settled along the Fox River in LaSalle County, Illinois. It is important to note that the largest number of subsequent Norwegian immigrants were Lutherans who came to find better economic conditions (Larsen, 1950; Lovoll, 1982). Between 1836 and 1840, twelve hundred Norwegians immigrated to America; seventeen thousand more arrived in the 1840s, and thirty-six thousand came to the New World in the 1850s.

Contributions

Norwegians founded several colleges, most of which were affiliated with the Lutheran Church: Lutheran College (1861) in Decorah, Iowa; Augsburg College (1869) in Minneapolis; Augustana College (1889) in Sioux Falls, South Dakota; Concordia College (1891) in Moorland, Minnesota; Pacific Lutheran College (1894) in Parkland, Washington; and St. Olaf College (1874) in Northfield, Minnesota. Norwegian Americans have contributed much to America in various fields. (Andersen, 1975). Ole E. Rølvaag was an outstanding author. His book *Giants in the Earth* was described by *The Nation* magazine on July 13, 1927, as "the fullest, finest and most powerful novel that has been written about pioneer life in America." Other famous Norwegian-American writers include Hjalmar Hjorth Boyesen, a professor at Cornell University and Columbia University before the turn of the century; Martha Ostenso, author of *Wild-Geese*; and Wallace Stegner, author of *The Big Rock Candy Mountain*. Thorstein B. Veblen, author of the famous works *The Theory of the Leisure Class* and *The Theory of Business Enterprise*, taught economics at the University of Chicago, Stanford University, and the University of Missouri. Rasmus B. Andersen taught Norwegian and Old Norse at the University of Wisconsin, the first university to establish a department of Scandinavian Studies. Victor Lawson, founder of the *Chicago Daily News*, helped start the Associated Press. He also originated the Postal Savings Bank.

Scientists and explorers of Norwegian-American ancestry include Ernest O. Lawrence, inventor of the cyclotron and winner of a Nobel Prize in physics in 1939. Lars Onsager was the winner of the Nobel Prize in chemistry in 1968. Gunner Randers and William Zachariasen were professors at the University of Chicago. Randers was an astronomer and Zachariasen a physicist. Finn Ronne mapped and claimed for the United States the last uncharted coastline in the Antarctic. Admiral Richard Byrd's pilot in the Antarctic was Bernt Balchen, who helped build Arctic bases for the U.S. Air Force. Thomas Barth was a world-famed geologist. Ludvic Hektoen was one of the world's foremost cancer specialists. Thomas G. Pihlfeldt was the engineer who improved on the bascule bridge that crosses the Chicago River at a number of points; Olaf Hoff did important work involving the practical problems of laying units of railroad tunnel in a prepared trench under the Detroit River; and Ole Singstad, often called the "dean of tunneling engineers," devised the unique ventilation of the Holland Tunnel between Manhattan and New Jersey. Also, he was the chief engineer on it when the tunnel was completed.

Leading Norwegian-American businessmen include Nelson Olson Nelson whose firm, the N. O. Nelson Manufacturing Company, was a major supplier of building and plumbing materials and supplies; Tinius Olsen founded the Olsen Testing Machine Company, and he was a pioneer of new methods of testing materials of all sorts; Magnus Bjorndal built the Tech Laboratories of New Jersey into a large manufacturing concern; Ole Evinrude was the founder of the Evinrude Outboard Motor Company in Milwaukee; Targe G. Mandt manufactured the Stoughton wagon; John A. Johnson founded the Gisholt Manufacturing Company, a corporation that turned out turret lathes; and Conrad Hilton was a hotel owner.

In athletics, Norwegians and Norwegian Americans who performed often in the United States included Sonja Henie, a famous ice skater and popularizer of the sport in America and Torge Tokle, a ski champion of the Western Hemisphere. Knute Rockne, the legendary football coach at Notre Dame University, won 105 games, tied 5, and lost 12. Molly B. Malory was a tennis champion; Ralph Gouldahl was a golf champion; and Mildred "Babe" Didrikson Zaharias was an all-around sports champion, who won the javelin throw in the 1932 Olympics.

Significant Norwegian Americans in politics include Hubert Humphrey, governor of Minnesota, a U.S. senator, vice president of the United States, and a presidential candidate. Nicolay Grevstad was appointed by President William Taft as minister to Uruguay and Paraguay in 1911; Knute Nelson, governor of Minnesota in the early 1890s, was both a congressman and a senator from that state. In the arts, ballerina Vera Zorina was acclaimed throughout the world for her performances. Kirsten Flagstad, Wagnerian, though not an American citizen, gave millions of people special enjoyment through her performances at the Metropolitan Opera Company and her many phonograph records.

Danes

Danes were residents of the New Amsterdam and New Netherland colonies. In 1619, when Jamestown was twelve years old, King Christian IV of Denmark commissioned Jens Munk of Norway to find the Northwest Passage to the Orient. Munk's expedition of two ships and sixty-five men landed in the Hudson Bay area, and claimed New Denmark for Denmark. After a severe winter in 1620, marked by illnesses and death, only Munk and two other men lived to return to Denmark. The first Danish family, that of Jan Johannson van Breestede, arrived in New Denmark a short time later. The majority of the early Danish immigrants came from the southern Jutland area of Denmark (Hale, 1984; Nielsen, 1981).

Two famous Danes, James Bronck and Jochem Peterson Kuyter, came to America in 1629 and, with the consent of the Dutch West India Company, Bronck purchased 500 acres of land from the Indians on what is now a part of New York City. The purchase price was six gold coins, two rifles, two axes, two kettles, two shirts, two overcoats, and one barrel of apple cider. The section of New York City called "the Bronx" is named for him. Bronck's brother-in-law, Kuyter, was the first settler of the Harlem section of New York. By 1675 nearly one hundred Danes had arrived in America. Danish converts to Moravian Pietism founded a mission at Bethlehem, Pennsylvania, in 1735, and after 1750 a large number of Pietist Danes came to the same area. Other Danes immigrated to America from the Danish West Indies (Virgin Islands) both before and after the Revolutionary War (Thernstrom, 1980).

Between the end of the Revolutionary War and the onset of the Civil War, relatively few Danes immigrated to the United States, but in 1857 more than a thousand Danish immigrants came to American shores. The first year in which more than ten thousand such immigrants arrived in America was 1882, with a decline taking place gradually until the 1920s. U.S. Census figures place the number of Danish immigrants to America between 1820 and 1970 at three hundred sixty-six thousand. The reasons for the immigration between the 1850s and World War I were quite similar to those given to authorities by Norwegians, Swedes, and Finns.

Contributions

There have been many Danish contributions to American life. In the Revolutionary War, Christian "Old Denmark" Feberger was a general who fought in the battles of Bunker Hill, Brandywine, Yorktown, and Monmouth. Danish writers in America have included Sophus Keith Winther, whose trilogy dealing with the difficult life of Danish tenant farmers in Nebraska was highly praised. Other writers include Carl Hansen, Adam Dan, and Kristian Østergaard. Anton Kvist was a successful poet. In the arts, sculptor Gutzon Borglum was world famous for his carving of four great American presidents on

Mount Rushmore. The renowned Danish Wagnerian tenor Lauritz Melchior sang for many years at the Metropolitan Opera, starred in films, and became an American citizen. Soprano Povla Frijsh, a celebrated singer of French and German art songs, came to the United States in the 1930s and taught for many years at the Juillard School of Music in New York City.

Christian Gulduger, a well-known painter, is best remembered for his portrait of George Washington and the symbol depicting the eagle standing on a shield clutching three arrows. Gunnar Johansen, a pianist, made many records and was artist-in-residence at the University of Wisconsin for several years. Perhaps the most famous Danish American at the turn of the century was Jacob Riis whose book *How the Other Half Lives* (1890) described the harsh slums of America's big cities. Theodore Roosevelt called him "New York's most useful citizen." Riis was also a well-known photographer, lecturer, and journalist. His newspaper articles focused on poverty-stricken people in America.

Danish Americans have excelled in the sciences. Niels Bohr, a Nobel Prize winner in physics in 1922, came to the United States during World War II, and later played a major role in the construction of the atomic bomb. Henrik Dam, a professor at the University of Rochester, won a Nobel Prize in medicine in 1943 for his work on Vitamin K. Jens Clausen, a world-famed botanist, taught for many years in American universities. Karl A. Strand and Bengt Stromgren were both professors of astronomy in the United States, and Stromgren served as director of the Yerkes and McDonald Observatories. Among outstanding Danish-American businessmen have been Charles Hansen, lumber king of California in the 1850s and 1860s; Christopher Nisson, founder of an incubator factory in Petaluma, California, in 1864; George Rasmussen, founder of the National Tea Company; and Nies Paulson, inventor of fireproof stairs and library book stacks.

In the field of politics and government, Lawrence Gronlund's writings influenced American socialist leaders Eugene V. Debs and Edward Bellamy. Danish-born politicians have served as governors of Minnesota, Wyoming, South Dakota, Iowa, and New Jersey, and at least two sons of Danish immigrants have also been governors: Culbert L. Olson (California) and Frederick V. Peterson (Nebraska). Lloyd M. Bentsen, a senator from Texas, achieved acclaim as the Democratic candidate for vice president in 1988 and secretary of treasury in the Clinton administration. Henry Hertz was a federal internal revenue collector for the first Illinois district.

Swiss

The Swiss certainly qualify as old immigrants in America. The earliest Swiss came in the sixteenth century as mercenary soldiers in the service of Ferdinand and Isabella of Spain. The first historical record of a Swiss in America lists Diebold von Erlach, a mercenary who died in Florida in 1565. Several Swiss were at Jamestown under John Smith's leadership. In 1687, Jean François Gignilliat was given 3,000 acres of land from the directors of the colony of South Carolina in order to bring more Swiss to America (Thernstrom, 1980). Christoph von Graffenreid led more than seven hundred immigrants, including about a hundred Swiss from the area of Bern, to North Carolina in 1710 and founded the colony of New Bern (Faust, 1916).

From the outset of their appearance in Switzerland in the sixteenth century, Mennonites were persecuted. Their Evangelical Protestant opposition to taking oaths, holding public office, or performing military service was too radical for their Zwinglian neighbors. Jacob Schumaker was the first Swiss Mennonite to come to America. He settled in Pennsylvania in 1683 and became a Quaker. Throughout the seventeenth century, single families and individuals fled Switzerland to join relatives already in America. In the early eighteenth century, large numbers of Swiss Mennonites settled in England where Queen Anne sent some of them to Ireland, but most of them were shipped to American plantations.

After 1710 a growing number of Mennonites went directly to America. Swiss officials had no objection to this exodus, for as early as 1705 the town councilmen of Bern tried to draw up a plan to eliminate what they considered "undesirable elements" of the population (Faust, 1916). In October 1710, a large number of Mennonites immigrated to a 10,000-acre tract at Conestoga along the Pequa Creek in Pennsylvania. Between 1710 and 1750, over four thousand Brethren settled there. From that area, Swiss Mennonites spread out to other counties in the Shenandoah Valley. A foremost reason for the immigration was that Swiss who had settled in the New World after 1700 wrote glowing letters back to the homeland, and thus many Swiss were inspired to make the journey.

Franz Karren organized a Swiss regiment for French expeditionary services in America in 1719. Those mercenaries fought against the British in the French and Indian War. In 1732, Jean-Pierre Purry asked the British government for land along the Spanish borderland of the Carolinas. With a few changes, his plan was approved, and he journeyed to Charleston, South Carolina, where he laid out the plans for the town of Purrysburg on 200,000 acres 25 miles up the Savannah River. When he returned to Europe, he brought back with him to America about four hundred fifty French-Swiss and German-Swiss (Thernstrom, 1980). A large number of the settlers were Mennonites. Interestingly, the Mennonites' nonresistance principle was respected by the Indian tribes they encountered and there was little conflict between the two groups. However, Mennonites were not unique in their pacifism. Quakers, who were mainly British, were also pacifists. Most of the Swiss immigrants in the eighteenth century came from the mountain districts around Bern or from the rural areas around Zurich rather than from the cities.

Contributions

Switzerland, a country divided among German-, French-, and Italian-speaking citizens, has no distinct national culture or national language. However, Swiss-American contributions to the development of the United States have been significant. In the fields of science and engineering, many Swiss have been outstanding. Henry Banga brought antiseptic surgery to the United States. Carl Voegtlin was the director of the National Cancer Institute. At Harvard University, one of the most honored intellectuals in the nineteenth century was Louis Agassiz, who as professor of natural history began collections now prominently displayed in the Harvard Museum of Comparative Zoology. Felix Bloch, the brilliant Swiss-born American theoretical physicist, arrived in the United States in 1934 and accepted a teaching position at Stanford University. His discovery of the principle of nuclear magnetic resonance won him a Nobel Prize in physics in 1952.

Wolfgang Wasow, a distinguished mathematician, taught at New York University. Hans Staub, a physicist, worked on the atomic bomb in Los Alamos during World War II. Gerhard Fankhauser had a productive career in the United States as a biologist. Louis Chevrolet was a major contributor to the development of the 3Der Wahrcombustion engine; a General Motors automobile bears his name. Othmar Ammann was the chief engineer and designer of five major New York City bridges, including the George Washington and the Verrazano-Narrows. William Lescaze was the designer of several skyscrapers in the United States, including the Borg-Warner Building in Chicago. In the tradition of his military ancestors, Christian Gatiot built Fort Monroe in Virginia.

Martin Henni became archbishop of Milwaukee in 1875, and Philip Schaff became a leading Reformed theologian at Union Theological

Seminary in New York City. Adolf Meyer and Raymond de Saussure were well-known psychiatrists. Kurt Seligmann and Fritz Glarner pursued their painting careers for many years in America. Wieland Herzfelde, a distinguished writer and publisher in Berlin, immigrated to New York in 1939 and opened the Seven Seas Book and Stamp Shop. Fritz Caspari had a much-praised career as a historian and teacher. Arnold Wolfers was a professor of international relations at Yale University before he joined the Johns Hopkins School of Advanced International Studies in Washington, D.C. Adolph Gatschet was a well-known ethnologist. Adolph Bandelier wrote extensively on the archaeology of the American Southwest, and he was on the staff of New York's Museum of Natural History. Jean Piccard was best known for his contributions to the study of cosmic rays and the development of high-altitude balloons. There were several leading Swiss-American psychiatrists.

Swiss-American businessmen who have contributed to the development of the United States include Jacques Anton Biderman, who became a partner in E. I. Du Pont de Nemours & Company. In 1837, he built Winterthur, which has become a museum of early Americana. Meyer Guggenheim opened a store in Philadelphia and later, with his sons, built a great fortune in smelting and refining. Milton Hershey founded Hershey, Pennsylvania, in 1903 as the site for his chocolate manufacturing business. He established the Hershey Industrial School, an institution for orphan boys in 1909, and in 1918 he donated $60 million for its maintenance. Oscar Tschirky founded the Waldorf Hotel in New York City in 1893. César Ritz founded the Ritz Carlton Hotel in New York City, and Lorenzo Delmonico, with his uncles, established Delmonico's Restaurant in New York City in 1834.

In government service, one of the most distinguished Swiss-American citizens was Albert Gallatin, secretary of the treasury under Presidents Thomas Jefferson and James Madison, as well as minister to France and to England. He founded the American Ethnological Society of New York (1842), and has been called "father of American ethnology." His great grandson, Albert Eugene Gallatin, was a well-known painter, art collector, and writer on art. Emanuel Philipp was governor of Wisconsin. Herbert Hoover was secretary of commerce and the thirty-first president of the United States.

Dutch

The first large wave of Dutch immigrants (about 20,000) came to the United States between 1840 and 1860. Less than three thousand came between 1820 and 1840. Several factors influenced their decision to immigrate (De Jong, 1975). First, King William I inserted the Dutch Reformed Church into the state bureaucracy by creating the State Department of Religion to oversee religious matters. In 1834, two congregations seceded from the National Reformed Church, and thus was born the Secession, in which over 120 churches took part by 1836. The Secession movement has been called the "Dutch branch of European Pietism," for its members wanted, among other things, a more "heartfelt experience" than that offered by the state church. Further, the secessionists wanted "internal diversity . . . and puritanical strictures regarding popular mores" (Bratt, 1984, pp. 3– 4). The king retaliated against the seceders by handing out heavy fines and prison sentences to dissenting ministers who refused to agree to his terms for recognizing the Secession (Wakeke, 1944). Many of the secessionists believed immigration was the only way to maintain the purity of their faith.

In the nineteenth century, the rural economy was in decline as a number of disasters struck. From 1845 to 1847, floods ruined farmlands, the potato blight laid waste the important crop, and rural famine devastated farm dwellers—80 percent of the potato crops were blighted. Food riots broke out in several communities. Also, land rents were high in the countryside, a condition that robbed tenants of the hope of being able to own their own farms (Wakeke, 1944). Seventy-five percent of all Dutch immigrants came from rural areas between 1820 and 1877 (Brinks, 1982).

Contributions

If we take into consideration the fact that in 1970 the Dutch ranked only eighteenth in size among immigrant groups in the United States, their contributions stand out even more. In the fields of science and mathematics, significant individuals of Dutch ancestry include Gerard Kuiper, a professor of astronomy at the University of Chicago and the University of Arizona; he also served at the Yerkes Observatory. Peter Debye won a Nobel Prize in chemistry in 1936, and he was a professor of chemistry and department chairman at Cornell University. Cornelius Bol invented the Bol lamp, a mercury vapor lamp that gives off intense light. Robert van de Graffe built the first electrostatic generator. George Uhlenbeck and Samuel Goudsmit were professors of physics at the University of Michigan. Jan Schilt and Dirk Brouwer were famous astronomers. Izaak Kolthoff, professor of chemistry, published over seven hundred research papers and articles. Lee De Forest perfected the electron tube and he is often called the "father of radio broadcasting." Bart Bok was a professor of astronomy at Harvard University and director of the Steward Observatory in Tucson. Arie Haagen-Smit, a professor of biochemistry at the California Institute of Technology and a pioneer in the chemistry of air pollution, discovered that smog is formed by the reaction of unburned hydrocarbons and nitrogen oxides in strong sunlight.

Outstanding Dutch in other fields include Tjalling Koopmans, professor of economics at the University of Chicago and Yale University, who developed linear programming; Henry Frankfort, a world-famed archaeologist at the Oriental Institute of the University of Chicago; Elizabeth Geleerd, a pioneer in child psychoanalysis; David Christian Henry, the chief engineer on the Hoover Dam. Authors of Dutch ancestry include Hendrick William van Loon, author of *The Story of the Bible*; Cyrenus Cole, author of *I Remember, I Remember*; Peter De Vries, author of *The Blood of the Lamb*; famed poet Walt Whitman; Edward Bok won a Pulitzer Prize in literature. Derek Bok is president of Harvard University. Walter Cronkite was a Columbia Broadcasting System (CBS) commentator. Herman Melville was a renowned writer.

In the arts, Egon Petri was one of the world's greatest pianists and he taught for many years at Cornell University and Mills College. Abstract painters William de Kooning and Piet Mondrian were world renowned; Gladys Swarthout was a mezzosoprano at the Metropolitan Opera Company. Hans Kindler founded and served as the first conductor of the National Symphony Orchestra in Washington, D.C. Influential business leaders include Cornelius Vanderbilt, a shipping and railroad tycoon. In the field of government, three presidents of the United States had Colonial Dutch ancestry: Martin Van Buren, Theodore Roosevelt, and Franklin D. Roosevelt. Michigan voters sent Arthur H. Vandenberg, a distinguished Dutch American, to the U.S. Senate. At first, he was an isolationist in foreign policy. Later, he became one of the strongest supporters of international cooperation and the United Nations.

The Dutch Reformed Church became greatly interested in education in America and it was responsible for establishing Queens College in the colony of New Jersey in 1766. The college later became one of the best in the United States and was renamed Rutgers College. The Church also built Hope College (1851) and Calvin College (1876) in western Michigan during the post-Civil War years. Dutch Catholics established St. Norbert College at De Pere, Wisconsin, in 1898 and Crosier Seminary in Onamia, Minnesota, in 1922. Dutch immigrants introduced ice skating, hockey, sleighing, the Christmas figure Santa Claus, and Easter eggs to Americans. Also, *yacht*, *boss*, *stoop*, and *cookie* are Dutch words which have become common in the English language.

French

In 1685, Louis XIV revoked the Edict of Nantes in which Henry IV had granted freedom of worship to French Huguenots (Protestants) in 1598. Louis gave the Huguenots the choice to either leave France or abjure their faith, which most of them did, albeit reluctantly. Some of the dissidents immigrated to the English colonies in America where they believed they would be secure. There is some question about just how many French Huguenots settled in America at that time. Authorities cite figures as high as fifteen thousand (Reich, 1989) and as low as fifteen hundred to two thousand (Butler, 1983). Whatever the number, the Huguenot settlements to the New World from the middle of the sixteenth century to the beginning of the seventeenth century did not last.

From 1680 to 1685, almost all of the Huguenots who lived in the French West Indies moved to North America in order to escape religious persecution. For a few years after 1685 Louis XIV tried deporting Huguenots to the colonies but the experiment failed. Pennsylvania had only five or six Huguenot families before 1700, and New Jersey had about twenty-five or thirty families living near New York City in 1700. The Huguenots who arrived in America from France after 1685 were generally young men skilled in areas of work useful in a new land. Most of them came from the western and northwestern parts of France, and they rapidly spread out across America after they arrived. Massachusetts, New York, and South Carolina were the colonies to which most of them were initially attracted.

As with other immigrants, a great many of the French were drawn to America because of the pamphlets which magnified the virtues of the American colonies. Some of them, or their descendants, rose to high positions in colonial society. Huguenots in South Carolina occupied positions in the colonial legislature at a rate more than twice their population (Daniels, 1990). James Bowdoin became governor of Massachusetts during the Revolution. Unfortunately, the Huguenots and their churches went out of existence within a relatively short time.

The next wave of French immigration to America came during the French Revolution, for the lives of aristocrats and priests were threatened during the reign of Robespierre. At least ten thousand refugees escaped to the United States during this period, and while many of them came from mainland France, most of them came from the

French West Indies (Thernstrom, 1980). After the defeat of Napoleon in 1815, many of his followers immigrated to the United States, where they tried to build settlements in Texas, Ohio, Florida, and Alabama. Following the French Revolution of 1848, nearly twenty thousand French royalists and refugees came to the United States.

French immigration to America during the nineteenth century seemed to diverge in character from other western Europeans. Whereas most of the latter group were largely unskilled rural laborers, most French immigrants were skilled, professional workers. Many of them were "modernizers," people who saw America as a land of opportunity and experimentation—unlike most parts of France. Nor did French immigrants generally band together in their own ethnic enclaves. Further, they married outside their ethnic group at a higher rate than did any other non-English-speaking immigrants. What they sought in many cases was a chance to get ahead, an opportunity to escape an Old World too often bound by archaic rules left over from the days of the medieval guilds.

Acadians

In the early seventeenth century, several French families crossed the ocean to settle Acadia, the area of Canada which then included Nova Scotia, New Brunswick, Prince Edward Island, and part of what is now Maine. After 1713, the Acadians resided mainly in Nova Scotia. Growing up in isolation, the descendants of those original settlers retained their language and their customs. By the Treaty of Utrecht in 1713, ending the War of Spanish Succession, France ceded Nova Scotia to England. The French Acadians (Cajuns) neither removed themselves to French territory nor did they acknowledge English dominion. Various compromises were worked out between the Acadians and the English colonial government until 1755, when the French settlers were forced to leave their homes to save their lives. Some of them migrated to Maryland, others to the Carolinas, and some to Georgia. Most of them, however, migrated to Louisiana, but they did not realize that the territory would be secretly transferred from France to Spain. Fortunately, the Spanish government was not hostile to the Acadians. To the contrary, the Spaniards welcomed such industrious people with grants of land and provisions of other necessities.

By 1788, nearly three thousand additional French Acadian exiles had arrived in Louisiana from France or the French West Indies. They began to raise livestock and work the land. Several wealthy French Acadians acquired slaves to work their plantations, although most of the settlers kept the same way of life they had enjoyed in Acadia years before. Cajuns remained devout Roman Catholics and they often lived in near isolation, for they were intent on maintaining the customs and traditions remembered from an earlier time. Large families, ten to fifteen children, were common among the Cajuns, and the bonds of family were very strong. Between 1815 and 1880, the number of French Acadian descendants in Louisiana climbed from thirty-five thousand to two hundred seventy thousand. Against the odds, they triumphed in their own manner.

Contributions

It is doubtful whether the American colonies would have won their freedom without the help of the Marquis de Lafayette, a major general in the Continental army. He gave strong support to George Washington during the most dire days of the war by going to France to seek help from the French government, an endeavor in which he was successful. Count Jean-Baptiste de Rochambeau commanded the French forces dispatched in 1779 to aid the American side of the Revolutionary War. He joined Washington's army, and the joint forces marched southward, besieged Cornwallis at Yorktown, and with a French fleet, prevented the English from escaping by sea. Cornwallis was forced to surrender. Many other Frenchmen joined the Continental forces to fight for the young nation. Paul Revere, silversmith and legendary hero, was of French ancestry.

Benjamin Bonneville was born in France and later joined the American armed forces. He served with distinction in the Mexican War and the Civil War on the Union side. Also, he explored the northwestern part of the United States between 1832 and 1835. Admirals Stephen Decatur and George Dewey (Douay) distinguished themselves in important naval engagements for the United States. General John J. Pershing, hero of World War I, was of Alsatian descent.

For several centuries France has been a cultural beacon to the world. She has produced outstanding individuals in virtually all the areas of the arts and in every discipline of the sciences and the liberal arts. At the same time, the cultural contributions of French Americans have paralleled contributions which France herself has bestowed on humankind. In music, French Americans and French citizens transplanted to the United States have given rich gifts. Pierre Monteux, a conductor, brought the San Francisco Symphony Orchestra to world recognition and made many phonograph records for his American public. Pierre Boulez conducted the New York

Philharmonic for a number of years and held master classes for young conductors. Paul Paray was musical director of the Detroit Symphony Orchestra during some of its finest years and gave record collectors some of their most cherished moments. Charles Munch became conductor of the Boston Symphony Orchestra after the retirement of Serge Koussevitsky and continued the tradition of excellence Koussevitsky had begun with his musicians. Jean Martinon conducted the Chicago Symphony. Philip Entremont won the admiration of American audiences as a concert pianist and conductor of the New Orleans Symphony. Perhaps the most recognized Cajun contributions to American culture are the Mardi Gras and the *fais-dodo* (public country dancing).

Members of the Casadesus family—Robert, Gaby, and Jean—were world-famed pianists and held classes for young American musicians both in the United States and in France. Nadia Boulanger, perhaps the most famous teacher of composition in the world for many years, taught such outstanding American composers as Howard Swanson, Roy Harris, Aaron Copland, and Virgil Thomson in her Paris studio. Alfred Cortot, the great French pianist, had many American students in piano study both before and after World War II. Marcel Moyse, one of the world's finest flautists, held master classes for years for many American students. Among singers, Lily Pons gave much pleasure to her audiences at the Metropolitan Opera Company; Martial Singher, a baritone, taught a large number of American students during his years in this country; Darius Milhaud, the distinguished French composer, gave composition lessons to countless American students at Mills College in California.

Also in the fine arts, Louis Bouche, John Lafarge and Victor Perand won acclaim as painters. Marcel Duchamp, the French Cubist, spent most of his life in the United States. Outstanding French-American sculptors include Leonard Crunelle, Raoul-Jean Josset, and Jules-Andre Meliodan. Pierre L'Enfant designed the eagle which symbolized the spirit of the United States and drew up the first plans for Washington, D.C.

In the field of literature, the following American authors of French ancestry enriched the world with their works: Henry David Thoreau, Philip Freneau, Henry Wadsworth Longfellow, John Greenleaf (Feuillevert) Whittier, Jacques Barzun, Richard Henry Dana, Sidney Lanier, Stephen Vincent Benét, and Edna St. Vincent Millay. Henri Peyre taught at Yale University; André Maurois, a French novelist, biographer, and literary critic, taught at the University of Kansas.

In the sciences, prominent French Americans and immigrant French include René Jules Dubos, bacteriologist and Pulitzer Prize-winning author. Hans Bethe, from Alsace-Lorraine, was a Nobel Prize winner for physics in 1967 and he was a professor at Cornell University. Andre Cournand, who codiscovered cardiac catheterization and won a Nobel Prize for medicine in 1956, taught at Columbia University. Leon Brillouin, a theoretical physicist, taught at Harvard University, Brown University, and the University of Wisconsin. Pierre V. Auger, an atomic physicist, taught in the United States for a number of years. Rudolph Minkowski, the famed astronomer and observer of nebulae, worked at the Palomar and the Mount Wilson observatories. Andre Weil, an outstanding mathematician, taught at the Institute for Advanced Study at Princeton University. In other academic fields, contributions to American intellectual life were made by Gustave Cohen, a philologist at the French Institute in the New School for Social Research in New York City; Yves Simon, a professor of philosophy at Notre Dame University; and Jean Wahl, a philosophy professor at the New School for Social Research.

Pioneers in the field of business include Paul Tulane, who gave heavily to the University of Louisiana and the name was later changed to Tulane University; Pierre Samuel du Pont de Nemours, an economist and statesman who fled France during the Revolution and established a gunpowder manufacturing plant—the beginning of the great industrial giant E. I. Du Pont de Nemours & Company. Stephen Girard, a businessman in Philadelphia in the 1770s, founded the Bank of Stephen Girard which helped the United States to finance the War of 1812. He also founded Girard College in Philadelphia to educate "poor, white, male orphans." Ellie Magloire Durand, a chemist and pharmacist, was the first person to bottle mineral water in the United States. Philip Armour was a successful meat packager, and Henry Oxnard was president of the American Beet Sugar Company. Jules Weber placed most of the American French chefs employed in American hotels.

French-American stars of screen and stage include Claudette Colbert, Charles Boyer, Adolphe Menjou, and Leslie Caron. In the field of education, Thomas Gallaudet, the pioneer teacher of the hearing-impaired people in America, established the first free school for the deaf in America. Gallaudet College is named for him.

In politics, a large number of Americans of French ancestry have been outstanding. Gifford Pinchot, one of the great advocates of the conservation of America's natural resources and scenic wonders, founded the Pinchot School of Forestry at Yale University. Later he also served two terms as governor of Pennsylvania. Senator Robert La Follette from Wisconsin was one of the most respected individuals who ever served in the U.S. Senate. In 1924, he ran as the presidential candidate of a third party, the Progressives. His son, Robert La Follette Jr., also served as senator from Wisconsin. Another son, Philip, served three terms as governor of the same state. Presidents George Washington, John Tyler, James A. Garfield, Theodore Roosevelt, and Franklin Roosevelt all had French ancestors. France gave the United States the Statue of Liberty as a gift in 1886. The monument has greeted millions of immigrants to America for more than a century.

Belgians

The Dutch usually receive credit for being the first white settlers of New York, but the first settlers were Belgian Walloons. The Catholic rulers of Spain persecuted Spanish Protestants, who fled in large numbers to other countries in Europe, especially Belgium and the Netherlands (O'Dell, 1957; Skardal, 1974). In 1623, Jesse De Forest, a Belgian Walloon, led the first group of Belgian colonists to Manhattan Island, arriving on the ship *New Netherland*. Further, Belgian Walloons were among the first Europeans to settle in New Jersey, Delaware, Connecticut, Pennsylvania, and the mid-Atlantic states.

Father Louis Hennepin, a Catholic priest from Flanders, explored throughout America in the seventeenth century and was the first white person to see Niagara Falls. His books, *A New Discovery of a Large Country in America, Description of Louisiana, Discovery of a Very Large Country*, and *A Trip Through a Country Larger than Europe*, document the role Belgians played in the exploration of America. A street in Minneapolis, a county in Minnesota, and a village in Illinois are named after Father Hennepin. Belgian explorers and missionaries who followed Father Hennepin to America include Father Croquet, known as the "saint of Oregon"; Archbishop Sauous, known as the "apostle of Alaska"; and Father De Smet, a Jesuit whose missionary work with the Indians extended from the Mississippi River to the Rocky Mountains.

Belgium has never been a source of a large number of immigrants to America, mainly because during most of the past two hundred years, it has generally been an exceptionally prosperous nation. About two hundred thousand Belgians immigrated to the United States between 1830 and 1975. During the middle of the nineteenth century, many farmers in Belgium felt the lack of land. From about 1840 to 1884, approximately twenty-two thousand Belgians left their homeland for America. The potato blight as well as overpopulation of the 1840s also motivated many Belgians to leave the countryside in the north and northwest for a journey across the Atlantic.

Contributions

Belgian Americans have contributed a great deal to their adopted country in the sciences. Leo Hendrick Baekeland, a chemist, invented the synthetic resin Bakelite and developed Velox, a highly sensitized photographic printing paper. Father Nieland discovered synthetic rubber. Karel Bossart has been called the "father of the Atlas missile." George Goethals, the chief engineer on the Panama Canal construction, was of Belgian ancestry. So too were Raymond de Roover, economic historian, and Charles Schepens, noted ophthalmologist. Pol Swings, an astrophysicist, was a professor at the University of Chicago and worked at the McDonald Observatory. Maurice Biot, the noted physicist, taught at several American universities. George Sarton has been outstanding in the field of history of science as an author and professor at Harvard University. In other academic fields, Paul de Man, the leading scholar of a literary theory called deconstruction, taught many years at Yale University. Raymond Goldsmith and Robert Triffin, noted economists, taught at several universities in the United States.

Desire Defauw conducted the Chicago Symphony Orchestra and made phonograph records in the United States. Alfred Jonniaux was an outstanding Belgian painter who immigrated to this country. Andrew Parmentier helped to establish landscape gardening in the United States. Violinist Eugens Ysaye played many concerts in the United States and taught numerous young American violinists in Belgium. Ernest van Dyck and Ramonde Delaunois gave great enjoyment to large audiences at the Metropolitan Opera Company. In addition to these individuals, Belgian Americans have distinguished themselves in furniture making, sculpture, woolen manufacturing, and education.

Finns

In the fourteenth century, Sweden completed its annexation of the land we know today as Finland, or Suomi as the Finnish people call their country (Kallas & Nickels, 1968). After that time, Finland became the eastern half of Sweden and enjoyed full equality and participation with Swedes. In 1638, Sweden established a trading colony called New Sweden on a 35-mile stretch of land along the Delaware River. The colony remained small, containing no more than two hundred forty people by the last year of its existence as a Swedish settlement in 1655. It is estimated that more than one-third of the colony's population was Finnish. In fact, the last expedition to the area by

Swedes in 1656 contained 92 Finns out of a total of 105 immigrants (Wuorinen, 1930). This contingent of settlers arrived in New Sweden not knowing that the settlement had been seized by the Dutch. Several of the Finns who came to New Sweden had been given the choice of imprisonment for poaching and burning forests or emigration. The site of the settlement was near the present city of Wilmington, Delaware. Some families in the area still trace their ancestry to the early Finnish immigrants. Finns of New Sweden are credited with introducing the log cabin into America (Haglund, 1960; Jalkanen, 1969). Not for another two hundred years was there a significant influx of Finnish immigrants to America.

Contributions

Around the turn of the century, Finnish Americans were among the pioneers of the cooperative store movement in the United States. Cooperatives were opened by Finns in Michigan and Massachusetts. Although he did not visit America, Jan Sibelius exerted a great influence on Finnish-American musicians and also on American symphony orchestras. Juan Wuorinen was an eminent historian of the Finnish-American immigration. Eliel Saarinen, an important Finnish-American architect, designed the Smithsonian Art Gallery. His son, Eero, was the architect who designed the Columbia Broadcasting System (CBS) Tower in New York City, as well as many other notable buildings. His work greatly influenced two generations of American architects. Vaino Hoover was a famous engineer. Peter Kalm visited the colonies of New York, Pennsylvania, and New Jersey from 1738 to 1741, collecting plants and seeds. His collection became the first scientific study of the fauna and flora of the United States. Elmer Forsberg was dean of the Chicago Institute of Art for many years. Bruno Nordberg was a builder of outstanding stationary engines. Herman Laitinen and Hiilo Hakala were renowned chemists. John Kolehmainen was an outstanding writer. However, the greatest Finnish contribution to the United States was the clearing of more than one million acres of frontier land for cultivation by immigrants.

References

Andersen, A. W. (1975). *The Norwegian-American*. Boston: Twayne.

Bailyn, B. (1986). *Voyagers to the West: A passage in the peopling of America on eve of the Revolution*. New York: Alfred A. Knopf.

Barton, H. A. (1975). *Letters from the promised land: Swedes in America, 1840–1914*. Minneapolis: University of Minnesota Press.

Bjork, K. O. (1976). *The Norwegians in America: Giants in the earth*. In F. J. Coppa and T. J. Curran (Eds.), *The immigrant experience in America*. Boston: Twayne.

Brancaforte, C. L. (Ed.). (1989). *The German forty-eighters in the United States*. New York: Peter Lang.

Bratt, J. D. (1984). *Dutch Calvinism in modern America: A history of a conservative subculture*. Grand Rapids, MI: William B. Eerdmans.

Brinks, H. J. (1982). Recent Dutch immigration to the United States. In D. L. Cuddy (Ed.), *Contemporary American immigration: Interpretive essays (European)*. Boston: Twayne.

Butler, J. (1983). *The Huguenots in America: A refugee people in a New World society*. Cambridge: Harvard University Press.

Coppa, F. J., & Curran, T. J. (1976). From the Rhine to the Mississippi: The German emigration to the United States. In F. J. Coppa & T. J. Curran (Eds.), *The immigrant experience in America*. Boston: Twayne.

Cuddy, D. L. (Ed.). (1982). *Contemporary American immigration: Interpretive essays (European)*. Boston: Twayne.

Daniels, R. (1990). *Coming to America: A history of immigration and ethnicity in American life*. New York: HarperCollins.

De Jong, G. F. (1975). *The Dutch in America: 1609–1974*. Boston: Twayne.

Faust, A. B. (1916). Guide to the materials for American history in Swiss and Austrian archives. Washington: Carnegie Institution of Washington.

Gjerde, J. (1985). *From peasants to farmers: The migration from Balestrand, Norway to the Upper Middle West*. Cambridge: Cambridge University Press.

Gonzales, J. L., Jr. (1990). *Racial and ethnic groups in America*. Dubuque, IA: Kendall/Hunt.

von Hagen, V. W. (1976). *The Germanic people in America*. Norman: University of Oklahoma Press.

Haglund, A. W. (1960). *Finnish immigrants in America*. Madison: University of Wisconsin Press.

Hale, F. (Ed.). (1984). *Danes in North America*. Seattle: University of Washington Press.

Hamerow, T. S. (1989). The two worlds of the Forty-Eighters. In C. L. Brancafort (Ed.), *The German Forty-Eighters in the United States*. New York: Peter Lang.

Handlin, O., & Harding, L. (1986). *Liberty in America: 1600 to the present: Volume I: Liberty and power: 1600–1760*. New York: Harper & Row.

Harris, J. F. (1989). *The Arrival of the Europamüde: Germans in America after 1848*. New York: Peter Lang.

Jalkanen, R. J. (Ed.). (1969). *The Finns in North America*. East Lansing: Michigan State University Press.

Kallas, H., & Nickels, S. (1968). *Finland: Creation and construction*. New York: Praeger.

Larsen, K. (1950). *A history of Norway*. Princeton: Princeton University Press.

Lovoll, O. S. (1982). From Norway to America: A tradition of immigration fades. In D. L. Cuddy (Ed.), *Contemporary American immigration: Interpretive essays (European)*, Boston: Twayne.

Moltmann, G. (1985). The pattern of German emigration to the United States in the nineteenth century. In F. Trommler & J. McVeigh (Eds.), *America and the Germans: An assessment of a three-hundred-year history: Volume I: Immigration, language, ethnicity*. Philadelphia: University of Pennsylvania Press.

Nadel, S. (1990). *Little Germany: Ethnicity, religion, and class in New York City 1845–1880*. Urbana IL: University of Illinois Press.

Nielsen, G. (1981). *The Danish Americans*. Boston: Twayne.

O'Connor, R. (1968). *The German-Americans: An informal history*. Boston: Little, Brown.

O'Dell, A. C. (1957). *The Scandinavian world*. London: Longmans, Green.

Reich, J. (1989). *Colonial America*. Englewood Cliffs, NJ: Prentice-Hall.

Rippley, L. V. J. (1976). *The German-Americans*. Boston: Twayne.

Scott, F. D. (1988). *Sweden: The nation's history*. Carbondale: Southern Illinois University Press.

Skardal, D. B. (1974). *The divided heart: Scandinavian immigrant experience through literary sources*. Lincoln: University of Nebraska Press.

Stephenson, G. M. (1932). *The religious aspects of Swedish immigration: A study of immigrant churches*. Minneapolis: University of Minnesota Press.

Taylor, P. (1971). *The distant magnet: European emigration to the U.S.A.* London: Eyre & Spottiswoode.

Thernstrom, S. (Ed.). (1980). *Harvard encyclopedia of American ethnic groups*. Cambridge: Harvard University Press.

Trommler, F., & McVeigh, J. (Eds.). (1985). *America and the Germans: An assessment of a three-hundred-year history: Volume I: Immigration, language, ethnicity*. Philadelphia: University of Pennsylvania Press.

Wakeke, B. H. (1944). *Dutch emigration to North America: 1624–1860*. New York: Netherlands Information Bureau.

Wefald, J. (1971). *A voice of protest: Norwegians in American politics, 1890–1917*. Northfield, MN: The Norwegian-American Historical Association.

Wokeck, M. (1985). German immigration to colonial America: Prototype of a transatlantic mass migration. In F. Trommler & J. McVeigh (Eds.), *America and the Germans: An assessment of a three-hundred-year history: Volume I: Immigration, language, ethnicity*. Philadelphia: University of Pennsylvania Press.

Wuorinen, J. C. (1930). *The Finns on the Delaware: 1638–1655: An essay in American colonial history*. New York: Columbia University Press.

The Furor Teutonicus: Upper Mississippi Abteilung
by George Mann

The German neighborhood in which I grew up stretched along both
sides of University Avenue, which ran west out of downtown St.
Paul toward Minneapolis. It began, more or less, at Rice Street—where the
Deutches Haus was located—and continued west to Dale, which ran
north to the German Lutheran Cemetery. The mile of University
Avenue between Dale and Rice was lined with small business establishments, largely operated by first- or second-generation immigrants—hardware stores, barber shops, confectioneries, variety
stores, groceries, dry goods stores, bakeries, butcher shops, drug
stores, a feed store, some of the earliest automobile agencies, and, in
a parenthesis around Prohibition, saloons ranging from the
respectable to the rowdy. Interspersed were an occasional herb doctor
and several well-patronized undertaking establishments, each with a
fiercely loyal patronage.

My maternal grandparents arrived in St. Paul in the early 1880's,
and built a two-room shanty with a self-contained barn in the area
just north of University Avenue. There my grandmother set up the
spinning wheel and wool-carding brushes she had brought with her,
first on the steerage and then on a steamboat up the Mississippi.
Prospering modestly, like their neighbors, they moved south two
blocks across University Avenue, where my grandfather built a five-
room house with a dormitory attic to house his boys and a separate
backyard barn for his horse. The backyard smokehouse where homemade sausages and hams were smoked was optional.

Here, roughly in the decade split by the end of the First World War,
I grew up, in an amazing homogeneous neighborhood of small frame
houses. After almost fifty years I can recall the roster of the neigh-
bors—Badtke, Leudtke, Zahlinger, Schimmel, Kaiser, Kramer,
Umland, Wolters, Schleh, Scherdin, Neujahr, Behrens, Gehrmann,
Klein, Tesman, Hesse, Ohde, Zaudtke, along with assorted clutches of
Beulkes and Muellers.

I grew up in my grandfather's house, which typically housed three
generations, my grandmother, my parents, and myself. Although the
members of my parents' generation were never to know a grandpar-
ent—who all remained behind in the Old Country—the senior citizens
of the neighborhood took a paternal interest in the children, perhaps
because there were fewer of them than in the enormous families that
marked the first generation on American soil. A retired carpenter,

with gnarled and arthritic hands, bribed me with *windkuchen* (*cream puffs*) to listen to his half-a-century-old horror at the uncivilized French civilians who poured boiling water over the Prussian infantry as it marched through in 1870. When my mother and I went for a walk, we would meet the proprietor of the neighborhood's most respectable saloon. Tall and portly (his size diminished trouble on Saturday nights) with an impressive white, close-cropped imperial—a style also favored by the major Lutheran clergy—he would bend down, not without effort, chuck me under the chin and inquire, "Und wie geht es Landsmann, mit d' Franszosen mit d' roten hosen?" [*And how are you, countryman, with the Frenchmen's red trousers?*] In 1916 this was a good question, the French with their red pants were not locally popular, although animosity toward the French was mixed with envy. It was generally understood that the truly lucky man lived "wie Gott im Frankreich" [like God in France].

The feeling toward the French was by and large cyclical. The real day-to-day animosity dated back to the Reformation and the Thirty Years' War, and was reserved for those whose ancestors had chosen the wrong and Catholic side. For German Lutheran families like mine, the sack of Magdeburg was as fresh and bleeding as whatever it was that Cromwell did to Drogheda was to the Irish. We were convinced that not only did our South German neighbors gloat over past outrages, but that they are momentarily plotting even more dastardly efforts on behalf of the Pope. When I sulked in stubbornness or erupted in a rage, I was quickly rebuked by being told, "Sei nicht so Katholisch,"—"don't be so Catholic." Intermarriage between Catholics and Protestants was substantially equated with miscegenation. When a baker uncle of mine married the daughter of a prolific German Catholic farming family from St. Cloud, the neighborhood expected my grandmother to take to her bed. Instead, she reacted so calmly that, whenever another erring son was ensnared by the wiles of a daughter of Rome, my grandmother was called in to consult with the groom's mother and convince her it might end almost as well as if he had married properly.

Thanks to the single focus of animosity, other nationality groups in the neighborhood were regarded with a curious calmness. The small resident Jewish population—like the corner grocer, mostly struggling shopkeepers, facing a tenacious Teutonic competition—were not only tolerated but often respected because they and the Negroes were often the first to send their children to college. But with the German Catholics it was at best a cold war that heated up five days a week when the competing parochial schools let out at about the same hour, filling the surrounding streets with ambulant mayhem.

Nor was fighting in the community confined to warring clans of schoolboys. A culturally accepted technique for emphasizing a strongly held personal conviction was putting your fist where your opponent's mouth was. My father, for example, in spite of a skinny boyhood, achieved a reputation as a bantamweight brawler that stretched from Rice Street to within two blocks of Dale. I remember on occasion during the Second World War when, in his late fifties and hampered by a tricky mitral valve, my father appeared at dinner wearing a shyly distinct black eye, following a streetcorner discussion of a fender-bending automobile accident.

The neighborhood champion for chronic adult belligerence was the hostler down the block, who lavished a lifetime of paranoia on the employees of the streetcar company. On his way to work, any suggestion of surliness on the part of the conductor led to immediate blows. Genuinely aroused, he was capable of moving down the aisle with the conductor under one arm and the motorman under the other before dumping them off the rear platform, leaving the other passengers to wait for the next streetcar.

Such belligerence was not essentially a love of fighting for its own sake; unlike the Irish who claim to fight gaily, the Germans fought solemnly and doggedly to extend their personal conviction of what was right and was wrong. Equal intensity carried over into arguments, especially if they involved religion or politics. Any opinion not expressed at the top of one's voice was not expected to be taken seriously. Forty years later, my mother remembered with a still quaking delight the theological battles between her father and his brother who had taken up farming in Watertown and lapsed into the Baptist Church. His periodic visits to St. Paul began amiably enough, but by the second beer, the theological argument reached its former decibel level. Pounding the table, the brothers challenged each other to cite where in the New Testament total immersion was prescribed or proscribed. During the din, half-frightened and completely enchanted, my mother and her brothers peeked around the edge of the kitchen doorway. In the early 1920's, my father, who equated trade unions with sin, and his brother-in-law, a carpenter who was still dazzled by the possibilities he had seen in the Seattle general strike of the International Workers of the World, calmly discussed socialism and trade unions in voices that could be heard halfway into the next block.

The fighting and arguments easily turned into animosities fuelled to survive decades, and routinely bequeathed, along with the insurance, to the immediate heirs. A major feud within the community existed between the two most popular doctors, whose loathing for each other was legendary. At a *Maennerchor* picnic, one of the doctors attacked the keg too enthusiastically and was last seen staggering toward the sunset, waving his stein and shouting encouragingly at adjacent females, "Drink beer, ladies, beer makes milk!" much to the scandalized amusement of my mother. Years later, I told mother's anecdote to the other doctor's son. At the mention of the hated name, his face reddened and almost before I could finish, he burst out, "That man was a damned quack!" He wasn't contradicting the widely accepted beer-milk hypothesis, but expressing an inherited opinion. The end of that feud is scarcely in sight.

The Germans possessed neither the equipment to manufacture charm nor the antennae to detect it. The one line of work for which they possessed absolutely no talent was that of the confidence man. . . .

By and large, the Germans lived well below the comfort level, eating well only at festivals, handing down clothing routinely from one sibling to another. And by today's standards, they were grossly underhoused, with families of a dozen children occupying five or six rooms. This occupancy at the turn of the century was often reduced by epidemics of typhoid and diphtheria, whose childish victims were aligned in neat rows of graves in the German Lutheran Cemetery.

Learning was respected, but literature received only a token nod, even though the statues of Goethe and Schiller began to appear in Midwestern parks whenever the first two local brewers accumulated any surplus money. Music was the culture of choice. The tradition produced few virtuosos, but almost an entire population equipped with a piano-playing daughter, a son with a fair lead baritone to dominate the family singing, while a neighborhood reputation awaited a reasonable performer on the violin, mandolin, or concertina. Music's prestige lifted choral directors high in the local hierarchy; church soloists were regarded as citizens of more than ordinary substance, and tryouts for the *Maennerchor* were taken seriously. . . .

Music, along with alcohol and food, formed the three legs of the stool of holiday celebrations. All three were enlisted to celebrate Christmas, as we gathered to serenade the Christmas tree with "O Tannenbaum," Luther's "Cradle Hymn," and "Morgan Kommt der Weinachtsmann" with his potential gifts of swords, guns, and "ein wirklich Kriegesheer." On Christmas Eve, we also replayed the well-guarded Red Seal record of Ernestine Schumann-Heink singing "Stille Nacht." Over Christmas, regiments of relatives gathered at each other's houses to consume mountains of cookies, pfeffernuss, windkuchen, and fruitcakes, which had been weeks in the baking, washed down with homemade elderberry and dandelion wine. The latter was even offered to the children in thimblesized glasses, while the older males periodically retired to the kitchen for private rites of their own.

Easter concentrated upon the Passions of the Cantor of Leipzig; brass quartets with frosty breath heralded the Resurrection from church steeples, and Bach bit deeply into the community. Some thirty years after he stopped singing in public, my father happened to hear an unannounced choral number coming in on the radio during a bridge game and commented, "The St. Matthew Passion." Briefly and expertly, he picked up the baritone part before doubling his opponents.

And finally, the dead were carried to their last place escorted by the German pick-up bands of the period. The cortege moved along University Avenue to Dale, and then turned north, relying on a repertoire alternating between "Ich Hat Ein Kameraden" and the "Dead March" from *Saul*. By prior arrangement, the band continued as far as the Dale Street Bridge. While the mourners proceeded on foot, the band wheeled about, struck up "Yankee Doodle" or "Marching Through Georgia," and double-timed it back to the saloons at Dale and University, where they drank up the proceeds of the engagement.

In between funerals, the musicians appeared in polka and schottische dates on Saturday nights in the dance halls which occupied the second floor of the neighborhood saloons. On Sunday afternoons in winter, they blew with cold lips and mittened fingers in a shed at the Hollow skating rink. No matter how cold, it became a family ritual to walk to the rink, and listen to the brass bounce Strauss and Waldteufel back and forth against the surrounding houses.

If the deceased had been a member of a fraternal organization whose insurance benefits were as simple as its ritual was elaborate the procession could be modestly spectacular, although the Missouri Lutheran Church, the dominant North German church group, eyed such organizational competition coldly. Perhaps the largest and certainly the most perspiring fraternal group was the *Turnverein*. In my youth it was quartered in a ramshackle rambling frame building on Wabash Street, halfway between the nearly abandoned red brick State capitol of the pioneers and Cass Gilbert's tribute to antiquity which houses the current majesty of the State. The turners, who concentrated upon formal gymnastics by the count, were the intellectual heirs of both libertarianism and German nationalism. Their solid skills on the horse, the parallel bars, and the flying rings were generally thought to imply free thinking. In New Ulm (founded by the Forty-Eighters, besieged by Little Crow and his Sioux, and the eventual source of a string of statewide candidates during the early days of the Farmer-Labor Party) an accepted conversational gambit with a newcomer was "Are you a turner or do you go to church?"

Far more powerful than these other institutions was the family. Basically, the German family—except when the father became, in the old Missouri phrase, a "bottle mechanic"—was an uneasy patriarchy. The father, hopefully operating under the imported tradition of "Ich bin der Herr" (*I am the master*)—which eroded fast in American air— exerted a family discipline as strict as he could get by with. Sons were rigorously disciplined until they reached their full strength, daughters treated more indulgently, although walled off from wandering males. When the father died, the oldest son often tried to rule his siblings by a kind of wistful primogeniture, sometimes with a temporary success. Only one thing was certain; in the fluctuating power structure of the German-American family, the classical image of the Jewish mother would have been greeted with total disbelief.

In spite of the music and the elaborately celebrated holidays this was not a society in which anyone rested easy, not even the children. Not only was too much work always waiting, there were rigid right and wrong ways to do work. The unending race after high standards applied to the carpenters, stereotypers, fur cutters, steam fitters, bakers, printing pressmen, lathers, shipping clerks who were my uncles, and flooded out to the small businessmen in their groceries, butcher shops, and saloons, and, ridiculous as the concept of workmanship in this connection may seem today, to the early automobile mechanics.

Consequently, it was a delightful society for the consumer, no matter how frustrating for the producer. A small tailor-made coat, given me on my third birthday, lasted through almost a dozen cousins. A compulsion toward workmanship produced a uniform high quality in shoe repairs and haircuts, and in the sausages and schnecken whose memories still set my tastebuds to itching. The concentration upon detail and on a perfection that expected no second chance tomorrow carried over into the disciplined gyrations of the turners and the meticulous *Takt* of the director of the *Maennerchor*. Even the undertakers took a serious pride in their handiwork. . . .

Outwardly self-contained, this musical, industrious, alcoholic society was amputated, part by part. The German language first eroded and then disappeared, as it previously had from the Pennsylvania legislature. Each succeeding wave of immigrants—most of whose passage money had been faithfully remitted by relatives gone before— integrated more easily into the community and adapted more enthusiastically to English. By the 1930's even my maternal grandmother conceded enough to her half a century in America to throw an occasional English word into the conversation just to make visitors comfortable.

Even though German words and phrases persisted in conversation, the quality of the language steadily declined. Only the Plattdeutsch of North Germany lingered on, largely as a vehicle for private conversation in public among the elders; the young understood only English and the local blurred facsimile of classical German.

Chapter 5

Eastern Europeans: Slavs

Countless European citizens were pushed out of their rural homes in the nineteenth century by industrialization. As fewer workers were needed on farms, the dislocated people moved into local towns and cities. Some of them migrated to other European countries; others traveled across the oceans to new continents. Most of those traveling abroad came to the United States. From 1880, when eastern Europeans began to immigrate to America in great waves, to 1930, when the United States passed immigration restriction laws, approximately twenty-seven million immigrants came to America.

All of the immigrants who came after 1880 are considered "new immigrants." The Slavic states, mainly Russia, Poland, Ukraine, Czechoslovakia, Bulgaria, and Yugoslavia, accounted for about one-fourth of the new immigrants. The ethnic groups of each Slavic country had distinctive customs, languages, and histories. Most of the immigrants scattered throughout the United States and either established their own ethnic communities or integrated with other Slavic groups (Golab, 1977). After Russian Jews and Italians, Poles were the third largest group of immigrants in the early twentieth century.

Differences Within

Slavs, or Slavonians, are a group of eastern European and Siberian peoples, mainly Russians, Poles, Czechs, Slovaks, Yugoslavs,

Bulgarians, and Ukrainians. The original Slav people were a division of Indo-European peoples. The early Slavs were mainly farmers and herders who lived in northwestern Ukraine and southeastern Poland. Between the years A.D. 200 and 500, they began to migrate to other regions of Europe, primarily Germany, Albania, Russia, and Montenegro. It is important to note that Slavs form *language groups* rather than racial groups. They vary in physical features according to the region in which they live. For example, some Slavs have brown hair and others are blond. Those who live near the Mediterranean Sea are much darker skinned than White Russians. Every Slav nation has a tragic history: Genghis Khan slaughtered thousands of Russians; Serbia lost its autonomy after the Austro-Serbian War; Bohemia (Czechoslovakia) was defeated at the battle of White Mountain in 1620; and Poland was divided three times among its enemies.

A Slavic nationalistic movement, known as Pan-Slavism, and led by Russia, spread throughout Europe during the 1830s. Pan-Slav congresses were held in Moscow, Prague, and Vienna to awaken within the scattered Slavic peoples of Europe the desire for national independence. While the congresses demanded freedom from foreign control, lack of cooperation among the various Slavic groups stalled the freedom movement. It was not until after World War I that the dream of freedom was partially realized. At that time Poland, Czechoslovakia, and Yugoslavia became independent Slav nations. Slavs in Ukraine formed a state in the Soviet Union.

The early Slavic immigrants to America tended to settle in communities where their relatives and friends lived. This resulted in their being concentrated in the industrial and mining regions of Illinois, Michigan, New York, Ohio, and western Pennsylvania. They were the largest group of workers in the slaughterhouses of Chicago and the steel mills of Pennsylvania. Approximately one-third of the Poles became farmers in the Northeast and Midwest. Slavic immigrants were particularly significant as truck gardeners on Long Island; tobacco, asparagus, and onion cultivators in the Connecticut Valley; and corn and wheat planters in the Midwest.

Sojourners

In the 1800s, thousands of eastern Europeans emigrated from their native countries to the United States in order to earn more money. In the 1870s, for example, immigrant laborers could earn between $1.50 and $2.00 a day working in the steel mills and coal mines. While that was less than U.S. citizens earned, it was considerably more than the

15 cents to 30 cents they could earn at home—if they could get one of the few jobs available. In violation of state laws, children of immigrants between the ages of nine and twelve also worked. Depending on their jobs, children earned between 30 cents and 90 cents a day.

Many of the sojourners who labored in coal mines, steel mills, and oil refineries during this period lived in company housing in the coal regions, and in row houses built around mills and refineries. When they saved enough money, they would move into surrounding areas and establish ethnic communities in which they built churches and operated lodges (fraternities) and women's organizations.

By the 1900s, the majority of the fraternal mutual aid societies and lodges—created to pay the workmen's compensation, disability insurance, and death benefits that American industrialists refused to pay—were formed along ethnoreligious lines such as Calvinists, Roman and Greek Catholics, and Lutherans. Excluded from organizations formed by men, women established their own societies.

Like many of the earliest immigrants from other countries, the first and second waves of Slavic immigrants maintained their cultural identities through their language and religion. Specifically, they spoke their native language at home, in the neighborhood, at church, at lodge and women's society meetings, and other gatherings of home folks. The children were taught the native language, but each successive generation deemphasized it, preferring instead to speak English. Gradually ethnic languages lost their prominence. Even so, many of the folk customs were passed to the next generation. The examples that follow illustrate traditional folkways.

On Christmas Eve, tradition-oriented Slovak families gathered in the home of their parents or grandparents to await the first sight of the evening star. Once sighted, the meal began. Straw and pine boughs covered the tablecloth to symbolize the manger, and traditional dishes were served: sauerkraut soup, fresh fish or *klobása* (garlic sausage), bean and potato salads, and *bobalky* (dumplings in crushed-poppyseed sauce), accompanied by mulled wine and assorted poppyseed and nut pastries and fruit. Prior to eating the meal, the father or grandfather recited an invocation, then the mother supervised the dipping of communion wafers in honey and smeared some of it on the forehead of each person in the sign of the cross. Apples were cut, and if a star-shaped design appeared in the center, it meant good luck but a cross signified bad luck. After the meal, the family sang Christmas carols, and then the children were allowed to open their presents.

In tradition-oriented Serbian-American families, godparents—*kum* (godfather) and *kuma* (godmother) were closest kin after parents. The spiritual bond between godparents and godchildren, whom they sponsored at baptism, was so venerated that intermarriage between the families was taboo. It was expected that godparents would be as concerned with the well-being of their godchildren as the parents would be. This custom bound Serbian-American families into close-knit religious, political, and economic colonies. Colony members celebrated Easter with colored eggs and observed Christmas with a Christmas tree and, often, the Serbian yule log (*badnjak*), the Christmas candle, spread straw on a portion or all the floor to recall the manager in which Christ was born, honey cake with a coin hidden in it for a lucky recipient, and a roast suckling for Christmas dinner. Christmas was observed on January 7 in accordance with the Gregorian calendar.

There was a familiar saying among the Czech immigrants: "*Co Cĕch, to muzikant*" ("If he's a Czech, he's a musician"). They brought musical instruments as well as feather quilts and Czech recipes to the New World. Even families that did not bring a musical instrument managed to pass on the tradition. They improvised for percussion effects. Frequently, Czech musicians joined with German neighbors to liven the community with melodious sounds. Czech polkas and waltzes still enliven American communities.

Russians

Russian immigrations to America began in 1741, when Captain Alexei Chirikoff led two expeditions to the Western Hemisphere. During the second expedition, his co-leader was Captain Vitus Bering, a Dane in the service of the czar. The Bering Strait and the Bering Sea are named after Captain Bering. The first permanent Russian settlements were established on Kodiak Island, Alaska, in 1784 (Khlebnikov, 1976). The settlements were set up primarily for trade. At the end of the eighteenth century, independent commercial enterprises were consolidated into the Russian-American Company, a corporation sponsored by the Russian government to regulate trade in Alaska and the Aleutian Islands (Wertsman, 1977). Led by Alexander Baranov, Nikolai Petrovich, and Nikolai Ivanovich Kushoff, expeditions from the settlements explored as far down as what today is Sonoma County, California.

During each expedition, a small group of Russian settlers were left behind. The colonization efforts peaked in 1812 when Russian settlers established the Fort Ross Colony at Bodega Bay near San Francisco. Fort Ross became large and economically strong with its own farms, churches, and schools. During this period, several high-ranking Russian officials advocated more permanent settlements in the Western Hemisphere. In 1822, Dimitri Zavalishin urged the Russian government to establish a Russian Empire in America. To avoid international conflict, the Russian government ordered the settlers to sell Fort Ross to John Sutter, a Mexican citizen of Swiss descent. (The settlement was subsequently sold several times and its last owner, William Randolph Hearst, donated the property to the state of California.) Alaska was sold to the United States in 1867, and a new wave of Russians emigrated from Alaska to California (Davis, 1922).

The Russian immigration to the eastern part of the United States was less dramatic. One of the earliest Russian immigrants, Prince Demetrius Gallitzin, arrived in Maryland in 1792. He converted to Roman Catholicism and became the first Catholic priest to be ordained in America. Gallitzin was also a missionary among white settlers and Indians in western Pennsylvania for more than forty years (Wertsman, 1977). Three main Russian motives for immigration to America were the desire for political freedom, religious freedom, and economic stability. Liberal political activities and deviations from the Russian Orthodox Church, the only recognized religious body in the Russian Empire, were punished with local imprisonment or a long-term deportation to Siberia. In addition to religious restrictions and political suppression, brutal nobles oppressed the peasants who lived on their estates.

Contributions

As with all the ethnic groups discussed in this book, the lesser-known people are just as important as the renowned individuals. Russian farmers and industrial workers were major contributors to American culture. Russian farmers brought many varieties of seeds with them, and some of them were suitable for cold American regions. The following people are among the most prominent Russian-American contributors to American culture.

Vladimir Stolishnikoff, an architect, helped to design Carnegie Hall. Peter Demyanoff-Demens was a businessman, railroad builder, and co-founder of St. Petersburg, Florida, which he named after his birthplace. Vladimir Nabokov was a well-known writer and teacher. Other writers include Mark Aldunov, Vassil Janovsky, and Gleb Struve. American colleges and universities were the major beneficiaries of the emigration from Russia. Hundreds of Russian scholars became teachers and researchers in American higher education institutions. The scholars included Michael Rostovzeff, archaeologist; Michael T. Florinsky, historian; Samuel Meltzer, physiologist; Pitirim Sorokin, sociologist; and Andrew Avinoff, zoologist. Most fields of study have been enriched by the contributions of Russian-American scholars.

Alexander Seversky, a pilot and aircraft designer, invented an automatic bombsight, an amphibian landing gear, hydraulic shock absorbers for aircraft, and skis for aircraft. In 1932, he founded Seversky Aero Corporation, which became Republic Aviation in 1939. His book, *Victory Through Airpower*, was made into a cartoon film by Walt Disney. Igor Sikorsky designed the first full engine aircraft in 1913, and he designed the Western Hemisphere's first helicopter in 1939.

In the field of music, outstanding Russians include Sergei Rachmaninoff, a pianist, conductor, and composer whose Piano Concerto No. 2 in C Minor and Piano Concerto No. 3 in D Minor are favorites with many pianists, and Igor Stravinsky, a composer, who influenced many American musicians by his ballet *The Rite of Spring* with its complex rhythms, fragmentary and repetitive melodies, and harmonies with two or more keys at once. His dissonance in music is well known. Other notable Russian musicians include pianists Vladimir Horowitz, Josef and Rosina Lhevinne, and Serge Tarnowsky; violinists Jascha Heifetz, Mischa Elman, and Nathan Milstein; cellist Gregor Pictigorsky; composers Luis Gruenberg, Irving Berlin, Vernon Duke, Dimitri Tiomkin, Nikolai Lopatnikoff, and Leo Ornstein; conductors Serge Koussevitsky, Nikolai Sokoloff, Alexander Koshetz, and Alexander Smallens; singers Sophie Braslau, Irene Pavlovska, Mari Barova, Mstislav Rostropovich, Nina Koshetz, and Maria Kurenko; dancers Natalia Makarova, Mikhail Baryshnikov, Rudolf Nureyev, and George Balanchine; pianist and composer Leopold Godowsky; and pianist and conductor Ossip Gabrilowitsch.

Poles

The first ship carrying Polish immigrants arrived in America in the colony of Jamestown in October 1608. Among the passengers the *Mary and Margaret* brought were Michal Lowicki, a merchant; Jan Mala, a soapmaker; Stanislaw Sadowski, a watermill constructor; Zbigniew Stefanski, a glassblower; and Jan Bogdan, a shipwright. Those skilled workers were among a group of technicians brought over by Governor John Smith to help with the new colony's economy (Davies, 1984). In June 1619, several Poles walked off their jobs to protest being denied the right to vote in America's first Assembly, the Virginia House of Burgesses. On July 21, 1619, they were enfranchised. From the mid-seventeenth century to nationhood, Poles immigrated to colonies in America, especially to New Netherland (Rienkiewicz, 1973; Wytrwal, 1969). In 1659, Alexander Kurchis arrived there by invitation of the Dutch. He founded an academy, the first higher educational institution in what is now New York. It was the second Latin school after Harvard in North America.

In 1662, Albert Zabriskie immigrated to New Amsterdam. Later, he moved across the Hudson to Bergen (now Jersey City) and was appointed the first justice of the peace for Upper Bergen County. Poles also settled in the Delaware valley, and a group of Polish Protestants settled in Pennsylvania and Virginia. In 1736, John Anthony Sadowski established an outpost along the Ohio River that grew into the town of Sandusky, Ohio. The first reliable map of the coast of New England was drawn by Karl Blaszhiewicz, a Polish surveyor. Paul Mostowski tried unsuccessfully in 1776 to found New Poland in the South.

Other Contributions

Polish contributions to America were numerous during the American Revolutionary War. Two well-known Poles fought on the side of the colonists: Count Kazimierz (Casimir) Pulaski, a cavalryman who gave his life during the Seige of Savannah in 1779; and Tadeusz Kościuszko, a military engineer who later led a liberal revolt against the forces of the czar in 1794 (Daniels, 1990). Kościuszko was a brilliant strategist who is often referred to as "the father of American artillery." There is a monument to Kościuszko at West Point and a bust of Pulaski in Washington, D.C., at the Capitol. Also, Feliks Miklaszewicz, a New England privateer, served in the Revolution. In 1848, Paul Wierzbicki, a surgeon in the U.S. Army Medical Corps, wrote a guide to California which was the first volume printed west of the Rockies.

Several decades later, Colonel Kasimir Gzowski, an engineer, helped build the first bridge at Niagara Falls, and Captain Karol Radziminski surveyed and assisted in establishing the U.S.-Mexico boundary. Joseph Turkolski surveyed Louisiana and Utah. Maria Zahrzewska, a physician, founded hospitals for women in New York and Boston. She also demanded professional training for African-American women, and the first African-American nurses in America graduated from her school of nursing. Ernestine Lewis Potowski-Rose, an ardent feminist and abolitionist, submitted the first American petition for a married women's property law. It reached the New York state legislature in 1836. General Wlodzimierz Krzyzanowski served the Union Army with distinction in the Civil War.

The largest number of Polish-American contributions to American culture have been in the fine arts and humanities. Leopold Stokowski, Jan Kiepura, Stanislaw Skrowaczewski, and Artur

Rodzinski were leading conductors of American orchestras. One of America's greatest actresses, Helena Modjeska, was a Polish immigrant. She won worldwide acclaim. Renowned Polish-American opera singers include Marcella Sembrich-Kochanska and Jan Kiepura. Although not Americans, Jean and Edouard de Roszke and Adam Didur sang for many years at the Metropolitan Opera and greatly influenced American singers with their teaching. Josef Hoffman, Artur Rubinstein, and Marylan Jonas were pianists beloved by American audiences. Moriz Rosenthal, one of the greatest pianists in music history, trained many young American pianists. Jazz drummer Gene Krupa was an outstanding entertainer. Jan Rosenand and Tade Styka were successful painters. Famous Polish-American writers have been numerous, including Norman Rosten, Sholem Asch, and Arthur Kober. Polish-American film stars of past years include Pola Negri, Carole Landis, Loretta Young, Mike Mazurki, Jean Wallace, and Estelle Clarke.

In the social and physical sciences, four Polish Americans stand out. Bronislaw Malinowski developed a functional approach in anthropology; Florian Znaniecki pioneered the case study method in sociology; Alfred Korzybski originated the system of general semantics; and Casimir Funk discovered the vitamins. In religion, John Cardinal Krol was archbishop of Philadelphia. In politics, former U.S. Senator Edmund Muskie from Maine also served as secretary of state; Zbigniew Brzezinski was national security adviser to President Jimmy Carter; and Edward Derwinski was the first secretary of veterans affairs. Outstanding sports figures include boxer Stan Ketchel, track star Stella Walsh, and baseball star Stan Musial. Polish Americans have been leaders in labor unions as well as state and federal officials.

Czechs and Slovaks

The traditional homelands of the Czechs, the westernmost branch of the Slavs, are Bohemia and Moravia. After World War I, in 1918, the Czechs and Slovaks were merged into one country, Czechoslovakia. (Today they have gone their separate ways to form distinct nations.) Nearly four hundred thousand Czechs immigrated to the United States, the great majority of them between 1848 and 1914. They made up the only significant Slavic farming group in America, and they came in groups of families. Highly skilled, the Czech immigrants possessed a literacy rate of 97 percent (Capek, 1969; Roucek, 1967).

The first Czech in America was Augustine Herman, a member of the Dutch West India Company in Holland. He arrived in New

Amsterdam in 1633 and received denization in 1644. In 1659, he was sent to Maryland by Governor Peter Stuyvesant to settle a boundary dispute between the Dutch and English. After the assignment, Herman was commissioned by the Calverts to map Maryland and Virginia. Ten years later, in 1670, he gave the map to Lord Baltimore and was rewarded with 5,000 acres of land on the northeast shore of Maryland. It was there that Herman cut the first road through New Bohemia and gave the Bohemia River its name. He is also credited with introducing tobacco into northern Virginia.

Early Czech immigrants to America were largely Moravian Brethren who settled in Pennsylvania, Georgia, and North Carolina along with German converts to the Moravian Church. In the eighteenth century, an edict of the Austrian emperor banned all non-Catholics from western Bohemian territory. The Moravian Brethren were among the religious refugees from Bohemia who immigrated and, as missionaries, they converted Indians and Africans. Bethlehem, Pennsylvania, was the headquarters of their missionary activities. The Brethren also established Moravian villages in Nazareth, Lutiz, and Salem, North Carolina. In the late 1700s, Moravian missionaries founded their first town, first church, and first school in the Ohio Territory.

Contributions

Czechoslovakians have made their greatest American contributions in the field of music. Antonín Dvořák, a composer, was not a citizen of the United States but he helped foster a national music in this country. He encouraged Jeanette Thurber to set up a national conservatory in New York City, where free musical instruction was given to talented persons who could not afford to pay. In 1892, Dvořák became head of the National Conservatory of Music in New York City, and he held that position until 1895 when he returned to Czechoslovakia. He attracted African-American musicians to the conservatory, and used African-American soloists and choirs in his concerts. Also, largely through Dvořák's efforts, American Indian music and Negro spirituals gained national acceptance. Famous Czech-American composers include Rudolph Friml, author of the light operas *The Firefly*, *Rose Marie*, and *The Three Musketeers*; and Jaromir Weinberger, author of the folk operas *Schwanda the Bagpiper* and *Under the Spreading Chestnut Tree*. Czech-American opera singers include Maria Jeritza and Jarmila Novotna. Czech singers Pavel Lukidar, Emmy Destinn, and Otakar Marak sang in the United States. Although not American citizens, they inspired countless young American singers.

Josef Sovak designed the Gothic spires of St. Patrick's Cathedral. Jaroslav Pelikan was one of the most distinguished historians of religion in the world. Aleš Hrdlička, a pioneer American physical anthropologist, founded the *American Journal of Physical Anthropology* in 1918, and the American Association of Physical Anthropologists in 1929. Frederick Novy, a foremost American bacteriologist, was awarded the Cross of a Chevalier of the French Legion of Honor. Aloise Kovarik, a physicist, helped to develop devices to detect German submarines. Biochemists Carl and Gerty Cori were co-recipients of the 1947 Nobel Prize in physiology or medicine. Eugene Cernan was one of the early astronauts. Walter Slezak was one of Hollywood's well-known actors.

In the field of business and industry there have been numerous successful Czech Americans, including James Triner, founder of Triner's Scale Company; Joseph Bulova, founder of the Bulova Watch Company; John David Hertz, creator of the Yellow Cab Corporation; John Shary, president of the Texas Fruit Growers Exchange and also the developer of the agricultural and citrus fruit industry in the Lower Rio Grande Valley, Texas; Henry Walters, manufacturer of zippers and fasteners; Cyrus Lazelle Warner, builder of the New York Times building; Mark Eidlitz, builder of the Metropolitan Opera House and the Presbyterian, St. Francis, and St. Vincent Hospitals in New York; Robert James Eidlitz and Otto Mark Eidlitz, builders of the New York Stock Exchange, Columbia University Library, and the Cloisters Museum.

Individuals distinguished in literary fields include writers Egon Hostovský, Zdeněk Němeček, Milada Součková, Jíří Hochman, Jan Beneš, Ota Ulč, Antonín Liehm, and Amošt Lustig. Historians of Czech origin include Otaker Odložilík, Francis Dvorník, and Robert Kerner. Among the distinguished American literary critics is René Wellek. Erazím Kohák is well known in the field of philosophy. Sports figures include Czecholovakian-American William Hartack, winner of five Kentucky Derbies.

Yugoslavs

The country of Yugoslavia was carved out of part of the defeated Austro-Hungarian Empire at the end of World War I. Austrians had occupied a large part of the area for more than four hundred years, and the Turks also held part of it for several centuries. Although there were several other smaller groups, the three major ethnic groups that made up the new nation were Croats, Slovenes, and Serbs. The official name of the new state was the Kingdom of Serbs,

Croats, and Slovenes until 1929, when it was changed to the Kingdom of Yugoslavia. Each group is related linguistically and racially to the other two. But there are major religious differences: the majority of the Croats and Slovenes are Roman Catholic, while the Serbs are Orthodox Protestants. The smallest group of Croats are Muslim whose ancestors converted centuries ago under Turkish rule (Colakovic, 1973; Govorchin, 1961; Prisland, 1968; Vlahovic, 1940). The recent dissolution of Yugoslavia and the resulting civil war among its racial and religious groups have brought to light the serious differences among the various peoples who made up the former Communist state. The differences were not apparent to the vast majority of people unfamiliar with the history of the area.

Bosnian Muslims are examples of similarities and differences between Christian and non-Christian Yugoslavian immigrants. Immigrants from both groups were employed in America mainly as laborers. Also, both groups formed their own ethnic organizations such as lodges. The first Muslim-American lodge, Džemijetul Hajrije (Beneficient Society), was established for insurance and burial assistance. However, because the early Muslims did not have a mosque they held Friday evening prayers in private homes. Nor did they have the wide range of employment and social opportunities that were available to Christian Yugoslavians.

Croats

In 1715, approximately twelve hundred Croatian and Slovenian Protestants, whose ancestors had left the Austrian Empire after unsuccessful peasant revolts in 1573 and the anti-Reformation edict of 1598, arrived in the American colony of Georgia. They settled on the right bank of the Savannah River where a creek, which they named Ebenezer, flows into the river. Those settlers introduced silkworm cultivation to Georgia. The community prospered for 150 years, until it was demolished during the Civil War. Earlier, in 1683, a Croat Jesuit named Juan Ratkay (Ivan Ratkaf) established a mission in northwest Mexico. In 1746, another Jesuit, Consago Gonzales (Ferdinand Konschak), drew the first dependable map of Baja California. Beginning in 1738, Joseph Kundek, a Croat missionary, helped to develop several midwestern towns, including Ferdinand and Jasper, both in Dubois County, Indiana. In the 1830s, various groups in the Austrian Empire sent thousands of dollars to America to support missionary activities.

In 1815, Austria received from the Congress of Vienna dominion over all eastern Adriatic shores from Trieste to the Albanian border.

Hundreds of Adriatic Croats chose to immigrate to the United States, and many of them settled in New Orleans and were employed as traders, artisans, and fishermen. By 1860, there were about six hundred Dalmatians in New Orleans. Several Croat families settled permanently in Alabama. During the Civil War, nearly three thousand Croats resided in the South, mostly in Louisiana, Alabama, and Mississippi. Hundreds of them volunteered for the Confederate Army and Navy. After the defeat of the Confederacy, in 1865, many Croats who had served in the Confederate military moved to the West.

Among Croatian artists who achieved fame in America were the sculptors Ivan Meštrović, Paul Kelečić Kufrin, and Joseph Turkalj. Three Croat American painters stand out: Ivan Benković, Maksimilian "Maro" Vanka, and Gustav Likan. One of the greatest sopranos in the history of the Metropolitan Opera Company was Zinka Kunc-Milanov. Mia Corak Slavenska was an outstanding ballerina at the Metropolitan Opera and elsewhere. Other Croatian musicians include violinists Louis Svecenski, one of the founders of the Curtis Institute of Music in Philadelphia, and Zlatko Baloković, who married Joyce Borden of the well-known Borden family.

The entertainment industry has had many Croat Americans: actors Peter Coe (Knego), John Miljan, John Northpole (Kovačevć), Slavko Vorkapić, Gloria Grey (Dragomanović), Walter Kray (Krajačić), and Guy Mitchell (Al Crnich). In the field of education, Croat Americans held high positions: Henry Suzzallo, a distinguished scholar, was a president of the University of Washington as well as president of the Carnegie Foundation. Milislav Demerec, a geneticist, taught at Columbia University and was later a senior geneticist at Brookhaven National Laboratory at Upton, Long Island. Other eminent scholars of Croatian-American background include Francis Preveden, Clement Mihanovich, and Dinko A. Tomasic. Bogdan Raditsa and Charles Jelavich are among distinguished historians and authors. Well-known writers include Joseph G. Hitrec, Vinko Nikolić, and Ante Bonifačić.

Croatian Americans have also left their mark in the field of business and enterprise: Peter J. Divizich built a thriving agricultural business in San Joaquin Valley; John Slavic founded the Delmonte Fruit Company; Marcus Nalley and Martin Bogdanovich were food processors. Nikola Bezmalinovic came to America as a poor 14-year-old boy and became a millionaire. In politics, distinguished Croats include Michael Stepovich, the first governor of Alaska; Nick Begich, the first Croatian-American congressman; Rudy Perpick, governor of Minnesota in 1977; Michael Bilandic, former mayor of Chicago; Dennis J. Kucinich, mayor of Cleveland in 1977 at the age of thirty-one. In sports, Fritzie Zivich of Pittsburgh won the world's welter-weight boxing championship in 1951. Hundreds of Croatian Americans gave their lives for their country in World War II, and at least four Croatian-American GIs were awarded the Congressional Medal of Honor.

Slovenes

Ethnically and linguistically distinct from all their close neighbors, most Slovenes lived in the northwest section of the former state of Yugoslavia. One of the earliest Slovenes to immigrate to America was Mark Kapus, a Jesuit missionary, who traveled throughout Arizona between 1687 and 1717. Along with a few Croats, Slovene Protestants migrated to Prussia in the late sixteenth century. In 1715, some of their descendants immigrated to America. Many Slovenians fought as soldiers in General Washington's army during the Revolutionary War (Prpic, 1978). Slovene missionaries, like Frederick Baraga who traveled throughout Wisconsin, upper Michigan, and northern Minnesota, made America known to their fellows in the Austrian Empire. A handful of Slovenes went to California during the days of the gold rush in 1849, and numerous Slovenes migrated to that state after serving in the army of Emperor Maximilian Hapsburg in Mexico.

Some of the early Slovene immigrants were pack-peddlers, who traveled with their wares and sold them to pioneers and Indians in Illinois, Michigan, Wisconsin, Minnesota, Iowa, and Nebraska. Chicago was their business base. They wrote to their relatives and friends in Europe and told them about the job opportunities in the copper and iron mines in Michigan and Minnesota. Their letters contributed to the first large number of immigrants from Slovenia and inland Croatia. During the 1870s and 1880s, most of the Slovenes who came to the United States settled in Michigan and Minnesota to work in the mines.

Slovenian Americans who contributed to the arts include Harvey G. Prusheck, a painter, and Franc Groshe, renowned for his sculptures. In the field of architecture, John Jager, Alexander Papesh, and Aldo Kousta are well known. Anton Schubel sang at the Metropolitan Opera Company for several years, and then became a talent scout for Carnegie. In films, Laura La Plante (Turk), Zala Zarana, and Zalka Srsen achieved success. Michael Lah achieved praise as a movie cartoon animator. Slovenian-American writers include Louis Adamic, author of numerous books and, undoubtably, the outstanding author of his ethnic group; Frank Mlakar wrote about Slovenian Americans in Cleveland, Ohio.

Politics is a field in which several Slovenian Americans have excelled. Among them have been Frank J. Lausche, mayor of Cleveland, governor of Ohio, and a U.S. senator from that state. John A. Blatnik, a congressman from Minnesota, was succeeded by James L. Oberstar. Ray P. Kogovsek was a congressman from Minnesota; Joseph Skubitz was a congressman from Kansas; Philip Ruppe was a congressman from Michigan. Ludwig J. Andolsek was appointed U.S. Civil Service commissioner by President Lyndon Johnson. In the military, Slovenian Americans include five admirals and five generals, among them Lieutenant General Ferdinand J. Chesarek who was supreme military representative of the United States to the United Nations. In the field of popular music, the name of Frank Yankovic, the "Polka King of America," is well known.

Serbs

Before World War I, Serbia was an independent nation in the Balkans, having won her full freedom from the Turks over a period of centuries. Only a few Serbs came to the United States from Serbia before World War II. However, a large number of them came from lands ruled by Austria-Hungary: from Croatia, Dalmatia, Bosnia Herzegovina, and Southern Hungary. At the end of World War I, Serbia, along with Croatia and Slovenia, became part of the new country of Yugoslavia.

Serbs made up about 15 percent of American immigrants from Yugoslavia. Early Serb immigrants to America included George Fisher, who arrived in Philadelphia in 1815, and later fought in Texas for American residents' independence from Mexico. Djordje Sagic was appointed a judge in California (Thernstrom, 1980). In the 1830s, Serbian sailors and fishermen seeking work immigrated from the Bay of Kotor and from Montenegro and Herzegovina to New Orleans. Serbs also immigrated to Alabama and Mississippi. Other Serbs settled in California, particularly around San Francisco, and joined the gold rush. In the 1880s, a large number of Serbian immigrants came to America.

Two of the most illustrious men in the history of science and invention were Serbs who immigrated to America: Nikola Tesla and Michael Pupin. Tesla has more than seven hundred inventions to his credit. Among them is a system of electrical transmission of power, an electromagnetic motor, a method of operating arc lamps, a dynamo electric machine, and an induction motor that powered moving vehicles. He also facilitated the delivery of electricity from powerhouses over great distances. Tesla's nephew, Nikola Terbo, was also an inven-

tor and his discoveries contributed greatly to the progress of the automobile industry. Pupin worked in the field of electricity, especially in
telephone and telegraph systems and xrays. He greatly enhanced the
range of long-distance telephone with the invention of the telephone
repeater, the Pupin coil. He was a member of the American delegation
to the Paris Peace Conference of 1919 and he was a fine writer; his
autobiography, *From Immigrant to Inventor* (1923), won a Pulitzer
Prize in 1924.

In the field of the arts, distinguished Serbs include Vuk Vucinich, a
painter and sculptor; Savo Radulovich, a painter; John David Brcin, a
sculptor; and Borislav Bogdanovich, an artist. In the field of music,
Danica Ilić, the soprano, won the admiration of American audiences for
a number of years at the Metropolitan Opera Company. Mia Novich
(Bosiljka Mijanavić), another soprano, sang in many cities of America.

Among the fine Serbian writers in America were Stoyan
Pribichevich and Mladin Zarubica. William Jovanovich was for many
years president of Harcourt, Brace, Jovanovich and Company, a large
publishing firm. Serbian Americans have held prominent positions in
government: Donald R. Perry was assistant commissioner of the
Immigration and Naturalization Service; and Helen Delich Bentley, a
newspaper woman, was appointed chair of the Federal Maritime
Commission in 1969 by President Richard Nixon. One of the most
famous Serbian Americans is Milan Panić, who came after World War
II. He was chairman of the International Chemical and Nuclear
Corporation, a healthcare corporation. He returned to Yugoslavia in
1992 to lead the Serbian government in an attempt to bring peace to
what was formerly Yugoslavia.

Bulgarians

Bulgarians are descendants of the Thracians whose civilization
goes back to 3500 B.C. The first known Thracian state was established
in the mid-fifth century B.C. Later, its kings acknowledged the
suzerainty of the Roman Empire, although they retained nominal
independence. In the first century A.D., under Emperor Vespasian, the
Romans absorbed Thrace. As the Roman Empire began to crumble,
Thrace underwent successive invasions by Goths, Huns, and Avars.
The northern section of mainly Macedonian Thrace was occupied by
Bulgarians in the Middle Ages, but when Constantinople fell to Turks
in 1453 the area was defenseless. Soon after, the Turks took Thrace
and Macedonia. The independent state of Bulgaria did not come into
being until 1878. When Bulgaria became an independent state,
Macedonia remained under Ottoman rule. By the time of the Turkish

invasion, the peoples of Thrace had adopted the Slavic languages and customs. Today, Macedonia is divided between Bulgaria, Greece, and the former government of Yugoslavia (Anastasoff, 1936).

In Bulgaria proper, spurs to immigration to America were overpopulation, heavy taxation, low living standards, and lack of employment as well as the desire of young men to escape harsh military service, and the persecution of the Eastern Orthodox faith. In Macedonia, the severe rule of the Turks as well as economic neglect caused many people to immigrate to America.

Contributions

Among the prominent Bulgarian-American academicians have been Radislav Sadoff, professor of philosophy at Rice University; Vangel Sugereff, professor of history at Texas A&M University; and George Dimitroff, director of the Harvard University Observatory. Alexander Georgiev invented a condenser used in electric motors and radios; Assen Jordanoff, a renowned aviation authority, was technical adviser to airlines and aircraft manufacturers. Strashimer Petroff's discovery that tuberculosis bacilli in animals comprises three types of bacteria provided clues to the composition of tuberculosis germs in humans. In the arts, Agop Agopoff created a well-known sculptured bust of Will Rogers, and Victor Sharenkov was a prominent art photographer. Among the Bulgarians who have sung at the Metropolitan Opera have been Ljuba Welitsch, although she is not an American citizen, and Lubomir Vishegonov. In politics, Stoyan Christowe was a state senator in Vermont, and he served on various federal boards.

Ukrainians

When large-scale Ukrainian immigration to the United States began in 1980, there existed no such thing as a Ukrainian state. The Ukrainian people were divided among Russia, Austria-Hungary, and Poland. However, nearly 85 percent of the Ukrainian immigration originated in the Austrian provinces of Galicia and Bukovin and in the Transcarpathia region of northeastern Hungary (Thernstrom, 1980). Those immigrants were not the first Ukrainians to come to America. Ivan Bodahn arrived in Jamestown, Virginia, with Captain John Smith in 1608. Not long after, between 1658 and 1662, several Ukrainian Protestants who were persecuted by the Polish Catholic Church immigrated to Holland. Later, several Ukrainian immigrants came to Pennsylvania with Dutch and German settlers. In 1772, Albert Zoboriwsky was the first Ukrainian to settle in New York.

Ukrainians were with the Russians who founded Fort Ross in California. A steady stream of Ukrainians came to America from Alaska with the Cossacks, and hundreds of Ukrainian Americans distinguished themselves in the Revolutionary War and the Civil War (Halich, 1937; Subtelny, 1988; Wertsman, 1976; Yaroslav, 1940).

Contributions

There have been a sizable number of distinguished Ukrainian-American artists, including sculptor Alexander Archipenko, who pioneered the art of sculpto-painting which unites form and color in a harmonious ensemble (the Cubist style). Other well-known sculptors include George Bobritzky, Slava Gerulak, Alexander Hunenko, and Mykola Holodnyk. Rosalia Rolenka, another artist, began teaching Easter egg painting in Detroit in 1915, and Severina Parylla, a nun, popularized Ukrainian wood carving in the United States. A group of neo-Byzantine painters such as Sviatoslav Hordynsky and Peter Kholodny created icons and other artistic elements in Ukrainian church interiors. Other Ukrainian-American painters and graphic artists include Wolodymyr Balas, Michael Moroz, Jacques Hnizdovsky, Petro Mehyk, and Myroslawa Lasowoska.

Well-known Ukrainian-American architects include George Kodak, Julian K. Jastremsky, Ivan Zukovsky, and Appollinaire Osadca. Distinguished Ukrainian-American musicians include Mychaylo Hayvoronsky and Roman Prydatkewych. In 1952, the Ukrainian Music Institute in New York City was established. Prominent composers include Ihor Bilohrud, Alexander Koshetz, Nicholas Fomenko, Volodymyr Hrudyn, Antin Rudnytsky, and Ihor Sonevytsky. Famous Ukrainian-American opera singers include Maria Sokil, Peters Ordynsky, Maria Hrebinetzka, and Olga Lepka. Orchestra conductors include Nicholas Malko and Anthony Rudnicky.

Ukrainian-American writers include the poets Sava Chemetskyi, Bohdan Boychuk, Bohdan Rubchak, and Iurii Tarnawsky; and novelists Ostap Tarnawsky, Evhen Malaniuk, Iurii Kosach, Teodosii Osmachka, and Vasyl Barka. In the sciences there is Sabin Sochocky, who invented a radium paint that led to the manufacture of luminous watch bands; Konstantin Sudzilovsky, a physician, was the first president of the Hawaii Senate after the incorporation of Hawaii into the United States; and George Kistiakowsky was a special adviser for science and technology to President Dwight D. Eisenhower. Joseph Charyk was an undersecretary of the U.S. Air Force from 1960 to 1963, and Myron Kuropas was a special adviser to the president for ethnic affairs in 1975–76.

Among actors in films have been Sandra Dee (Alexandra Zhuk), Nick Adams (Adamschock), Jack Palance (Palaniuk), and John Hodiak. Outstanding Ukrainian-American athletes include professional football players Bronislav "Bronko" Nagurski, famous during the 1930s, and Charles "Chuck" Bednarik, with the Philadelphia Eagles; and hockey players Bill Mosienko and Terry Sawchuk.

References

Anastasoff, C. (1936). *The tragic peninsula*. St. Louis: Blackwell Vieland.

Capek, T. (1969). *The Czechs in America*. New York: AMS Press.

Colakovic, B. M. (1973). *Yugoslav migrations to America*. San Francisco: R&E Research Associates.

Daniels, R. (1990). *Coming to America: A history of immigration and ethnicity in American life*. New York: HarperCollins.

Davies, N. (1984). *God's playground: A history of Poland. Volume II: 1795 to the present*. New York: Columbia University Press.

Davis, J. (1922). *The Russian immigrant*. New York: Macmillan.

Golab, C. (1977). *Immigrant destinations*. Philadelphia: Temple University Press.

Govorchin, G. S. (1961). *Americans from Yugoslavia*. Gainesville: University of Florida Press.

Halich, W. (1937). *Ukrainians in the United States*. Chicago: University of Chicago Press.

Khlebnikov, K. T. (1976). *Colonial Russian America*. Portland, OR: Historical Society.

Prisland, M. (1968). *From Slovenia to America*. Chicago: Slovenian Women's Union of America.

Prpic, G. J. (1978). *South Slavic immigration to America*. Boston: Twayne.

Rienkiewicz, F. (1973). *The Poles in America. 1608–1972*. Dobbs Ferry, NY: Oceana.

Roucek, J. S. (1967). *The Czechs and Slovaks in America*. Minneapolis: Lerner.

Subtelny, O. (1988). *Ukraine: A History. Toronto*: University of Toronto Press.

Thernstrom, S. (Ed.). (1980). *Harvard encyclopedia of American ethnic groups*. Cambridge: Harvard University Press.

Vlahovic, V. S. (1940). *Slavic personalities: Past and present*. New York: Slavic Press.

Wertsman, V. (Ed.). (1976). *The Ukrainians in America, 1608–1975: A chronology and fact book*. Dobbs Ferry, NY: Oceana.

Wertsman, V. (Ed.). (1977). *The Russians in America, 1727–1970*. Dobbs Ferry, NY: Oceana.

Wytrwal, J. A. (1969). *Poles in American history and tradition*. Detroit: Endurance.

Yaroslav, J. C. (1940). *The Ukrainian immigration in the United States*. Scranton, PA: Ukrainian Workingman's Association.

Russians and Slavs at Scranton, PA 1913
by Stephen Graham

I came into Forest City along a road made of coaldust. A black by-path led off to the right down a long gradual slope, and was lost among the culmheaps of a devastated country side. Miners with sooty faces and heavy coal-dusty moustaches came up in ones and twos and threes, wearing old peakhats, from the center of the front of which rose their black nine-inch lamps looking like cockades. They carried large tarnished "grub-cans," they wore old cotton blouses, and showed by unbuttoned buttons their packed, muscular bodies. Shuffling forward up the hill they looked like a different race of men—these divers of the earth. And they were nearly all Russians or Lithuanians or Slavs of one kind or another. "Mostly foreigners here," said I to an American whom I overtook.

"You can go into that saloon among the crowd and not hear a word of white the whole night," he replied. He addressed a collier in English.

"Are you an American?"

"No Speak English," he replied, and frowned.

"From Russia?" I inquired, in his own tongue.

"And you from where?" he asked with a smile. "Are you looking for a job?"

But before I could answer he sped away to meet a trolley that was just whizzing along to a stopping-place. Presently I myself got into a car and watched in rapid procession the suburbs of Carbondale and Scranton. Black-faced miners waited in knots at the stations all along the road. I read on many rocks and railings the scrawled advertisement, "Buy diamonds from Scurry." Girls crowded into the car from the emptying silk-mills, and they were in slashed skirts, some of them, and all in loud colours, and over-decorated with frills, ribbons, and shoddy jewellery. We came to dreary Iceville, all little grey houses in the shadow of an immense slack mountain. We came into the fumes of Carbondale, where the mines have been on fire ten years; we got glimpses of the far, beautiful hills and the tender green of spring woods set against the soft darkness of abundant mountains. We dived into wretched purlieus where the frame-buildings seemed like flotsam that had drifted together into ridges on the bending earth. We saw dainty little wooden churches with green and yellow domes, the worshipping places of Orthodox Greeks, Hungarians, Ruthenians, and at every turn of the road saw the broad-faced, cavernous-eyed men and the bright-eyed, full-bosomed women of the Slavish nations. I realised that I had reached the barracks of a portion of America's great army of industrial mercenaries.

I stayed three days at Casey's Hotel in Scranton, and slept nights under a roof once more, after many under the stars. I suppose there was a journalist in the foyer of the hotel, for next morning, when I opened one of the local papers, I read the following impression of my arrival:

> With an Alpine rucksack strapped to his back, his shoes thick with coal-dust, and a slouch hat pulled down on all sides to shut out the sun, a tall, raw-boned stranger walked up Lackawanna Avenue yesterday afternoon, walked into the rotunda of the Hotel Casey and actually obtained a room.

Every paper told that I was an Englishman specially interested in Russians and the America of the immigrant. So I needed no further introduction to the people of the town.

Just as I was going into the breakfast-room a bright boy came up to me and asked me in Russian if I were Stephen Graham. "My name is Kuzma," said he. "I am a Little Russian. I read you wanted to know about the Russians here, so I came along to see you."

"Come and have breakfast," said I.

We sat down at a table for two, and considered each a delicately printed sheet entitled, "Some suggestions for your breakfast." Kuzma was thrilled to sit in such a place; he had never been inside the hotel before. It was pretty daring of him to call and seek me there. But Russians are like that, and America is a free country.

As we had our grape-fruit and our coffee and banana cream and various other "suggestions," Kuzma told me his story. He was a Little Russian, or rather a Red Russian or Ruthenian, and came from Galicia. Three years previously he had arrived in New York and found a job as dish-washer at a restaurant. After three months of that he progressed to being bottle-washer at a druggist's, then he became ice-carrier at a hotel. Then another friendly Ruthenian introduced him to a Polish estate agent, who was doing a large business in selling farms to Polish immigrants. As Kuzma knew half a dozen Slavonic dialects the Pole took him away from New York, and sat him in his office at Scranton, putting him into smart American attire, and making a citizen out of a "Kike." I should say for the benefit of English readers that illiterate Russians and Russian Jews are called Kikes, illiterate Italians are "Wops," Hungarians are "Hunkies." These are rather terms of contempt, and the immigrant is happy when he can speak and understand and answer in English, and so can take his stand as an American. After six months clerking and interpreting Kuzma began to do a little business on his own account, and actually learned how to deal in real estate and sell to his brother Slavs at a profit.

Kuzma, as he sat before me at breakfast, was a bright, well-dressed business American. You'd never guess that but three years before he had entered the New World and taken a job as dish-washer. He had seized the opportunity.

"You're a rich man now?" said I.

"So-so. Richer than I could ever be in Galicia. I'm learning English at the High School here, and when I pass my examination I shall begin to do well."

"You are studying?"

"I do a composition every day, on any subject, sometimes I write a little story. I try to write my life for the teacher, but he says I am too ambitious."

"Do you love your Ruthenian brothers and sisters here?"

"No, I prefer the Great Russians."

"You're a very handsome young man. I expect you've got a young lady in your mind now. Is she an American, or one of your own people? Does she live here, or did you leave her away over there, in Europe?"

"I don't think of them. I shall, however, marry a Russian girl."

"Have you many friends here?"

"Very many."

"You will take me to them?"

"Oh yes, with pleasure."

"And where shall we go first? It is Sunday morning. Shall we go to church?"

We left the hotel and went to a large Baptist chapel. When we arrived there we found the whole congregation engaged in Bible study. The people were divided into three sections—Russians, Ruthenians, Poles. Russians sat together, Ruthenians and Little Russians together, and Poles together. I was most heartily welcomed, and took a place among the circle of Russians, Kuzma being admitted there also, though by rights he should have gone to the other Ruthenians. He was evidently a favourite.

We took the forty-second chapter of Genesis, reading aloud the first verse in Russian, the second in Ruthenian, and the third in Polish. When that was accomplished we prayed in Ruthenian, then we listened to an evangelical sermon in Russian, and then sang, "Nearer, my God, to Thee!" in the same manner as we had read the chapter of

Genesis—first verse in Russian, second in Ruthenian, third in Polish. It was strange to find myself singing with Kuzma:

Do Ciebie Boze moj!

Przblizam sie.

. I have never seen Poles and Ruthenians and Russians so happy together as in this chapel, and indeed in America generally. In Russia they more or less detest one another. They are certainly of different faiths, and they do not care about one another's language. But here there is a real Pan-Slavism. It will hold the Slavic peoples together a long time, and separate them from other Americans. Still there are not many cities in the United States resembling Scranton ethnologically. The wandering Slav when he moves to another city is generally obliged to go to a chapel where only English is spoken, and he strains his mind and his emotions to comprehend the American spirit.

After the hymn the congregation divided into classes, and talked about the Sermon on the Mount, and to me they were like very earnest children at a Sunday School. I was able to look round. There were few women in the place; nearly all of us were working men, miners whose wan faces peered out from the grime that showed the limit of their washing. At least half the men were suffering from blood-poisoning caused by coal bruises, and their foreheads and temples showed dents and discolorations. They had been "up against it." They would not have been marked that way in Russia, but I don't think they grudged anything to America. They had smiles on their lips and warmth in their eyes; they were very much alive. "Tough fellows, these Russians," wrote Gorky. "Pound them to bits and they'll come up smiling."

They were nearly all peasants who had been Orthodox, but had been "converted"; they were strictly abstinent; they sighed for Russia, but they were proud to feel themselves part of the great Baptist community, and knit to America by religious ties. None of them entirely approved of Scranton. They felt that a mining town was worse than anything they had come from in Russia, but they were glad of the high wages they obtained, and were saving up either to go back to Russia and buy land or to buy land in America. They craved to settle on the land again.

It seemed to me Kuzma's business of agent for real estate among the Slavs was likely to prove a very profitable one. I shall come back to Scranton one day and find him a millionaire. He evidently had the business instinct—an example of the Slav who does not want the land again. The fact that he sought me out showed that he was on the *qui vive* in life.

When the service was concluded we went over the church with a young Russian who had fled to America to escape conscription, and who averred that he would never go back to his own country. His nose was broken, and of a peculiar blue hue, owing to blood-poisoning. His finger-nails were cut short to the quick, but even so, the coal-dust was deep between the flesh and the nail. He was most cordial, his handshake was something to remember, even to rue a little. He had been one of those who took the collection, and he emptied the money on to a table—a clatter of cents and nickels. He showed us with much edification the big bath behind the pulpit where the converted miners upon occasion walked the plank to the songs of fellow-worshippers. They were no doubt attracted by the holiness of water, considering the dirt in which they lived. . . .

In the afternoon Kuzma took me to the Public Library and showed me its resources. In the evening we went to supper at the house of a dear old Slovak lady, who had come from Hungary on a visit thirty years ago, and had never returned to her native land. She had been courted and won and married within three weeks of her arrival—her husband a rich Galician Slav. Now she was a widow, and had three or four daughters, who were so American you'd never suspect their foreign parentage.

She told me of the many Austrian and Hungarian Slavs in Pennsylvania, and gave it as her opinion that whenever a political party was badly worsted in southeastern Europe the beaten wanted to emigrate *en bloc* to the land of freedom. When they came over they held to the national traditions and discussed national happenings for a while, but they gradually forgot, and seldom went back to the European imbroglio.

A touching thing about this lady's house was a ruined chapel I found on the lawn—a broken-down wooden hut with a cross above it, built when the Slav tradition had been strong, and used then to pray in before the Ikon, but now only accommodating the spade and the rake and a garden-roller.

We had a long talk, partly in Russian, partly in English—the old lady had forgotten the one and only knew the other badly. So it was a strange conversation, but very informing and pleasant.

Slavs always talk of human, interesting things.

Kuzma was very happy, having spent a long day with an Englishman whose name had been in the newspaper. We walked back to the hotel, and for a memory he took away with him a newspaper-cutting of a review of one of my books and a portrait of the tramp himself.

Next day, through the kindness of a young American whom I had met the week before entirely by chance, I was enabled to go down one of the coalmines of Scranton, and see the place where the men work. The whole of the city is undermined, and during the daytime there are more men under Scranton than above it.

I was put into the charge of a very intelligent Welshman, who was a foreman, and we stepped into the cage and shot down the black shaft through a blizzard of coaldust, crouching because the cage was so small, and holding on to a grimy steel bar to steady ourselves in the swift descent. In a few seconds we reached the foot—a place where there was ceaseless drip of water on glistening coal—and we walked out into the gloom.

Black men were moving about with flaming lamps at their heads, electric cars came whizzing out of the darkness, drawing trucks of coal. Whole trucks were elevated in the opposite shaft from that in which we had descended, elevated to the pit-mouth with a roar and a rush and a scattering of lumps of coal. I gained a lively realisation of one way in which it is possible to get a coal-bruise.

My guide showed me a map of the mine, and we went along dark tunnels to the telephone cavern, and were enabled to give greeting to miners as far as three miles away underground. Every man working in the mine was in telephonic communication with the pit-mouth. I saw the men at work, watched small trucks of coal being drawn by asses to the main line where the train was made up. I talked with Poles, Ruthenians, Russians—actually meeting underground several of those whom I had seen the day before in the Baptist Chapel. They were all very cheerful, and smiled as they worked with their picks. Some were miners, some labourers. The miner directs the blasting and drilling, puts in the powder and blows out the coal; the labourer works with pick and shovel. A man has to serve two years in a mine as a labourer before he can be a miner. Even a British immigrant, who has worked in South Wales or Northumberland or elsewhere has to serve his term as a labourer. This discourages British men. Scranton used to be almost entirely Welsh; but it goes against the grain in an English-speaking man to fetch and carry for a Slovak or a Pole. On the other hand, this rule safeguards American strikers against imported miners.

After I had wandered about the mine a while I went up to the "Breaker's" tower, to the top of which each truck of coal was hoisted by the elevator; and I watched the fanning and screening and guiding and sifting of this wonderful machine, which in collaboration with the force of gravity can sort a ton of coal a second. I talked with Polish boys sitting in the stream of the rolling, hurrying coal; their task was to pick out bits of slate and ore; and I watched the platemen splitting lumps of coal with their long-handled hammers, and casting out the impurities. I saw the wee washhouse where the collier may bathe if he wish.

"Well, America or Russia, which is it?" I asked of almost every Russian I met. "Which do you prefer? Are you Americans now or Russians?"

And nearly all replied, "America; we will be Americans. What does one get in Russia?—fifty cents a day." Only a few said that America was bad, that the mining was dangerous and degrading. Strange to say, the astonishment at America's wealth and the wages they get from her had not died away. They admired America for the wages she gave; not for the things for which the people of culture in the great cities admire her. America gave them money, the power to buy land, the power to buy low pleasures, the power to get back to Russia, or to journey onward to some other country—to the Argentine or to Canada.

I then spent a day visiting people at random. I went into Police Station No. 4, and found Sergeant Goerlitz sitting at a desk reading his morning paper, and he was very ready to talk to me. From him I gathered that the Slavs were the best citizens—quiet, industrious, and law-abiding. By Slavs he meant Huns, Bulgarians, Galicians, Ruthenians. The Russians were vulgar and pushing. He probably meant Russian Jews and Russians. The Italians were the most dangerous people; they committed most crimes, and never gave one another away to the police. The Poles and Jews were the most successful people.

I went to the house of a communicative, broad-nosed, broad-lipped little Ruthenian priest—an Austrian subject—and he told me that Russia could take India whenever she wanted to, American could take Canada, and that Germany would break our naval power. But the English would still be the greatest people in the world. In the near future the whole of North America would be one empire, and the whole of South America another—one Anglo-Saxon, the other Latin. He was evidently a student of contemporary possibilities. Despite his belief in America he was proud of his own nationality, and jealous of the loss of any of his flock. To his church there came three hundred Little Russians and about thirty Great Russians. He reckoned there were fifty families in Scranton purely Nihilist—by that he meant atheistic and pleasure-seeking. At his church the service was in Slavonic and the sermon in Ruthenian. He was sorry to say there were comparatively few marriages. People came to the town to make money rather than to live.

Then I went to the official Russian priest, away on Divison Street. He shepherded one hundred and thirty-seven families, and four hundred and sixty-two unmarried people. His church had been burned down the year before, but had sprung up again immediately. Some of the congregation had succeeded in business, and having come as poor colonists were now rich and respected citizens, professional men, large storekeepers, responsible clerks. Scranton was more like a Russian city than an American, and it was possible to flourish as a lawyer or a doctor or an estate agent although you knew very little of the English language. And out in the country round about were many Russian farms with real Russian peasants on them; and he spent many weeks in the year travelling about in the rural districts giving the consolation of Orthodoxy to the faithful.

A pathetic thing happened whilst I was taking leave of the priest; a young workman came in to ask advice, and in salutation he took the priest's hand to kiss it, but the latter was ashamed to receive that homage before me, and so tried to pull his hand away. Despite the churchman's enthusiastic account of his work I felt that little action was symbolical of the ebb-tide. It was to me as if I had looked at the sea of faith, and said, "The tide is just turning."

Chapter 6

Eastern Europeans: Non-Slavs

The eastern European immigrants who came to America were similar
to the other European immigrants in their reasons for moving from
their native lands: bad economic conditions, war, and political and
religious oppression (Goldhagen, 1968; Karklis & Streips, 1974).
More than anything else, lack of economic opportunity caused their
desire to seek a new home and, like other immigrants, their unique
ethnic group histories made them strangers in the new land. It is a
truism that people who speak different languages live in different
worlds, and the immigrants who could not speak English were not
only different from those who lived in English-speaking communities,
they were also assigned inferior or low-status jobs. Even so, large
numbers of eastern European immigrants and their descendants distinguished themselves in numerous ways and contributed immensely
to the cultures of America.

Kinship Ties

Kinship ties are important to all ethnic groups, and the non-Slavic
eastern Europeans illustrate this (Coppa & Curran, 1976; Cuddy,
1982). It was usually a relative in the New World who helped them
find employment and learn to speak English. Equally important is
the fact that kin helped immigrants preserve family rituals and cul-

tural traditions while they simultaneously learned American ways. Whether they came to the United States in family units, reconstructed separated families, or formed new families, kin served as a valuable link for immigrants torn between the past, present, and future. Only when immigrants became Americanized did the utilitarian value of kin diminish.

Albanian Americans illustrate the fusion, and sometimes confusion, between old country and new country values and traditions. In Albania, the husband was the absolute authority of the family, and the wife's place was at home. It was an embarrassment to the family for her to work outside the home. Females were socialized to become wives and mothers, and it was not even expected that they would get a highschool diploma. Too much education would, according to traditional belief, damage their moral purity and strength of character. This was an elaborate rationalization for perpetuating male dominance. Initially, Americanization altered the nearly absolute authority of the husband but it did not significantly weaken other traditions. Albanian immigrants were able to maintain close contact with their relatives and observe numerous traditional customs and courtesies. For example Albanian food, song, and dance characterized the manner in which they celebrated national and religious holidays. Chicken and roast lamb, olives and feta cheese, spinach, squash-filled pies (lakror), and pastries (kurabie, brushtull, and baklava) were served. Further, tradition-oriented Albanian Americans celebrated name days instead of birthdays. Orthodox Christians celebrated Easter and Christmas, and Muslims observed Bairam and other religious holidays.

Estonians and Latvians also illustrate the importance of culture for non-Slavic eastern European peoples. Despite a long history of foreign domination, they maintained a distinct national culture in the homelands and in the United States too. Much of their culture was passed on in songs, poetry, and ethnic-language journals and newspapers. In each instance, the political goal of free, independent nations kept Latvian and Estonian cultures intact. For example, Latvian *dainas* (folk songs), which have more than a million original verses and variant texts, and Latvian choirs and theatrical groups expressed the Latvian desire to become members of a sovereign nation. Estonian folk dancing groups and scholars provided a similar message during the 1960s, 1970s, and 1980s.

Austrians

The Austro-Hungarian Empire was an unstable, multinational, and multilingual coalition formed by the union of Austria, Hungary,

Bohemia, and portions of Poland, Italy, Yugoslavia, and Romania. The peoples of Austria-Hungary included Austrians, Hungarians, Germans, Czechs, Poles, Slovaks, Croats, Slovenes, Serbs, Romanians, and Russians. In 1867, Franz Joseph, emperor of Austria and king of Hungary, established a dual monarchy with Hungary. After that event, Hungary and Austria had separate constitutions but shared ministries of war, finance, and foreign affairs. When Franz Joseph died in 1916, the dual monarchy began coming apart. The Czechs demanded independence; the Slovaks sought independence or, at minimum, reunification with Czech-Bohemia; and the Serbs wanted an independent state in Transcarpathia. In 1919, the Treaty of Versailles separated Austria and Hungary and created the independent nations of Poland, Czechoslovakia, and Yugoslavia.

The first major immigration of German-speaking Austrians came after 1848, the year in which revolutions swept over Europe. Prince Klemens Metternich, Austrian minister of foreign affairs for nearly forty years, spent several years beginning in 1815 trying to eradicate from Europe the ideas of the American and French revolutions. In 1848, protests against Metternich's policies reached violent levels; most of the revolts failed, and the revolutionaries of Austria were forced to flee their country. Large numbers of them, the so-called "Forty-Eighters," immigrated to the United States (Spaulding, 1968). Some of them came with their families, although most of them were young, unmarried men. Intellectual in their approach to life and politics, they were well received in the new country. Many of the Forty-eighters were Jews. Within two years, the Austrian Catholics and Austrian revolutionaries in America became the targets of the Know-Nothings, formed in the 1850s to subjugate foreigners. Many of the immigrants became ardent abolitionists and fought in the Union Army during the Civil War.

Contributions

Frederick Brandies was a composer, pianist, and organist. Ernestine Schumann-Heink, the greatest operatic contralto of her time, was a longtime star of the Metropolitan Opera Company. Leo Slezak, a leading singer in the Vienna State Opera, was also a member of the Metropolitan Opera Company for many years. Arthur Bodanzky was a noted symphonic and operatic conductor. Fritz Kreisler, a noted composer, was one of the great concert violinists in music history. Erich Wolfgang Korngold was a symphonist and one of the finest composers of music for the films.

Heinrich Confried was manager of the Metropolitan Opera

Company during some of its greatest seasons. Anton Seidl was a famed conductor of the Metropolitan Opera Company and of the New York Philharmonic. Arnold Schoenberg, one of the greatest composers of the twentieth century, was also a noted teacher. Bruno Walter was a famous symphonic and operatic conductor. Artur Schnabel was one of the most significant concert pianists of the twentieth century. In addition, he was a teacher of considerable importance. Otto Preminger was a noted film producer. Max Reinhardt was one of the most important stage directors of the twentieth century.

Viktor Hess was winner of the Nobel Prize in physics in 1936. Isidor Rabi was winner of the Nobel Prize in physics in 1944. Wolfgang Pauli was winner of the Nobel Prize in physics in 1945. Karl Landsteiner discovered that there are four main types of blood, and he was winner of the Nobel Prize in medicine in 1930. Julius Hausen was the surgeon-general of the Union Army of the Potomac. Ernest Krackowitzer, a physician, introduced the laryngoscope to the United States.

John L. Smithmeyer was the architect of the Library of Congress. Rabbi Benjamin Szold was an ardent advocate for the education of black Americans in Baltimore. Fannie Bloomfield-Zeisler and Moriz Rosenthal were noted pianists. Nathan Ohrbach founded Ohrbach Stores; August Brentano founded Brentano's Bookstores; Charles Louis Fleischmann founded the General Baking Company; Jennie Grossinger founded Grossinger's Country Club. Bruno Bettleheim and Theodor Reik were famous psychoanalysts.

Hungarians

When Hungarians began arriving in large numbers in the United States, immigration officials made no ethnic distinctions between them. Later, differences were noted and the label "Hungarian American" was used to describe the Magyar-speaking people from Hungary and their descendants. The first Hungarian to arrive in the New World, Parmenius of Buda, was a classical scholar and poet who came with the English explorer Sir Humphrey Gilbert to Newfoundland in 1583 (Széplaki, 1975). Nearly one hundred years intervened before the first Hungarian settlers arrived. István Zádora, a Reformed clergyman, landed in Boston in 1682. Soon Johannes Kelp, a Pietist who led a group of Transylvanian Saxons to Pennsylvania in 1694, followed and the next year Izsak Ferdinánd Sárosy settled in Germantown, Pennsylvania. But long before 1682 a Jesuit missionary, Johannes Rátkey, had explored the southwestern part of what later became the United States. He wrote detailed reports about his adventures (Vardy, 1975).

A small group of Hungarian professional officers fought on the American side during the Revolutionary War. One of them, Mihály Kováts de Fabricy, was killed at the battle of Charleston. Before his death, he helped organize a hussar regiment in Count Casimir Pulaski's army. Another Hungarian, Major John Ladislaud Pollereczky, led a group of Hungarian hussars in the war. Pollereczky later settled in Dresden, Maine, and his grave is still there. Later, Agoston Haraszthy came to the United States to visit and settled in California, where he introduced Hungarian Tokay grapes to America. He became one of the nation's first winemakers (Daniels, 1990).

The First Large Wave

The first group of Hungarians of any size to settle in the United States were followers of Louis Kossuth, the leader of the 1848 Revolution in Hungary, which failed (Lengyel, 1974; Schuchat, 1971). Thousands of Hungarian nationalists fled from the Austrian police, and nearly four thousand of them came to the United States between 1849 and 1851. One of them, Nicholas Fejérváry, founded a Hungarian colony in Davenport, Iowa. Many of the refugees distinguished themselves as volunteers in the Union Army during the Civil War, and it is estimated that about eight hundred Hungarians served President Lincoln, of whom one hundred were officers. Major General Julius Stahel (Gyula Szamvald), received the Congressional Medal of Honor (Vardy, 1975).

Contributions

Joseph Pulitzer was founder of the *St. Louis Post-Dispatch* and the *New York Evening World*. Pulitzer also established the Pulitzer Prizes "for the encouragement of public service, public morals, American literature, and the advancement of education." István Nádas was a prominent concert pianist and teacher who fled Hungary in 1956. Hungarians have been prominent in science, including Leo Szilard, a physicist, who first asked Albert Einstein to write to President Franklin Roosevelt to suggest the feasibility of an atomic bomb. Hungarian Nobel Prize winners who taught at American universities include Eugene Wigner (physics, 1963), Albert Szent-Györgyi (medicine or physiology, 1937), Georg von Békésy (medicine or physiology, 1961), Georg de Hevesy (chemistry, 1943), and Daniel Gajdusek (medicine or physiology, 1976). All of these scientists taught at American universities. Edward Teller was a famed physicist and "father of the hydrogen bomb." John von Neumann was one of the world's greatest mathematicians. John George Kemeny was one of the greatest twentieth-century mathematicians and a president of Dartmouth College. Theodore von Kármán, a famous aerodynamicist, was known as the "father of the jet age."

Eugene Ormandy was conductor of the Philadelphia Orchestra for many years. Fritz Reiner, Antal Doráti, and Georg Solti were conductors of the Chicago Symphony Orchestra; George Szell was conductor of the Cleveland Orchestra. Béla Bartók was one of the foremost composers of the twentieth century. Ferenc Molnár was a distinguished playwright and novelist. Adolph Zukor was one of the most important film producers in Hollywood. William Fox was a noted film producer and one of the founders of Twentieth Century Fox Studio. Miklós Rózsa was a composer of both symphonic music and music for the films.

Lithuanians

Some historians speculate that the first Lithuanians in America were craftsmen in the group of colonists who came with Captain John Smith in 1608. In any case, Lithuanians fought on the side of American troops in the Revolutionary War. Significant immigration by Lithuanians to the United States did not begin until after the Civil War, however. By 1795, Russia had annexed most of Lithuania. After 1864, the czar banned Lithuanian literature, seriously oppressed the Catholic Church, and restricted ownership of land. In the 1860s, serfdom was abolished and this gave the masses of Lithuanians freedom of movement that they had not previously known (Budreckis, 1981). The Lithuanian railroad system allowed a way of escape to other countries in Europe. Finally, a terrible famine did serious harm to the Lithuanian peasant economy in the late 1860s (Kucas, 1975; Roucek, 1940; Thernstrom, 1980). The exodus accelerated.

Contributions

Mikas Petrauskas was a composer of operettas and an opera. Ana Kaskas was a contralto who sang for several seasons with the Metropolitan Opera Company in New York. Polyna Stoska, Algera Brazis, and Lillian Sukis sang during various seasons with the Metropolitan Opera Company. Charles Bronson is a noted film actor. Bruce Bielaski was the director of the Federal Bureau of Investigation from 1912 to 1919. Johnny Unitas and Dick Butkus were outstanding professional football players. Jack Sharkey was the world heavyweight boxing champion in 1932. Paulius Angius, Adomos Varnas, Alfonso Dargis, Kazyk Varnelis, and Liudas Silimas were artists who came to the United States during World War II. Frank Lubin was captain of the 1936 U.S. Olympic Basketball Team. Albina Osipavich was winner of the 100-meter dash in the 1928 Olympics. Bill Burke achieved fame as a golfer. Andy Kondrat was one of America's leading wrestlers.

Estonians

Like the Baltic states Lithuania and Latvia, Estonia has enjoyed only a few decades of freedom and, until very recently, most of her people had lost hope of being independent again. Estonia was part of the Swedish territories in the seventeenth century when Sweden established settlements in the New World. Even so, only a few Estonians immigrated to America during the colonial period. Sweden lost Estonia to Russia in the Great Northern War (1700–1721). Under czarist rule no known Estonians came to America until 1855. However, it is possible that there were Estonian sailors in the czar's navy during Russian explorations to Alaska and northern California. If that is true, some of them may have participated in the California gold rush in 1848. The actual size of the Estonian immigration during that period is not known because no records of Estonians were kept by American immigration officials until 1922. Before then Estonian immigrants were counted as Russians (Pennar, 1975).

Contributions

Prominent Estonian Americans include Carl Sunbach, a mechanical engineer who invented a freezer which reduced the bulk freezing of fish to one-third of the time required previously. Otto Lellep, a metallurgical engineer, contributed to the use of oxygen in steel processing. He also developed the Leopold Baking Oven. George Valley made several scientific discoveries, including Bella-cydine, a typhoid killer. Harold Oliver helped construct the moon vehicle used in the 1971 National Aeronautics and Space Administration moon expedition. Arthur Ermates is a prominent photographer. Alexander Yaron and Andrew Winter received awards for their paintings. Evi Liivak was a renowned concert violinist. Ludwig Juht is an outstanding contrabass soloist. Louis Kahn is one of the great architects of the twentieth century. Hermann Eduard von Holst was a noted historian and head of the department of history at the University of Chicago from 1892 to 1900. Vladmir Padwa gained fame as a composer and pianist. Ivan

Romanenko was a concertmaster of American orchestras. Elmer Leppik achieved recognition as an outstanding biologist.

Latvians

The first Latvians came to New Sweden in Delaware and Pennsylvania in 1640. In 1687, a large contingent of Latvians from Tobago emigrated to Boston. A few Latvian sailors prospected for gold in California in 1848 and 1849. During a large part of the nineteenth century, a stream of Latvians immigrated to the United States, most of them settling in the Midwest. In 1861, Martin Bucia, a Latvian sailor, was one of the first casualties in the American Civil War. The 1900 U.S. Census recorded 4,309 Latvians in the United States, although quite often Latvians were counted as Russians, Germans, and Scandinavians (Karklis & Straips, 1974).

Contributions

Augusts Pinepuka was a composer who arrived in 1906 and later became director of the New York Latvian Choir and Orchestra. Orswalt Tippo was provost and chancellor of the University of Massachusetts and editor of the *American Journal of Botany*. Edward Stockman was a ship mechanic on the first American ship to sail through the Panama Canal. Henry Brown developed a nonstinging strain of honey bee by crossing Italian and Cypriot strains. Andrew Murnek was president of the Society of Plant Physiology and a professor at the University of Missouri. Arthur Osol was a pharmacist and also editor of several professional journals. August Krastin built one of the first automobiles in America in 1896. From 1901 to 1942, his plant in Cleveland, Ohio, made gasoline and electric automobiles, farm machines, refrigerators and electrical appliances.

Thomas Blau was commandant of the U.S. Maritime Service. The Reverend John Kweetin coordinated the Welfare Library for the American Tract Society on Ellis Island. Edmar Mednis gained recognition as a chess master. Sigurda Grava, a U.N. adviser on city planning, developed the master plan for New York City's metropolitan transportation system in 1972. Nara Kristberga-Culp won the Powder Puff Derby in 1969 when she flew her airplane from San Diego to Washington, D.C., in record time. Jacob Sieberg founded the first Latvian Evangelical Lutheran Church in 1891, and he published America's first Latvian newspaper. John Ozolins-Burtnieks and Jūlijs Vecozols were well-known authors. Hugo Stikhewitz wrote under the name "Hermits" and published several collections of poems in English and Latvian, including *Hermits Religion* and *Love Poems*. Anslavs Eglitis was a novelist, playwright, and social satirist. Gunars B. Birkerts was a well-known architect. Janis Annus, Svens Lūins, and Ivars Hirss achieved prominence as artists. Alfred Kalnins was a composer and organ virtuoso.

Romanians

Although Romanians immigrated to the United States from the Kingdom of Romania, some of them came from Austria-Hungary, Russia, Turkey, and Greece. Despite differences in citizenship, the Romanians, although scattered throughout Europe, maintained common ethnic group characteristics (Galitzi, 1929). Actually, very few Romanians came to the United States before 1890 (Wertsman, 1975). A few joined in the gold rush in 1849 and at least two fought in the Civil War. Captain Nicolae Dunca served with the 9th New York Volunteers and was killed in the battle of Cross Keyes. General Georghe Pomutz joined the 5th Iowa Volunteer Regiment. He fought at Shiloh, Vicksburg, Corinth, and Atlanta. He became the first and only Romanian promoted to the rank of brigadier general. Later, he was appointed U.S. consul general in St. Petersburg (Wertsman, 1975).

Contributions

Ionel Gardescu was the first Romanian petroleum engineer to earn a doctorate at the University of California. Dagobert Runes established a publishing company, the Philosophical Library. Theodor Andrica organized and was the first president of the Cultural Association for Americans of Romanian descent. John Popa-Deleu achieved national recognition as a professor of history. George Brodschi was a nationally acclaimed professor of international law. Mircea Eliade was one of the foremost historians of religion. Stella Roman was a soprano star of the Metropolitan Opera Company. George Zolnay's monuments and memorials are scattered throughout the United States.

Outstanding Romanian-American writers include Conrad Bercovici, Eugene Ravage, Peter Neagoe, and Anisoara Stan. Yolanda Marcoulescou, an outstanding opera soprano in Romania, came to the United States in 1968 and gave numerous recitals. She taught voice at the University of Wisconsin at Milwaukee, and her records received great praise. George E. Palade won a 1974 Nobel Prize for his work in medicine. George Stănescu and Alexander Seceni earned great reputations in the field of sculpture. Traian Leucutia contributed greatly to radiology and nuclear medicine with his inventions. Marilena Bocu and Anisoara Stan became well known as folklorists and artists.

Nicolae Novac and Vasile Posteuca are acclaimed for their poetry. John Florea distinguished himself in the fields of journalism and photography. Radu Florescu produced works dealing with Transylvanian folklore. Ştefan Florescu inspired many people with disabilities by founding the Rolling Romanians, a track-and-field group in Detroit. Franz Kneisel, a violinist, founded one of the world's leading string quartets. Jean Negulesco was for many years one of the most successful film directors in Hollywood and elsewhere. Jacque Kapralik was one of modern art's most praised curators. Ely Culbertson was a popularizer of contract bridge and one of the game's greatest players.

Albanians

It is estimated that there are now about seventy thousand Albanian Americans, including original immigrants and their descendants. Nicholas Christopher (Kole Kristofor) came to the United States in 1886 and settled in Boston. In subsequent trips to Albania, he convinced nine of his relatives and friends to join him in America. Thus the first enclave of Albanians in the United States came from the same village. The letters that they wrote their friends in Albania prompted additional compatriots to come to America. Prior to 1912, only a few Albanian Americans used the term Albania. They called themselves *Shugapatary* (Sons of the Eagle) and named their country *Shugapateria* (Land of the Eagle) (Skendi, 1967).

The earliest Albanian immigrants were mostly Orthodox Christian Tosks from the south of Albania. They came to earn money to send to their families in Albania. There are no reliable statistics for pre-World War I Albanian immigrants because passports were not required for entry. Muslim Albanians were frequently classified as Turks, and Christian Albanians were frequently classified as Greeks. Almost all of the Albanian immigrants who came to the United States before World War II were from southern Albania and were mainly farmers, sheepherders, and soldiers. The first immigrants settled in Boston and then went to other areas of New England—New Hampshire, Maine, and Connecticut. Still others located in New York City, Rochester, Philadelphia, Pittsburgh, Cleveland, Detroit, Chicago, and St. Louis. Most of the later Albanian immigrants settled in the same areas. The early immigrants were mostly illiterate, although many later learned how to read and write both English and

Albanian. Lacking skills, they took jobs in industry or low-skilled work in restaurants and hotels. Over a period of time, many of them rose into the middle class and began to value education for their children. The largest concentration of Albanian Americans was in the Bronx.

The first Albanian Orthodox Church was founded in the United States on March 22, 1908, and Fan S. Noli, in many ways the guiding spirit of the early Albanian community, became its priest. The Albanians had for centuries been under the rule of the Ottoman Empire, but their desire for freedom from the Turks could not be extinguished. The Albanian Orthodox Church in the United States became a leading propagandist organ for Albanian freedom. In April 1912, the Pan-Albanian Federation of America, called *Vatra* (Hearth), was formed for the purpose of furthering the cause of Albanian independence. A few months later, in August, the prayers of Albanians were answered: Turkey granted freedom to Albania (Skendi, 1967, p. 453).

The Albanian Orthodox Church of America became an independent diocese under the Eastern Orthodox Church. Its mother church is in Boston, and the archdiocese includes thirteen parishes. Albanian Muslims established their first colony in 1915 in Biddeford, Maine, and in 1949 Imam Vehbi Ismail formed the Albanian-American Muslim Society in Detroit. Albanian Catholic parishes were established in the Bronx and Detroit. Albanian communities in the United States were augmented at the end of World War II by refugees fleeing from the new communist governments installed by the Russians and Yugoslavs in Albania. The new immigrants contained several professionals and intellectuals.

Contributions

In addition to Bishop Fan Noli, founder of the Albanian Orthodox church in America, special mention should also be made of Potier Petsi, the first editor of *Combi*, the earliest Albanian-American newspaper. Nexhmie Zaimi was a successful Albanian-American author. Thomas Nassi founded the Boston Albanian Mandolin Club and the Albanian String Orchestra in 1915. Later, he was the conductor of the Cape Cod Philharmonic Society. Arshi Pipa and Fan Noli wrote several volumes of poetry. Louis Theodos was one of the founders of Crown Food Stores. Tom La Bache was nationally known for his silhouette cuttings. Nicholas Prift and Dimitra Elia were prominent Albanian-American physicians.

References

Budreckis, A. M. (1981). Reluctant immigrants: The Lithuanian displaced persons. In D. L. Cuddy (Ed.), *Contemporary American immigration: Interpretive essays (European)*. Boston: Twayne.

Coppa, F. J., & Curran, T. J. (1976). *The immigrant experience in America*. Boston: Twayne.

Cuddy, D. L. (Ed.). (1982). *Contemporary American immigration: Interpretive essays (European)*. Boston: Twayne.

Daniels, R. (1990). *Coming to America: A history of immigration and ethnicity in American life*. New York: HarperCollins.

Galitzi, C. A. (1929). *A study of assimilation among the Romanians in America*. New York: Columbia University Press.

Goldhagen, E. (Ed.). (1968). *Ethnic minorities in the Soviet Union*. New York: Praeger.

Karklis, M., & Streips L. (Eds.). (1974). *The Latvians in America*. Dobbs Ferry, NY: Oceana.

Kucas, A. (1975). *Lithuanians in America*. Trans. by Joseph Boldy. Boston: Encyclopedia Lithuania.

Lengyel, E. (1974). *Americans from Hungary*. Philadelphia: J.B. Lippincott.

Pennar, J. (Ed.). (1975). *The Estonians in America, 1627–1975: A chronology and fact book*. Dobbs Ferry, NY: Oceana.

Roucek, J. S. (1940). *American Lithuanians*. New York: Lithuanian Alliance of America.

Schuchat, M. G. (1971). *Hungarian refugees in America and the counterparts in Hungary*. Unpublished Master's Thesis, Washington, D.C.: Catholic University of America.

Skendi, S. (1967). *The Albanian national awakening: 1878–1912*. Princeton, N.J.: Princeton University Press.

Spaulding, E. W. (1968). *The quiet invaders: The story of the Austrian impact upon America*. Vienna: Becvar.

Széplaki, J. (1975). *The Hungarians in America, 1583–1974: A chronology and fact book*. Dobbs Ferry, NY: Oceana.

Thernstrom, S. (Ed.). (1980). *Harvard encyclopedia of American ethnic groups*. Cambridge: Harvard University Press.

Vardy, S. B. (1975). *The Hungarian-Americans*. Boston: Twayne.

Wertsman, V. (Ed.). (1975). *The Romanians in America, 1748–1974: A chronology and fact book*. Dobbs Ferry, NY: Oceana.

From Lithuania, 1901
by Pauline Newman

*The calamitous Triangle Shirtwaist Factory fire of 1911, in which 146
women and girls lost their lives, was a landmark in American labor
history. It galvanized public opinion behind the movement to improve
conditions, hours, and wages in the sweatshops. Pauline Newman
went to work in the Triangle Shirtwaist Factory at the age of eight,
shortly after coming to the Lower East Side of New York City. Many of
her friends lost their lives in the fire. She went on to become an organizer and later an executive of the newly formed International Ladies
Garment Workers Union, of which she is now, at the age of eighty-six,
educational director.*

The village I came from was very small. One department store, one
synagogue, and one church. There was a little square where the peasants would bring their produce, you know, for sale. And there was one
teahouse where you could have a glass of tea for a penny and sit all
day long and play checkers if you wanted.

In the winter we would skate down the hilltop toward the lake, and
in the summer we'd walk to the woods and get mushrooms, raspber-
ries. The peasants lived on one side of the lake, and the Jewish people
on the other, in little square, thatched-roofed houses. In order to go to
school you had to own land and we didn't own land, of course. Very
few Jews did. But we were allowed to go to Sunday School and I never
missed going to Sunday School. They would sing Russian folk songs
and recite poetry. I like it very much. It was a narrow life, but you
didn't miss anything because you didn't know what you were missing.

That was the time, you see, when America was known to foreigners
as the land where you'd get rich. There's gold on the sidewalk—all
you have to do is pick it up. So people left that little village and went
to America. My brother first and then he sent for one sister, and after
that, a few years after that, my father died and they sent for my
mother and my other two sisters and me. I was seven or eight at the
time. I'm not sure exactly how old, because the village I came from
had no registration of birth, and we lost the family Bible on the ship
and that was where the records were.

Of course we came steerage. That's the bottom of the ship and three
layers of bunks. One, two, three, one above the other. If you were
lucky, you got the first bunk. Of course you can understand that it
wasn't all that pleasant when the people on the second bunk or the

third bunk were ill. You had to suffer and endure not only your own misery, but the misery from the people above you.

My mother baked rolls and things like that for us to take along, because all you got on the boat was water, boiled water. If you had tea, you could make tea, but otherwise you just had the hot water. Sometimes they gave you a watery soup, more like a mud puddle than soup. It was stormy, cold, uncomfortable. I wasn't sick, but the other members of my family were.

When we landed at Ellis Island our luggage was lost. We inquired for it and they said, "Come another time. Come another time. You'll find it. We haven't got time now." So we left and we never saw our luggage again. We had bedding, linen, beautiful copper utensils, that sort of thing.

From Ellis Island we went by wagon to my brother's apartment on Hester Street. Hester Street and Essex on the Lower East Side. We were all bewildered to see so many people. Remember we were from a little village. And here you had people coming and going and shouting. Peddlers, people on the streets. Everything was new, you know.

At first we stayed in a tiny apartment with my brother and then, finally, we got one of our own. Two rooms. The bedroom had no windows. The toilets were in the yard. Just a coal stove for heat. The rent was ten dollars a month.

A cousin of mine worked for the Triangle Shirtwaist Company and she got me on there in October of 1901. It was probably the largest shirtwaist factory in the city of New York then. They had more than two hundred operators, cutters, examiners, finishers. Altogether more than four hundred people on two floors. The fire took place on one floor, the floor where we worked. You've probably heard about that. But that was years later.

We started work at seven-thirty in the morning, and during the busy season we worked until nine in the evening. They didn't pay you any overtime and they didn't give you anything for supper money. Sometimes they'd give you a little apple pie if you had to work very late. That was all. Very generous.

What I had to do was not really very difficult. It was just monotonous. When the shirtwaists were finished at the machine there were some threads that were left, and all the youngsters—we had a corner on the floor that resembled a kindergarten—we were given little scissors to cut the threads off. It wasn't heavy work, but it was monotonous, because you did the same thing from seven-thirty in the morning till nine at night.

What about the child labor laws?

Well, of course, there were laws on the books, but no one bothered to enforce them. The employers were always tipped off if there was going to be an inspection. "Quick," they'd say, "into the boxes!" And we children would climb into the big boxes the finished shirts were stored in. Then some shirts were piled on top of us, and when the inspector came—no children. The factory always got an okay from the inspector, and I suppose someone at City Hall got a little something, too.

The employers didn't recognize anyone working for them as a human being. You were not allowed to sing. Operators would have liked to have sung, because they, too, had the same thing to do and weren't allowed to sing. We weren't allowed to talk to each other. Oh, no, they would sneak up behind if you were found talking to your next colleague. You were admonished: "If you keep on you'll be fired." If you went to the toilet and you were there longer than the floor lady thought you should be, you would be laid off for half a day and sent your lunch on the fire escape in the summertime. The door was locked to keep us in. That's why so many people were trapped when the fire broke out.

My pay was $1.50 a week no matter how many hours I worked. My sisters made $6.00 a week; and the cutters, they were the skilled workers, they might get as much as $12.00. The employers had a sign in the elevator that said: "If you don't come in on Sunday, don't come in on Monday." You were expected to work every day if they needed you and the pay was the same whether you worked extra or not. You had to be there at seven-thirty, so you got up at five-thirty, took the horse car, then the electric trolley to Greene Street, to be there on time.

At first I tried to get somebody who could teach me English in the evening, but that didn't work out because I don't think he was a very good teacher, and, anyhow, the overtime interfered with private lessons. But I mingled with people. I joined the Socialist Literary Society. Young as I was and not very able to express myself, I decided that it wouldn't hurt if I listened. There was a Dr. Newman, no relation of mine, who was teaching in City College. He would come down to the Literary Society twice a week and teach us literature, English literature. He was very helpful. He gave me a list of books to read, and, as I said, if there is a will you can learn. We read Dickens, George Eliot, the poets. I remember when we first heard Thomas Hood's "Song of the Shirt." I figured that it was written for us. You know, because it told the long hours of "stitch, stitch, stitch." I remember one of the girls said, "He didn't know us, did he?" And I said, "No, he didn't." But it had an impact on us. Later on, of course, we got to know Shelley. Shelley's known for his lyrics, but very few people know his poem dealing with slavery, called "The Masque of Anarchy." It appealed to us, too, because it was a time when we were ready to rise and that helped us a great deal. [*Recites*: "Rise like Lions after slumber."]

I regretted that I couldn't go even to evening school, let alone going to day school; but it didn't prevent me from trying to learn and it doesn't have to prevent anybody who wants to. I was then and still am an avid reader. Even if I didn't go to school I think I can hold my own with anyone, as far as literature is concerned.

Conditions were dreadful in those days. We didn't have anything. If the season was over, we were told, "You're laid off. Shift for yourself." How did you live? After all, you didn't earn enough to save any money. Well, the butcher trusted you. He knew you'd pay him when you started work again. Your landlord, he couldn't do anything but wait, you know. Sometimes relatives helped out. There was no welfare, no pension, no unemployment insurance. There was nothing. We were much worse off than the poor are today because we had nothing to lean on; nothing to hope for except to hope that the shop would open again and that we'd have work.

But despite that, we had good times. In the summer we'd go to Central Park and stay out and watch the moon rise; go to the Palisades and spend the day. We went to meetings, too, of course. We had friends and we enjoyed what we were doing. We had picnics. And, remember, in that time you could go and hear Caruso for twenty-five cents. We heard all the giants of the artistic world—Kreisler, Pavlova. We only had to pay twenty-five cents. Of course, we went upstairs, but we heard the greatest soloists, all for a quarter, and we enjoyed it immensely. We loved it. We'd go Saturday night and stand in line no matter what the weather. In the winter we'd bring blankets along. Just imagine, the greatest artists in the world, from here and abroad, available to you for twenty-five cents. The first English play I went to was *Peer Gynt*. The actor's name was Mansfield. I remember it very well. So, in spite of everything, we had fun and we enjoyed what we learned and what we saw and what we heard.

I stopped working at the Triangle Factory during the strike in 1909 and I didn't go back. The union sent me out to raise money for the strikers. I apparently was able to articulate my feelings and opinions about the criminal conditions, and they didn't have anyone else who could do better, so they assigned me. And I was successful getting money. After my first speech before the Central Trade and Labor Council I got front-page publicity, including my picture. I was only about fifteen then. Everybody saw it. Wealthy women were curious and they asked me if I would speak to them in their homes. I said I would if they would contribute to the strike, and they agreed. So I spent my time from November to the end of March upstate in New York, speaking to the ladies of the Four Hundred (the elite of New York's society) and sending money back.

Those ladies were very kind and generous. I had never seen or dreamed of such wealth. One Sunday, after I had spoken, one of the women asked me to come to dinner. And we were sitting in the living room in front of a fireplace; remember it was winter. A beautiful library and comfort that I'd never seen before and I'm sure the likes of me had never seen anything like it either. And the butler announced that dinner was ready and we went into the dining room and for the first time I saw the silver and the crystal and the china and the beautiful tablecloth and vases—beautiful vases, you know. At that moment I didn't know what the hell I was doing there. The butler had probably never seen anything like me before. After the day was over, a beautiful limousine took me back to the YWCA where I stayed.

In Buffalo, in Rochester, it was the same thing. The wealthy ladies all asked me to speak, and they would invite me into their homes and contribute money to the strike. I told them what the conditions were that made us get up: the living conditions, the wages, the shop conditions. They'd probably never heard anything like this. I didn't exaggerate. I didn't have to. I remember one time in Syracuse a young woman sitting in front of me wept.

We didn't gain very much at the end of the strike. I think the hours were reduced to fifty-six a week or something like that. We got a 10 percent increase in wages. I think that the best thing that the strike did was to lay a foundation on which to build a union. There was so much feeling against unions then. The judge, when one of our girls came before him, said to her: "You're not striking against your employer, you know, young lady. You're striking against God," and sentenced her to two weeks on Blackwell's Island, which is now Welfare Island. And a lot of them got a taste of the club.

I can look back and find that there were some members of the union who might very well be compared to the unknown soldier. I'll never forget one member in the Philadelphia union. She was an immigrant, a beautiful young woman from Russia, and she was very devoted to the local union. And one Friday, we were going to distribute leaflets to a shop that was not organized. They had refused to sign any agreement and we tried to work it that way to get the girls to join. But that particular day—God, I'll never forget the weather. Hail, snow, rain, cold. It was no weather for any human being to be out in, but she came into my office. I'd decided not to go home because

of the weather and I'd stayed in the office. She came in and I said,
"You're not going out tonight. I wouldn't send a dog out in weather
like this." And I went to the window and I said, "Look." And while my
back was turned, she grabbed a batch of leaflets and left the office.
And she went out. And the next thing I heard was that she had pneumonia and she went to the hospital and in four days she was gone. I
can't ever forget her. Of course, perhaps it was a bit unrealistic on her
part, but on the other hand, I can't do anything but think of her with
admiration. She had the faith and the will the help build the organization and, as I often tell other people, she was really one of the
unknown soldiers.

After the 1909 strike I worked with the union, organizing in
Philadelphia and Cleveland and other places, so I wasn't at the
Triangle Shirtwaist Factory when the fire broke out, but a lot of my
friends were. I was in Philadelphia for the union and, of course, someone from here called me immediately and I came back. It's very difficult to describe the feeling because I knew the place and I knew so
many of the girls. The thing that bothered me was the employers got
a lawyer. How anyone could have *defended* them!—because I'm quite
sure that the fire was planned for insurance purposes. And no one is
going to convince me otherwise. And when they testified that the door
to the fire escape was open, it was a lie! It was never open. Locked all
the time. One hundred and forty-six people were sacrificed, and the
judge fined Blank and Harris seventy-five dollars!

Conditions were dreadful in those days. But there was something
that is lacking today and I think it was the devotion and the belief.
We *believed* in what we were doing. We fought and we bled and we
died. Today they don't have to.

You sit down at the table, you negotiate with the employers, you
ask for 20 percent, they say 15, but the girls are working. People are
working. They're not disturbed, and when the negotiations are over
they get the increases. They don't really have to fight. Of course,
they'll belong to the union and they'll go on strike if you tell them to,
but it's the inner faith that people had in those days that I don't see
today. It was a terrible time, but it was interesting. I'm glad I lived
then.

Even when things were terrible, I always had that faith. . . . Only
now, I'm a little discouraged sometimes when I see the workers
spending their free hours watching television—trash. We fought so
hard for those hours and they waste them. We used to read Tolstoy,
Dickens, Shelley, by candlelight, and they watch the "Hollywood
Squares." Well, they're free to do what they want. That's what we
fought for.

Chapter 7

Southern Europeans

Southern European immigrants from Italy, Albania, Greece, Portugal, and Spain were barely tolerated by Americans whose European relatives lived in western Europe. The peoples from the southern parts of Europe were thought by many westerners to be of inferior stock (Cuddy, 1982). Slightly more than thirty thousand immigrants came to America from the Mediterranean countries before 1860, compared to five million who came from western Europe. Contrary to popular opinion, few of the early Southern European immigrants were unskilled. The transition to American life was easy for them because almost all of them were skilled workers, merchants, professionals, or Catholic missionaries. However, during the period between 1880 and 1924, more than five million of the nearly twenty million European immigrants who came to the United States were peasants from southern Europe. It was during this period that the negative stereotypes of southern Europeans were rampant. Americanized immigrants began acting out their fears and prejudices by verbally and physically attacking recent southern European immigrants and denying them complete access to housing and jobs.

Patterns of Adjustment

In order to survive the strange customs and languages in America, most southern European immigrants established their own housing areas, churches, newspapers, magazines, and fraternal organizations. Because the first wave of immigrants had more men than women, they married at an older age than did the second and third generations. As the second generation became Americanized through learning English and practicing American customs, a culture gap widened between them and their first-generation relatives and friends. Gradually, through acculturation, most of the southern European ethnic groups lost their unique Old World identities and became conglomerate American ethnic groups (Feagin, 1984). For example, Sicilians, Calabrians, Abruzzians, and Neapolitans merged into Italian Americans; Bravos and Continentals merged into Portuguese Americans. And, like other European immigrants, they became "white people."

The pace of assimilation varied from group-to-group but all southern European immigrants underwent some form of assimilation. Distinctions based on race, religion, and social class have always been major factors facilitating or impeding cultural assimilation. The Americanization process was akin to *amalgamation* for most of the western European immigrants. But it was closer to *accommodation* for the first and second generations of nonwestern European immigrants. People who came from villages and farms were more quickly accepted if they shared a common sense of history, religion, social class, and language with dominant-group American citizens. The more an individual differed from western European Anglo-Americans, the more problems he or she had gaining acceptance. The ethnic peoples discussed in this chapter not only differed significantly from those groups but they also competed with them for unskilled and artisan jobs.

Economic mobility and job competition were the precipitating causes of violent ethnic group confrontations in nineteenth-century New England factories, in Southwest and Midwest mines, and in big-city industries. English and Irish workers generally resented Italians, Greeks, Albanians, and Portuguese because they worked for lower wages and were used by employers as strikebreakers. In addition to job competition, fear of unfamiliar groups was a contributing factor to the enmity English and Irish workers felt for the new immigrants. Often the different languages, smells, colors, and values associated with southern European immigrants were defined by majority-group Americans as "strange," and the presence of such differences made it easier to rationalize discriminatory behaviors.

Italians

Christopher Columbus is given credit for being the first white person to discover America but the country is named after another Italian: Amerigo Vespucci. Vespucci made voyages to the New World—the first in 1499—but he never commanded an expedition nor did he discover the new continent. Yet, many people believed his story of discovering a continent. Martin Waldseemueller, a German cartographer, was one who believed Vespucci. He applied the term *America* to the unexplored portion of the Western Hemisphere on the maps he drew. An unknown author wrote the following about Columbus: "When he started out, he didn't know where he was and when he got back, he didn't know where he had been." On August 3, 1492, Columbus set sail from Spain in the *Santa María*, accompanied by two other ships, the *Niña* and the *Pinta*. On October 12, 1492, a lookout on the *Pinta* sighted land which turned out to be an island in the Bahamas.

Italian soldiers traveled throughout Florida with Hernando de Soto, the Spanish explorer, and more than one hundred Italians established a colony at New Smyrna shortly after 1763. Although the settlement failed, many of the Italians migrated to St. Augustine. Italian priests founded missions in southern Arizona and northern Mexico between 1698 and 1711. Besides converting many Indians to Christianity, priests helped them to farm and to raise animals. Twenty-four missions were established by Father Kino. He mapped many of the areas that he traveled and was the first person to prove that Baja California is a peninsula, not an island.

During the 1760s and the early 1770s, numerous prominent Italians fled to America because of political persecution in their homeland. Among them was Filippo Mazzei, a physician, merchant, author, and horticulturist. Benjamin Franklin persuaded Mazzei to go to Virginia in order to cultivate Italian agricultural products in the colony. Mazzei tried unsuccessfully to introduce silk culture and to cultivate wine grapes and olives. During his stay, he became a friend and confidant of Thomas Jefferson, near whose estate he settled in 1773. Jefferson shared his ideas on liberty and government with the learned Italian. Later, Mazzei raised funds for the Revolution and recruited Italians as soldiers for the Revolutionary Army. Italian masons and agricultural experts followed Mazzei to America. When Jefferson became president, he sent for Italian musicians who made up a large part of what became the U.S. Marine Band (Fuchs, 1990).

Other Italians soon immigrated to the United States from Italy, among them Lorenzo da Ponte, who had been the librettist for three of Mozart's operas. He had been forced to flee several countries in Europe, including his native Italy. To him the United States proved to be a haven in time of a storm. He established the first opera house in America: the Italian Opera House in New York. Beginning in 1825, he served as an unpaid professor of literature at Columbia University and gave classes in Italian as well. Another Italian contributor to early American culture was Constantino Brumidi, who painted the large frescoes in the dome of the Capitol in Washington, D.C. He painted many works in his adopted country.

Except for a small number of Waldensians who immigrated to the United States from Italy, almost all of the Italians who arrived in the nineteenth century were Catholics. A special missionary community of priests and brothers, founded in 1877 by Bishop John-Baptist Scalabrini, ministered to the Italian immigrants. They were supplemented by other religious orders sent from Italy: Franciscans, Servites, and Salesians. Because Italian Americans were not proportionately represented among American clergy or in the religious orders, young Italian Americans were not encouraged by their families to go into the service of the Church. Nor did the Church aggressively recruit them. Furthermore, some Italian-American parents viewed the clergy as low-status and marginal-income jobs. The explosive, sentimental, and often superstitious piety of Italian Americans, largely immigrants from southern Italy, did not fit smoothly into the Catholicism of Rome, Florence, or Milan.

The vast majority of Italian immigrants who came to America before the American Civil War were from the northern provinces of Italy. Many of them were highly skilled professionals in various fields. A number of them were teachers, artists, craftsmen, and businessmen. Between 1820 and 1860, nearly fourteen thousand Italian immigrants arrived in the United States (Gonzales, 1990). Most of them left their homeland in order to avoid military conscription, to find religious liberty, to enjoy political freedom, or to enjoy the great economic opportunities which America offered (Thernstrom, 1980). Many of them migrated to California where they put their talents to work in introducing new crops and viticulture.

Most of the Italians who came to America before the Civil War settled in New York, Louisiana, and California (Nelli, 1983). Giuseppe Garibaldi, the illustrious Italian revolutionary, lived on Staten Island as a candlemaker for a few years before becoming a naturalized American citizen. A Garibaldi Guard in New York served in the Union Army. More than two hundred Italians were officers in both the Union and Confederate armies (Iorizzo & Mondello, 1971). Approximately sixty-eight thousand Italians immigrated to the United States between 1860 and 1880, and they settled mainly in New York City, New Orleans, Galveston, San Francisco, Boston, Charleston, Key West, Memphis, Mobile, and Philadelphia (Rolle, 1982).

Contributions

Americans of Italian ancestry have made outstanding contributions to the United States in many fields of achievement. Unfortunately, their contributions have often been overshadowed by the criminal activities of organized crime figures such as Al Capone, Philip Musica (known as Dr. F. Daniel Coster), Frank Costello, Charles "Lucky" Luciano, and John Gotti. More Americans remember the fictional crime lords in Mario Puzo's novel and movie series *The Godfather* than the positive contributions made by millions of Italian-American citizens.

Music is a field in which Italian Americans have given their fellow citizens wonderful gifts. Opera, in particular, would hardly exist in the United States were it not for the great Italian singers who enthralled audiences. Rosa Ponselle is considered by many critics to have been the greatest dramatic operatic soprano in this century. Her sister, Carmela, also had a fine voice and sang many concerts. Another well-known dramatic soprano was Dusolina Giannini, an outstanding star at the Metropolitan Opera Company. Her father, Ferruccio, was a tenor who emigrated from Italy before 1900, and her brother, Vittorio, was one of America's outstanding composers. Anna Moffo, possessor of one of the most beautiful lyric soprano voices in the world, was acclaimed at Metropolitan Opera for many years.

One of the most renowned operatic tenors of this century was Enrico Caruso, an Italian American who poured out his brilliant voice to countless opera lovers during the eighteen years he spent at the Metropolitan Opera Company. Even though he died in 1921, his records are still in demand by the music public. Amelita Galli-Curci possessed of one of the most wondrous soprano voices since the turn of the century. Ezio Pinza, a basso, made successful careers both at the Metropolitan Opera and on the Broadway musical stage. Giuseppe De Luca and Pasquale Amato were two of the finest baritones at the Metropolitan Opera for decades and, after their careers ended, they taught scores of students. Arturo Toscanini, a refugee from Italian fascism, was the most celebrated conductor the Metropolitan Opera Company ever had. Later, he became the director of the New York Philharmonic and the National Broadcasting Company Symphony Orchestra. Cleofonte Campanini was the first conductor of the Metropolitan Opera, and Massimo Freccia conducted the Baltimore and New Orleans orchestras after World War II.

Distinguished Italian-American instrumentalists include Guila Bustabo, a violinist; Aldo Mancinelli, a pianist who was the first American to win the coveted Busoni Prize in Italy; Pietro Yon, a composer and organist; and Fernando Valenti, a well-known harpsichord player. Giulio Gatti-Casazza was the manager of the Metropolitan Opera Company from 1908 to 1934. Mario Castelnuovo-Tedesco, acclaimed composer, was a refugee from Mussolini's tyranny in the late 1930s. Other distinguished Italian-American composers include Gian Carlo Menotti, John Corigliano, and David Del Tredici.

Outstanding Italian-American actors include Rudolph Valentino, Al Pacino, Robert De Niro, Sylvestor Stallone, and Liza Minnelli. Frank Capra, Francis Ford Coppola, and Vincent Minnelli will go down in cinema history as three of Hollywood's greatest directors. Among popular singers are Frank Sinatra, Dean Martin, Russ Colombo, Tony Bennett, and Frankie Vale. In sports, there was boxing champion Rocky Marciano; baseball stars Joe DiMaggio, Domonic DiMaggio, Yogi Berra, Tony Lazzeri, Phil Rizzuto, and Frankie Crosetti; golfing greats Henry Ciuci, John Turnesa, John Muraro, and Gene Sarazen. Hank Luisetta popularized the one-handed shot, the jump-shot, and the behind the back dribble in basketball. In football, Vince Lombardi and George Musso are among the famous Italian American stars. Distinguishing themselves in painting and sculpture were Giovanni Castano, Patsy Santo, Joseph Coletti, Ettore Cadorin, Ercole Cartotto, Nicola D'Ascenzo, Luigi Lucioni, Salvatore Scarpitta, Carlo Ciampaglia, Leo Lentelli, Onorio Ruotolo, Oronzio Maldarelli, and Victor Salvatore.

There have been many outstanding Italian Americans in the sciences, including three Nobel Prize winners: Enrico Fermi for physics in 1938, Emilio Segrè for physics in 1959, and Salvador Luria for medicine in 1969. Fermi, a professor for many years at the University of Chicago, was one of the major contributors to the building of the first atomic bomb. He was the first person to build an atomic pile, a step which led to the ultimate success of the weapon. Segrè taught at the University of California, and Luria was a professor at the University of Indiana and the Massachusetts Institute of Technology in the field of virology. Other distinguished Italian Americans in the sciences include Camillo Artom, a biochemist and professor at the Bowman Gray School of Medicine; Ugo Fani, a physicist at the University of Chicago; Sergio de Benedetti, a physicist who worked on the Manhattan Project; Piero Foá, a leading physiologist; and Eugene G. Fubini, an electronics engineer who was vice president of International Business Machines and assistant secretary of defense. Prominent Italian-American surgeons include Andre Crotti, William Verdi, Gaston Carlucci, and Vincent Lapenta. Giorgio de Santillana is one of the outstanding historians of science.

Leading Italian-American scholars include Renato Poggioli, professor of Italian and Slavic literature at Harvard University; Gaetano Salvemini, professor of history at Harvard University; Guido Weiss, professor of mathematics at Washington University in St. Louis; Franco Modigliani, professor of economics at the Massachusetts Institute of Technology; and Giuseppe Borgese, professor of Italian literature at the University of Chicago.

Well-known Italian-American writers include Max Ascoli, Mario Puzo, and Pietro di Donato. In the field of law, Judge John Sirica performed great public service during the Watergate trials, and Antonin Scalia is an associate justice of the U.S. Supreme Court. Among many significant Roman Catholic nuns have been St. Frances Xavier Cabrini (Mother Cabrini) who founded orphanages and hospitals and was the first native-born saint in the United States. Joseph Cardinal Bernardin was a leader in American Roman Catholicism as archbishop of the diocese of Chicago, as well as an important voice in national church affairs.

Well-known Italian-American businessmen who contributed not only to the business world but also to the world of public affairs and philanthropy include A. P. Giannini, founder of the Bank of America; Amadeo Obici, founder of the Planter Peanut Company; and Lee Iacocca, former chairman of Chrysler Motor Company. There have been many successful Italian-American politicians, including Fiorello La Guardia, congressman and later reform mayor of New York City; John Pastore, the first Italian-American governor of a state and U. S. senator from Rhode Island and the first Italian-American U.S. senator; Joseph Alioto, mayor of San Francisco; Senator Dennis De Concini of Arizona; Robert S. Maestri, former mayor of New Orleans; John Volpe, governor of Massachusetts and secretary of transportation under President Richard Nixon; Senator Alfonse D'Amato of New York; Geraldine Ferraro, congresswoman and a Democratic vice-presidential nominee—the first woman to be a vice presidential nominee of a major political party in America; Mario Cuomo, governor of New York. The first Italian American to play a leading role in American government was William Paca, a member of the Continental Congress and a signer of the Declaration of Independence.

Greeks

It is said by some historians that a Greek sailor, John Griego, sailed with Christopher Columbus on his first journey to the New World, and that the first Greek to have landed in America was a man named Don Teodoro. Some writers say that Juan de Fuca, the Spanish explorer who discovered the strait between Vancouver Island and the present state of Washington in 1592 and after whom the strait is named, was really a Greek sea captain named Ioannis Phocas (Scourby, 1984, p. 23). In any case, in addition to a few Greeks who came to the American colonies by their own means, approximately four hundred Greek indentured servants arrived in 1768 under the sponsorship of Andrew Turnbull.

Funded by the Board of Trade in London, Turnbull recruited 1,403 residents of Mediterranean lands to work the area he owned some seventy-five miles south of St. Augustine. He named the colony New Smyrna after the birthplace of his wife in Asia Minor. More than half the colonists of New Smyrna died within two years of their arrival in the mosquito-infested swampland. Approximately one hundred survivors fled to St. Augustine in 1777; many of them became successful merchants. One of those men, a Greek named John Geannopoulos, established a school in his house. It is the oldest standing wooden schoolbuilding in the United States. Because the Greeks in St. Augustine were not large enough as a group to form a separate enclave, they were gradually assimilated into the population of the town (Saloutos, 1964).

Contributions

Greek contributions to American culture have been many and varied. Perhaps they contributed most in the field of medicine. Some of the most distinguished Greek-American physicians include John Pantazopoulos, a specialist in cardiovascular disease and director of the Cardiac Catheterization Laboratory at Mount Sinai Hospital in New York City. He was also a professor of medicine at the Mount Sinai School of Medicine. Constantine E. Anagnostopoulos was a specialist in cardiac surgery and a professor of surgery at the University of Chicago; Panagiotis N. Symbas was a specialist in thoracic and cardiovascular surgery and professor of surgery at Emory University School of Medicine; Pete Poolos Jr. was a specialist in neurological surgery and a professor of neurosurgery at Case Western Reserve University; Theodore Drapanas was a specialist in surgery and professor and chairman of the Department of Surgery at Tulane University School of Medicine; Angelos Papatestas was a specialist in surgery and professor of surgery at Mount Sinai School of Medicine; Chryssanthos P. Chryssanthou was a specialist in pathology and director of laboratories and research at Beth Israel Medical Center, New York City.

Other distinguished Greek-American physicians include George S. Ioannides, a specialist in anatomic pathology and dermatology and a professor at the University of Miami School of Medicine. George Kotzias was a professor of neurology at Mount Sinai Hospital in New York City and a senior scientist at the Brookhaven National Laboratory. He developed l-dopa, a treatment for Parkinson's disease. Kontras Bicouvaris was a specialist in pediatrics, hematology, and genetics, and a professor at Ohio State University College of Medicine. Basil Strates was a specialist in biochemistry and medicine and a professor at the University of California School of Medicine. Antonia Vernadakis was a specialist in neuropharmacology and a professor at the University of Colorado Medical Center. George Papanicolaou invented of the Pap test used for the detection of uterine and cervical cancer.

Leading Greek-American academics include Stamatios Krimigis, professor of applied physics at the Johns Hopkins University; Evangelos Anastassakis, professor of physics at Northwestern University; Loucas Christophorou, head of the Atomic and Molecular Physics Group, Oak Ridge National Laboratory; John Papaconstantinou, specialist in molecular-developmental biology and senior staff member at Oak Ridge National Laboratory; Ann Arpajolu, chair of the Modern Greek Language Department at the Defense Language Institute, Monterey, California; Deno Geanakoplos, professor of Byzantine history at Yale University; Constantine Cavarnos, director of the Institute for Byzantine and Modern Greek Studies; John Rexine, professor and chairman of the Classics Department at Colgate University; Chris Argyris, professor of education and organizational behavior at Harvard University; Xenophon Diamantopoulos, chairman of the Department of Education at Hellenic College; and Louis Stamatakos, professor of education at Michigan State University.

In the field of music, leading Greek-American artists include operatic soprano Maria Callas, whose performances on stage and on records enriched the lives of millions of opera lovers; Teresa Stratas, whose dramatic portrayals were acclaimed at the Metropolitan Opera Company and elsewhere throughout the world; Dimitri Mitropoulos, a conductor of the Minneapolis Symphony Orchestra and the New York Philharmonic; Maurice Abravanel, a conductor of the Utah Symphony Orchestra and a professor of music at the University of Utah; and Gina Bachauer, one of the world's greatest pianists. Noted Greek-American academics in the field of music include Constantine Poulimas, a professor of music at Butler University, and George Soulos, professor of composition at Windham College.

Noted Greek Americans in politics include Michael Dukakis, governor of Massachusetts and the Democratic nominee for president in 1988; Paul Tsongas, U.S. senator from Massachusetts; Congressman

John Brademas of Indiana; U.S. Senator Paul Sarbanes of Maryland; and Spiro T. Agnew, governor of Maryland and vice president of the United States under President Richard Nixon. Significant Greek contributions were made in the field of business by Spyros Skouras and his brothers, Charles and George, who controlled Twentieth Century Fox studios and also operated 750 movie houses scattered throughout the world. Anastasios Stathopoulos founded Ethephone which gained a reputation for producing the world's finest stringed instruments; Constantine Nicholson invented the storm screens, a storm window in the winter and a screen in the summer. Lucas Kyrides discovered Neurcurasol, a drug for syphilis, and was the developer of the first American process for making synthetic rubber from isoprin and mutadine. Emmanuel Nicholides invented with Hugo Lieber the microphone amplifier hearing aid device. Alexander Pantages developed one of the largest theater chains showing both films and vaudeville acts.

In the field of entertainment, outstanding Greek-American actors include Telly Savalas, George Chakiris, and John Cassavetes. Cassavetes also achieved acclaim as a director, as did Elia Kazan. In fashion merchandizing, James Galanos and Marie Dorros earned worldwide reputations. John Vassos was a leading designer of automobile bodies, stoves, cosmetic containers, radio cabinets, turnstiles, and the Coca-Cola dispenser. George Lykos, Stamo Papdaki, and Socrates Stathes earned fame as architects. Greek-American stars in sports include Jimmy "Golden Greek" Londos, a wrestler; Harry Agganis, and Alex Karras, football players; and baseball players Harry Agganis, Alex Grammas, and Milt Pappas.

Portuguese

Although Christopher Columbus was Italian and sailed under the Spanish banner to the New World, it was during an extended stay in Portugal that he decided to become a discoverer of unexplored lands. In Lisbon, he absorbed the knowledge of some of the most outstanding geographers and seamen of his time. This prepared him for the momentous mission he would later accomplish. In 1525, thirty-three years after Columbus's first voyage, Estévao Gomes, who came from Portugal, charted the coasts of the present states of Maine, Massachusetts, Connecticut, New York, New Jersey, and Delaware (Pap, 1981). Sixteen years later, in 1541, a handful of Portuguese accompanied Hernándo de Soto on his ill-fated journey of exploration along the Mississippi and most of them perished with him.

The most notable accomplishment of Portuguese explorers in North

America was undoubtedly the voyage of navigator Juan Rodrígues Cabrillo (Joao Rodrigues Cabrilho). In the autumn of 1542, while searching for a strait connecting the Atlantic with the Pacific Ocean, he sailed into San Diego Bay and disembarked. Thus Cabrillo became the first European to land on the coast of what is now the state of California. After discovering Santa Catalina and San Clemente islands, Santa Monica Bay, and San Buenaventura, he continued to an area near Fort Ross in northern California. Although he died a few months later, Cabrillo's pilot Bartolomé Ferrelo, sailed to the northern border of California.

Mathias de Sousa was the first Portuguese settler in the American colonies. He came to Maryland in 1634. Almost ten years later, there were only a few Portuguese, most of them Jews who lived in New Amsterdam. In fact, most of the Portuguese in the New World during the seventeenth century were Jews. A group of Spanish-Portuguese Jews came to New Amsterdam in 1654 and some of them migrated to Newport, Rhode Island, a short time later. A handful of Portuguese settled Martha's Vineyard, Massachusetts, during the last decade of the colonial era. Portuguese immigrants helped the colonists to win their freedom from England. John Paul Jones had twenty-eight Portuguese sailors among his crew. They enlisted in France in the summer of 1779; eleven of them died in the sea battle between the *Bonhomme Richard* and the *Serapis*. Peter Francisco served with Washington's army in the Revolutionary War and later became sergeant-at-arms of the Virginia House of Delegates.

According to the U.S. Immigration and Naturalization Service records, thirty-five Portuguese immigrants came to the United States in 1820 (Thernstrom, 1980). The vast majority of Portuguese immigrants did not come from the European mainland. Instead, they came from the Azores, the Madeiras, and the Cape Verde Islands—possessions of Portugal since the fifteenth century. Because their ranks were frequently depleted by desertions and illness, the early Yankee whaling ships would often stop in the Azores and the Cape Verde Islands to pick up extra hands as they voyaged to the Pacific. A large number of Portuguese welcomed the chance to see the world and leave their homes, because life was hard on the islands and most males had no desire to serve in the military.

Many of the Azoreans returned to New England towns and settled there after a life at sea. And they sent for relatives left behind on the islands. New Bedford, Massachusetts, became a home for hundreds of Portuguese immigrants in the 1850s. In 1865, New Bedford had a population of more than eight hundred Portuguese. By 1875, the state of Massachusetts had 3,705 Portuguese (Pap, 1981). Earlier, in 1849, a group of Portuguese Protestants from Madeira Island, refugees from religious persecution, fled their home and settled in Springfield, Illinois. In 1858, Abraham Lincoln employed a Portuguese woman, Frances Affonsa, to do the family washing; she became a cook for the Lincoln family.

The California gold rush brought thousands of fortune seekers from around the world to the former Mexican territory. Sailors from Portugal and Portuguese island possessions deserted their ships and joined in the quest for riches. Most of them soon realized that the chance for wealth was slight. Many of the disillusioned fortune hunters settled in California and earned a living in fishing and agriculture. Eventually some of the immigrants took up dairy farming and a few of them became quite successful (Avêndaño, 1982). Halfway across the Pacific from California, as early as 1794, a few Portuguese had taken up residence in the Sandwich Islands (now Hawaii). The first Portuguese dignitary on the islands was John Elliot de Castro, who arrived in 1814. King Kamehameha I was so impressed with de Castro that he made him his personal physician. De Castro left the islands a year later to live in Alaska. He returned for two additional years to serve as the king's foreign minister. By 1878 there were several hundred Portuguese living in Hawaii. Many of them had deserted whaling vessels to try their luck in the islands. The *Poquehe*, as Hawaiian natives called the Portuguese, became familiar people throughout the islands.

Contributions

Even though Portuguese immigrants are a relatively small group in the United States, they have been quite active as political leaders in local, state, and national governments. Mariano S. Bishop (Bispo) became executive vice president of the Textile Workers Union of America in 1953, and Michael Botelho was elected a vice president. Joseph F. Francis was the first Portuguese American to be elected to a state legislature in the eastern part of the United States. He was a Massachusetts state senator in the 1940s. John Arruda was elected mayor of Fall River, Massachusetts, in 1957. João G. Mattos Jr. was the first Portuguese American to be elected to the California state legislature. He later became a state senator and a judge. Helen L. C. Lawrence (Silveira) was chairperson of the City Council of San Leandro, California, in 1941. Manuel Caetano Pacheco chaired Hawaii's Democratic Territorial Committee and was later supervisor of Honolulu.

Other Portuguese Americans in politics include Antonio Rogers, the second Portuguese American to be elected to the California Assembly

(1911). Mary Fonseca was a member of the Massachusetts state senate in 1952; Clarence Azevedo was the first Portuguese-American mayor of Sacramento, (1959). Antonio Perry (Pereira) was chief justice of Hawaii from 1926 to 1934; Cyrus Nils Tavares was attorney general of the Hawaii Territory and later a federal district judge in the 1950s. Peter "Tony" Coelho, the first Portuguese American in the U.S. House of Representatives, was the Democratic Party majority whip; Benjamin Cardozo, associate justice of the U.S. Supreme Court from 1932 to 1938, is generally regarded as one of the greatest justices in the history of the Court.

In the field of music, Ilda Stichini and Maria Silveira were opera singers in the 1930s; John Philip Sousa, the "March King," gave America some of its most stirring music. Elmar de Oliveira won the gold medal for violin in the prestigious Tchaikovsky Competition in Moscow in 1978. He was the first American to win a gold medal in the violin category. Raul da Silva Pereira, from Lisbon, moved to California in the early 1920s and became a noted composer and conductor. Sequeira Costa was a professor of piano at the Lisbon Conservatory and the University of Kansas.

Outstanding Portuguese-American novelist John Dos Passos was author of the great trilogy *USA*. Portuguese Americans in show business include Harold Peary (Pereira de Faria), "The Great Gildersleeve" on the long-running radio comedy show; Henry da Sylva, director and actor in Hollywood in the 1920s; Rod de Medecis, another actor in early Hollywood films; and John Mendes, known as Prince Mendes, a touring magician.

Portuguese Americans who excelled in sports include Bernie de Viveiros, Manuel Gomes, and Lou Fonseca, all in baseball; Al Melo (Alfonso Tavares de Melo), boxing champion of New England and an American Olympic representative in 1924; George Araujo and Johnny Gonsalves, boxing championship contenders; Justiniano Silva, a professional wrestler in the 1920s; and Henrique Santos, U.S. fencing champion in 1942.

Three Portuguese Americans stand out in religion. Humberto Medeiros, born on the island of São Miguel in the Azores, immigrated with his family to Fall River, Massachusetts, in 1931 and became a bishop of the Roman Catholic Church in Texas. He succeeded Cardinal Cushing as archbishop of Boston, and in 1973 became a cardinal of the church. Stephen Peter Alencastre became a Roman Catholic bishop of Hawaii in 1924. "Daddy" Grace (Marcelino Manuel Graça, later Charles M. Grace), a Cape Verdean, founded over 350 Houses of Prayer in sixty American cities. His followers totaled over three million.

Painters Henrique Medina and Palmira Pimentel were both natives of Portugal, and they became well known in American art circles after settling in this country. Influential Portuguese-American businessmen include William Wood, who founded the American Woolen Company, which operated fifty-nine textile mills; Joseph E. Fernandes, a native of Madeira, who established a grocery chain of over thirty supermarkets in southeastern Massachusetts and did considerable works of philanthropy; Lawrence Oliver, who founded various successful business enterprises; and Joaquim de Silveira and Manuel T. Freitas, who were founders and developers of the Portuguese-American Bank in San Francisco. Portuguese-American inventors include John Lobato, developer of a new type of armored car and an accommodation airplane; Abilio da Silva Greaves, creator of the Thermophone fire alarm and a patent holder of a number of aviation-related devices; Steve Abrantes, developer of a new wool carding system; José dos Santos Fernandes, holder of a patent for a successful stable cleaner; José Pacheco Correia, developer of an electric needle machine for cotton combing; and Sebastião Luiz Dias, who developed a new irrigation control system. In medicine, Mathias Figueira helped found the American College of Surgeons, and Carlos Fernandes was director of St. John's Hospital in San Francisco.

Spanish

During the fifteenth century, Portugal monopolized trade along the African coast and Italy controlled trade with the Near East. In order to break the monopolies, Spanish monarchs decided to find new treasures and routes by circling the globe. Thus the Spanish government accepted a plan to sail west in order to reach the East. Success at that venture would, the proponents of the plan argued, bring Spain national glory as well as break the Portuguese and Italian cartels. The decision to implement the plan set into motion a series of Spanish explorations that would be unmatched in history. Christopher Columbus "discovered" the Bahamas, Cuba, and Haiti in 1492. In his following three voyages, Columbus explored the northern coast of South America and Central America.

In 1499 and 1500, Alonso de Ojeda, Juan de la Cosa, and Peralonso Niña explored Venezuela and the Gulf of Maracaibo. In 1530, Vasco de Balboa was the first European to sail on the Pacific Ocean, and Juan Ponce de León explored Florida. Earlier, in 1519, Ferdinand Magellan began a journey that ended only after his ship had sailed around the globe, although he was killed by natives on the island of Mactan midway in the voyage. During the same year, Hernán Cortés and seven hundred soldiers invaded Mexico and two years later conquered the Aztecs. Hernándo de Soto landed in Florida in 1539. From there, he led an expedition to what are now Georgia, North Carolina, South Carolina, Tennessee, and Alabama. In 1565, the Spaniards founded St. Augustine, the oldest community in the United States established by Europeans. That was the beginning of Spanish settlements in America. From 1565 to 1770, Spanish colonization efforts were uncoordinated ventures and logistical nightmares. Most of the Spanish colonies were isolated and difficult to reach. Spanish communities were also developed in Louisiana, although Spain held that territory only from 1762 to 1800 (Daniels, 1990, p. 96).

Spanish explorers established settlements in what is now the state of New Mexico in 1598, and Santa Fé was founded about 1610. By 1680, Santa Fé had about twenty-five hundred Spaniards; however, in that same year, the Indians revolted and killed more than five hundred Spanish settlers. Twelve years later Spanish soldiers came back to the area and waged war for four years before they retook the territory. Father Eusebio Kino, a Jesuit priest, founded missions in Arizona and lower California in the 1700s. Moving against the possibility of English or Russian settlement in upper California, the Spanish sent troops into the area. Franciscan fathers assumed religious jurisdiction over the territory in 1767, and Father Junipero Serra led the establishment of twenty missions, the last of which reached to what is now San Francisco. Countless Indians were converted by the fathers, who also introduced them to European techniques of farming and cattle raising as well as various crafts (Reich, 1989).

Until the end of the Spanish colonial era, Spanish settlers included government officials, large landowners and various professionals. At the end of this period, the Spanish colonists numbered over three million. Whites from Spain ruled all the colonial areas. Spanish rule over the Southwest came to an end when Mexico won independence from the mother country in 1821. The Spanish immigrants in the United States formed enclaves in such cities as New Orleans, Tampa, New York, Philadelphia, Newark, Chicago, Cleveland, and Bridgeport, Connecticut. A large number of the immigrants established regional associations. In the New York-Connecticut-New Jersey area alone it is estimated that there were fourteen associations for Spaniards. Some of the immigrants chose to define themselves not as Spaniards but as Galicians, Basques, Asturians, or Catalonians. It is impossible to trace accurately the Spanish immigrants because the 1848 Treaty of Guadalupe Hidalgo gave Spanish-speaking people their choice of citizenship—Mexican or American. Some of the Spanish who became U.S. citizens later identified themselves as Mexican Americans instead of Spanish Americans.

Contributions

The foremost Spanish contributions to America were sixteenth-century explorations and settlements that helped to carve an Anglo nation out of the American wilderness. Spanish architecture, especially as exemplified in the Catholic churches found in numerous American cities, has had a deep influence on American architecture in general, particularly in Florida and California. In music, José Iturbi, a pianist, enthralled millions of American music lovers with his concerts, phonograph records, and films. He was also known as an outstanding conductor, directing the Rochester Philharmonic for several years before World War II. His sister, Amparo Iturbi, also played many concerts in the United States and made phonograph records as well. American music would be less rich if Pablo Casals, a cellist, conductor, and composer, had not spent a good deal of time in the United States. Casals had many outstanding American students who came to him in Marlboro, Vermont, at the annual music festival. Before his death, he organized a yearly music series in Puerto Rico.

In the sciences, Spanish-American biochemist Severo Ochoa won the Nobel Prize in medicine in 1959 for his work in synthesizing a long chain of nucleotides that resembled naturally occurring RNA. Rafael Lorente de Nó, a physiologist, worked in the United States for many years. In the fine arts, Salvador Dalí worked for many years in the United States and had a profound influence on several American painters. Louis Quintanilla, Julia de Diego, and Frederico Castellon were well-known Spanish-American artists. José de Creeft, a sculptor and painter, came to the United States in 1929 and produced a most significant body of work. One of the world's greatest architects, José Luis Sert, joined the faculty of Harvard University in 1953. Soon after, he was appointed dean of the Graduate School of Design and chairman of the Department of Architecture.

José Lopez-Rey, an outstanding art historian, came to the United States in 1944 to teach and write. One of the world's greatest philosophers, George Santayana, came to America from Spain in 1872. He graduated from Harvard University and remained there to teach until 1912. His influence is still widely felt in academic circles. Historian Américo Castro was born in Brazil and educated in Spain before coming to the United States. Although continuing to write in Spanish, he taught at the University of Wisconsin, the University of Texas and Princeton University. Countless Americans are familiar with Spanish-American dancer José Grecó's success as a flamenco dancer. Al Lopez achieved success as a baseball star Hall-of-Famer and manager.

References

Avendaño, F. (1982). Portuguese immigration into the United States. In D. L. Cuddy (Ed.), *Contemporary American immigration: Interpretive essays (European)*. Boston: Twayne.

Cuddy, D. L. (Ed.). (1982). *Contemporary American immigration: Interpretive essays (European)*. Boston: Twayne.

Daniels, R. (1990). *Coming to America: A history of immigration and ethnicity in American life*. New York: HarperCollins.

Feagin, J. R. (1984). *Racial and ethnic relations*. Englewood Cliffs, NJ: Prentice-Hall.

Gonzales, Jr., J. L. (1990). *Racial and ethnic groups in America*. Dubuque, IA: Kendall/Hunt.

Iorizzo, L. J., & and Mondello, S. (1971). *The Italian-Americans*. New York: Twayne.

Nelli, H. S. (1983). *From immigrants to ethnics: The Italian Americans*. Oxford: Oxford University Press.

Pap, L. (1981). *The Portuguese Americans*. Boston: Twayne.

Reich, J. (1989). *Colonial America*. Englewood Cliffs, NJ: Prentice-Hall.

Rolle, A. (1982). The American Italian: Upraised or uprooted? In D. L. Cuddy, (Ed.) *Contemporary American immigration: Interpretive essays (European)*. Boston: Twayne.

Saloutos, T. (1964). *The Greeks in the United States*. Cambridge: Harvard University Press.

Scourby, A. (1984). *The Greek Americans*. Boston: Twayne.

Thernstrom, S. (Ed.). (1980). *Harvard encyclopedia of American ethnic groups*. Cambridge: Harvard University Press.

To the Land of Promise: The Italian Exodus to America
by Alexander DeConde

Within a century, or from the time of the American Revolution, Italy's population had doubled, producing unemployment and widespread unrest. Emigration worked as a kind of social safety valve. Italy became an exporter of strong human bodies to other regions that needed labor and could offer food. New, relatively cheap, easy to obtain, and what was then considered swift transportation also stimulated a mass overseas migration. Despite improvements in travel, for most Italian peasants the voyage through the Mediterranean and across the Atlantic, taking from two to three weeks, was an agonizing experience. They were packed in steerage in row after row of dirty bunks, like herring in a barrel. There they ate, slept, inadequately took care of toilet functions, and often huddled in fright.

When the exhausted immigrants landed in the United States, exploiters swarmed around them. Runners who spoke Italian, or one of its various dialects, piloted the newcomers to boarding houses where they were cheated and robbed. Employment agents also swindled the immigrants, as did railroad representatives who sold them counterfeit or worthless railroad tickets.

Aware of these indignities, some of the leaders of the new Italy urged the people not to emigrate. In more than one instance the *contadini* (peasants) answered, explaining why they were forced to abandon their country. "We plant and we reap, but never do we taste white bread," they said. "We cultivate the grape but we drink no wine. We raise animals for food but we eat no meat. We are clothed in rags. . . ."

Most of the Italians who stepped off the trans-Atlantic steamers in the seventies settled in the large industrial centers of the East and Middle West. Their first homes were in the deteriorating sections of those cities. There, as around Mulberry Street in New York City, they formed "Little Italies." In Philadelphia and elsewhere newspapers were already carrying stories of squalor, drunken brawls, and crime in the Italian neighborhoods.

By the end of the seventies the character of Italian immigration had changed. Now instead of northern Italians the great majority of newcomers were swarthy, illiterate *contadini* from the south. They

From American History Illustrated, (August 1972), 13-23. Reprinted through the courtesy of *American History Illustrated*, published by the National Historical Society, Gettysburg, PA.

seemed particularly strange because Americans had not previously encountered Italians of this kind in large numbers. Earlier immigrants had experienced prejudice, but these newcomers met almost instant hostility. As early as 1872 *The New York Times* reported that in the city's "business community there is an almost unanimous refusal to hire Italians." In 1874 the Armstrong Coal Works in western Pennsylvania brought in a group of Italian laborers to break a strike. Immediately, hatred of strikebreakers and prejudice against Italians produced violence. The other workers rioted, attacked, and killed several of the Italians. Even the earlier northern Italian immigrants, concerned about damage to their own precarious status, looked with contempt on the Sicilians, Neapolitans, and other southerners.

With these peasants came something seemingly new, the worker who took seasonal employment to earn a little money and then return to Italy, "as a bird in springtime repairs to its old nest." Although others, such as Irishmen, Poles, and French Canadians, came seasonally and migratory workers were familiar to Europe, no previous immigrants had brought with them as many temporary laborers as did the Italians. These "birds of passage" angered old stock Americans who considered them flighty and lacking in character. Actually, the relative swiftness of the steamship and the cheapness of steerage accommodations did more to stimulate temporary immigration than did Italian traits.

Disliking the seasonal job hunter and Italians in general, native Americans grumbled about this large ethnic group, which could not be fitted into what they considered the desirable pattern of American life. Nativists began to talk about an unpleasant change from an "old" to a less desirable "new" immigration, and to concern themselves with the nation's "unguarded" gates.

Ironically, the formative years of Italian immigration ended and massive immigration began at a time when a reborn nativism was on the rise in the United States. The coming of the southern Italian intensified this nativism, leading to demands by old stock Americans for some kind of Federal control—really restriction—over immigration. Despite this hostility the *contadini* kept coming. . . .

Many more Italians came than stayed permanently, and more arrived than official sources indicate. Thousands entered the country illegally. Throughout the eighties and nineties a third or more who came returned to Italy. In the eighties the new pattern of Italian emigration became clear. As many Italians were pulling up roots to go overseas as were migrating to neighboring countries, such as France or Switzerland. In the nineties the United States became their favorite goal.

Like that from other countries, this southern Italian migration followed a pattern. Most immigrants were young men between the ages of 14 and 45. Italy sent a higher proportion of males to the United States than did any other European country. So the average Italian immigrant was a young, robust male, uneducated and unskilled, but in the most productive years of his life. When he became reasonably settled and acquired enough money for the passage he sent for his family in Italy.

In the first years of the 20th century fewer immigrants returned to Italy than in the past. Many visited their old homes briefly, but few stayed. Most returned to America and what they regarded as home.

This outpouring of humanity from the Italian peninsula surprised Americans. Italian immigrant had, the sociologist Edward A. Ross said, "shot up like Jonah's gourd." Since their arrival contributed noticeably to the changing character of immigration to the United States, and of the ethnic composition of the population, though not as abruptly as nativists maintained, old stock Americans became increasingly critical. Why, they asked, did Italians keep rushing to a strange and often hostile land?

Italians kept coming in greater numbers than anticipated for the same reasons that caused other peoples to emigrate, and for unique reasons also. The United States had a reputation of a land of plenty with an expanding economy that required workers. The inexperienced and unlettered could find jobs quickly in mines or factories because technology had eliminated the need for skills.

This economic attraction, as well as the improvements in travel, was not enough in itself to force conservative *contadini*, for whom emigration amounted to an admission of failure at home, to desert the soil. Students of emigration believe that few people leave home by true free choice, or according to an Italian proverb, *chi sta bene non si muove*, or "he who is well off doesn't move." The Italians also came because, as in the seventies, their homeland virtually expelled them; they left in a mass act of protest against intolerable conditions. For the *Mezzogiorno*, southern Italy, the last decades of the 19th century were a time of economic stagnation. Agriculture, the nation's main economic activity, suffered a severe depression, much of it resulting from competition with other countries. The new national government did little to help alleviate the economic distress. Its leaders talked about agricultural reform in the *Mezzogiorno* but poured resources into industrialization of the north.

More peasants than ever from Calabria, the Abruzzi, or Sicily came to feel that they could not do worse in other lands than in their own.

Even though they may never have ventured beyond their native village, more and more responded to the posters of emigration agents giving the prices and dates of voyages to America and became willing to encounter the perils of a strange environment. They borrowed money for the voyage, sometimes paying as high as 50 percent interest.

Most of the emigrants from southern Italy might have followed the northerners who had in earlier decades converged on South America except that conditions there, temporarily at least, seemed uninviting. An outbreak of yellow fever in Brazil claimed some 9,000 Italian victims and led the Italian Government temporarily to ban immigration to that country. In Argentina political disturbances, financial crises, and a war with Paraguay crippled economic life and caused prospective immigrants to think twice about going there. . . .

At first the government of the new Italy deplored or ignored the exodus. Slowly, despite the influence of land-owners in parliament who opposed emigration, the attitude of the government changed. Seeing advantages in emigration, officials even encouraged it. In emigrating to a richer land, such as the United States, Italians often helped themselves and their country by relieving the economic pressure at home. Immigrants continued to help by sending home some of the money they earned. These remittances gave the Italian Government badly needed cash and became important to Italy's effort to balance her economy. Immigrants in the United States, like those in South America, bought Italian foods and other products. By creating a demand for Italian goods they also helped in building Italy's foreign markets.

Emigration also had negative aspects. In the *Mezzogiorno* it thinned out the population, emptying whole villages of able-bodied men, and leaving streets choked with grass and weeds. The cry *Ci manca la mano d'opera* ("We lack the working hand") could be heard through the countryside. "The young men have all gone to America," one villager explained in 1908. "We are rearing good strong men to spend their strength in America."

"American letters" from relatives and friends who had emigrated to the United States often awakened desires in *contadini* for a better life. Even though sometimes stained with tears, these letters, and the cash or money orders they often contained, told of the material advancement available in the New World for those who were prepared to bend and strain in a strange land. If you are willing to sweat, the American letters said, come and join us.

This message appealed to the *contadini* whose main assets were strong arms and a willingness to work. On the average, southern Italians brought with them about half as much money as did northerners, who carried into the United States slightly more cash than the average immigrant of any other nationality. The southerner usually had so little capital and education that he could work only with pick and shovel, or at some other job requiring no skills, such as hod carrier or mortar mixer. "Whenever you see a shovel, a steamroller, or a dredging machine," one observer noted in 1909, "there also you see Italians."

Two characteristics that Italians brought with them, although often criticized, helped them in facing life in the jungles of strange cities— tightly knit family ties and loyalty to their *paese,* or "home village." "Italy for me," immigrants would say, "is the little village where I was raised." In New York, Boston, Chicago, and elsewhere Italians congregated in deteriorating neighborhoods with their *paesani* (others from the same region) recreating what sociologists call urban villages, or the Italian country town in a city environment. Such settlements were often divided into almost as many groups as there were sections of Italy represented. Few were exclusively Italian, and the make-up of all was in a state of flux.

It was logical for immigrants who could speak no English to want to seek familiar faces, to be near relatives or those who language and customs they understood. *Paesani* could assist in finding a job or place to live, and could help in emergencies. By custom and tradition Italians expected aid from relatives. Their family cohesiveness and provincial clannishness was not unusual. Earlier immigrants—the English, the Irish, the Germans, and others—had also settled among relatives or countrymen from the same region, and they too had created urban villages. But the Italian, who often continued to think of himself as a Calabrese, a Veneziano, an Abruzzese, or a Siciliano, seemed stranger, more conspicuous, less capable of national feeling, more clannish than earlier immigrants.

Density of population was usually greater in the Little Italies than elsewhere. In 1904 a tenement-house inspector described Philadelphia's Little Italy as thirty-five blocks of tightly packed humanity. Under such conditions life could be tolerable only when people appreciated each other's customs. In California social conditions differed from those in the East. Little Italies were less crowded there, less provincial, and more prosperous.

The narrow loyalties of the Italians also brought disadvantages. Along with illiteracy, they hampered the development of Italians into a cohesive ethnic group capable of exerting pressure on a statewide or national level for the advantage of all. Italians often did not work together as effectively as immigrants in other ethnic groups; differences in dialect and the lack of widespread written communication kept them apart.

Like the Poles, Ukranians, Jews, and other immigrants, Italians banded together in fraternal organizations, especially in mutual aid societies similar to those they had known in the homeland. These societies provided a kind of group-benefit insurance for workmen, small shopkeepers, and others. Here Italians showed a capacity to help each other in meeting the problems of America's industrial society. In New York City alone, in 1910, there were more than 2,000 Italian mutual-benefit societies.

In time, out of the experience of living together within American communities, immigrants discovered the larger ethnic bond—that they were Italians, not just *paesani*, with a common heritage and common interests. Italian newspapers, magazines, and other publications, despite shortcomings, contributed to the growth of this ethnic identity. . . .

Italian immigrants generally avoided the South, mainly because of low wages, the plantation-tenant system, and the religious and ethnic bigotry common there.

The southern experience was unusual only because it was extreme; almost everywhere Italians found themselves culturally isolated. Even in their crowded urban villages many, especially unmarried males, were overcome by dreadful loneliness. The long separation of the sexes produced an unwholesome situation, but Italians were probably no worse off than other immigrants, many of whom had also come as single men. Loneliness did not seem to spur assimilation; Italians and old-stock Americans seldom intermarried. Since Italian women were relatively scarce, the male was the one who usually married outside his ethnic group.

Outsiders considered Italian women passive; they were not. When men could not obtain jobs or earned wages too low to maintain the family, the wives worked. Some, like native Americans, took jobs just to get ahead. So eager were Italian women to earn that at the turn of the century they gained the reputation of accepting lower wages than any other women in the United States. Few birds of passage could be found among them. Once settled with husband and family, they usually had no intention of returning to Italy. These women were the churchgoers. Far more than the men they kept alive the traditional Italian adherence to the Catholic faith. This clinging to the church was significant, for one of the striking changes in life for Italians in the United States occurred in religion.

Contadini were as ignorant in religion as in other matters. They found the Catholic churches in the United States different from anything they had known in the old country. "The fact is," an Irish Catholic observed, "the Catholic Church in America is to the mass of Italians almost like a new religion." Italians considered the American Catholic church cold and uncongenial, mainly because the Irish dominated it and infused it with a harsh militancy. *Contadini* could not speak intimately with Irish priests as they did with their own clergy in Italy. At first they had little choice; they had to use the Irish priests or dispense with religion. Some chose to abandon Catholicism; most remained loyal, or nominally so, but in their own way. The church dilemma of the Italians was aggravated by the fact that they were the first Catholic people to come to the United States in large numbers without bringing their own religious leaders with them.

Chapter 8

Asians

Until the early 1970s, American high school and college students enrolled in courses speciously entitled "World History." The textbooks used in the courses postulated that the most significant cultural developments occurred first in Europe and later in the United States. History was Eurocentric—mainly Western Europe (Seller, 1977; Takaki, 1989). Other peoples and their cultures were mentioned only peripherally and then usually when Anglo-Saxons discovered them. For example, early textbook references to the Orient generally focused on China as being a cradle of civilization; being discovered by Marco Polo; being under European domination; and being an emerging nation. The Japanese fared even worse, for their history in U.S. textbooks began when Japan was opened to trade by Commodore Matthew Perry in 1854. There was even less mention of Filipinos, Koreans, Vietnamese, Asian Indians, and Thais.

Examples of Differences

The diversity within Asian ethnic groups is as pronounced as it is within other ethnic groups. For example, cultural items such as languages, religions, customs, and foods differ widely. Yet, throughout U.S. history, Asian groups have been lumped together, particularly during xenophobic periods. A 1790 federal law restricted naturalization to "free white persons." Even when black slaves were freed and granted citizenship after the Civil War, Asians were denied citizenship. The xenophobic political climate of the 1800s culminated in the Exclusion Act of 1882—the only federal law restricting the admission of a specific nationality: Chinese. The act prevented Chinese immigrants, most of whom were men, from bringing their spouses to the United States. Thus the Chinese became largely a society of bachelors. Indeed, the mutilated family was the dominant form of Chinese family life until 1946, when several legislative acts permitted the reunion of some families.

The experience of Japanese immigrants was different from that of Chinese immigrants. Japanese male immigrants brought or imported brides to the United States. Citizens by birth, second-generation Japanese Americans (*Nisei*) became immersed in American communities. They founded the Japanese American Citizen League and used it as a base for extending political and economic activities. World War II put a temporary end to their cultural ascension. The internment of more than one hundred thousand Japanese, two-thirds of them U.S. citizens, was the low point in the history of Asians in America (Iyenago, 1921; Miyamota, 1973).

At various points in history, masses of Chinese and Japanese were deported, relocated, or tragically murdered (Barth, 1964; Hosakawa, 1969). Surrounded by hostile neighbors, small enclaves of Chinese and Japanese evolved into Chinatowns and Little Tokyos. From 1924 until the passage of the McCarran-Walters Bill in 1952, Asian immigration almost came to a halt. Only a few qualified businessmen, preferred professionals, and scholars were allowed to enter the United States. But even they were classified as "aliens" ineligible for U.S. citizenship. It was not until the enactment of Public Law 89-232 in 1965 that discrimination against Asians in immigration laws was eliminated, thus lifting the restrictions that had been enforced for over eighty years.

East Meets West

Unlike European settlers, Chinese immigrants did not come to America to discover an undeveloped country. The first Chinese settlers were predominately men who migrated in the nineteenth century to improve their economic conditions. There were even fewer Japanese immigrants in the nineteenth century, and the gender ratio was as lopsided among the Japanese as it was among the Chinese. By the 1880s, Chinese males outnumbered females by more than twenty to one (Daniels, 1953). The majority of early Chinese immigrants made San Francisco their port of entry; more than one-fifth of all Chinese Americans lived there.

Similar to most other ethnic groups discussed in the earlier chapters, the first wave of Asian immigrants tended to be poorly educated, had little or no financial resources, and did not speak English. They came to the United States in order to earn a fortune and then return to their native lands. Actually, few of them returned and even fewer earned a fortune. Between 1833 and 1882, China was stricken with a series of natural disasters such as typhoons, plagues, and droughts that resulted in much dislocation. The country was also grappling with a very serious overpopulation problem. Estimates cite the population of China in 1741 as 143 million; it doubled to 286 million in 1789; and it escalated to 430 million by 1850 (Tsai, 1956). These factors made the Chinese vulnerable to emigration even though they were for the most part treated like unwanted strangers in almost every country to which they moved.

All of the early Asian immigrants were subjected to conditions of racial segregation and discrimination. The extent of their tribulations is reflected in the various legal actions undertaken to exclude them from entering the United States. Virulent anti-Asian hostility culminated in laws which almost brought Asian immigration to a halt from 1924 until 1932. Despite hardships, a large number of Asian immigrants and their descendants made significant contributions to American agriculture, mining, lumbering, and railroad construction. And they excelled as individuals in the sciences, the arts, education, and business. Unfortunately, many Americans viewed people of Asian descent as a homogeneous group which shared the same physical characteristics, personality traits, and cultural adjustments. This stereotypical assessment did not take into account the broad historical, cultural, social, and emotional differences that individuated people and differentiated the ethnic groups broadly labeled "Asians" (Gardner et al., 1985).

Chinese

Among specific Asian groups, the Chinese have the largest population in America. Historians disagree on the date the first Chinese came to America. Some historians believe that Chinese were shipbuilders in Baja California between 1571 and 1748. Other authorities believe that a Buddhist priest sailed east across the Pacific to North America in the fifth century A.D. This theory is based on a seventh-century A.D. Chinese source, but little evidence can be found to support the claim. It has been established, however, that there were Chinese among the servants of the Spaniards who sailed between the

Philippines and Mexico after 1565 (Thernstrom, 1980). Chinese laborers were used in several areas of the Far West in the late 1700s.

The *Empress of China* was the first American clipper to reach China. It sailed up the Pearl River and set anchor in Canton in 1784. It is possible, however, that trade existed between American colonies and China before the Revolutionary War. Some writers speculate that the tea destroyed at the Boston Tea Party came from China through the East India Trading Company, whose ships sailed in Chinese waters as early as 1620. The company established a four-way trade system between India, China, England, and the American colonies.

It was not until 1784 that trading ships from the United States began regular voyages to Canton, the city designated for such purposes by the Manchu emperor. In 1786, President George Washington appointed Major Samuel Shaw, a Boston merchant who shared expenses for the *Empress of China*, the first American consul to China. His assignment was to promote closer cultural and trade relations between the two countries. Shaw's success was evident in historic centers of the United States: Williamsburg, Monticello, Mount Vernon, and other sites of colonial America imported intricate Chinese arts and crafts. Consequently, Chinese objects in ivory, jade, porcelain, lacquer, bronze, copper, and other precious metals and stones became highly prized by many Americans, most of whom never saw a Chinese.

The first Chinese name recorded in California was Ah Nam (d. 1817). He came to Monterey in 1815 and was employed as a cook for the Spanish governor. There is no dispute about the 1840 census which listed the presence of eight Chinese in the United States. After this scant beginning of immigration, the number of Chinese soon rose dramatically. For example, in 1850 there were 758 Chinese in America; by 1860 the number had risen to 34,933 and most of them resided in California. Large numbers of Chinese laborers were imported between 1850 and 1860 to help build the transcontinental railroads.

Labor contractors discovered that "coolies," as they called the Chinese, were cheap laborers compared with European immigrants who required more money to live. It is important to note that not all of the Chinese immigrants were unskilled laborers. A few upper-class Chinese students and intellectuals came to the United States to further their education. Immigration policies were formulated based on four basic factors: public sentiment regarding further immigration, the demands of foreign policy makers, goals and interests of elected officials, and perhaps most important, the human resource needed for the American economy (Gonzales, 1990).

The majority of the ninteenth-century Chinese immigrants came from districts in Kwangtung and Fukien. The outmigration was triggered by China's high-density population, primitive agricultural techniques, periodic crop failures, and high unemployment rates. When the news of high wages and the discovery of gold in California reached Kwangtung, thousands of men were eager to immigrate to the New World to seek their fortune. Most of them started out as temporary immigrants, or sojourners, who planned to work until they were fifty or sixty years old. By then, according to the plan, they would have saved enough money to return home and live their remaining years in comfort. In the interim they sent money to their families.

Several formal organizations of merchants in San Francisco evolved by 1854 to assist Chinese to immigrate to America. Known as the "Chinese Six Companies," they represented the nine major districts from which the majority of Chinese immigrants came. These companies sponsored a "credit ticket" system and also furnished a variety of social services such as meeting new arrivals, providing interpreters, securing temporary housing, putting Chinese in contact with other immigrants from their home areas, and most importantly, finding them jobs (Commonwealth, 1946). Ninety percent of all Chinese laborers in America were secured through the Chinese Six Companies. The remainder of Chinese immigration was organized by kinsmen or fellow villagers who acted as agents and sponsors. Through this process, the loyalties and institutions of the villages were transported overseas to the New World.

The immigrants identified with members of their Old World clan, village, dialect groups, or secret societies. Frequently, the elders who arranged work groups became community leaders who acted as the immigrants' spokesmen in the white society. Most often, however, the traditional clans controlled immigration, regulated commerce, settled disputes, meted out punishment, and levied taxes and fines. Blood feuds and turf wars were commonplace in the early Chinatowns. Filling the void in leadership, secret societies controlled intracommunity conflicts as well as Chinatown gambling houses, brothels, and drug distribution.

The Period of Coolie Labor

The large number of hardworking Chinese in California in 1852 prompted Governor John MacDougall to call them "the most desirable of America's adopted people." He was cognizant of the fact that Chinese laborers were contributing significantly to the building of the Union Pacific, the Southern Pacific, and the Northern Pacific railroads. Also, they were used to build levies and roads; reclaim swamps; mine coal, copper, and ore; and do jobs typically reserved for women such as cooking, gardening, washing, and sewing. From 1850 to 1870, many of the Chinese immigrants prospected for gold. Hundreds of others worked in mining camps as cooks, laundrymen and domestic servants. A few Chinese established commercial laundries, restaurants, bars, and general stores. In 1855 there were an estimated twenty thousand Chinese miners living in California.

By 1862, there were thirty thousand Chinese miners (Barth, 1964). An occupational survey conducted in San Francisco in 1870 documented a heavy concentration of Chinese immigrants in cigar manufacturing—91 percent of all cigars manufactured in San Francisco were provided by Chinese. They also constituted two-thirds of the people employed in the garment industry, and 19 percent of bootmakers (Coolidge, 1969). In the 1860s and 1870s, Japanese women were brought to the United States for the Chinese railroad construction workers. Also, Japanese slave girls were brought to the West by Japanese farmers who sold them to Chinese merchants.

American tolerance of Chinese laborers came to an abrupt end when unemployment for whites increased. White workers began to compete with Chinese for what they once considered "coolie jobs." Chinese industriousness and frugality, strange-sounding languages, different food customs, and shuffling walk were no longer considered quaint. Almost overnight Chinese immigrants became targets of verbal and physical abuse. As targets, they were readily identifiable: most Chinese males had distinctive characteristics that contributed to their high visibility—a long braid of hair down their back (a queue), loose pajamalike clothes with baggy trousers, Chinese shoes, and when working in the fields, circular bamboo hats.

Some angry white Californians attributed the economic depression of 1876 and the resulting business failures to Chinese who were frequently attacked on the streets. Chinese houses and business buildings were burned or wrecked, and white politicians in California were elected on platforms that included expelling all the Chinese from the state. Concurrently, legal acts which discriminated against the Chinese were passed by the state of California and local governments. As an example, San Francisco passed an ordinance which assessed laundry license fees: $8.00 per year for laundries using one horse vehicles, $16.00 per year for those using two horses, and $60.00 per year for those using no horses. Because Chinese laundries mainly did not use horses, the ordinance was obviously aimed at them. Another example of discrimination was the San Francisco ordinance that made walking on the sidewalks carrying a basket (a common Chinese behavior) a misdemeanor. Stereotypes depicted Chinese as cruel, dishonest, crafty, cowardly (Miller, 1969). San Francisco became the home for agitators who sought the cessation of Chinese immigration. Several groups—including unemployed white workers, members of labor unions, newspaper editors, and politicians—lobbied for laws to stop Chinese immigration. By 1867 there was an Anti-Coolie Club in every ward in San Francisco.

Other inequities included a California law that required miners to pay a $4.00 per month tax, but it was frequently reduced for white miners who could not pay the full amount. The various laws and ordinances which discriminated against Chinese workers were preceded by an 1868 U.S. treaty with China which allowed Chinese to come to America but they could not become naturalized citizens. Both Rutherford Hayes and Samuel Tilden had anti-Chinese proposals in their 1876 presidential platforms. In 1882, the Chinese Exclusion Act was passed. It specifically barred Chinese laborers from immigrating to the United States for ten years, and it prohibited state courts from granting citizenship to any Chinese already in the United States. The slogan "The Chinese must go!" became one of the most popular chants of organized labor at political meetings. Denis Kearney's Workingman's Party led the denunciations. The Knights of Labor picked up the cry. Finally, the Exclusion Act was revised in 1892 and Chinese immigration was suspended indefinitely until 1902.

Some of the most blatant forms of harassment in early twentieth-century San Francisco included the following: Chinese children were not allowed to attend public schools and were refused admission to the city hospital; Chinese could not be hired on public works projects; they were prohibited from using poles to transport laundry and vegetables; they were prohibited from using firecrackers and Chinese ceremonial gongs; a queue ordinance required all inmates in the county jail to have their hair cut within one inch of their scalp (Pajus, 1913). The California Supreme Court upheld a law that Chinese could not testify in court against white people; Chinese were prohibited from owning land in California; and Chinese were prohibited from working on municipal work projects (Gonzales, 1990). Because they could purchase land in Hawaii, an opportunity not available in California, hundreds of Chinese males left California and moved to Hawaii. Some of the migrants married local native Hawaiian women and became rice farmers in an industry they soon dominated.

Atrocities against them forced almost all Chinese into self-contained ethnic enclaves called Chinatowns. The first Chinatown used as a racial quarter was established about 1850. Unlike most ethnic communities, its inception and growth were based on the need for self-protection and survival. Specifically, Chinatowns became occupied by people who were beaten, burned, lynched, and subjected to other flagrant acts of racial oppression—all reasons for colonization in the United States. The early Chinatowns were dirty, overcrowded, rodent- and insect-infested; and they were poorly constructed with narrow alleys and underground cellars that frequently had secret passages.

Over time Chinatowns became clean, colorful, and often exotic places. Clan associations—whose memberships were determined by dialect, old country region, place of origin, and tong affiliation—were secret organizations that controlled most of the vital activities within the Chinese communities. More than half the Chinese immigrants were concentrated in urban enclaves in California, Washington, Oregon, Hawaii, New York, and Illinois. Chinese immigrants observed the major Chinese festivals: the New Year, the Dragon Boat, Mid-Autumn, and Winter Solstice. Also, they made annual offerings to all spirits at the *Shaoi* ("burning mock clothes") ceremony in summer—a Chinese version of All Souls' Day; and they visited graves of relatives and friends during spring and fall. The ritual most difficult for them to observe was exhuming and returning their dead for burial in the native village.

Contributions

Chinese immigrants have made numerous cultural contributions to America. In 1957, Tsung-dao Lee and Chen Ning Yang were awarded Nobel Prizes in physics, and Samuel Ting won it in 1976. Chien Shiung was recognized as the world's foremost female experimental physicist. Kuan Sun, a former manager of the Westinghouse Radiation and Nucleonics Laboratory, was the first person to use the powder method to make a photographic pattern of neutron defraction. Cho Hao Li, a protein chemist, isolated five of the six major pituitary hormones, including ACTH, which has cured diseases once considered incurable. George Chu, a bacteriologist and parasitologist, discovered the cause of a seaweed dermatitis in the Pacific Ocean. The fact that Chinese Americans have demonstrated great horticultural skills is seen in such legacies as the cherry named for Ah Bing, a foreman who worked in Milwaukie, Oregon, and an orange developed by pomologist Lue Gim Gong.

Chao-Chen Wang, an engineer, helped develop an electronic tube that produces 4 million watts of radar power. Other prominent Chinese-American engineers include Jeffrey Chu, Eng Lung Chu, Julius Tou, Frederick Fuliu, and Yuan Chu'en Lee. I. M. Pei achieved international acclaim for his architectural designs. Francis L. K. Hsu, an anthropologist, wrote a much-quoted book entitled *American and Chinese: Two Ways of Life*. Rose Hum Lee was the first Chinese American to head a department of sociology. Loh Seng Tsai, a psychologist, posited a biological foundation for a theoretical possibility of world peace. Yi Kwei Sze was the first Chinese singer to win international fame as an interpreter of leading roles in classical operas. Wen Chung was the first Chinese singer to be given a Guggenheim fellowship. Numerous Chinese Americans gained fame by establishing businesses, including Joe Shoong, who founded the National Dollar Stores.

Yung Wing was the first Chinese graduate from an American college (Yale University, 1854). Ng Poon Chew was a nationally known lecturer on China and the Chinese in America. In the 1920s, cinematographer James Wong Howe and actress Anna May Wong attained recognition in Hollywood for their contributions. Dong Kingman gained a national reputation as an artist and Lin Yutang interpreted his version of Chinese culture for Americans. Nationally known musical artists include bass-baritone Yi Kwei Sze and composer Wen-chung Chou. In politics, Wing Ong of Arizona was the first Chinese American on the mainland to be elected to the state legislature, and Thomas Tang became a judge in the 9th Circuit Court of Appeals. Computer magnate An Wang is reported to be the largest single contributor to philanthropic causes in Boston.

Japanese

In 1834, Manjiro Nakahama, or John Mung as the Americans called him, came to the United States aboard the *John Howland*. He was the first Japanese to settle in the United States, and he came during a time when Japan prohibited immigration to America. Several years later, in 1851, a shipwrecked thirteen-year-old Japanese boy named Hikozo Hamada (Joseph Heco) was brought to San Francisco aboard the *Auckland*. In 1858, he became the first Japanese to become a naturalized American citizen. Several other Japanese visited the United States before the mass migrations, including Korekiyo Takahashi, who became Japan's minister of finance; and Joseph Niishima, the founder of Doshisha, one of Japan's Christian colleges.

The Early Immigrants

For several centuries Japan was an isolated nation that prohibited emigration of its citizens under penalty of death. In 1870, the U.S. Census Bureau reported fifty-five Japanese immigrants—forty-seven males and eight females. Official emigration from Japan was not approved until 1886. The first wave of immigrants consisted of students rather than unskilled laborers. The glowing letters they sent to relatives in Japan inspired others to come to the United States in order to improve their economic situation. In 1890, only 2,039 Japanese immigrated to the United States. The largest number of Japanese, 12,626, came to the United States in 1900. However, many more thousands of Japanese immigrated to Hawaii. As the Hawaiian native population declined, Japanese workers were recruited by sugar planters to augment the Chinese laborers who had been recruited beginning in 1850.

The first Japanese who settled in Hawaii had numerous benefits negotiated for them by the Japanese government: full passage for them and their families, free housing, a minimum wage, medical care, and a maximum ten-hour workday. No other immigrants had their government negotiate such an attractive relocation package. The first 148 Japanese laborers immigrated to Hawaii in 1868 to work for the owners of commercial sugar production cartels. They were assigned to work on six plantations under a six-year contract to work for $4.00 a month (Gonzales, 1990). Almost thirty thousand Japanese immigrated to Hawaii between 1868 and 1894 and soon they became Hawaii's largest ethnic group. Beginning in the 1890s, a small but significant number of Japanese arrived directly from Japan and North American Pacific ports such as San Francisco and Seattle (Daniels, 1953). After 1898, when Hawaii was annexed by the United States, hundreds of Japanese plantation workers moved from Hawaii to the Pacific Coast.

Many of the first generation Japanese (*Issei*) who immigrated to America in the early 1900s were employed as laborers in agriculture, on the railroads, in mining, in canneries and in lumbering (Niiya, 1993). However, the majority of the immigrants were not laborers (Pajus, 1913). An undetermined number of Japanese female slaves were brought to America and sold to Japanese and Chinese workers who were laborers for the transcontinental railroads. The earliest Japanese farmers came to Fresno, California, in 1880 as servants. In 1888, Japanese started working in apricot orchards of Vacaville, California, and by 1890 there were more than three hundred Japanese working in Vacaville farms and orchards. Japanese laborers became migrant workers, moving to whatever area had the greatest need for labor. By 1904, they had become the major harvesters of grapes, beets, and cantaloupes in California; by 1910, a large number of Japanese were farm owners. Japanese farm workers established the first ethnic group labor union (Fuller, 1939).

While most Japanese lived in or around the port cities of Seattle and San Francisco, several colonies were established as far inland as Texas.

In fact, large Japanese colonies were settled in Texas. But those immigrants were wealthy persons who came with substantial capital to invest in rice farms. The Mayakawa family became so successful in growing rice in Houston that a railroad company built special tracks to their farm to pick up the produce. The Saibara family also settled in Texas to grow rice. Beginning with $10,000 in capital and accompanied by rice-growing specialists, they settled in Webster, Texas.

The major ethnic conflict did not really begin until 1900. On May 7, 1900, white people attending a mass meeting in San Francisco urged Congress to exclude all Japanese from coming to the United States. The California legislature passed a resolution in 1901 urging Congress to protect American labor by greatly restricting Japanese immigration. The state legislatures of California and Nevada passed resolutions in 1905 demanding that Congress immediately restrict Asian immigration. In accordance with the 1907 Gentleman's Agreement, the Japanese government limited Japanese passports to the United States to nonlaborers seeking to join a parent, husband or child, and to laborers already in America. In reality, only picture brides—women in Japan who Japanese workers selected by viewing pictures of them—came to the United States from 1907 to 1920. But this did not stop the anti-Japanese forces. Hostile resolutions were passed in the California, Oregon, Nevada, and Montana legislatures. In 1920, the Japanese government initiated a Ladies Agreement which ended passports to Japanese brides to immigrate the United States. The U.S. Supreme Court ruled in *Takao Ozawa* (1924) that Japanese could not become naturalized American citizens.

Contributions

Henry Ayao was a silversmith whose creations won numerous awards. Hideyo Noguchi was one of the world's greatest chemists. He discovered the cause of locomotor ataxia. He also was the first person to isolate the pure culture of the germ syphilis, and he died investigating yellow fever. Jin Kinoshita, an ophthalmologist, pioneered research in the formation of cataracts. Yasuo Kuniyoshi and Isamu Noguchi were among the world's finest architects. Sono Osata was a successful ballerina, and Sessue Hayakawa was one of Hollywood's most proficient actors. In 1910, Kinji Ushijima, better known as George Shima, purchased the only land available to him in the Sacramento delta and within ten years he became known as the "potato king." He cornered the potato market in San Francisco. Shima operated 60,000 acres and owned his own barges. Keisaburo Koda was known as the "rice king." He pioneered the method of planting rice using airplanes, built his own mill, and established the Kokuho brand. In 1915, a Japanese named Sato first planted lettuce as a field crop. It is ironic that the successful Japanese farmers could only purchase or lease land unwanted by white farmers.

Other notable Japanese-American business achievements include the Oriental Trading Company of Seattle, established by Tetsu Takahashi and Otataka Yamaoka in 1898; the Tacoma (Washington) Construction and Maintenance Company was founded by W. H. Remington and Hifumi Kumamoto in 1898; a fishing boat specially designed to catch tuna in Hawaiian waters was built by Gorokichi Nakasuji in 1899; the Hawaii Shoyu (Soy Sauce) Company was established by Nobuyuki Yamashiro in 1906; winter celery was introduced to Chula Vista, California, by Mitsusaburo Yamamoto and Fukutaro Muraoka in 1912.

Bill Hosokawa was the first foreign correspondent for the *Denver Post*. John Aiso was the first Japanese American named to a judicial post. In 1953, he was appointed to the municipal court in Los Angeles. Tomi Kanazawa was the first *Nisei* singer to appear in a leading role with the Metropolitan Opera Company. Hiroshi "Ford" Konna was one of America's greatest swimmers; he won the 1500-meter free-style competition in the 1952 Olympic Games; Yoshinobu Oyakawa won a gold medal in the 100-meter backstroke; Tommy Kono, a weightlifter, won Olympic gold medals in 1952 and 1956. Yoshiro Uchida was a manager-coach of the U.S. 1964 Olympic judo team. Takemoto "Patsy" Mink was the first American woman of Asian descent to be elected to the U.S. House of Representatives. She was also the first Asian woman in the state of Hawaii to be admitted to the practice of law.

Daniel Inouye, a war hero, was the first U.S. representative from Hawaii; in 1962 he was elected to the U.S. Senate. In 1976, Samuel Hayakawa was elected the Republican U.S. senator from California. Also in 1976, Norman Mineta became the first Japanese-American U.S. representative from the mainland. Norman Matsui was also a congressional representative. Robert Takasugi and Wallace Toshima were federal district judges. Takasugi presided over the nineteen drug trials of defendant John DeLorean, a millionaire industrialist. Jack Soo (Guro Suzuki) was a successful actor. Teiko Tomita, a pioneer Japanese woman in the Pacific Northwest, was an acclaimed poet who wrote about the *Issei* in America.

Filipinos

In 1898, after a decisive naval engagement in the Spanish-American War, the Spanish fleet was defeated by Admiral George Dewey.

On December 10, 1898, by terms of the Treaty of Paris, Spain ceded the Philippine Islands to the United States. The treaty ended more than three hundred years of Spanish rule. In the 1890s, the United States looked abroad for ways to assert itself. American businesses needed more raw materials and new export markets; Protestant missionaries wanted new heathens to convert to Christianity; and the military wanted strategic outposts from which they could more effectively monitor the Pacific Ocean areas. The Philippines was such a place. It was a prime area for American businesses to get raw materials, for missionaries to convert natives, and for the U.S. Navy to establish a military base. It also soon became the major place to acquire Far East laborers (Crouchett, 1982; Keeley, 1973).

Most Filipinos came to the United States in three waves during the twentieth century. The first wave began in 1903 when hundreds of government-sponsored Filipino students (*penchinados*) enrolled at American colleges and universities (Melendy, 1977). They majored in a variety of subjects, including education, agriculture, civil engineering, mechanical engineering, and medicine. The second wave occurred from 1907 to 1934. These were mostly Ilocanos from the island of Luzon which provided cheap labor to both Hawaii and the Pacific Coast states (Cuddy, 1982). The largest wave, 210,269 Filipinos, came between 1965 and 1974. The overwhelming majority of Filipino workers who came between 1907 and 1935 were young males under thirty years of age (Melendy, 1977).

In the 1900s Hawaii was in need of unskilled labor for its plantations and sugar mills. In 1909, the Chinese, Japanese, and Koreans, who had been heavily recruited in the past, were barred from emigrating. Furthermore, most of the Europeans (Germans, Scots, Scandinavians, and Russians) who were brought to Hawaiian plantations to work as unskilled laborers had long since found jobs in the cities as skilled laborers and small business owners. Other early immigrants became independent farmers and the remainder returned to their homelands or moved to the western states. Thus the Philippines became the major country of recruitment for Hawaiian labor (Clifford, 1967). By the end of 1910, almost 5,000 Filipinos had been recruited to work in Hawaii.

Mainland Immigration

The decade of the 1920s was a time of mass Filipino migration to the United States. From 1920 to 1929, more than thirty-one thousand Filipino immigrants came to San Francisco and Los Angeles. A large number of them came from Hawaii where an unsuccessful strike resulted in hundreds of workers being blacklisted (denied employment). While most Filipino immigrants settled on the West Coast, a sizeable number moved to Chicago, Detroit, New York, and Philadelphia. The gender ratio of Filipino immigrants was fourteen males to one female. Most of the immigrants had little formal education and they spoke neither English nor Spanish. Once they arrived, they were recruited for a wide variety of unskilled urban and rural jobs. Filipino migratory workers were employed largely in salmon canneries, fruit farms, vegetable gardens, and sugar-beet ranches. They were transported from job to job in trucks owned by labor contractors. When economic conditions worsened, white workers vented their frustrations on the Filipinos.

A large-scale migration of Filipino agricultural laborers to the mainland coincided with a similar influx to Hawaii. The mainland movement started early in 1920 and continued until the 1930 Depression. The combination of the Depression and the Tydings-McDuffie Act virtually stopped any significant traffic after 1934 (Melendy, 1977). By the time of the outbreak of World War II mainland immigration had stabilized at a very low level. As was true of the Chinese immigrants, prior to 1945, almost all of the Filipinos came to the United States with the idea of making a fortune and returning home. However, the dream of becoming rich and returning to the Philippine Islands turned into nightmares. Instead of becoming financially secure, some of the workers became migrant workers, who moved from one crop to another barely eking out a living. Others joined the large pool of marginally employed cooks, janitors, dishwashers, and other unskilled laborers. They lived in farm labor camps and city boarding and rooming houses. In the large cities, their neighborhoods were called Little Manilas.

Dark skin and faulty English set Filipino immigrants apart from their white neighbors and fellow workers. On the West Coast, they were treated like African Americans were treated in other parts of the country. They were denied service in restaurants, barbershops, and beauty shops; barred from movies, swimming pools, and other public facilities. White real estate owners restricted Filipinos to slum enclaves. Consequently, Little Manilas became some of the few places where Filipinos could find accessible housing, food, and recreation. To make up for the absence of wives and other close relatives, the early immigrants associated with friends and shared housing and meals, thus producing the *company* (surrogate family) in which the eldest male acted as head of the household.

Because they came from a U.S.-owned island, Filipino immigrants were unprepared for the prejudice they encountered. In the Philippines, they thought of themselves as loyal Americans. They learned English in the schools, and learned to salute the American flag, and had no vigorous race line drawn. In the United States, Filipinos, like Chinese and Japanese, were treated as people of color with low social status. But, unlike Chinese and Japanese, a large number of Filipinos crossed the race line and dated white females. One of the first anti-Filipino riots occurred in Yakima, Washington, on September 19, 1928. Later, in the 1930s, whites in California attacked and killed several Filipinos.

Contributions

Silvers Capistrano invented the machine believed to be the first rice-planting machine of its kind. Juan Urbane invented the Urbaro electric pencil and flashlight. Carlos Bulosan, author of the book *Laughter of My Father*, was a successful writer. Dalisay Aldaba was a lead singer with the New York City Opera Company. There were other individual achievements, but the foremost Filipino contribution to the development of the United States consisted of the thousands of people who performed menial jobs and provided countless services needed to keep the society functioning. Like the other ethnic minority groups included in this book, early generations of Filipinos were denied equal opportunities to achieve educational and economic success. Even so, they achieved excellence as workers.

Koreans

The first official Korean immigrants to the United States moved to Honolulu on January 15, 1900 (Kim & Wong, 1977; Romerantz, 1984). The Hawaiian Sugar Planters Association began formal negotiations in 1902 for Korean laborers. Emperor Konjong established a Department of Immigration which authorized the sugar association to recruit Korean workers (Romerantz, 1984). The first Korean contract laborers on the mainland arrived on the West Coast in 1903. They worked as railroad laborers for $1.20 to $1.50 per day. Most of them abandoned railroad construction and service jobs to become farmers in California. The workers who came during the first six months of 1903 fulfilled their employers' expectations. Word of the success was sent back to Korea by American companies as a recruiting tool. American labor agents continued to recruit Korean workers until April 1, 1905, when the Korean Foreign Office prohibited all emigration abroad. The U.S. Department of Immigration was closed in November, 1905 (Melendy, 1977). One of the last students who came to

America before the 1905 edict was Syngman Rhee who later became a leader in Korea. More than five hundred young Korean political activists, struggling against Japanese oppression, entered the United States via Shanghai or Manchuria between 1910 and 1918. After Korean independence in 1945, approximately six thousand Korean students came to the United States to continue their education.

Before the U.S. Immigration Reform Act of 1965 liberalized the immigration policy, the number of Koreans residing in the United States consisted of only a few thousand. Since 1965, thousands of Koreans have arrived, and this has made them the third fastest-growing ethnic group in the United States. As a whole, they immigrated to America to find a better way of life (Kim & Wong, 1977). However, the matter is somewhat more complex. Two additional push factors were population pressure and political instability. The political uncertainty between North and South Korea since the Korean War (1950–53) prompted many middle-class and even more affluent Koreans to emigrate from their homeland to the United States for fear of another war.

Employment and compensation for Koreans in the 1970s followed distinct patterns. Second- and third-generation Koreans who had made the adjustment to American culture became successful business executives and professionals. Unfortunately, those who arrived in West Coast cities, Honolulu, and New York City in the 1980s did not readily attain economic success. Many Koreans settled in large groups in Pennsylvania, Ohio, Michigan, and New Jersey with very few of them residing in rural areas (Cuddy, 1982). Almost all recent Korean immigrants have settled in large urban areas. The largest community of Koreans is in Los Angeles, followed by New York, and then Chicago. A significant number of Korean females entered the United States as war brides after the Korean War. Almost all of them married non-Asian-American servicemen (Daniels, 1953). During the 1960s, nearly 70 percent of all Korean immigrants were females. As a group, Korean immigrants learned to play the immigration game very well. The 1990 census figures reveal they have managed to gain economic security and educational successes—feats which are commonplace among other Asian immigrants.

Contributions

Kwan Doo Park earned a baccalaureate degree from the University of Hawaii and a master's degree in engineering from Massachusetts Institute of Technology. He later gained statewide recognition for his architectural firm's pioneering use of prestressed concrete construction. Hawaiian-born Joseph Park was a leading chemical engineer. He worked for the DuPont Company and Frigidaire and developed a variety of refrigerants. Following his retirement in 1972, Park was named president of the Korean Advanced Institute of Science in Seoul where he remained until 1974. In California, Alfred Song was the first individual of Asian ancestry to serve in the state senate. He was elected to the first of his two terms as state assemblyman in 1962.

Philip Minn, born in Maui, graduated from the University of Hawaii and served in the U.S. Army during World War II. He was elected to the Hawaii House of Representatives from the Ewa-Waianae district in 1963 where he served until his death in 1966. Richard K. C. Lee was a director of the Hawaii State Health Department, and he later became dean of the newly created School of Public Health at the University of Hawaii. Herbert Y. C. Choy was one of four Koreans honored in 1973 by his fellow Koreans as a distinguished citizen. He graduated from the University of Hawaii and from Harvard Law School. He was admitted to the bar in 1941. In 1957, Hiram Fong was named territorial attorney general. In 1971, President Richard Nixon appointed Choy a judge on the 9th Circuit Court of Appeals. In 1992, Jay Kim became the first Korean American elected to the U.S. House of Representatives.

Vietnamese

The Vietnamese do not have a long history of immigration to the United States. Many early immigrants were poorly equipped to live in the United States. It was only after the United States took over the responsibility from the French to resist communism in Southeast Asia in the mid-1950s that a few Vietnamese came to the United States, mostly as students. If they had not been refugees to whom the United States related with a guilty conscience, most of them would not have qualified for immigration admission. There is a direct correlation between America's involvement in Vietnam and Vietnamese immigration to the United States (Daniels, 1953). The end of racial quotas in the 1960s, coupled with special refugee admittance, made a significant difference in the number of Vietnamese who came to the United States for respite from their country's economic and political woes. The number of Asian immigrants to the United States increased dramatically from 1969 to the early 1980s—including the Vietnamese. In the decade of the 1980s the United States accepted over five hundred thousand Indo-Chinese immigrants; two-thirds of them were Vietnamese (Feagin, 1984).

When the first Vietnamese arrived in the United States, they were confronted with an explicit federal policy of dispersing them through-out every state. The policy was adopted to minimize racial hostility, and to dampen hostility in the economic areas toward a growing number of immigrants who came to America when unemployment was at very high levels. As a part of the policy, thirty-seven Korean families were relocated in the metropolitan Lexington, Kentucky, area. Most of them spoke English, had contact with Americans in Vietnam, and had the financial resources and skills needed to qualify them for employment. Also, some of them enrolled in college to expand their professional training for increased job opportunities. As the Viet-namese gained economic security, they were able to thwart the U.S. government's plan to disperse them in groups to California, Texas, Pennsylvania, Virginia (near the District of Columbia), and Louisiana (*U.S. News & World Report, 1977*). Thus they were able to live in colonies where traditional holidays were observed, and Vietnamese food and Vietnamese music were readily available.

Because of the Vietnamese independence and economic success, several U.S. citizens and groups raised public opposition to the new immigrants. A strange group of people joined forces against them: the Ku Klux Klan, unions leaders, political conservatives, and liberals. Union members were concerned that the Vietnamese would take away jobs; political conservatives feared the Vietnamese would join the forces with people trying to alter the values and morals that are typically American; and liberals were fearful that the newcomers would adopt right-wing political ideologies and shift voting patterns to the right (Feagin, 1984).

The plight of the boat people from Vietnam also created a crisis of conscience for the United States. At one time during the war in Viet-nam, South Vietnamese fled their country at the rate of sixty-five thousand per month, but no other Asian country would accept them. Those refugees differed from the original Vietnamese immigrants, many of whom had language skills and economic resources (Cuddy, 1982). Most of the Vietnamese boat people had little or no money. Those who started their journey with money had it taken from them by pirates or greedy officials in the countries of first asylum.

As recent immigrants, the cultural contributions of the Vietnamese in the United States have yet to be found in large numbers. Even so, their educational and business skills will be significant in the twenty-first century.

References

Barth, G. (1964). *Bitter strength: A history of Chinese in the United States, 1850–1870*. Cambridge: Harvard University Press.

Clifford, M. D. (1967). *The Hawaiian sugar plantation association and Filippino exclusion movement, 1927–1935.* Quezon City: University of the Philippines: Institute of Asian Studies.

Commonwealth Club of California. (1946). *The population of California.* San Francisco: Parker.

Coolidge, M. P. (1969). *Chinese immigration.* New York: Arno Press.

Crouchett, L. J. (1982). *Filippinos in California: From the days of the Galleons to the present.* El Cerrito, CA: Downey Place.

Cuddy, D. L. (1982). *Contemporary American immigration.* Boston: Twayne.

Daniels, R. (1953). *The Japanese frontier in Hawaii, 1868–1898.* Berkeley: University of California Press.

Feagin, J. R. (1984). *Racial and ethnic relations.* 2nd ed. Englewood Cliffs, NJ: Prentice Hall.

Fuchs, L. H. (1990). *American kaleidoscope: Race, ethnicity and civic culture.* Hanover, MA: Wesleyan University Press.

Fuller, V. L. (1939). *The supply of agricultural labor as a factor in the evolution of farm organization in California.* Doctoral Dissertation. Berkeley: University of California.

Gardner, W., et al. (1985). *Asian Americans: Growth, change and diversity.* Population Bulletin, 40 (4): 1–10.

Gonzales, J. L., Jr. (1990). *Racial and ethnic groups in America.* Dubuque, IA: Kendall/Hunt.

Hosakawa, B. (1969). Neisei: The quiet Americans. New York: William Morrow.

Iyenago, T. (1921). *Japan and the California problem.* New York: Putnam.

Keeley, C. B. (1973). *Phillippine migration: Internal movements and emigration to the United States.* International Migration Review, 7: 177–187.

Kim, D. S., & Wong, C. C. (1977). *Business development in Koreatown, Los Angeles.* Santa Barbara, CA, CLEO.

Melendy, H. B. (1977). *Asians in America, Filippinos, Koreans and East Indians.* Boston: Twayne.

Miller, S. (1969). *The unwelcome immigrant: The American image of the Chinese, 1785–1882.* Berkeley: University of California Press.

Miyamota, S. F. (1973). *The forced evacuation of the Japanese minority during World War II.* Journal of Social Issues, 29: 11–29.

Niiya, B. (Ed.). (1993). *Japanese American history, 1868 to the present.* New York: Facts on File.

Pajus, J. (1913). *The real Japanese California.* Berkeley: Gillick.

Romerantz, L. (1984). The background of Korean emigration. In L. Cheng & E. Bonacich (Eds.), *Labor immigration under capitalism: Asian workers in the United States before World War II.* Berkeley: University of California Press.

Seller, M. (1977). *To seek America: A history of ethnic life in the United States.* New York: Jerome S. Ozer.

Takaki, R. (1989). *Strangers from a different shore: A history of Asian Americans.* New York: Little, Brown.

Thernstrom, S. (Ed.). (1980). *Harvard encyclopedia of American ethnic groups*. Cambridge: Harvard University Press.

Tsai, H. S. (1956). *The Chinese experience in America*. Bloomington: Indiana University Press.

U.S. News & World Report. (1977). June 13: 46.

The *Nisei* Arrive
by Bill Hosokawa

In 1930 fewer than 4,000 *Nisei* in the entire United States were of
voting age. The *Issei*, in their productive prime, were firmly in control
of their communities. Their wandering days were ended; their little
businesses in Los Angeles, Fresno, San Jose, San Francisco, Stockton,
Sacramento, Portland, Tacoma, Seattle, Spokane and way points provided them with a measure of security and a sense of permanence
that they had never known previously. Despite the land laws, they
had sunk their roots in the soil of valleys with names like Imperial
and San Joaquin, Yakima and Puyallup; they had learned to gauge
the weather and they won as often as they lost in the gamble on market prices which is all a farmer can expect. The *Issei* held the purse
strings. They established standards of behavior, planned the routine
of their community life, ruled their families. Their world was a pot-
pourri of the Japanese culture in which they had been reared and
which they remembered and revered with a fierce tenacity until
oftentimes the memory was more vivid than the reality; the American
culture that had rubbed off on them and which they absorbed into
their lives, sometimes unconsciously; and finally, the pressures that
compressed them largely into their own ethnic communities.

The result for the *Nisei* was a world that was both secure and con-
fining, comfortable and frustrating, challenging and stultifying, warm
and hostile. In a word, although they rarely had either time or incli-
nation to brood about it, theirs was a confusing life. Pervading all was
the influence of the public schools. They learned English in their
classes and spoke Japanese at home; in time, as English won the linguistic tug of war, the parents spoke to them in Japanese and they
replied in English and somehow they understood each other very
well. They took peanut butter and jelly sandwiches to school for lunch
and for supper shoveled rice into their mouths with chopsticks together with fish or vegetables flavored with soy sauce.

The shock absorber that enabled them to survive the jolting and buf-
feting of divergent cultures was the home, reassuring despite its meager comforts, warm with often unarticulated love even though both
parents worked themselves close to exhaustion, closeknit and secure
because of—as well as in spite of—outside forces beyond their control.

For the *Issei*, home was security after the daily struggle of making
a living in a white man's world where the language was difficult and

strange, the competition harsh, the laws and those who enforced them hostile. At home the *Issei* could eat rice with hot tea and make his delicious *tsukemono* pickles in a malodorous jar of fermenting *nuka* without prying blue eyes to embarrass him. He could listen to the wailing music that had soothed and moved his parents and grandparents before him and evoke memories of home. He could observe his own holidays, like New Year's Day which in Japan is New Year's, Thanksgiving, Labor Day and two or three other holidays rolled into one. On New Year's Eve he observed the tradition of paying off as many of his debts as he could, so their burden would not follow him into the upcoming year; scrubbed and dusted his shop or office or home from top to bottom; luxuriated in a long hot bath to rid himself of the past year's grime—a symbolic rite since he bathed daily—and at midnight shared with his family a large pot of buckwheat noodles floating in chicken broth. His wife, meanwhile, was cooking all the wonderful and traditional dishes of the New Year's feast—bamboo shoots and taro, kelp neatly rolled and tied, spicily flavored burdock root, shrimp, a lobster if she could afford it, whole red snapper grilled after it had been trussed to make it look as if it were alive and flipping off the platter, filet of raw tuna and seabass, salted herring roe soaked in soy sauce, fried soybean cake, black beans and chestnuts, fishcakes, vinegar-flavored rice wrapped like a jelly roll in sheets of seaweed, and *mochi*—rice pounded into a glutinous mass and shaped into little buns. City people bought their *mochi* in the stores. Country folks gathered a few days before New Year's in gay, boisterous *mochi*-making parties not unlike husking bees in early America.

Early on New Year's Day—it would not do to linger in bed, for what one did on January 1 set the pattern for the rest of the year—the *Issei* man of the house would don his best suit and pay formal calls on his employer, his neighbors and friends. He followed an age-old ritual, bowing deeply, repeating the prescribed phrases: "*Akemashite omedeto gozaimasu*: Happy New Year. I am much indebted to you for your many favors the past year. I ask your benevolence once again this coming year." Then, with the host and hostess apologizing profusely for the "untasty, miserably prepared, unworthy food," he would be invited to sample the feast laid out in colorful array on huge platters. He could not tarry long. There were many calls to be made, and he had to hurry home to receive guests, too. In the afternoon the whole family might visit relatives or particularly close friends, gorge themselves, reminisce, play Japanese games.

As the years slipped by, the reminiscences about Japan grew less frequent; in their stead stories about adventures and amusing times in America in the earliest years were told with pride and relish as the

Nisei listened in fascination. Memories grew mellow, the loneliness and pain and frustration, the humiliation of being denied service in public accommodations and of being relegated to "Nigger heaven" in the movie theaters, could be forgotten on happy occasions. They even laughed when they told about being stoned and beaten by hooligans on the street just because they were Japanese, and many men related stories like these because it was a common occurrence. But they laughed even harder when they recalled how a self-appointed squad of young *Issei* judo experts turned the tables on the roughnecks, prowling the alleys and backstreets and inviting attack, to which they retaliated with wondrous swiftness and dispatch so that in time the toughs came to associate judo with Japanese and left even the scrawniest specimen alone. And because their bellies were comfortably full, they could remember without pain how they had drooled in front of bakeries, torturing themselves with the aroma of cakes and cookies they couldn't afford to buy, and how they would slip into a restaurant booth to order a cup of coffee and then sprinkle sugar on the bread that was on every table and take these "sandwiches" outside to ease the pain of hunger

Because of their *Nisei* children, the families found themselves celebrating Christmas, Thanksgiving and the Fourth of July with gusto comparable to that of the New Year festivities. But nothing quite replaced New Year's. If he owned a business, the *Issei* kept the doors closed at least three days, and New Year parties were celebrated throughout January and sometimes even into February. The most important of these were staged by the *Kenjin-kai*, an association made up of people from the same prefecture. A *kenjin*, someone from one's own native prefecture, was almost like a blood brother even if he were a stranger—to be fostered, assisted when in trouble, to be trusted, tolerated, and to be treated gently and affectionately. Whenever possible, one took his business to a *kenjin*. An insurance agent born in Hiroshima or Okayama or Yamaguchi Prefecture, which had sent many *kenjin* to the States, was more likely to be successful than one from a prefecture that had exported few immigrants. People from other *ken* were Japanese, all right, but still they were considered a wee bit different from one's own kind, and various characteristics were attributed to the people of each prefecture. For example, Hiroshima people were said to be industrious and tight-fisted; Wakayama people aggressive and hot-tempered; Tokyoites generous, people from Kumamoto stubborn, Okayama shrewd and clever, the northern provinces patient as a result of their long, cold winters.

A *Kenjin-kai* New Year's party was like a clan reunion at which feasting, singing of ancient ballads, performances of traditional dances, and drinking (even during Prohibition years a generous supply of bootleg *sake* always seemed to be available, camouflaged discreetly by being served in teapots) helped the *Issei* to unwind and forget their pressing cares, however briefly. If the *Issei* father attended the party alone, he was given neatly packaged portions of food to take home to his family. More often, all the children went along, for these were primarily family parties and babysitters were unknown. These were customs that could be cherished and perpetuated in the cloistered security of the Little Tokyos.

The *Kenjin-kai* were also sponsors of elaborate outings each summer, with the various associations competing to see who could put on the biggest show. The young *Nisei* could appreciate these functions more than the New Year parties. The *Kenjin-kai* picnic was usually preceded by a shopping expedition on which each youngster was outfitted with a new pair of rubber-soled canvas shoes. Everyone called them tennis shoes, although few ever played tennis. The shoes, guaranteed to make even the dumpiest child a little lighter on his feet, were for the variety of footraces around a circular course marked by rope attached to posts hammered into the ground. The winners were given merchandise prizes and the also-rans were consoled with pencils and nickel tablets. It was astonishing how much loot even an unathletic family could gather in the course of a day. The picnics were also an opportunity for *Issei* mothers to assemble magnificent Japanese lunches—including fried chicken and potato salad—which were packed into treasured lacquer boxes. The food was washed down with an endless supply of free lemonade and topped off with free ice cream and watermelon. Before the Depression, several of the larger *Kenjin-kai* in Seattle customarily chartered excursion boats to take their members and their families to picnic sites on beaches across Puget Sound, no small undertaking even by today's standards.

The *Kenjin-kai* also served as welfare organizations. If a member became ill and could not work, the *Kenjin-kai* quietly offered help. When a member died, his compatriots made the funeral arrangements for the bereaved family. His friends came to the services with two or three dollars in an envelope which was dropped off at a desk set up to receive these offerings. After the funeral all those who had a part in making the arrangements would gather to enjoy a meal together, usually prepared by the ladies of the Christian church or Buddhist temple. Almost always there were enough cash offerings to pay all expenses and provide the widow with a small nest egg. In a way, these funeral offerings were like a mutual insurance policy. One paid a small premium each time a friend or *kenjin* died, knowing when his turn came, his family would be taken care of. That was the way the requirements of life and death had been met in the villages back home. Yet the bereaved family could not let such gifts go unacknowledged, even though the deceased may have been paying his "premiums" faithfully over many years. The *Issei's* sense of *on*, of obligation, required at least a token acknowledgement—a handkerchief for each person who had brought a contribution to the funeral, a tiny box of sweets, a little package of tea, and sometimes even a pound of coffee or a book of postage stamps.

These *Issei* customs, particularly in New Year parties and summer picnics, were matters the *Nisei* could understand, participate in and enjoy. But their first appreciable breach with their parents developed over language. The *Issei* who spoke English well was an exception; the linguistic problems that almost all immigrants face were complicated in this case by the total dissimilarity between Japanese and English. The fact that most *Issei* were confined to a racial ghetto where they lived, associated and did business with their own countrymen, made mastery of English largely unnecessary. The Reverend Daisuke Kitagawa, Japan-born Episcopalian minister who came to the United States in 1937, offers another explanation: "Because of his uncritical admiration for America and his neurotic desire to be able to speak English like an American, the *Issei* was overwhelmed by the tremendous difficulty of the English language—which no one can deny—and could not bring himself to speak it unless he could do so perfectly. Knowing that he could not possibly do so, he felt ashamed, and was afraid to open his mouth." Yet he could not avoid a certain absorption, and adaptation, of English to his needs.

"Oh lie," he would say when he meant "all right." "Thank you" became "sun kyu." If something went haywire, it was "waya." He said "osu mala you" when he asked his friend "what's the matter with you," and the reply might be "no guru" meaning "no good." He liked "cohee" with toast and "buttuh" for breakfast, and because he rarely had much money he ate hamburger steak which he called "hamboku stekki."

The *Nisei* had comparable trouble learning to speak Japanese adequately. As pre-schoolers many of them spoke Japanese better than English because this was the language of the family. But the Japanese they used was "baby talk," totally inappropriate and ridiculous coming from the mouths of adults or even teenagers. Professor Edward K. Strong Jr. of Stanford University, in his *The Second-Generation Japanese Problem* published in 1934, found "Japanese Americans are mastering neither language." Although he was writing about *Nisei*, he reported he "never met a Japanese who was free from accent, always used the article correctly, and did not occasionally employ the Japanese order of words in a sentence"—certainly an excessively broad evaluation based on limited observation. In ghetto type primary schools where the overwhelming percentage of pupils were of Japanese parentage—and there were many of these—Dr. Strong's observation could be applicable. However, it was the Japanese language that suffered as the *Nisei* progressed in school, wrote English, buried their noses in English language novels, read the daily English language newspapers, shouted and quarreled on the playgrounds in English, and resorted to Japanese only to communicate with their parents.

The *Issei* viewed this Americanization of their children with mixed emotions. They were proud that their offspring took so naturally to a language that they themselves were incapable of mastering. They knew their children must absorb the American culture, must be Americans, to make their way in the land of their birth. But they were also disturbed that the *Nisei* were ignoring, and in some cases rejecting, their Japanese heritage. The gradual change from Japanese-language-orientation to English-language-orientation was evidence of this change; how could one understand Japan when one could not even speak the language?

Basic to *Issei* concern was the feeling—the expectation, even the likelihood—that some day they would return to Japan with their families. Japan was still "home"; America was a temporary residence, and what would the children do if they could not read and write and speak Japanese? For most *Issei* this possible eventuality was a vague something in the distant future, and they had no way of knowing whether their decision, when the time came, would be voluntary or forced by even more oppressive legislation of the kind they had experienced. They were also acutely aware of the economic barriers ahead of their children despite their American citizenship and education. Few doors to jobs were open outside the communities. Everyone knew of older *Nisei* trained as engineers who worked in service stations, men with degrees in business administration helping run the family grocery. So *Issei* leaders pointed out that if one hoped to do business in the Japanese community, he had to know Japanese. And if he would capitalize on his knowledge of the English language and American customs to work for a Japanese trading firm, he still had to know Japanese.

Thus the *Issei* scraped up the tuition and the *Nisei* were sent to Japanese language school to learn the rudiments of this strange and difficult tongue. Until 3 p.m. the *Nisei* youngster was exposed to an education system calculated to make him as good an American as his classmates named O'Brien, Swanson, Santucci or Koblykovich. But when the bell rang and they ran off to play ball, many a *Nisei* trudged off for another hour or two of classes. . . .

Monica Stone, in her autobiographical *Nisei Daughter*, writes vividly of a *Tenchosetsu* program sponsored by the Japanese language school in Seattle, honoring the Emperor's birthday. (It is perhaps significant that the school was named *Kokugo Gakko*, meaning National Language School.) Attendance at the program was compulsory, she reports. The youngsters sat bored and uncomprehending as community leaders conducted, as solemnly and formally as a religious rite, the reading of the Imperial Rescript on Education. "We did not understand a single word of the Imperial message since it was written in a style of speech used exclusively by the Emperor," she says. Then the assembly sang the Japanese national anthem and shouted three *banzais* for the Emperor's health. She recalls that some of the older *Nisei* girls once showed up wearing hats, as was proper at an important American afternoon affair, and were loudly ordered by the chairman to bare their heads and censured for "insulting" the Son of Heaven. The *Nisei* attitude toward the entire program can be summed up in the words of a boy who exclaimed on dismissal: "Thank God that's over. Come on, Bozo, let's get going."

Chapter 9

Immigrants from the Americas, the West Indies, and the Caribbean

Not all of the immigrants who helped create the United States of America came from great distances. Mexicans are a classic example. At one time, they occupied U.S. land called the Southwest. That was before it was cut up into several North American states. The first Mexicans did not immigrate to the United States of their own free will. Mexican land and the people who occupied it were brought into the United States by force (Alvarez, 1973; Feagin, 1984). Those Mexicans suffered the experience of being aliens on their own land. Through a series of wars and conquests, the titles to property long recognized in Mexican courts were voided in U.S. courts. Other immigrants from the Americas include Canadians and peoples from Haiti, Cuba, the Dominican Republic, Central, and South America (Alers-Montalvo, 1985; Boswell & Curtis, 1984; Cardosa, 1980; Portes & Bach, 1985).

North and South

The Congressional Land Act of 1851, which required the United States to validate landownership, had the ultimate effect of making thousands of Mexicans landless. Instead of turning their backs on the

U.S. government, most Mexicans became loyal American citizens who, like the other ethnic groups similarly disestablished, died in subsequent wars to prove their loyalty (Kanellos, 1993; Meir, 1988; Telgen & Kamp, 1993). Even so, a part of their loyalty resided with Mexico as is evident in a *corrida* sung by Mexican workers in the 1920s: *An Emigrant's Farewell* tells of the anguish of a young man about to depart for the United States to work. "I bear you in my heart," he sang about Mexico, his family, and the beloved Virgin of Guadalupe. "I go sad and heavy hearted/ to suffer and endure . . ." (Fuchs, 1990, p. 110).

The area immediately north of the uppermost U.S. boundary (now Canada) has also been a source of thousands of people who became temporary or permanent workers. But often when the history of the United States is written, the contributions of Canadians are omitted. This is unfortunate because the history of the United States is complete only when we acknowledge the presence of Canadian migrants and immigrants. In many ways, the United States developed at the expense of Canada. If the immigrants discussed in the previous chapters had settled in Canada instead of the United States, North America and South America probably would have developed much differently.

While they are relatively recent migrants to the United States, Puerto Ricans have enriched American culture with contributions unique to them (Frizpatrick, 1971). Puerto Ricans' preoccupation with their island's freedom has periodically prompted mainland citizens to reevaluate their own freedom. The presence of Puerto Ricans vividly reminds North Americans that skin color is a poor determinant of a person's ethnicity. As seen in Figure 9.1, large numbers of immigrants came from Mexico, Canada, and Cuba in 1960. In 1985 and 1988, large numbers came from Mexico, the Dominican Republic, Cuba, and Jamaica.

Mexicans

Compared with their sixteenth-century neighbors, Mexicans were extremely advanced people. This is evident from the ruins of the cities of Teotihuacán, Chichén Itzá, Monte Alban, and others. At the time of the Spanish conquest, Tenochtitlán (which became Mexico City) was probably the largest and most modern city in the world. The ancient Mexicans excelled as village planners, architects, craftsmen, artists, astronomers, and warriors. In addition, they established centers of higher education and produced meaningful written works. Mexican traders (*pochteca*) traveled extensively throughout the adjacent areas

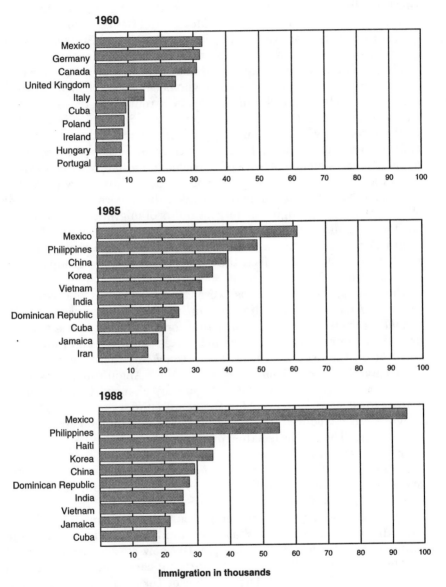

1960

1985

1988

Immigration in thousands

Source: U. S. Immigration and Naturalization Service

Figure 9.1. Major Source of Immigrants: 1960, 1985 and 1988

and spread Mexican culture as far north as California, and as far south as Nicaragua. By the 1520s the Mexican language was the common language of north and central Mexico and Central America.

Mexico was very active in what is now the United States. Particularly, Mexican miners were scattered throughout the Southwest; their mining techniques dominated until the invention of steam-powered machinery. Furthermore, Mexicans who became established in North America founded schools and opened new routes for travelers. And the new routes facilitated the discovery of gold in California which in turn altered forever the ethnic composition of the Southwest. The discovery of gold also resulted in the total transformation of the economy of California. A steady stream of Mexicans migrated from New Mexico to California to mine for gold. But it was the discovery of gold in the Sierra Nevada foothills and the end of the Mexican-United States War in 1848 that brought the largest influx of migrants. Besides looking for gold, Mexicans were hired by cattle barons in Los Angeles and Santa Barbara to take care of their herds and move their cattle to market (Pitt, 1971). In effect, they were the first large group of cowboys in America.

The first ranchers (*rancheros*) were Canary Islanders who settled in the San Antonio and Goliad areas in 1731. The success of the *rancheros* is evidenced by the fact that for a long time cattle was the only export item produced in Spanish Texas—in hides and tallow and as meat on the hoof. However, before *rancheros* there were Spanish cowboys or *vaqueros* (from *vaca*: cow). Most Anglo-Americans were unable to pronounce bah-CARE-oh, so they changed it to buckaroo. The earliest cowboys cared for the conquistadors' cattle and mustangs—both introduced into the New World by Columbus on his second voyage. The cattle fed the conquistadors and the horses helped them to conquer the natives.

In the late 1700s, there were *rodeos*, roundups of wild stock. For example, more than seven thousand wild cattle and almost two hundred wild horses were rounded up in San Antonio in 1788. As cattle, horses, sheep, and goats were being accumulated, Spanish and Mexican officials acknowledged that more land was needed for grazing animals than for farming. Consequently, new settlers were granted one labor of land (177.1 acres) for farming compared to one league (4,428.4 acres) for grazing. The Republic of Texas continued the tradition in 1836 by granting a first-class headright of one league and one labor of land to heads of families.

In the process of learning to be cowboys, Anglos adopted and adapted numerous Mexican words: *riata* became lariat, *lazo* became lasso, *chaparreros* was changed to chaps, and *espuelas* to spurs. Other words such as *patio, grande, corral, arroyo*, and *adobe* also became part of the Anglo cowboy vocabulary. Some of the more colorful lingo (*lengua*: tongue) includes vamoose (*vamos*: let's go), hoosegow (*juzgado*: court), calaboose (*calabezo*: jail), and desperado (*desesperado*: desperate one). Even the word Texas has Spanish origin (*tejas*). And, of course, the ten-gallon hat is a copy of the *tan galán* (very decorative) *sombrero* worn by the *charros* (expert horsemen). Thus Spaniards and Mexicans conquered the Southwest culturally instead of physically.

Mexican Americans

At the end of the Mexican-United States War, Mexico ceded to the United States the vast territories of California, Nevada, Utah, Arizona, and New Mexico as well as the previously annexed state of Texas. In return Mexico received $15 million, and Mexicans who chose to remain for a year in the territory that now belonged to the United States were granted citizenship. Protocol to the treaty signed by United States emissaries (according to interpretation by Mexico) guaranteed to the Mexicans land and water rights and religious and cultural integrity (Fuchs, 1990). At the time of the signing of the Treaty of Guadalupe Hidalgo in 1848, approximately seventy-five thousand Mexicans lived in the United States and almost all of them opted to become U.S. citizens.

For several years little change occurred in the newly acquired United States territories except that English became the dominant language and Mexican miners were forced out of the Sierra Nevada mines. Even so, Spanish-speaking community leaders, judges, and elected officials dominated the region until the 1870s. However, the prevailing North American Anglo attitude was that Mexican Americans were present merely to serve as cheap labor and were therefore apolitical. Interestingly, Mexican Americans were viewed as being very political by Anglos when their votes were needed to ensure the election of a local Anglo *patrón*. Then they were expected to vote. The most blatant examples of this Southwestern version of the Yankee political machine occurred in New Mexico.

The Southwest underwent considerable change after the 1870s when the railroads opened new economic opportunities in the rapidly expanding West. Also, minerals and lumber, fruits and vegetables, cattle and sheep, cotton and corn became major industries. The bulk of the people brought in to satisfy the labor needs of these new industries came from Mexico instead of Europe. Agricultural development in the Southwest was strongly encouraged by the U.S. government through the Reclamation Act of 1902, which provided funds to facilitate the construction of huge irrigation projects. This created the need for thousands of Mexican laborers in the construction of canals, dikes, and reservoirs. Thousands more were recruited to clear the deserts and prepare the soil for cultivation (Fernandez, 1977; Reisler, 1976).

Most of the early immigrants, legal and illegal, were unskilled agricultural workers. Beginning in 1821, when the Santa Fe Railroad aggressively recruited Mexican laborers to replace Anglo section hands in Arizona, the unskilled railroad labor pool throughout the United States became largely Mexicans and African Americans. Also, when Chinese immigration ended in the agricultural industry, Mexican laborers were brought in as a suitable substitute. Completion of the transcontinental railroads in 1869 immediately increased the demand for labor. Agricultural products in California could now be transported to the lucrative Eastern markets (McWilliams, 1971). In the middle 1880s, Mexican workers constituted 90 percent of the railroad labor crews. By the turn of the century, the railroad companies were still vigorously recruiting laborers in Mexico.

Several industries began using Mexican workers and, like other minority groups, they were frequently used as strikebreakers. Heeding the complaints of labor union leaders, American congressional legislators drafted state resolutions into federal bills aimed at greatly limiting the number of Mexican migrant workers. The failure of thousands of businesses in the United States and the loss of millions of jobs during the 1930s Depression made countless U.S. workers critical of all foreign workers in U.S. businesses and industries. In particular, Mexicans were perceived by white labor unions as unwanted competition (Majka & Majka, 1982).

The U.S. government's response to the economic conditions during the depression was a repatriation program which encouraged Mexicans, many of whom were actually American citizens, to consent to voluntary repatriation. The program resulted in the deportation of five hundred thousand Mexicans, mainly from Texas and California (Meier & Rivera, 1972). Growing national sentiment against cheap foreign labor was prophetic of the discrimination that would follow. The Mexican Revolution of 1910 contributed to an atmosphere of banditry and violence on both sides of the Texas-Mexico border. Rioting, lynchings, and other vigilante activities were more pronounced in the Southwest between 1848 and 1925 than in any other region of the United States. It was as if the migrants were considered fair game— it was open season on Mexicans. Anglos, or *gringos* as the Mexicans called them, openly attacked Mexicans. And the Mexicans retaliated in kind.

Discrimination and Segregation

Discrimination against Mexicans and Mexican Americans was similar to discrimination against other U.S. minority groups, particularly African Americans. The most vicious form of discrimination against Mexicans occurred in the West and Southwest. Some states permitted discrimination in public facilities such as hotels, public toilets, lunch counters and restaurants, bars, movies, recreation centers, and hospitals. Separate and unequal schools were established in many Southwest communities. In other communities children whose first language was Spanish were put in segregated classes within racially segregated schools. Segregated education and housing, coupled with discrimination in employment, isolated Mexicans and Mexican Americans from Anglo-Americans. These acts of discrimination gave the barrios added importance. They were no longer merely places to live, they had become Mexican-American havens—safe places in which to live (Paz, 1961).

At the beginning of World War II, unemployment and underemployment in Mexico were comparatively low. Even so, farm owners in the United States who needed additional laborers looked to Mexico for their workers. Unhappy with the way America handled the Mexican migrant repatriation in the 1930s, Mexico was reluctant to supply the workers. However, after Mexico declared war on the Axis powers, the United States and Mexico worked out a new bracero program in July 1942. In essence, the agreement stated that Mexican workers would not be used to replace American workers or to lower wages, and that Mexican laborers would receive minimum guarantees on wages and working conditions. Braceros were essentially limited to the agricultural sector labor market. And although they were free from the draft, they also were unable to join labor unions and therefore they earned less than an average of $500 per year each in wartime wages (Fuchs, 1990).

When job opportunities increased in the cities, many migrant Mexican workers took them. However, almost all the jobs in cities available to them were menial labor. The low wages paid for such work forced the newcomers to accept cheap housing which for the most part was racially segregated (De La Garza, et al. 1984). Mexicans found themselves living in close proximity to African Americans, with whom they became lumped socially. It is ironic that during World War II Mexican Americans earned proportionately more citations in combat than any other ethnic group but, again like African Americans, they were subjected to physical abuse at home. Several incidences of racial discrimination against Mexican Americans made local and national newspaper headlines. In La Junta, Colorado, a Mexican-American soldier who was a decorated war hero was refused service in a night-club. During the fight which followed, the soldier was killed. No one was indicted nor did the proprietor lose his liquor license. But the most graphic examples of discrimination were the zoot suit riots and the Sleepy Lagoon case, both in Los Angeles.

The zoot suit was a popular style of clothing worn by many Mexican Americans and African Americans. The clothing was popularized by Mexican youths—baggy trousers, long draped jackets, wide-brimmed hats, and a long key chain. Zoot suiters often sported tattoos and ducktail haircuts. On June 3, 1943, looking for zoot suiters to beat up, two hundred Anglo citizens cruised in taxis throughout downtown Los Angeles and the Mexican-American section of Los Angeles. The police did nothing to prevent the violence. To the contrary, forty-four severely beaten Mexican-American youths, who had unsuccessfully tried to defend themselves against their assailants, were arrested. A negative image emerged that reinforced a racial stereotype: Mexicans were prone to violence. The zoot suit riots set the tone for some rather harsh feelings in the *barrios* against Anglos. Equally important, the incidents made it more difficult for Mexican Americans to receive equal treatment under the law, whether in the courts or on the streets (Morales, 1972).

The Sleepy Lagoon case involved the murder of a young Mexican American in an abandoned gravel pit. He was apparently slain in an altercation between gangs on the night of August 2, 1942. Newspapers sensationalized the death as part of a Mexican-American crime wave. The police, with the stealth and determination of avengers, reacted with a mass roundup of suspects. They arrested twenty-four young Mexican-American men for the murder and subsequently indicted seventeen of them. The suspects were beaten by police officers and forced to appear disheveled in court. All of the suspects were convicted despite the lack of any tangible evidence against them. In fact, it was a blatant case of reasonable doubt. The convictions were reversed on appeal but bitterness remained between Los Angeles law enforcement officers and Mexican-American citizens (Daniels, 1990).

Those incidences of discrimination, segregation, and violence occurred at a time when Mexican Americans had served the United States honorably. The three hundred thousand Mexican Americans in the armed forces greatly overrepresented their population in both casualties and medals. For example, eleven Mexican Americans received the Congressional Medal of Honor. While they encountered little discrimination in the armed forces, Mexican-American GIs received little positive recognition back home. Similar to other ethnic minorities, they were not as welcome on the streets of America as they had been on the battlefields abroad.

Despite the enactment of the Immigration Reform Act of 1986, which imposed severe employer sanctions for hiring undocumented aliens, the number of undocumented Mexican aliens was approximately two million to four million in the 1980s. A growing Chicano movement of alienation from North American life and a return to traditional values characterizes a growing minority of Mexicans and Mexican Americans. Reconciliation with Anglos is problematic because Chicano history began in conflict, conquest, and subordination. Although Mexicans in the U.S. territories were granted citizenship at the end of the nineteenth century, many of their descendants have remained second-class citizens and part of the dispossessed in American history.

Other Contributions

Until recently, most U.S. history books did not mention the early cultural contributions of Mexican Americans. Instead, they would sometimes mention a few contemporary Mexican Americans such as Carlos Castañeda, anthropologist and writer; Lee Trevino, golfer; community organizers César Chávez, Rodolfo Gonzáles, and Reies López Tijerina; and politicians Jerry Apodaca and Raúl Castro. The accomplishments of these individuals were made possible by the achievements of their ancestors. For example, it is significant to note that Tomás Sánchez founded Laredo, Texas, in 1761. His grandson, Benavides Sánchez, was commissioned captain of a Texas Ranger company in 1861, and he served as a brigadier general in the Confederate army. Jose Villarreal made extensive studies of South Texas animals. Luisa García sent her children to the first English-speaking school in California. Her husband, Manuel, was the U.S. consul of Tepic, Mexico. Romulado Rachero was the state treasurer of California from 1863 to 1867; he was lieutenant governor from 1877 to 1883; and he was minister of the Central American States in 1890. Miguel Antonio Otero was the territorial governor of New Mexico from 1897 to 1906. Octavio Larrazolo was governor of New Mexico from 1918 to 1922, and a U.S. senator from 1928 to 1930.

Camelo Tranchese, a Jesuit activist, helped organize four thousand San Antonio Mexican pecan shellers who carried out strikes to protest wage cuts and deplorable working conditions between 1933 and 1936. He was also an advocate for migrant workers in Oklahoma, Arkansas, Michigan, and parts of Texas. Emma Tennayuca, a pecan sheller in the San Antonio area, was a successful labor activist during the 1930s, but eventually her Communist party affiliation led to her downfall as a leader. The earliest Mexican-American organizations were the forerunners of today's Chicano activist groups, a movement that evolved during the 1960s. The name Chicano was adopted to indicate Mexican allegiance and political activism. The movement encourages Mexican community activities, ethnicity, and political militancy; it rejects assimilation; it supports the goal of self-determination (Meier & Rivera, 1988).

Octavio Paz achieved fame as a world-renowned philosopher and poet and received the Nobel Prize in literature in 1990. Diego Rivera is the most prominent painter of the modern Mexican mural movement; his work still graces the walls of some of Mexico's most imposing buildings. Bert Corona was a nationally known Congress of Industrial Organization (CIO) union organizer in Southern California between 1936 and 1942. Indeed, Mexicans and Mexican Americans have played an important role in the development of America's culture. Waldo Frank was a very insightful commentator when he said, "We all go forth to seek America. And in the seeking we create her. And in the quality of our search shall be the nature of the America we create" (Seller quoting Frank, 1977, title page).

The Spanish-language professional theater in the United States began as early as 1789, when a three-act play, *Astucias por heredar un sobrino a su tío (The Clever Acts of a Nephew in Order to Inherit His Uncle's Wealth)*, toured through California. In 1848, Don Antonio Coronel, who later became mayor of Los Angeles, built a 300-seat theater as an addition to his house. Other prominent early Hispanic theaters that produced both Spanish- and English-language productions include Vicente Guerrero's Union Theater (1852–54), Abel Stearn's Hall (1859–75), and Juan Temple's theater (1859–92). Authors José Zorrilla, Manuel Bretón de los Herreros, and Mariana José de Larra wrote many of the melodramas performed by touring theater companies. Gerardo López del Castillo and his wife, Amalia Estrella del Castillo, were among the best performers in California in the 1860s. Years later, in the 1920s and 1930s, Eduardo Carrillo, Antonio Guzmán Aguilera, Gabriel Navarro, and Adalberto Elías Gonzalez established their credentials as playwrights.

Contemporary playwrights include Leonardo García Astol, Carlos Morton, and Rafael Trujillo Herrera. Manuel Noriega was the first Hispanic director and impresario to establish, rent, and buy theaters in New York. In 1919, in partnership with several persons, he opened the first Spanish-language theater in New York. Luis Valdez is considered the "father of Chicano theater." Anthony Quinn, an acclaimed actor, won two Academy Awards (1952 and 1956). Carmen Zapata, actress and producer, founded the Bilingual Foundation for the Arts in Los Angeles. Edward James Olmos is an outstanding actor, singer, and producer. One of the first Hispanic actors to have a leading role in a long-lasting television dramatic series ("Miami Vice"), he received a Los Angeles Drama Critics Circle Award and an Emmy for Best Supporting Actor.

Luis Walter Alvarez, an experimental physicist, is a pioneer in particle physics, geophysics, air navigation, television optics, and astrophysics. Another Mexican-American physicist, Alberto Vinicio made significant contributions to research in x-ray radiation, optics, and microsopy. Mary Janet M. Cárdenas is a renowned biochemist. Carlos Ernesto García (mechanical engineer), Elma González (cell biologist), Paul González (physiologist), and Héctor Rolando Nava-Villarreal (oncologist) have made important contributions in science.

Richard Alonzo González ("Pancho" González), Lee Trevino, and Nancy López are three of the best known Mexican-American athletes. In 1948, González won the U.S. tennis singles championship at Forest Hills, New York, and he played on the U.S. Davis Cup team. An International Tennis Hall of Fame inductee, he was the world singles tennis champion from 1954 to 1962. In 1968, Trevino won the U.S. Golf Open, and became the first player in history to shoot all four rounds under par. His many Professional Golf Association victories resulted in his being elected to the Texas Sports, American Golf, and World Golf Halls of Fame. López, Ladies Professional Golf Association player, has received numerous awards, including Rookie of the Year, Player of the Year, Golfer of the Year, and Female Athlete of the Year.

Canadian Americans

At the end of the nineteenth century, the United States and Canada were being settled by people who crisscrossed the forty-ninth degree of latitude, an artificial boundary line ignored by land seekers who gave little thought to political or legal jurisdiction. For several decades, Canada and the United States shared the most undefended border between any two sovereign nations in the world (Cuddy, 1982). Most of the settlers tended to follow the same beaten paths or marked trails as they made their way across the United States and Canada, which resulted in population clusters of Canadians in the United States. The eastern half of Lake Erie had several Canadian and American settlements. The upper lakes were well traveled by Irish immigrants who landed in Montreal and proceeded up the Saint Lawrence River, and the Germans disembarked in New York and followed the route of the Hudson River and Lake Erie to Canada.

Prior to that time, approximately twenty thousand British loyalists, who lived in the American colonies during the American Revolution, fled to Canada, primarily to Nova Scotia. Some of the loyalists took their slaves with them to Canada, but the institution of slavery was short-lived in the upper provinces. A 1793 Canadian law prohibited future introduction of slaves and provided for the gradual emancipation of those who were in bondage. Furthermore, slaves who escaped to Canada were beyond the jurisdiction of American states that had fugitive slave laws. Nor were there any Canadian laws which restricted the economic and social activities of emancipated slaves. Canada therefore became a desirable home for both refugee slaves and freed Africans. In fact, the Canadian government allocated land to freed Africans and, in 1833, the Parliament decreed that no slave could be extradited to the United States except for murder, larceny, or similar crimes. Settlements scattered along the Great Lakes—eastward from Detroit along the edge of Lake Erie—became the destinations of the underground railroad for fugitive American slaves.

The Beginning of Mass Migrations

Political rebellions occurred in the upper and lower Canadian Provinces in 1837 and 1839. The executive branch of the Canadian government disregarded the representative branch in matters pertaining to land reform, business monopoly, and education. In Lower Canada, the French-speaking citizens and the English-speaking citizens, who dominated them politically and economically, were divided culturally. A repressive policy of punishing political dissenters drove many French-speaking Canadians across the border to the United States. Some of the political refugees used the United States as a base for confronting government officials back home. A few of them even organized unsuccessful raids and demonstrations aimed at overthrowing the Canadian government. Despite a partial amnesty in 1843 and a general amnesty in 1849, few political refugees returned to Canada.

An economic depression in 1837 was more important than repressive political policies in inducing emigration from Canada. During the depression, all plans for government public improvement projects were terminated; shipbuilding was at a standstill, and the influx of immigrants dropped to a mere trickle. The departure of native-born Canadians was further encouraged by a false rumor that the U.S. government was setting aside large tracts of land for people willing to become American citizens. In 1838, several hundred Canadians a week crossed the Niagara River into New York. A similar number may have migrated to Detroit. Thousands of Canadians were involved in settling the West. Many other Canadians found jobs in logging and lumbering on the Great Lakes.

The interplay of population was so natural on the North American scene that it constituted perhaps the largest reciprocity in international migration in history (Gates, 1934; Hanson, 1940). Beginning in 1837, the demand for laborers in New England mill towns and railroad camps drew large numbers of French Canadians. Canadians were also hired as farm workers in New Hampshire and Vermont. Others found jobs in the industrial centers of Massachusetts and Rhode Island. Still others were employed as laborers in brickyards throughout the Midwest.

During the Civil War in the United States, there was very little emigration from Canada to the United States but things changed dramatically after the war. The new wave of Canadians was not directed toward any particular region or industry. They found jobs in fishing, lumbering, and manufacturing in the East; and agriculture and commerce in the West. The only distinguishing features of the Canadian immigrants were found among French Canadians, whose French language and Catholic religion set them apart from their Protestant neighbors. Few of the first-generation French Canadians opted to be anglicized. Conversely, because the Protestant Canadians were already anglicized, they were highly mobile and they readily moved wherever their labor was needed. French Canadians migrated mostly to New England. This migration was unique in another aspect: the French Canadians were the only ethnic group whose migration was mainly by rail (Daniels, 1990).

Contributions

Canadian Americans have made numerous contributions to the development of the United States—contributions that are best measured in terms of mass activities rather than individual achievements. Canadian immigrants and their descendants worked in the industries in New England, cleared forests in Michigan and Wisconsin, established farms in the Mississippi valley, helped organize and operate a network of transcontinental railroads whose center was Chicago, and were among the builders of towns and cities from the Atlantic Ocean to the Pacific Ocean. Canadians and Canadian Americans have done exceptionally well in the United States in business, education, science, and entertainment. John Kenneth Galbraith, a renowned economist, was born in Canada. Three Nobel Prize winners in chemistry were Canadians: John Polanyi (1986), Henry Taube (1983), and Gerhard Herzberg (1971). The list of prominent Canadian-American scientists includes Frances Kelsey of the U.S. Food and Drug Administration, who kept thalidomide out of circulation in the United States. Many Hollywood directors, writers, dancers and actors came from Canada, including Walter Pidgeon, Glenn Ford, Rich Little, Mary Pickford, Norma Shearer, Raymond Burr, Allan Blye, and Ron Clark. Gordie Howe and Bobby Orr were premier hockey players.

Puerto Ricans

The eighteenth century was the beginning of a modern Puerto Rican society. Commerce was expanded and the cultivation of coffee had begun. A phenomenal population growth occurred between 1765 and 1800. In 1765, the population was 44,883. It increased to 70,000 by 1776, and in 1800 it was 155,426. By that time, the Puerto Rican economy was dominated by sugarcane, tobacco, cotton, and coffee. When the United States gained control of Puerto Rico, after the Spanish-American War in 1898, it acquired an island that had too many people and too few job opportunities. But it was not until the 1917 Jones Act that Puerto Ricans were made American citizens. That set in motion a mass migration between Puerto Rico and the United States.

Migration and Migrants

There were about 1,500 Puerto Ricans in the continental United States in 1910; there were over 12,000 in 1920; there were 53,000 in 1930; and in 1940 there were 70,000 (Maldono-Denis, 1980). In 1950, there were 300,000 Puerto Ricans on the mainland—90 percent of them residing in New York City. The first Puerto Rican migrants were political exiles who came to escape the island's Spanish dictatorship. Labor shortages in the postwar United States served as a pull factor for Puerto Ricans who migrated to the mainland. Other factors were the high rate of unemployment in Puerto Rico, the postwar economic boom in the United States, less stringent immigration laws passed by Congress, and the Puerto Rican government's encouragement of widespread migration to the United States as an escape valve for surplus population (Maldono-Dennis, 1980; Stevens-Arroyo & Diaz-Ramirez, 1982).

The early Puerto Rican migrants consisted mainly of urban dwellers from San Juan and Ponce, Puerto Rico's two largest cities. Although most of them settled in New York City, farm workers from

Puerto Rican rural areas spread throughout the rural areas of New Jersey, New York, Michigan, and Pennsylvania. They were frequently used to replace Mexicans and Mexican-American migrant farm workers in seasonal, low-paying jobs. Wherever they settled in the United States, Puerto Ricans tended to be viewed as foreigners. Life on the mainland was considerably different from that on the island. Traditional Puerto Rican values and lifestyles clashed with mainland American values and lifestyles, which frequently changed.

Color was an alienating aspect of the mainland to Puerto Ricans. They found themselves caught in a black-white social status dichotomy, where light skin was equated with high social status and dark skin was equated with low social status. Discrimination based on skin color was less severe in Puerto Rico. Although there was less emphasis on color discrimination in Puerto Rico, white skin was more desirable there too. But poor whites and poor blacks mixed freely and intermarriage between people of black and white skin pigmentation was commonplace in Puerto Rico. On the mainland, however, dark-skinned Puerto Ricans were treated like black Americans, whether or not they wished to be perceived that way. Culturally, they were neither black nor white. Puerto Ricans are a distinctive group of Americans who are endowed with an ancient and diverse heritage. As is true of Mexican Americans, they represent a fusion of aborigine, Spanish, and African heritages.

Contributions

Many of the Puerto Rican contributions to the United States have been as a pool of unskilled laborers who filled the void left by earlier immigrants as they moved up the social and economic ladders. Individual contributions have been made by people such as Francisco Gonzalos Marín, publisher of a newspaper called *El Postillon*. He published the newspaper in New York after it had been suppressed in Puerto Rico. Santiago Iglesias, founder of Puerto Rico's Socialist Party, is one of the leaders who never stopped fighting for independence. Luis Muñoz Marín was the first governor elected by the people of Puerto Rico. Another prominent Puerto Rican was Ramón Emeterio Betances, who organized Puerto Rico's first attempt at establishing an independent republic. Albizu Campos was a renowned nationalist leader.

Miriam Colón is considered by many writers as the "first lady of Hispanic theater" in New York. She founded the Puerto Rican Traveling Theater. Juan Nadal de Santa Coloma was a leading actor, singer, director, and impresario. José Ferrer achieved excellence as an actor and director in plays and movies. His awards include the Gold Medal from the American Academy of Arts and Sciences (1949) and the Academy Award for Best Actor (1950). José Enamorado Cuesta and Franca de Armiño (a pseudonym) were two of the first Puerto Rican playwrights on the mainland to achieve fame. Enamorado Cuesta wrote *El pueblo en marcha* (*The People on the March*). De Armiño wrote *Los hipocritas* (*The Hypocrites*). Gonzalo O'Neill is best known for writing *Bajo una sola bandera* (*Under Just One Flag*).

Raúl Juliá, one of the most popular stage and screen actors in the United States, received four Tony Award nominations. René Marqués was Puerto Rico's foremost playwright and writer of short fiction. He achieved international fame. Rita Moreno (Rosita Dolores Alverio), an outstanding actress, won an Oscar for Best Supporting Actress, a Grammy, a Tony, and two Emmy awards. Miguel Piñero was a famous dramatic actor. Martina Arroya and Justino Diaz were successful opera singers.

Puerto Ricans have made numerous scientific contributions in various fields, including José Ramón Alcalá (discovered the first clear delineation of the protein composition of lens fiber plasma membranes), César Cáceres (improvements in electrocardiography and computers in medicine), Guillermo Cintrón (heart disease researcher), Teresa Mercado (research in parasitic diseases, especially malaria and typonosomiases), Margarita Silva-Hunter (research in morphology, taxonomy, and biology of pathogenic fungi), and Gladys Torres-Blasini (research in bacteriology).

Among the renowned Puerto Rican athletes are Roberto Clemente and Orlando Cepeda (baseball); Angel Cordero (horse racing); Carlos Ortiz, Jose Luis Torres, and Sixto Escobar (boxing). Escobar was the first Puerto Rican to win a world championship.

Cubans

On February 15, 1898, the U.S. battleship *Maine*, on a friendly visit, was mysteriously blown up in Havana harbor and 260 U.S. sailors were killed. That provoked war between the United States and Spain. The ensuing Spanish-American War was short and decisive. On August 12, 1898, a peace agreement was signed ending hostilities. Spain gave up its claim to Cuba and withdrew from the island. Based on the 1898 treaty, the United States established its trusteeship over Cuba, which lasted nearly two years. While the United States occupied Cuba, it helped to prepare the Cuban people for eventual self-government. On May 20, 1902, the United States turned the island over to the newly elected administration of Tomás Estrada Palma and the Republic of Cuba was established.

Refugees

The first large wave of Cuban refugees were called the "golden exiles" because they were members of the upper economic class. Sixty-four percent of them had held white-collar positions; 31 percent left professional-managerial jobs and 33 percent had held clerical-sales positions (Fagen et al., 1968; Kunz, 1973). Their departure constituted a Cuban brain drain. The 1962 Cuban missile crisis caused an additional decrease in Cuba's population. Most of the refugees who immigrated to the United States between 1962 and 1965 used various methods of subterfuge to leave. For example, some of them went to Mexico or Spain and then to the United States. In 1965, the United States and Cuba signed an agreement allowing refugees to be airlifted to Miami. Two daily "freedom flights" brought more than 340,000 refugees to the United States between 1965 and 1973 (Pedraza-Bailey, 1985). The *Mariel* boat lift in 1980 brought the last significant flow of Cuban refugees. During the five-month period between May and September 1980, one hundred twenty-five thousand refugees arrived. A large number of them were detained in U.S. government camps because they were suspected of being mental patients or convicts (Boswell & Curtis, 1984; Portes & Bach, 1985).

Contributions

Like all recent immigrants to the United States, Cubans and Cuban Americans have not had much time to compile a long list of cultural contributions. But they have some notable achievements. Tomás Estrada Palma, from his exile in New York City, proclaimed Cuba an independent republic. He was inspired by the passion of poet-warrior José Martí and the patriot guerrillas who championed the revolutionary movement. Led by Marti, Máximo Gómez, Antonio Maceo, and Calixto Garcia Iniquez, Cuba gained its freedom on January 1, 1898, when the Spanish government authorized the directorship of Marshal Ramón Blanco y Erenas. In 1902, under the newly elected administration of Estrada Palma, the Republic of Cuba came into being. General José Miguel Gómez was elected president and assumed office on January 28, 1909. Despite frequent revolts and internal political upheavals, he completed his term of office. So too did General Mario Garcia Menocal who replaced Gómez. After General Gerardo Machado y Morales took office in 1925, progress was made toward greater Cuban participation in its own industries and development.

Iván Acosta gained fame as a playwright. His play *Elsuper* (*The Super*) is often cited by critics as the most successful Hispanic play produced in an ethnic theater house. Manuel Alberto O'Farrill was an accomplished actor. Aparicio was an outstanding actor and director. Contemporary Cuban exile playwrights in the United States include Julio Matas, José Cid Pérez, Celedonio Gonzáles, Matias Montes Huidobro, Leopoldo Hernández Raúl de Cardenas, and Miguel González Pando. Beatriz Escalona (La Chata Noloesca) was one of the greatest Hispanic stage performers. Maria Irene Fornés has had more than thirty plays produced.

Famous Cuban-American actors include Mel Ferrer (Melchior Gastón Ferrer), who also achieved success as a director and producer of movies. César Romero played the Cisco Kid in the Hollywood films from the 1930s until the early 1940s. He also starred in several other films. Desi Arnaz (Desidero Alberto Arnaz y de Acha III) started as an actor-musician and built a multimillion-dollar production company.

Prominent Cuban-American scientists include Michael Louis Ibáñez, a pathologist who conducted cancer research; Diana Montes de Oca López, a microbiologist whose research focuses on tumor immunology, cell kinetics, and viral oncogenesis; Fausto Ramírez, an organic chemist who was awarded the Cresy-Morrison Award from the New York Academy of Sciences in 1968 and the Silver Medal of the City of Paris in 1969 for his research of phosphorus and sulfur compounds; and Aída Soto, an organic chemist whose research is in clinical enzymology and the use of immunologic techniques in chemistry.

Among prominent Cuban athletes are José Méndez, an outstanding baseball pitcher and infielder in the Negro National League from 1908 until 1926; Pedro "Tony" Oliva, an outfielder and the only player to win batting championships during his first two major league seasons; and Alberto Bauduy Salazar, track and field star, who set distance race records. Salazar also won New York and Boston marathons.

Dominicans

In November 1916, the United States proclaimed that the Dominican Republic was under U.S. military administration, and President Woodrow Wilson sent forces to occupy the island. Shortly thereafter the Dominican congress was suspended and the United States, under leadership of Captain Harry Knapp, assumed virtually dictatorial powers. However, American occupation brought about material improvements and reforms: roads were constructed, sanitary conditions were improved, educational opportunities were advanced, and public finances were placed on a more sound footing. But none of this erased the Dominican resentment against the harshness of military rule. In September 1924, American occupation forces were recalled, a new Dominican constitution was adopted, and General Horacio Vasquez was elected president. In 1930, Rafael Trujillo was elected president and he ruled the country until May 1961.

Immigration Patterns

Most early Dominican immigrants and illegal aliens clustered in the urban areas of the Northeast, in Florida, and in Puerto Rico. Similar to many European immigrants, the Dominican migration occurred in a family-connected sequence. Often young male family members immigrated to the United States and, when they became financially able, obtained immigrant visas for other family members. The Dominican newcomers to the United States during the first half of the twentieth century settled almost entirely in fairly circumscribed New York City culture enclaves. And they consisted of both urban and rural people.

Most rural immigrants came with little education and few job skills. As a whole, they entered the labor force in jobs such as unskilled restaurant workers, laborers in clothing manufacturing, assembly-line workers, and janitors. Also, they retained a strong interest in Dominican politics. Identity with their homeland was facilitated by the proximity of the Dominican Republic to the United States and immigration laws that made it easy to have family reunions. This slowed Dominican acculturation to the dominant English-speaking society of the United States. The Catholic Church is the one institution in the United States in which the majority of Dominicans have historically participated.

The most dramatic change brought about by the Dominicans' immigration to the United States occurred in the lives of women, the largest group of Dominican immigrants to come to New York City (Pessar, 1987). When they started working outside the home, the traditional female subordinate role was altered. Also, when they achieved status as wage earners, the women tended to lose the desire to permanently return to the Dominican Republic where there was considerably less freedom for them. In terms of occupations, most of the Dominican female immigrants worked as semiskilled operatives, service workers, and unskilled nonfarm laborers. Further, there was a large concentration of Dominican women workers in the garment industry. In 1981, 61 percent of the Dominican women in the New York labor force worked in manufacturing, and 42 percent of them were employed in the garment industry (Gurzak & Kritz, 1982). They provided the labor resources New York needed to maintain a competitive edge against foreign markets (Waldinger, 1985).

Contributions

The Dominican Republic is the seat of the oldest European culture in the Americas and its citizens have made some of their contributions to the United States. A society organized and headed by Edna Garrido studied and collected much of the Dominican folk music, most of which reflects strong African influences. Among some of the best known writers of the Dominican Republic are Pedro Henríquez-Ureña and Max Henríquez-Ureña, two of the most distinguished writers and thinkers of Latin America. Pedro worked with José Vasconelos, the well known Mexican writer and philosopher. He was the director of the Institute of Philology at the University of Buenos Aires. In 1941, he gave a series of lectures at Harvard University. His lectures are in a book entitled *Literary Currents in Hispanic America*. He also wrote *Historia de la Cultura en la America Hispana*, a general history of Latin American culture. Pedro taught in the United States and throughout Latin America. Other Dominican writers include Gastón Fernando Deligne, a modernist often called the "national Dominican poet"; Fabio Fiallo, author of ethereal love lyrics; Manuel de Jesús Galván, author of *Enriquillo*, a historical novel based on an early Indian revolt against the Spaniards; and Menel del Cabral, a versatile poet who has written much literature with strong African overtones. Oscar de la Renta, a world-renowned fashion designer and perfumer, is a Dominican. Dominicans who achieved success in baseball include Juan Marichal, César Cedeno, Manny Mota, Rico Carty, César Geronimo, and the Alou brothers—Matty, Felipe, and Jesus.

Jamaicans

Through the 1970s and the 1980s, several thousand Jamaicans immigrated to the United States. A large percentage of them settled in the New York City metropolitan area. Some of the streets in Brooklyn were changed into bustling extensions of Kingston, Jamaica (Buckley, 1974). Along with other West Indians, Jamaicans superimposed their culture on the new surroundings. Yet the Jamaican immigrants were profoundly affected by both race and ethnic relations in the United States. They were identified by white New Yorkers as blacks and thus they shared a racial identification with African Americans, which is a salient point in understanding the Jamaican North American immigration experience (Foner, 1987).

There are a number of factors that precipitated the mass emigration from Jamaica to the United States. Some of those factors were a population that was too large for the available job opportunities; the domination of the island's economy by plantation agriculture; and since independence in 1962, continued dependency on neocolonial powers and multinational corporations. Additionally, there was unequal land distribution and the jobs that were available frequently were only part-time work with low earnings and no prospects for advancement. So oppressive were these conditions that a national opinion poll conducted in 1977 showed that 60 percent of Jamaicans would have immigrated to the United States if they had the opportunity (Palmer, 1974; Stone, 1982).

The 1965 Immigration and Nationality Act eliminated the small quota assigned to the West Indies and that, in turn, opened the door for a patterned mass migration: One migrant would come first and then exert pressure on his or her significant others, mainly family members, to follow. The presence of relatives and friends and the growing West Indian neighborhoods in the United States were important inducements in making New York the city of first choice for West Indies immigrants.

Contributions

Joel A. Rogers was one of the first black historians in the United States. His publications were challenged by other historians in terms of accuracy regarding the contributions of blacks throughout the world. His books include *From Superman to Man* (1917), *World's Greatest Men of African Descent* (1931), and *World's Greatest Men of Color* (1947). Marcus (Mosiah) Garvey, orator and black nationalist, was another prominent Jamaican. In 1914, he founded the Universal Negro Improvement and Conservation Association and African Communities League (UNIA), an organization that promoted social pride, education, and businesses for black Americans. It also encouraged black emigration to Africa. Thus Garvey could be called the "father of the black power movement" in the United States. Harry Belafonte Jr., a contemporary Jamaican, has achieved success as a singer, civil rights activist, actor, and composer. He introduced American audiences to West Indian and African music and musicians.

Haitians

While Haitian immigration to the United States is generally perceived to be a very recent phenomenon, actually it dates back to the eighteenth century. French colonists and freed mulattoes fled with their slaves the revolutionary debacle of Saint-Dominque (Haiti's colonial name) in the late 1790s and formed colonies along the Ameri-

can Eastern seaboard. Although Haitians immigrated sporadically to
the United States during the nineteenth century, no significant immigration occurred during that period because racial discrimination pre-
vailed in the United States (Souffrant, 1974). Most of the immigrants
were hard working people and proud citizens of the first black republic—descendants of Toussaint L'Ouverture. Rejecting the "minority
group" label, some Haitian mulattoes declared themselves white on
census surveys; black Haitians frequently spoke Creole or French to
each other in public or exaggerated their French accent to make sure
that they were not mistaken for African Americans. Family members
were closeknit and sustained each other through economic and emotional support.

Immigration Patterns

The number of Haitian immigrants was small before 1966, but
since then they have become one of the largest West Indian groups in
the United States. There have been four main surges of Haitian
immigration to the United States: the period of French colonization;
the period of the Haitian Revolution (1791–1803); the occupation of
Haiti by the United States (1915–34); and the rulership of the Duvaliers beginning in 1957. French colonists and their slaves were probably the first group of Haitian immigrants to the United States. They
came to Charleston County, South Carolina, to work on the rich plantations in the mid-1600s.

During the Haitian Revolution, more than fifty thousand white
planters, free blacks, and slaves came to the United States and settled in New York, Philadelphia, Norfolk, Virginia, Boston, New
Orleans, and Charleston. The third group of Haitians arrived in the
United States during the 1915–34 period when the United States
occupied the Republic of Haiti. The immigration was supported by the
U.S. government to discourage political instability that was a threat
to American investments in Haiti. About five hundred of those
migrants left Port-au-Prince and moved to Harlem in 1925. The fourth
major period of Haitian emigration commenced in 1957, when
François "Papa Doc" Duvalier was elected president of Haiti. Through
manipulation of the vote in 1964, Duvalier was elected president
for life. He died in 1971 and his son, Jean-Claude, took his place as
president—also for life. Even though the Duvaliers no longer rule, the
Haitian exodus has continued.

Port-au-Prince became a transition place for most Haitians before
immigrating (Mangin, 1967). For example, a peasant who decided to
immigrate to New York would go first to Port-au-Prince to become

accustomed to urban ways, to learn some English, to start transactions with a travel agent (who would help him with paperwork and legalities), to develop a network of contacts, and finally, to apply for an exit visa from the Haitian government and an American visa from the U.S. Consulate (Laguere, 1984). New York and Miami provided the greatest economic opportunities for the immigrants. When they returned home for a visit, they would usually relate the positive aspects of their newly adopted land in an effort to persuade family members and friends to join them. Family and kinship relationships have historically been important aspects of social organization within the Haitian community. Having relatives in the United States was crucial to the immigration process (Foner, 1987).

Unlike Cubans, who were welcomed as refugees from communism, Haitians were unwanted refugees from hunger (Daniels, 1990). One of the factors that preceded the "boat people migration" was the closing of the Cuban, Dominican, and Bahamian markets to Haitian workers (Chierici, 1991). "Emigration has been used as a safety valve in periods of crisis to allay the pressures of economic, social and political demands which threaten to blow up the system" (Fontaine, 1976, p. 126). Like most immigrants, when Haitians finally decided to leave home, they searched for the best opportunity and right time to leave in order to maximize their gains. In the early 1970s, the boat people started reaching the shores of Florida. Many of them were Haitian peasants who fled drastic rural poverty or, in some cases, the harassment of Tontons Macoutes, the secret police force of the Duvalier government. When the Creole-speaking illegal immigrants landed, they were interrogated by English-speaking officials whom they had difficulty understanding. They were often sent to jail to await eventual deportation. This has been repeated in the 1990s.

Contributions

Despite frequent rejections, Haitians have made many positive cultural contributions to the United States. One prominent Haitian émigré was a naturalist named John James Audubon. Born in Les Cayes, Saint-Dominque on April 26, 1785, he immigrated to the United States during the summer of 1803. His drawings of birds in America are still an invaluable source of information for naturalists and ornithologists (Ford, 1964). Two Haitian Americans in particular left their mark on Louisiana history. Victor Sejour, mulatto son of a Saint-Dominque émigré to New Orleans, wrote a number of plays that were presented on the stage in Paris. He became one of the secretaries of Napoleon III (Logan, 1941). Also of note was Julien Dejour, who became known for his works of charity in New Orleans. Haitian immigrants contributed to the architecture of Louisiana and South Carolina. Many of the buildings of old Charleston were constructed according to plans of immigrants from Saint-Dominque. The equally famous wrought-iron railings on many of the buildings in the Vieux Carré of New Orleans were forged by Haitian slaves (Logan, 1941).

Charles Reason was a professor belles-lettres and of French language and a professor of mathematics at the New York Central College in 1849 (Simmons, 1986). William De Florville, known as Billy the Barber, was both the personal barber and confidant of Abraham Lincoln. "Only two men in Springfield understood Lincoln, his law partner, William H. Herndon, and his barber, William De Florville" (Washington, 1942, p. 190). Several Haitians occupied positions in the Universal Negro Improvement Association (UNIA), Marcus Garvey's back-to-Africa movement. Among them were Jean-Joseph Adam, Eliézer Cadet, and Eli Garcia. Notable too is Jean-Baptiste Pointe de Sable, a trader credited with being the first permanent settler on the site of what is now Chicago. General Colin Powell, chairman of the U.S. military Joint Chiefs of Staff under Presidents George Bush and Bill Clinton, also served as a close adviser to President Ronald Reagan.

Central and South Americans

Between 1820 and 1980, more than one million immigrants from Central and South America settled in the United States. They represented a variety of national and ethnic groups, some speaking languages other than Spanish (Masud-Piloto, 1988). In 1976, the U.S. Census Bureau estimated that immigrants from Spanish-speaking Central and South American countries accounted for 7 percent of the Spanish-origin population in the United States. Immigrants from Central and South America represent different social strata, regional attachments, and ethnocultural backgrounds (Thernstrom, 1980). Four major ethnocultural groups have been identified: the descendants of the indigenous Indians; Africans and people of mixed African and Indian descent; people of European descent; and *mestizos*, people of mixed European and Indian stock.

During the nineteenth century, almost ten times as many South Americans as Central Americans came to the United States. Initially, immigrants from South America had a more balanced gender ratio than immigrants from Central America, with women initially holding only a small numerical majority over men. Later the balance tipped in favor of men. Immigrants from South America have differed somewhat in occupational characteristics from Central Americans, with a higher percentage from South America being professionals. The largest number of professionals have come from Bolivia. The largest number of immigrants have come from Argentina, Colombia, and Ecuador. Similar to Haitians, entire families have come to the United States and have clustered in urban areas, particularly in large metropolitan areas.

References

Alers-Montalvo, M. (1985). *The Puerto Rican migrants of New York City: A study of anomie.* New York: AMS Press.

Alvarez, R. (1973). *The psycho-historical and socioeconomic development of the Chicano community in the United States.* Social Science Quarterly, 53: 931–942.

Boswell, T., & Curtis, D. (1984). *The Cuban-American experience: Culture, images and perspectives.* Totowa, NJ: Rowman & Allanheld.

Cardosa, L.A. (1980). *Mexican emigration to the U.S. 1897–1931: Socioeconomic patterns.* Tucson: University of Arizona Press.

Chierici, R. M. C. (1991). *Migration and adaptation among Haitian boat people in the United States.* New York: A.M.S. Press.

Cuddy, D. L. (Ed.). (1982). *Contemporary American immigration.* Boston: Twayne.

De La Garza, A., et al. (1984). *The Mexican American experience: An interdisciplinary anthology.* Austin: University of Texas Press.

Daniels, R. (1990). *Coming to America: A history of immigration and ethnicity in American life.* New York: HarperCollins.

Fagen, R. R., Brody, R. A., & O'Leary, T. J. (1968). *Cubans in exile: Disaffection and the revolution.* Stanford: Stanford University Press.

Fernandez, R. (1977). *The United States-Mexico border: A Political-economic profile.* South Bend: University of Notre Dame Press.

Foner, N. (1987). *New immigrants in New York.* New York: Columbia University Press.

Fontaine, P. M. (1976). Haitian immigrants in Boston: A commentary. In R. S. Bryce-Laporte & D. Mortimer (Eds.), *Caribbean immigration in the United States.* Washington, D.C.: Smithsonian Institution.

Ford, A. (1964). *John James Audubon.* Norman: University of Oklahoma Press.

Frizpatrick, J. (1971). *Puerto Rican Americans: The meaning of migration to the mainland.* Englewood Cliffs, NJ: Prentice-Hall.

Fuchs, L. H. (1990). *The American kaleidoscope: Race, ethnicity and the civic culture.* Hanover, CT: University Press of New England.

Gates, P. W. (1934). Official encouragement to immigration by the provinces of Canada. *Canadian Historical Review*, March: 20–27.

Gurzak, D., & Kritz, M. (1982). *Settlement and immigration processes of Dominicans and Colombians in New York City.* Paper presented at the Annual Meeting of the American Sociological Association, San Francisco, California.

Hanson, M. L. (1940). *The mingling of the Canadian American peoples.* New Haven: Yale University Press.

Kanellos, N. (Ed.). (1993). *Reference library of Hispanic America,* 3 vols. Detroit: Gale Research.

Kunz, E. F. (1973). *The refugee in flight: Kinetic models and forms of displacement.* International Migration Review, 10: 131–35.

Laguere, M. S. (1984) *American odyssey: Haitians in New York City.* Ithaca, NY: Cornell University Press.

Logan, R. W. (1941). *The diplomatic relations of the United States with Haiti: 1776–1891.* Chapel Hill: University of North Carolina Press.

Majka, L. C., & Majka, T. U. (1982). *Farm workers agribusiness and the state.* Philadelphia: Temple University Press.

Maldono-Denis, M. (1980). *The emigration dialectic: Puerto Rico and the United States.* New York: International.

Mangin, W. (1967). *Latin American squatter settlements: A problem and a solution.* Latin American Research Review, 2(3): 65–98.

Masud-Piloto, F. R. (1988). *With open arms.* Totowa, NJ: Rowman & Littlefield.

McWilliams, C. (1971). *Getting rid of the Mexicans.* The American Mercury, March.

Meier, M. S. (1988). *Mexican American biographies: A historical dictionary, 1836–1987.* Westport, CT: Greenwood Press.

Meier, M. S. & Rivera, F. (1972). *The Chicanos.* New York: Wang & Hill.

Morales, A. (1972). *I am bleeding: A study of Mexican American police conflict.* Fairlawn, NJ: Burdick.

Palmer, R. W. (1974). A Decade of West Indian migration to the United States, 1962–1972: An economic analysis. *Social and Economic Studies,* 23: 570–76.

Paz, O. (1961). *The labyrinth of solitude: Life and thought in Mexico.* New York: Grove Press.

Pedraza-Bailey, S. (1985). *Political and economic migrants in America: Cubans and Mexicans.* Austin: University of Texas Press.

Pessar, P. R. (1987). The Dominicans: Women in the household and the garment industry. In N. Foner (Ed.), *New immigrants in New York,* New York: Columbia University Press.

Pitt, L. (1971). *The decline of the Californios: A social history of the Spanish-speaking Californians, 1846–1890.* Berkeley: University of California Press.

Portes, A., & Bach, R. L. (1985). *Latin journey: Cuban and Mexican immigrants in the United States.* Berkeley: University of California Press.

Reisler, M. (1976). *Mexican immigrant labor in the United States, 1900–1940.* Westport, CT: Greenwood Press.

Seller, M. C. (1977). *To seek America: A history of ethnic life in the United States.* New York: Ozer.

Simmons, W. J. (1986). *Men of mark: Eminent, progressive, and rising.* New York: Arno Press.

Souffrant, C. (1974). *Les Haitiens aux Etats-Unis.* Population, 2: 133–145.

Stevens-Arroyo, A. M., & Diaz-Ramirez, A. M. (1982). *Puerto Ricans in the United States: A struggle for identity.* New York: Holt, Rinehart & Winston.

Stone, C. (1982). *The political opinions of Jamaican people, 1976–1981.* Kingston: Blackett.

Telgen, R. C., & Kamp, J. (Eds.). (1993). *Notable Hispanic women.* Detroit, MI: Gale Research.

Thernstrom, S. (Ed). (1980). *Harvard encyclopedia of American ethnic groups.* Cambridge: Harvard University Press.

Waldinger, R. (1985). Immigration and industrial change in the New York apparel industry. In M. Tienda & G. Borfas (Eds.), *Hispanics in the United States economy.* New York: Academic Press.

Washington, J. E. (1942). *They knew Lincoln.* New York: Dutton.

With His Pistol In His Hand
by Américo Paredes

Most of the Border people did not live in the towns. The typical
community was the ranch or the ranching village. Here lived small,
tightly knit groups whose basic social structure was the family or the
clan. The early settlements had begun as great ranches, but succeeding generations multiplied the number of owners of each of the original land grants. The earliest practice was to divide the grant among
the original owner's children. Later many descendants simply held
the land in common, grouping their houses in small villages around
what had been the ancestral home. In time almost everyone in any
given area came to be related to everyone else.

The cohesiveness of the Border communities owed a great deal to
geography. Nuevo Santander was settled comparatively late because
of its isolated location. In 1846 it took Taylor a month to move his
troops the 160 miles from Corpus Christi to Brownsville. In 1900 communications had improved but little, and it was not until 1904 that a
railroad connected Brownsville with trans-Nueces areas, while a
paved highway did not join Matamoros with the interior of Mexico
until the 1940s.

The brush around Brownsville in the 1870s was so heavy that
herds of stolen beef or horses could be hidden a few miles from town
in perfect secrecy. Even in the late 1920s the thick chaparral isolated
many parts of the Border. Ranches and farms that are now within
sight of each other across a flat, dusty cotton land were remote in
those days of winding trails through the brush. The nearest neighbors
were across the river, and most north-bank communities were in fact
extensions of those on the south bank.

The simple pastoral life led by most Border people fostered a natural equality among men. Much has been written about the democratiz-
ing influence of a horse culture. More important was the fact that on
the Border the landowner lived and worked upon his land. There was
almost no gap between the owner and his cowhand, who often was
related to him anyway. The simplicity of the life led by both employer
and employee also helped make them feel that they were not different
kinds of men, even if one was richer than the other.

Border economy was largely self-sufficient. Corn, beans, melons,
and vegetables were planted on the fertile, easily irrigated lands at

Reprinted from *With His Pistol in His Hand: A Border Ballad and Its Hero* by Américo
Paredes, copyright © 1958, revised in 1986. By Permission of the Author and the University of Texas Press.

the river's edge. Sheep and goats were also raised in quantity. For these more menial, pedestrian tasks the peón was employed in earlier days. The peón was usually a *fuereño*, an "outsider" from central Mexico, but on the Border he was not a serf. *Peón* in Nuevo Santander had preserved much of its old meaning of "man on foot." The gap between the peón and the vaquero was not extreme, though the man on horseback had a job with more prestige, one which was considered to involve more danger and more skill.

The peón, however, could and did rise in the social scale. People along the Border who like to remember genealogies and study family trees can tell of instances in which a man came to the Border as a peon (today he would be called a *bracero*) and ended his life as a vaquero, while his son began life as a vaquero and ended it as a small landowner, and the grandson married into the old family that had employed his grandfather—the whole process taking place before the Madero Revolution. In few parts of Greater Mexico before 1910 could people of all degrees—including landowners—have circulated and obviously enjoyed the story of Juan, the peón who knew his right, and who not only outwitted his landowning employer but gave him a good beating besides, so that the landowner afterward would never hire a peón who "walked like Juan."

This is not to say that there was democracy on the Border as Americans recognize it or that the average Borderer had been influenced by eighteenth-century ideas about the rights of man. Social conduct was regulated and formal, and men lived under a patriarchal system that made them conscious of degree. The original settlements had been made on a patriarchal basis, with the "captain" of each community playing the part of father to his people.

Town life became more complex, but in rural areas the eldest member of his family remained the final authority, exercising more real power than the church or the state. There was a domestic hierarchy in which the representative of God on earth was the father. Obedience depended on custom and training rather than force, but a father's curse was thought to be the most terrible thing on earth.

A grown son with a family of his own could not smoke in his father's presence, much less talk back to him. Elder brothers and elder cousins received a corresponding respect, with the eldest brother having almost parental authority over the younger. It was disrespectful to address an older brother, especially the eldest, by his name. He was called "Brother" and addressed in the formal *usted* used for the parents. In referring to him, one mentioned him as "My Brother So-and-So," never by his name alone. The same form of address was used toward cousins-german.

Such customs are only now disappearing among some of the old

Border families. In the summer of 1954 I was present while a tough inspector of rural police questioned some suspects in a little south-bank Border town. He was sitting carelessly in his chair, smoking a cigarette, when he heard his father's voice in an outer room. The man straightened up in his chair, hurriedly threw his cigarette out the window, and fanned away the smoke with his hat before turning back to the prisoners.

If the mother was a strong character, she could very well receive the same sort of respect as the father. In his study of Juan N. Cortina, Charles W. Goldfinch recounts an incident which was far from being an isolated case. After his border-raider period Cortina was forced to abandon Texas, and he became an officer in the Mexican army. At the same time his desertion of his wife set him at odds with his mother. Later Cortina returned to the Border and was reconciled with his mother. "They met just across from her ranch on the Mexican side of the river. As they met, the son handed his mother the riding crop and, as he knelt before her, in the presence of his officers, she whipped him across the shoulders. Then the chastised son, Brigadier General Cortina, arose and embraced his mother."

These same parent-child customs formerly were applied to the community, when the community was an extended family. Decisions were made, arguments were settled, and sanctions were decided upon by the old men of the group, with the leader usually being the patriarch, the eldest son of the eldest son, so that primogeniture played its part in social organization though it did not often do so in the inheritance of property.

The patriarchal system not only made the Border community more cohesive, by emphasizing its clanlike characteristics, but it also minimized outside interference, because it allowed the community to govern itself to a great extent. If officials saw fit to appoint an *encargado* to represent the state, they usually chose the patriarch, merely giving official recognition to a choice already made by custom.

Thus the Rio Grande people lived in tight little groups—usually straddling the river—surrounded by an alien world. From the north came the *gringo*, which term meant "foreigner." From the south came the *fuereño*, or outsider, as the Mexican of the interior was called. Nuevo Santander had been settled as a way station to Texas, but there was no heavy traffic over these routes, except during wartime. Even in the larger towns the inhabitants ignored strangers for the most part, while the people of the remoter communities were oblivious of them altogether. The era of border conflict was to bring greater numbers of outsiders to the Border, but most Borderers treated them either as transients or as social excrescences. During the American

Civil War and the Mexican Empire, Matamoros became a cosmopolitan city without affecting appreciably the life of the villages and ranches around it. On the north bank it took several generations for the new English-speaking owners of the country to make an impression on the old mores. The Border Mexican simply ignored strangers, except when disturbed by violence or some other transgression of what he believed was "the right." In the wildest years of the Border, the swirl of events and the coming and going of strange faces was but froth on the surface of life.

In such closely knit groups most tasks and amusements were engaged in communally. Roundups and brandings were community projects, undertaken according to the advice of the old men. When the river was in flood, the patriarchal council decided whether the levees should be opened to irrigate the fields or whether they should be reinforced to keep the water out, and the work of levee-building or irrigation was carried out by the community as a whole. Planting and harvesting were individual for the most part, but the exchange of the best fruits of the harvest (though all raised the same things) was a usual practice. In the 1920s, when I used to spend my summers in one of the south-bank ranch communities, the communal provision of fresh beef was still a standard practice. Each family slaughtered in turn and distributed the meat among the rest, ensuring a supply of fresh beef every week.

Amusements were also communal, though the statement in no way should suggest the "dancing, singing throng" creating as a group. Group singing, in fact, was rare. The community got together, usually at the patriarch's house, to enjoy the performance of individuals, though sometimes all the individuals in a group might participate in turn.

The dance played but little part in Border folkways, though in the twentieth century the Mexicanized polka has become something very close to native folk form. Native folk dances were not produced, nor were they imported from fringe areas like southern Tamaulipas, where the *huapango* was danced. Polkas, mazurkas, waltzes, lancers, *contra-danzas*, and other forms then in vogue were preferred. Many Border families had prejudices against dancing. It brought the sexes too close together and gave rise to quarrels and bloody fights among the men. There were community dances at public spots and some private dances in the homes, usually to celebrate weddings, but the dance on the Border was a modern importation, reflecting European vogues.

Horse racing was, of course, a favorite sport among the men. In the home, amusements usually took the form of singing, the presentation of religious plays at Christmas, tableaux, and the like. This material came from oral tradition. Literacy among the old Border families was relatively high, but the reading habit of the Protestant Anglo-Saxon, fostered on a veneration of the written words in the Bible, was foreign to the Borderer. His religion was oral and traditional.

On most occasions the common amusement was singing to the accompaniment of the guitar: in the informal community gatherings, where the song alternated with the tale; at weddings, which had their own special songs, the *golondrinas,* at Christmastime, with its *pastorelas* and *aguinaldos*; and even at some kinds of funerals, those of infants, at which special songs were sung to the guitar.

The Nuevo Santander people also sang ballads. Some were songs remembered from their Spanish origins, and perhaps an occasional ballad came to them from the older frontier colony of Nuevo Mexico. But chiefly they made their own. They committed their daily affairs and their history to the ballad form: the fights against the Indians, the horse races, and the domestic triumphs and tragedies—and later the border conflicts and the civil wars. The ballads, and the tradition of ballad-making as well, were handed down from father to son, and thus the people of the Lower Rio Grande developed a truly native balladry.

It was the Treaty of Guadalupe that added the final element to Rio Grande society, a border. The river, which had been a focal point, became a dividing line. Men were expected to consider their relatives and closest neighbors, the people just across the river, as foreigners in a foreign land. A restless and acquisitive people, exercising the rights of conquest, disturbed the old ways.

Out of the conflict that arose on the new border came men like Gregorio Cortez. Legends were told about these men, and ballads were sung in their memory. And this state of affairs persisted for one hundred years after Santa Anna stormed the Alamo.

Chapter 10

Africans and African Americans

Of all the ethnic groups in the United States, African Americans have had the most unique relationship with the rest of the nation's immigrant peoples (Greene, 1974; Hawkins, 1992; Hine, 1993; Kranz, 1992; Smith, 1992). This uniqueness stems from a distinct historical and cultural pattern. Only the ancestors of present-day African Americans were brought to the New World specifically to be slaves.

Like No Others

Because it was based on racism, slavery in North America was one of the cruelest forms of human oppression recorded in history. African slaves were treated like animals instead of human beings. Slave trade merchants and shipowners frequently discussed their human cargoes in terms of the most efficient ways to deliver loads. A continuing dialogue focused on whether it was better to pack slaves loosely in the holds of the ships in order that more might survive the rugged voyage, or to pack them tightly and hope that the greater number would make up for the deaths en route to America. Both loose and tight packers chained their cargoes to the floors of the hold, which provided only two or three feet of headroom, little air, and no sanitary facilities. Disease and sickness were commonplace during the sea voyages; one-third or more of the slaves died at sea—usually from flux or smallpox. Some slaves even committed suicide by flinging themselves overboard in order to escape the horrible conditions on board; others went on hunger strikes in order to protest their treatment (Franklin, 1988). It was common for slaves to drown in their own excrement. Countless Africans died during "seasoning in the islands," which was a process of making them terrified of whites and left them feeling helpless while in bondage. They underwent extremely inhumane treatment for two or three months on a Caribbean island before being transferred to the North American mainland (Gonzales, 1990).

Africans

Some writers speculate that Pedro Alonso Niño, who sailed with Christopher Columbus's crew on his first voyage, was an African. Whether that is fact or not, it is true that thirty Africans were with Vasco Núñoz de Balboa when he sailed the Pacific Ocean; and Hernán Cortés brought Africans with him when he entered Mexico—one of them planted and harvested the first wheat crop in America (Franklin, 1988). An outstanding African explorer named Esteban, or Estevanico ("Little Stephen" as he was known to his friends), was a member of Pánfilo de Narváez's ill-fated expedition of 1527. Esteban was the first non-Indian to explore what is now New Mexico and Arizona. The Spanish expeditions throughout the southwestern areas of the United States were successful in part because of Esteban's skill as a guide. Africans accompanied Francisco Pizarro, Francisco Vásquez de Coronado, Cristóbal Vaca de Castro, Diego Velásquez, Diego de Almargo, and Pedro de Valdivia, to mention a few. They also came to America in the sixteenth century with the French who explored the Mississippi Valley, where some of them settled along the Mississippi River.

The Peculiar Institution

It was the Portuguese and the Spanish who introduced African slaves into the New World. Portuguese sailors took African captives to Portugal around 1450 and later transported slaves to New World settlements. Pope Leo X approved the petition by Bishop Bartholomé de Las Casas in 1517 to allow Spaniards to import African slaves to the New World. This began what the noted historian John Hope Franklin (1988) called "the big business of slave trading" in America. Las Casas made his request of the Pope so that the Indians would not be used as slaves. A few years later Las Casas realized that he had made a dreadful error and denounced the trade in human beings as an evil institution. However, the process has been set irrevocably in motion. Neither the Portuguese nor the Spaniards could stop the slave trade. Equally important, there was no large-scale sentiment to do so.

Dutch, French, and English merchants controlled the slave trade during the greater part of the seventeenth century (Feagin, 1984). There are no reliable statistics of the number of Africans captured and sold into slavery but some historians estimate the total at nearly ten million, with only about 5 percent of them going to England's colonies or the mainland (Curtin, 1969; Reich, 1989). The majority of the slaves were taken from the coast of tropical Africa between the Senegal and Congo Rivers. A few of them were captured more than 300 miles inland (Daniels, 1990). Most of the slaves came from the Guinea Coast (Dormon & Jones, 1974). Others were taken from the Ivory Coast, the Congo, the Niger Valley (now Nigeria), the Cameroons, the Bengira, Angola, Ghana, Senegal, Gambia, and Sierra Leone (Thernstrom, 1980). They were a mixed group of Arabs, Bantus, Moors, and Hottentots who were as different from each other as the various European immigrants were from each other.

Not all the African slaves came from slave-free societies. To the contrary, some of them—a small minority—had experienced firsthand the horrors of human bondage in their native countries. Some were prisoners captured in intertribal wars; others were sold by family members to get food during famine; some were children enslaved to pay for crimes committed by other family members; and some were enslaved to pay off tribal debts. The essential differences between enslavement in Africa and America were economic and racial. There was no economic system in precolonial Africa that needed an exploited labor force to produce crops for profit. Ethnic and, to a lesser degree, religious differences characterized African masters and their slaves, but racist ideologies did not condemn for life the enslaved and their descendants. On the contrary, slaves in Africa were often absorbed into their owners' families.

By the end of the seventeenth century, England had become the dominant slave-trading power in the world (Reich, 1989). Triangular trade routes were instituted by the slave traders so that they could extract the greatest profits from their human cargoes. That is, ships from the New England Coast—many of them based in Newport, Rhode Island—carried African slaves to the West Indies. There the ships took on quantities of molasses, a by-product of refined sugar which was a basic necessity for making New England rum. In turn, the traders carried the rum to Africa and used it toward the purchase of a fresh boatload of slaves. Profits from this triangular trade were invested by Northern businessmen in various enterprises. One of the most popular enterprises was the manufacture of textiles. Thus the

African slave trade provided funds for American capitalism (Daniels, 1990).

Africans often resisted capture and transportation. In fact, there were more than 150 slave revolts on board ships even though resistance was almost always futile. The crews were heavily armed and the slaves at best had crude weapons of their own. Yet the desire to be free gave them the courage to defy their captors (Dormon & Jones, 1974).

Life in the Colonies

Contrary to popular literature, the twenty Africans brought to Virginia in 1619 by the Dutch were not sold as slaves. They were indentured servants whose status was the same as that of white indentured servants (Gonzales, 1990). The labor shortage in the English colonies was such that the British permitted almost anyone to relocate to America. Immigrants who had neither the money to pay their fare nor the resources to establish themselves once they arrived had to sign a work contract that usually bonded them for seven years of service. Indentured persons were given their freedom and sometimes land, when they fulfilled the contract. During the first half of the seventeenth century, Virginia had a large number of black indentured servants and, by 1640, many of them had become bondmen for life (Franklin, 1988). A few African indentured servants had earned their freedom before 1640, and some of them became landowners and acquired their own indentured servants. The loss of white indentured servants and the growing need for a cheap and plentiful labor supply led to changing the term of indentured service for Africans from a few years to life. Earlier, Indians had been enslaved by the colonists but they were much less compliant than Africans. Further, Africans offered landowners a practically inexhaustible supply of cheap labor (Redding, 1973).

Statutory slavery was not widespread in America before the 1660s. Although the words "slaves" and "servants" were frequently used interchangeably, whites were never in servitude in the same way Africans became slaves—serving for life and conveying the obligation to their offspring. Simultaneously with the Africans' descent to slavery, indentured whites were also affected. Ironically, slavery for Africans resulted in freedom for white indentured servants. Or as C. N. Degler (1959) noted, "Even Irishmen who were held to be literally 'beyond the Pale,' and some were referred to as 'slaves' were accorded higher social and legal status than black slaves" (p. 30). Indeed, the scorned Irish and other non-English white indentured servants were culturally more similar to the English than were the

Africans. It is not surprising that the English settlers made distinctions between various ethnic groups.

The differential treatment of Africans and Indians was not entirely due to color prejudice. In fact, color was not initially important in determining Indian and African social status. Instead, the major reason for their low status was because they were non-Christians or "heathens." Religion took priority over color. Early colonial laws, for example, focused more on prohibiting Christians from marrying non-Christians than white-black marriages. During and after the 1660s, laws were enacted regulating racial intermarriage but for a long time their emphases were upon religion, nationality, or some other non-racial basis. As an example, a 1681 Maryland law described marriage between white women and Negro men as lascivious and "to the disgrace not only of the English but also [sic] of many other Christian Nations" (Jordan, 1968, pp. 79–80).

In 1661, Virginia became the first colony to legalize slavery. The following year, the colony passed a second law concerning slavery: it made perpetual servitude hereditary according to the status of the mother (Franklin, 1988). The colonies of Maryland and the Carolinas legalized slavery in 1663. Those colonies further decreed that the child of a black mother would have the legal status of a slave. In 1667, the legislature of Virginia passed a law that whether a person was baptized or not had nothing to do with "the condition of the person as to his bondage or freedom" (Reich, 1989, p. 124). When the colony of Georgia was established in 1733, slavery was prohibited within its borders but the prohibition was bitterly resented by the landowners. Seventeen years later, the landowners succeeded in getting slavery legalized. Almost all of the slaves in the United States lived south of the demarcation of what was later drawn as the Mason-Dixon Line, and almost all of the free Africans lived north of it. While only a few slaves were kept in New England, several New Englanders made their fortune from it (Daniels, 1990). New York had the largest proportion (14%) of slaves in a colony outside the South and slaves accounted for 20 percent of New York City's population by the end of the colonial period (Reich, 1989).

Slavery was an economic success in the Southern colonies because conditions there were right for the industry. The climate was mild, the soil was fertile, and a large number of people were needed to cultivate crops. A majority of the slaves were used on large plantations to cultivate tobacco, rice, indigo, sugarcane, and cotton. Also, slaves were used as domestics and unskilled laborers in nonagricultural jobs (Gonzales, 1990). A few of them were trained as artisans and mechanics because there were seldom enough white artisans to do all the work needed in the South. In fact, most of the building and repairing was done by slaves.

Slave Rebellions

While most slaves accepted their fate with resignation, many of them did not. Those who did not destroyed tools, burned barns, injured themselves, or simply ran away when they had the chance. The one constant fear of Southern whites was the slave revolt. The first major conspiracy occurred in Gloucester County, Virginia, in 1663, but it was revealed by an informer before it could break into violence. The alleged conspirators were drawn and quartered with their heads placed on posts for the public to see. By 1710 at least twelve slave revolts had been plotted or carried out in Maryland, New Jersey, Massachusetts, and Virginia (Redding, 1973). In April 1712, twenty slaves in New York City burned a house and then waited for whites to arrive. The plotters killed nine white men and wounded nine others before the revolt was crushed by the militia. Eight slaves were killed, six killed themselves, and six were later executed.

In 1739, the Stono Rebellion took place 20 miles west of Charleston, South Carolina. Slaves murdered two guards and seized weapons from a warehouse; the revolt was put down. During the altercation, thirty-four blacks and thirty whites were killed. In 1741, believing stories that Africans and poor whites in New York City were going to seize power, city officials offered rewards for information about the alleged conspiracy. Nearly two hundred whites and blacks were arrested. Almost one hundred blacks were convicted, and eighteen of them were hanged, thirteen were burned alive, and seventy were exiled (Franklin, 1988).

Slave Codes

All of the colonies passed slave codes to repress and control blacks. Most of the codes were similar. Slaves could not own property. Most of the codes prohibited slaves from gathering in large groups unless white supervisors were present. Nor were slaves allowed to carry weapons, and they could not show disrespect for whites in any way. Slaves could not testify in court or leave plantations without their owner's permission. The slaveowner's authority was absolute. As one authority commented, "Behind the owner stood an elaborate and complex system of military control. In the cities were guards and police, for the countryside there were the ubiquitous patrols, armed men on horseback" (Aptheker, 1941, p. 67).

In summary, the codes deprived slaves of virtually all human rights—social, economic, political, familial, civic, and judicial. Slaves were defined as chattel property that could be bought and sold at the will of the owner (Gonzales, 1990). The codes were simply an age-old process of subjugation: before one can fully reduce a subject people to total obedience, one must rob them of their humanity; they must be portrayed as not fully human so that the majority group can work its brutal will without feeling remorse or conscious of the need for atonement. The slave codes of South Carolina and Georgia, for example, were enforced with brutal punishment. Burning, maiming, whipping, branding, and cropping slaves were commonplace. On the whole, the slave codes of the Southern colonies were considerably more harsh than those of the Northern colonies.

It was in the institution of family where slaves in the North and the South suffered the most indignities. Except for Northern codes, neither slave marriages nor fatherhood was legally recognized. Members of slave families could be divided at the will of their owners. Some owners insisted on religious ceremonies to unite slave couples. Other owners chose not to interfere when slave couples had informal marriages. A few states even had laws prohibiting the sale of mothers away from their children under a certain age. But there were no such laws pertaining to fathers. In all instances, however, when it was economically advantageous, slaveowners would sell mothers away from their children.

Despite laws against it, miscegenation was commonplace, especially between white men and slave women. The rape of a slave woman by someone other than her master was not a felony. Rather, it was merely a legal act of trespass on the property of her master. Children of miscegenational relationships were classified as slaves. The extent of race mixing is evidenced in the more than four hundred thousand mulatto slaves in the United States in 1860. They comprised 10 percent of the slave population. Relatedly, slave breeding was a widespread means of gaining money when African slave trade was prohibited in the United States in 1808. As long as cotton was the major cash crop, slave breeding was the inevitable way to replenish lost slaves and get additional ones to pick cotton. Breeders were generally not overworked, and most slave owners let slaves pick their own mates because contented slaves were more likely to produce offspring. A large number of slave mothers maintained a semblance of stable families and taught their children how to survive racism.

Life in the North

Blacks in the North established separate community institutions in an attempt to improve their lives. Before the Civil War, they had established and supported numerous schools; founded literary societies, libraries, and reading rooms; established independent churches, civic organizations, and benevolent and fraternal organizations. It is important to note that the Northern states committed their share of transgressions against Africans. For example, many businessmen in New England profited from the slave trade in various ways long after it had ceased in the North.

By 1702, New York decreed that whites could not trade with blacks, but New York City also declared that slaves could not be on the streets after sunset. Nor were slaves allowed to appear as witnesses at the trial of a free person. In 1704, the governor of Connecticut maintained that all offspring of African women in slavery were themselves born into slavery. The same colony prohibited blacks to own land in 1717. In fairness, however, it should be pointed out that while the Northern colonies had slave codes, they were far less oppressive than were those in the South and, in most cases, the codes were abolished more than a century before the Civil War brought slavery to an end in the South. The Northern codes never countenanced separation of slave family members—a common practice in the South (Reich, 1989).

Nor should it be forgotten that many white colonists condemned slavery and fought against it, often in the face of great danger. The first formal protest to reach a legislative body was made by Quakers of Germantown, Pennsylvania, in 1688, and they renewed it in 1693 and 1696 (Redding, 1973). These protests ignited a debate that spread throughout the colonies. A few brave slaves also joined in public outcries by asking for their freedom from bondage, and a large number of free African Americans demanded that colonial legislatures put an end to slavery. In 1764, James Otis wrote a pamphlet, *Rights of the British Colonies*, in which he declared that blacks had an inalienable right to freedom (Franklin, 1988). Theologians, including Samuel Hopkins of Rhode Island, Ezra Stiles of Connecticut, and Jeremy Belknap of Massachusetts, publicly advocated the abolition of slavery.

Quaker minister John Woolman epitomized the individual efforts of white colonists to abolish slavery. Beginning in 1743 he traveled throughout the South, the middle colonies, and New England encouraging slaveholders to accept the necessity of manumission (freeing) of slaves. His 1754 publication, *Some Considerations on the Keeping of Negroes*, was the first public proclamation by a religious body condemning slavery. Prominent leaders in the fight for colonial independence, including Benjamin Franklin and Benjamin Rush, agitated for abolition of slavery. Influential lawyers like Zepheniah Swift, Noah

Webster, and Theodore Dwight presented legal arguments for the abolition of slavery. In 1785, John Jay became president of the newly formed New York Society for Promoting the Manumission of Slaves. Other Founding Fathers who spoke out against slavery were John Adams, Albert Gallatin, Alexander Hamilton, George Washington, Patrick Henry, and Thomas Jefferson (Dormon & Jones, 1974). In fact, in the first draft of the Declaration of Independence, Jefferson took George III to task for not abolishing the slave trade. But Southern representatives in the Continental Congress were able to get the language stricken from the final document.

In the 1800s, there were many vocal abolitionists. In 1829, David Walker, a free black, wrote *Appeal*, a book that described the oppressive conditions of slavery, encouraged all blacks to seek the best education available to them, chided white Christians for allowing slavery to exist, and encouraged slaves to rebel. Georgia offered a $10,000 reward for the capture of Walker. The best-known black abolitionist, however, was Frederick Douglass. Born a slave in 1817, he escaped to New York in 1838. His best-selling book *Narrative* recounted his life. Douglass established a newspaper, *The North Star*, in which his poignant editorials stirred countless readers to condemn slavery.

The most notorious white abolitionist in the 1800s was William Lloyd Garrison, editor of an anti-slavery newspaper, *The Liberator*, established in 1831. Garrison's antislavery editorials incited a white mob in Boston to physically attack him in 1835. Other well-known white abolitionists included Theodore Weld, author of the book *Slavery as it is*; Horace Greeley, editor of an antislavery newspaper, *The New York Tribune*; writers Ralph Waldo Emerson, Julia Ward Howe, Harriet Beecher Stowe, Henry Wadsworth Longfellow, Lydia M. Child, Walt Whitman, and John Greenleaf Whittier.

Early Black Contributions

There were a large number of blacks in colonial America whose talents and courage contributed to the building of the nation. For example, in the 1760s, Phillis Wheatley was the first black poet to be published and receive wide acclaim. Her collected poems were printed in London and reprinted for five editions. Although she was born in Africa, Wheatley lived in Boston as a slave without formal education. Many of her poems were used by others in the crusade against slavery. Richard Allen and Absalom Jones, both ministers, were active civil rights leaders in Philadelphia. Benjamin Banneker—a self-educated mathematician, almanac maker, astronomer, and surveyor—was chosen by Secretary of State Thomas Jefferson to survey the national district which later became Washington, D.C. Prince Hall, a leader of the black community in Boston, established a Masonic order.

In March 1770, the people of Boston rose against the British soldiers quartered in the city. Led by Crispus Attucks, a runaway slave, a group of colonists charged soldiers in Captain Preston's company. The patriots were fired on; Attucks fell first, mortally wounded, as were four others. The Boston massacre helped to rouse Americans to stand up for freedom. Attucks was the first to die in the cause of colonial independence. The greater importance of his sacrifice was that it made numerous whites realize that a black American, who was not really free in the fullest sense, had been willing to lay down his life in order to make them free. Consequently, the death of a brave man who was himself legally a slave turned many colonists into abolitionists opposed to the barbarous practice of slavery.

Five thousand free and slave blacks distinguished themselves during the American Revolution, but this was not surprising because black soldiers were previously cited for bravery in the wars against the French and Indians. On November 12, 1775, Lord Dunmore, the governor of Virginia, announced that "all indentured servants, Negroes, or others" would be free if they joined the king's armed forces. Eight hundred slaves accepted the call. Later, in 1779, the British commander in chief, Sir Henry Clinton, extended in a similar offer to all blacks in the colonies. Initially, George Washington ordered recruiters not to enlist blacks, slave or free, in the Continental Army. But after Dunmore's offer, he changed his policy. On December 31, 1775, Washington recruited free blacks to the revolutionary cause. By 1778, all of the colonies, except Georgia and South Carolina, allowed the recruitment of slaves to the state militia. Most of the blacks fought in integrated units, although there were a few all-black companies. By the end of the war it was generally agreed that the five thousand black soldiers and sailors who served the revolutionary cause had fought well and bravely.

At the time of independence, there were approximately seven hundred fifty thousand blacks in the United States. Of these, about 59,000 were free; in 1830 there were 319,000 free blacks; by the time of the Civil War there were 488,000—44 percent in the South Atlantic states and 46 percent in the North, with the rest residing in the South Central states and the West. Many years earlier, hundreds of blacks had been given their freedom after they fought in the Revolution. A large number of blacks had gained their liberty in Northern states which had abolished legal servitude. Some masters manumitted their slaves; others provided for their slaves' freedom in wills.

A few blacks were able to purchase their freedom by saving money for several years. Still others were the children of white plantation owners and their slaves, having been set free upon the death of their fathers.

Free at Last

Few novels have had the social impact of Harriet Beecher Stowe's book, *Uncle Tom's Cabin* (1852), which is often cited as one of the causes of the Civil War. The antislavery movement was based on her novel's recollections of slavery. She further pricked the conscience of readers with two additional scathing challenges to slavery: *The Key to Uncle Tom's Cabin* (1853) and *Dred: A Tale of the Great Dismal Swamp* (1856). She was recognized in the United States and abroad as one of America's foremost authors.

The outbreak of the Civil War in 1861 was no panacea for patriotic blacks, for initially they were allowed to serve the North only as non-participants—as cooks, butlers, laborers, and teamsters. However, by the end of the war most of the Northern states had at least one black regiment. There were more than one hundred eighty-six thousand black soldiers and they fought in every area and under almost every command. They first saw action against Confederate forces in the fall of 1862. Many Americans protested that they should be trusted in battle rather than used simply as servants in uniform. Ultimately, more than thirty-eight thousand black soldiers died for the Union cause in general and for black freedom in particular. That they fought bravely is testified to by the fact that the mortality rate of black soldiers was almost 40 percent greater than for whites.

On July 28, 1866, the Congress of the United States passed an act that established six black regiments in the regular U.S. Army. Two of them, the 9th and 10th Cavalry Regiments, later became known as "Buffalo Soldiers" by the Indians they fought. That name was bestowed on them in recognition for the respect they earned as warriors. The 10th Regiment protected white Texans from Indians, and the 9th regiment protected Indian lands from white intruders—mainly horse thieves and cattle rustlers. The Buffalo Soldiers built the original Fort Sill in Oklahoma. In that group was Henry O. Flipper, who in 1877 became the first black cadet to graduate from the U.S. Military Academy. Twelve Buffalo Soldiers were awarded the Congressional Medal of Honor between 1870 and 1890; five others were awarded the Congressional Medal of Honor during the Spanish-American War of 1898.

Although the Emancipation Proclamation was issued in 1863 by

President Abraham Lincoln, legal freedom for black slaves did not come until 1865 when the Civil War ended. The black population of the United States totaled nearly five million by 1870, making up almost 13 percent of the American people (Gonzales, 1990). For a while in the Southern states life was very different from what it had been before the war. Having been given the vote as Reconstruction commenced, blacks turned out in large numbers for elections. As a result, twenty blacks were elected to the U.S. House of Representatives between 1870 and 1901, and between 1870 and 1881 two black U.S. senators were elected. When Reconstruction ended in 1877 and federal troops withdrew from the last Southern state in which they were stationed, black Americans in the South found themselves once again at the mercy of the Southern white power structure.

Fearing that blacks and poor whites might join together to effect sweeping changes in the political system, Southern legislatures decreed in various ways that the races were to be separated in community activities. The so-called "Jim Crow" laws were passed in order to segregate blacks from whites in all public facilities, including schools, transportation, libraries, housing, lodging, public bathrooms, public water fountains, and public beaches. Legal segregation in the South received the approval of the U.S. Supreme Court when it declared in the case of *Plessy v. Ferguson* (1896) that "separate but equal" accommodations for blacks were "reasonable" and within the jurisdiction of state governments. The Ku Klux Klan, founded in Tennessee in 1865, used terror and murder to impede the newly enfranchised African-American citizens from going to the polls. Whether the barriers to African-American voting were legal or extra-legal, they were effective. For example, between 1896 and 1900 the number of African-American voters in Louisiana fell from 130,000 to 5,300 (Stone, 1970).

In 1900, nine out of ten African Americans lived in the South where the largest number of skilled African Americans were employed in the building trades. As the black population grew (Table 10.1), unskilled African-American laborers had considerably more difficulty obtaining jobs than did their skilled peers. Throughout the United States, unskilled African-American workers competed with European immigrants for jobs. It was unfair competition because railroad companies, textile industries, and iron and steel mills preferred white workers. It was not until after 1914 that iron and steel mill owners began recruiting African-American workers from the South to replace upwardly mobile white immigrants. The mining industry provided proportionally more jobs for black Americans than did any other industry. Nor did the mine owners make distinction between ethnic

Table 10.1
The Black Population of the United States, 1790-1990

Year	Black Population (in thousands)	Black Percentage of Total Population	Percentage of Blacks Enslaved
1790	757	19.3 %	92.1 %
1800	1,002	18.9	89.2
1810	1,378	19.0	86.5
1820	1,772	18.4	87.4
1830	2,329	18.1	86.9
1840	2,874	16.8	87.0
1850	3,639	15.7	88.5
1860	4,442	14.1	89.5
1870	4,880	12.7	—
1880	6,581	13.1	—
1890	7,489	11.9	—
1900	8,834	11.6	—
1910	9,828	10.7	—
1920	10,463	9.9	—
1930	11,891	9.7	—
1940	12,866	9.8	—
1950	15,042	10.0	—
1960	18,872	10.5	—
1970	22,581	11.1	—
1980	26,495	11.7	—
1990	29,986	12.1	—

Source: Statistical Abstract, 1988

groups in terms of wages. While few African Americans were employed in textile mills, many were employed in the clothing industry which actually provided the widest range of economic opportunities for African Americans. The number of African-American workers in the clothing industry increased significantly during World War I when manufacturers in New York, Philadelphia, and Chicago began to recruit them actively.

Black workers were frequently used as strikebreakers and that caused considerable friction between them and white union members. Blacks in urban areas were often victims of racial discrimination and overt hostility. Many whites, in both the North and the South, were not willing to work side by side with black Americans. The majority of Black Americans lacked the skills to work in craft industries and thus found it difficult to join craft unions. However, the Knights of Labor were not particularly interested in skilled workers, enthusiastically recruited black American members. Some of the locals were integrated but most of them were divided by race. By 1886, the Knights had about sixty thousand black members.

At first the American Federation of Labor (AFL) welcomed black members but that soon changed when most of its white members protested. Through a loophole in its constitution, the AFL allowed its locals to exclude black Americans. Rejected black workers organized their own unions, including the National Association of Afro-American Steam and Gas Engineers and the Skilled Workers of Pittsburgh. But these unions did not make significant gains because white labor unions dominated the various industries. It was not until the 1930s that the AFL began to actively recruit black workers. And that was done to try to win a heated competition with the newly formed and nondiscriminating Congress of Industrial Organizations (CIO) (Feagin, 1984).

From 1860 to 1920, several African Americans founded their own businesses. The types of enterprises they established tended to reflect previous opportunities and training as freedmen and slaves. Booker T. Washington strongly urged African Americans to start their own businesses, and he organized the National Negro Business League in 1900. By 1907, the league had 320 branches. African Americans owned grocery stores, general merchandise stores, drugstores, restaurants, catering services, bakeries, tailor shops, contracting companies, shirt factories, cotton mills, rubber goods shops, lumber mills, and carpet factories—to mention a few. Almost without exception, African-American businesses were located in black neighborhoods and almost always were business activities that whites did not want for themselves. Insurance companies whose clients were mostly

African Americans and companies that manufactured skin and hair products for African Americans were the most successful African-American enterprises in the early 1900s.

World War I and the events following it tested African Americans in ways no white Americans had ever been tested. Almost three hundred seventy thousand African Americans served in the armed forces. They comprised 13 percent of all inductees. But African-American soldiers served in segregated units and trained in segregated camps. They could not serve in the Marines or pilot airplanes, and they were assigned the lowliest chores in the Navy. Even though African-American army officers trained in segregated units and were allowed to command only African-American troops, blacks served in almost all the branches of the U.S. Army.

African-American soldiers of the 24th Infantry Regiment were involved in a riot with whites in Houston, Texas, in August, 1917. The soldiers killed seventeen whites and, in reprisal, the army hanged 13 of them for murder and mutiny, forty-one received life imprisonment, and forty others were detained for investigation. In October 1917, a trivial incident in Spartanburg, South Carolina, involving a racial slight to a black soldier nearly sparked a race riot of tragic proportion. The soldier involved in the altercation and his friends had made plans to avenge the slight by "shooting up" Spartanburg. Violence was averted when the soldiers' unit, the 15th New York Regiment (later named the 369th Regiment), was sent to France as the first African American troops to fight in Europe.

African-American troops fought well and often in World War I, and the 369th Regiment was awarded the Croix de Guerre by the French government. The regiment was in action almost daily from July 1918 to the conclusion of the war and it was the first of Allied soldiers to reach the Rhine. Other units of African-American soldiers received honors in France because of their bravery and skill in fighting the Germans. For example, twenty-one soldiers of the 370th Regiment were honored with the Distinguished Service Cross, one soldier received the Distinguished Service Medal, and sixty-eight soldiers were given various grades of the Croix de Guerre. Three officers of the 371st Infantry Regiment received the French Legion of Honor; thirty-four officers and eighty-nine enlisted men were honored with the croix de guerre, while fourteen officers and twelve enlisted men were given the Distinguished Service Cross. These are but a few examples of the courage and combat efficiency of African Americans in World War I. African Americans on the home front bought more than $250 million worth of war bonds and stamps.

Between 1916 and 1930, more than three million African Americans migrated from the South to the North and West, where they found considerably better employment opportunities than were available in the South. African Americans who moved to the North relieved the critical labor shortage during World War I. They were employed in the shipbuilding industry as well as in the manufacture of ammunition and iron and steel. Also, jobs in meatpacking, automobile and truck manufacturing, and the production of electrical goods provided incomes at higher pay than most African Americans had ever received. Over 150,000 African Americans helped to keep the railroads running in order to facilitate the shipment of crucial war material. While blacks were losing their lives in Europe and giving their labor in America, at least thirty-seven African Americans were lynched in 1917 and fifty-eight were lynched in 1918. On February 17, 1919, the much-decorated 369th Regiment returned to New York from Europe in a triumphant victory parade. The next day, an African American was lynched in Georgia. Also in 1919, at least seventy-five more blacks were lynched in the South. Some of them were still in uniform (Redding, 1973).

When the war ended, racial violence erupted in the North as well as in the South. White Northerners were no less racist than white Southerners. The summer of 1919 was the greatest period of interracial conflict the United States had ever experienced. There were racial disturbances in at least twenty-seven cities. In Chicago, a fight between blacks and whites led to a riot and the deaths of twenty-two blacks and sixteen whites. Between 1916 and 1920, there were fifty-eight bombings of newly purchased black homes in Chicago. In 1919, often referred to as "Red Summer," riots occurred in Knoxville, Tennessee, Omaha, Nebraska, and Elaine, Arkansas—among other places. Hundreds of African Americans and scores of whites were killed; thousands of people were injured. An entire black community was destroyed in Tulsa, Oklahoma. Also during those years, the Ku Klux Klan was responsible for hundreds of lynchings. According to the U.S. Bureau of the Census, between 1882 and 1931, 3,317 African Americans were lynched. No doubt there were other deaths that were not recorded.

Black Protests

The modern history of the black, or African-American, protest began in 1905 when W. E. B. Du Bois organized a group of fellow black intellectuals in a Negro movement, founded at the Niagara Conference. The purpose of the conference was to protest segregation and to encourage blacks throughout America to seek the equality promised in the Emancipation Proclamation of 1863. In 1910, the National Association for the Advancement of Colored People (NAACP) was created, followed by the organization of the Urban League in 1912. Disillusioned by the slow-paced tactics of the NAACP and the Urban League, some African Americans began to espouse separatist philosophies. Marcus Garvey's unsuccessful back-to-Africa movement of the 1920s was the forerunner to present-day African-American separatist ideologies. The urge to separate was fanned by white violence. World War I took many black GIs to Europe, where they often received better treatment than they had in America. Many of the survivors returned home unwilling to accept their prewar second-class citizenship.

The Depression of the 1930s and the onset of World War II exploded the African-American dream of equality. During this period, black Americans lost ground socially and economically when compared with their white counterparts. Nonviolent direct-action civil rights activities grew out of this period. A. Philip Randolph's March on Washington of 1940 was the first mass African-American protest officially endorsing the principle of nonviolent direct action. On June 16, 1942, black Americans turned out their lights in Harlem to protest racial discrimination. Later that year, the Congress of Racial Equality (CORE) was founded in Chicago. CORE took over many of the principles laid down by Randolph and began to work in the area of public accommodations, especially restaurants. The most promising development came in 1954 in the U.S. Supreme Court's decision in *Brown v. Board of Education*. The Court ruled: "We conclude that in the field of public education the doctrine of 'separate but equal' has no place. Separate educational facilities are inherently unequal."

The late 1950s and early 1960s were characterized by sit-ins, kneel-ins, wade-ins, and sleep-ins. The first formal sit-in took place in Oklahoma City on August 19, 1958, when the NAACP Youth Council, led by fourteen-year-old Barbara Ann Posey, sat at public lunchcounters. Throughout this period, less innovative but equally determined hostile whites responded with traditional tactics, ranging from setting dogs on blacks to burning churches to killing civil rights workers. In April 1960, the Student Nonviolent Coordinating Committee (SNCC) was organized in Raleigh, North Carolina. At this point, the civil rights campaign took on a collegiate, interstate character, with black and white college students testing the integration of interstate transportation. Later, they focused on voting rights. Such slogans as "Black and White Together" echoed the integrated nature of the activities.

Cultural Contributions

Despite racial violence and antagonism all over the United States, particularly in the South, African Americans began a period of unparalleled artistic creativity in the 1920s. In 1924, for example, Harlem had more African-American residents than any city in the South. Harlem became home to some of America's most talented black writers, musicians, and artists. It was here that a black renaissance was born. Black actors and musicians performed to packed houses. Legendary dance and vaudeville teams performed for both black and white audiences. Ethel Waters, Adelaide Hall, Ada Ward, Bill Robinson, and Florence Mills were just a few of the revue artists who enthralled New York audiences. About forty years later the full impact of the creativity of the Harlem experience was grasped and appreciated. The Harlem experiences gave special meaning to the song *We Shall Overcome*.

Almost all aspects of modern-day America have been influenced directly or indirectly by the contributions of African Americans. Their recent achievements are built on the success of the earlier performers. For instance, America is indebted to James Bland for composing *Carry Me Back to Old Virginny*, the official state song of Virginia. W. C. Handy's *Saint Louis Blues* is a masterpiece of the blues genre. "Ma" (Gertrude Pridgett) Rainey is best known as "Mother of the Blues." Bessie Smith was another founding mother of the blues. William Grant Still's *Afro-American Symphony* is one of America's symphonic masterpieces, as is Howard Swanson's *Short Symphony* that was recorded by conductor Dimitri Mitropoulos. Sissieri Jones, Marian Anderson, Paul Robeson, Roland Hayes, and Dorothy Maynor were world-acclaimed concert and opera singers. Marian Anderson was the first black singer to perform at the Metropolitan Opera in a leading role. Katherine Dunham and Pearl Primus introduced Caribbean and African dances to American audiences. Harry Burleigh, R. Nathaniel Dett, Carl Diton, and J. Rosamond Johnson's musical compositions paved the way for other African-American musicians. Bunk Johnson, Jelly Roll Morton, Meade Lux Lewis, Art Tatum, Fats Waller, Louis Armstrong, Duke Ellington, Earl "Father" Hines, and Bessie Smith laid the foundation for jazz—America's original art form.

Hattie McDaniel was the first black to win an Academy Award. She was named the Best Supporting Actress for her role as Mammy in *Gone With the Wind* (1939). Since then, the award has been won by three other black performers—Sidney Poitier, Whoopi Goldberg, and Denzel Washington. Canada Lee (Lionel C. Canegata) was a leading theater and film actor during the 1940s and 1950s. Mary McLeod Bethune, Booker T. Washington, and George Washington Carver set new education standards for blacks. In 1904, Bethune established a school for Black children in Daytona Beach, Florida. She was president of Bethune Cookman College for twenty-five years and adviser to four U.S. presidents, beginning with Herbert Hoover in 1930. Washington was born into slavery, acquired an education after emancipation, and was the principal of the Tuskegee Institute in Alabama from 1881 to 1915. Carver, a botanist and chemist, was born a slave. After earning a master's degree at Iowa State Agricultural College in 1889, he was appointed head of Tuskegee Institute's Department of Agriculture. While at Tuskegee, Carver developed over three hundred uses for peanuts and sweet potatoes. He was one of America's most honored scientists. Booker T. Washington made the Tuskegee Institute a national leader in industrial and vocational education.

Gwendolyn Brooks won the 1950 Pulitzer Prize for poetry; Toni Morrison won the 1993 Nobel Prize in literature. Other prominent early black writers include Paul Laurence Dunbar, Countee Cullen, Langston Hughes, Mari E. Evans, Leroi Jones, Sterling Brown, Zora Neale Hurston, and James Weldon Johnson. African-American fiction writers who set standards that even white writers strove to reach include Richard Wright, Frank Yerby, Jessie Fauset, Jean Toomer, James Baldwin, and Claude McKay. Lorraine Hansberry was an award-winning playwright. Her most famous work, *Raisin in the Sun*, was also made into movie.

The formal literature of social protest written by Frederick Douglass, Samuel Ringold Williams, and W. E. B. Du Bois has been cited by numerous social activists throughout the world. Du Bois was the author of the first monograph in the Harvard Historical Series, and he wrote the first autobiographical study of the African-American community. George Williams, author of *History of the Negro Race in America*, and Carter G. Woodson, founder of the *Journal of Negro History*, became the first renowned authors of information about African-American history. Charles S. Johnson, E. Franklin Frazier, and Ira De A. Reid were renowned sociologists. W. Allison Davis achieved honors in childhood education, and Abraham Harris was a successful economist.

African-American inventors include Norbert Rillieux, who invented the vacuum pan that revolutionized the sugar-refining industry; Lewis Temple invented the toggle harpoon; Jan Matzeliger invented a shoe lasting machine which made it possible to produce four hundred pairs of shoes a day, compared to 60 pairs by hand work; Elijah McCoy invented a lubricating cup for oiling locomotive engines; Andrew J. Beard invented the automatic coupler for railroad trains; and Garrett A. Morgan invented the automatic traffic light. Granville Woods invented the third rail which permitted the electrification of the New York City transportation system; Woods was called "Black Edison" because he had more than sixty patents to his credit. Charles Drew, a physician, was one of the pioneers in the development of blood plasma preservation. George Cleveland Hall, a physician, performed the first successful operation on the human heart; and Daniel Hale Williams, a physician, performed the first successful open-heart surgery.

Ralph Bunche was awarded the Nobel Peace Prize in 1950, and Martin Luther King Jr. received it in 1964. Bunche received the prize for successfully mediating an end to the Arab-Israeli conflict that was caused when Israel was founded. In the field of law, Thurgood Marshall was the first black to serve as a U.S. Supreme Court Justice. He was appointed in 1967 by President Lyndon Johnson.

African-American pioneers in professional sports include Bill Pickett, star of rodeos; basketball players Charles Cooper Jr. of the Boston Celtics and Nat Sweetwater Clifton of the New York Knickerbockers; baseball player Jackie Robinson of the Brooklyn Dodgers; football players Fritz Pollard of the Akron Indians, Joe Lillard of the Chicago Cardinals, Kenny Washington and Woody Strode of the Los Angeles Rams, and Bill Willis and Marion Motley of the Cleveland Browns; boxing champion Jack Johnson; golfer Charlie Sifford, the Long Beach Open champion in 1957; and the 1875 (first) Kentucky Derby winner Oliver Lewis. Althea Gibson was the Wimbledon tennis champion in 1957 and U.S. champion in 1958. Arthur Ashe was the Wimbledon tennis champion in 1975. Of special mention is Henry Armstrong, the first and only fighter to hold three titles at once: featherweight, lightweight, and welterweight.

REFERENCES

Aptheker, H. (1941). *The Negro in the abolitionist movement.* New York: International.

Curtin, P. D. (1969). *The Atlantic slave trade.* Madison: University of Wisconsin Press.

Daniels, R. (1990). *Coming to America: A history of immigration and ethnicity in American life.* New York: HarperCollins.

Degler, C. N. (1959). *Out of our past.* New York: Harper & Row.

Dormon, J. H., & Jones, R. R. (1974). *The Afro-American experience: A cultural history through emancipation.* New York: John Wiley & Sons.

Feagin, J. R. (1984). *Racial and ethnic relations*, 2nd ed. Englewood Cliffs, N.J.: Prentice-Hall.

Franklin, J. H. (1988). *From slavery to freedom: A history of Negro Americans*. 6th ed. New York: Alfred A. Knopf.

Gonzales, J. L., Jr. (1990). *Racial and ethnic groups in America*. Dubuque, IA: Kendall/Hunt.

Greene, R. E. (1974). *Black defenders of America, 1775–1973*. Chicago: Johnson.

Hawkins, W. L. (1992). *African American biographies: Profiles of 558 current men and women*. Jefferson, NC: McFarland.

Hine, D. C. (Ed.). (1993). *Black women in America: An historical encyclopedia*. 2 vols. Brooklyn: Carlson.

Jordon, W. D. (1968). *White over black*. Chapel Hill: University of North Carolina Press.

Kranz, R. C. (1992). *The biographical dictionary of black Americans*. New York: Facts on File.

Redding, S. (1973). *They came in chains: Americans from Africa*. Philadelphia: J. B. Lippincott.

Reich, J. R. (1989). *Colonial America*. Englewood Cliffs, NJ: Prentice-Hall.

Smith, J. C. (Ed.). (1992). *Notable black women*. Detroit: Gale Research.

Stone, C. (1970). *Black political power in America*, rev. ed. New York: Dell.

Thernstrom, S. (Ed.). (1980). *Harvard encyclopedia of American ethnic groups*. Cambridge: Harvard University Press.

The Negro Pitches His Tent
by Roi Ottley

Harlem was yet a vague, faraway place in the minds of most Negroes at the turn of this century—though New York's black population had jumped to sixty thousand, and was desperately fumbling about for elbowroom. External forces led the way finally—race riots.

Mass shifts of the Negro population in New York—as elsewhere— have always been accelerated by racial conflicts. The first great movement followed the Draft Riots on the lower East Side in the midst of the Civil War, when white men rioting against the draft law diverted their attack to Negroes, who were seen as the reason for the conflict. Blacks were dragged through the streets, beaten, hanged from lamp posts, and their homes burned. The riot raged for three days and nights before it was put down by soldiers summoned from the front. Four thousand persons, white and black, were killed and a thousand wounded. Relief had to be given to ten thousand victims. Two million dollars in property was destroyed. Thousands of Negroes, in fear of future violence, moved across the river to Brooklyn and up to midtown Manhattan—a section that came to be called "Black Bohemia"— where Negro life began to take the form in which it is seen today.

Fighting with white men became a part of everyday living in Black Bohemia, as well as in the Tenderloin, Hell's Kitchen, and San Juan Hill areas. The most innocent incident stirred the smoldering ill-feeling between the races. When a Negro, Granville T. Woods, inventor and Edison pioneer, perfected the third rail, and electricity replaced steam on the elevated railway, the white men who lost their jobs as steam engineers attacked Negroes whom they met on the streets because some "damn nigger" devised the innovation. The Negro who drove one of the first automobiles seen in New York—a white man's chauffeur, no doubt—was beaten, the car smashed, and afterward the homes of other Negroes were stoned.

New York's fourth great race riot, which occurred in 1900, marked the beginning of the wholly turbulent career of Harlem. This disorder was touched off in the Tenderloin by the fatal stabbing of a white man, later found to be a policeman in civilian clothes, who had made unwelcome advances to a Negro woman. Within a short time hundreds of white people poured into the streets, attacking every black man, woman, and child. Houses were sacked and burned, and places

Reprinted with permission from *New World A-Coming: Inside Black America* by Roi Ottley. Copyright © 1969 Arno/Ayren Co. Available from Ayren Company Publishers, P.O. Box 958, Salem, NJ 03029.

that employed Negroes were raided. When Negroes appealed to the police, they were cracked over the head with nightsticks, refused refuge at the police stations, and thrown back to the raging mob.

Demands for an investigation met with excuses and delays, while the buck was shuttled gingerly between city officials and police authorities, with the fine hand of Tammany Hall operating behind the scenes. Negroes took steps to force action. A mass meeting was held at Carnegie Hall, the Citizens' Protective League formed, and funds raised to carry on a vigorous fight. An aroused Negro public brought the league's membership up to five thousand within a few weeks. The organization retained as counsel Israel Ludlow, who brought claims against the city for nearly a half-million dollars; one in behalf of the poet, Paul Laurence Dunbar, and another for the well-known pugilist, Joe Walcott. Finally, a police department investigation was held that turned out to be a sham and whitewash.

The air grew tense. Tempers were at trigger-point. Then, the Negro pulpit and press began a strange campaign, terrifying in its implications. "Have your houses made ready," ran a typical warning, "to afford protection against the fury of white mobs. Carry a revolver. Don't get caught again!"

When the storm cleared, the historic exodus of Negroes began to the elegant green pastures of Harlem. Certain strong social factors also contributed to this wholesale movement. The principal Negro neighborhood, Black Bohemia—wedged between the Tenderloin and San Juan Hill sections—embodied the new and more daring phases of Negro life; and it was here that most of the clubs frequented by the sporting and theatrical people were situated. While life in this area was perhaps a little more colorful than in other districts, actually it was no more than a glorified slum. Its population had increased from three hundred families to almost five thousand. This human landslide, contained in three blocks, paid exorbitant rents, and lived in dilapidated, ill-ventilated, overcrowded lodging-houses. Many lived in cold-water flats, washtubs in the kitchen furnishing the only bathing facilities. The Negro, when he worked, averaged five or six dollars a week, and in the local theaters, comedians were singing: "Rufus Rastus Johnson Brown? What you gwine do when de rent comes roun?"

The sidewalks were choked with sweaty, irritable pedestrians. Disease was rampant. Epidemics were frequent, the toll of life enormous: two babies in every seven died under the age of one year. Besides, the area was a notorious red-light district, with bands of negro and white whores roving the streets like hungry wolf packs. To make men follow them, they would snatch their hats and run into dark hallways, where their victims were robbed by accomplices. Harlots, dressed in "unbuttoned Mother Hubbards," stood in front of churches Sunday evenings and openly solicited men as they emerged.

Finally, a delegation of Negro clergymen appealed to Mayor Gaynor, a Tammany Hall politician.

"Don't come down here," he said, "bothering me with any more protests about assignation houses until you can bring concrete evidence of such houses. . . . One of your men must pay a woman for the privilege of having intimate relationships with her, and you must bring a witness that she accepted the money."

Negroes returned to Black Bohemia and attempted to combat these conditions themselves. Under a thirty-day Gospel bombardment, led by the Reverend A. Clayton Powell, Sr., of the Abyssinian Baptist church, the neighborhood's pimps, prostitutes, and keepers of dives and gambling dens were drawn to the revival meetings, confessed conversion, and were baptized. "Many of them remained faithful until death," the Reverend Powell reports, "but the majority went back to wallowing in the mire because they had no place else to go." Without official support, efforts to change conditions seemed futile, so it was only natural the Negroes sought escape to the more desirable areas of the city.

The Harlem they first entered, about 1900, was a cheerful neighborhood of broad drives, brownstone dwellings, and large apartment houses, with the streets carefully laid out in the pattern of a gridiron. The white gentry resided here in suburban aloofness. People spoke of the section as an area of "Brownstone fronts and Saratoga trunks." Lenox Avenue was used for the showing of thoroughbred horses, and polo was actually being played on the Polo Grounds. The main thoroughfare was a favorite track of many wealthy horsemen toward the close of the last century. Here, any afternoon, the finest trotting stock could be seen driven by such men as Commodore Vanderbilt, Colonel Kip Rhinelander, and Russell Sage. A nice cultural touch was contributed by Oscar Hammerstein, who erected the Harlem Opera House.

Odd street names still commemorated some incident or honored some figure in the earlier life of the city and nation, and vividly recalled the days of Dutch and English occupation. The name Jumel Place, for example, commemorated Stephen Jumel, a wealthy wine merchant who died in 1832, and his wife, generally referred to as Madame Jumel. She added to her fame, or notoriety, by marrying Aaron Burr in 1833. The mansion in which the Jumel family lived still stands as a museum high on a hill overlooking the Polo Grounds—marking the northernmost tip of Harlem—and is in the custody of the Daughters of the American Revolution. It was built in

1765 by Colonel Roger Morris, who gave it to his bride, Mary Philipse, on their wedding day. During the Revolutionary War it was the headquarters of George Washington for a time and of General Henry Clinton and his British officers.

If this bit of almost-forgotten lore had little significance to new Negroes, certainly exciting connotation was attached to Hamilton Place, where Alexander Hamilton had built his beautiful mansion, "The Grange," which still stands on the western boundary of Harlem as a historic landmark. Legend has it that the great revolutionary figure, once a slaveholder, was himself a Negro and the father of the Reverend Williams Hamilton, one of the prominent Negroes in New York at the beginning of the nineteenth century. Some historians say that his fatal duel with Aaron Burr was fought over the accusation that he had Negro blood—no doubt an apocryphal tale. What is a fact, however, is that so convinced were Negro historians of Hamilton's Negro ancestry that one industrious scholar made a trip to his birthplace, Nevis, B.W.I., to check the facts.

In Hamilton's day Harlem was a section of elaborate estates and quiet aloofness, and was said to be "a community which knew nothing of sensational issues." Real-estate speculators looked upon this locality as "a far off country" too remote, without adequate transportation to be available for city lots, and no doubt, too aristocratic for republican popularity—the Astors nevertheless shrewdly invested in Harlem land, laying the foundation for one of the great American fortunes. The few scattered and less affluent dwellers used stagecoaches to travel downtown. Hostelries dotted the roads at convenient distances.

There were still some Negro oldtimers who remembered that before the Civil War Cato Alexander, a Negro caterer, operated a popular roadhouse at what was then the southernmost end of Harlem—situated at Beekman Place. His inn had a diminutive sitting-room with a bar, sanded floors, and coarse white walls covered with engravings. It was frequented by those socially prominent people who believed in the marked superiority of colored cooks. Its hospitality was described as "unbiased by any modern abolition doctrines." Mr. Alexander, it appears, was a remarkable host—as other records suggest that his place was actually a station of the Underground Railroad and he an active conductor.

The Third Avenue horse-drawn railroad, erected in 1853, took the place of stagecoaches, but it took an hour and twenty minutes to travel from lower Manhattan to Harlem—provided, travelers complained, no horse balked or fell dead across the tracks. It appears that the Harlem Navigation Line, operating boats on the Hudson River, was the more practical means of conveyance, making the journey from

Harlem to Wall Street in an hour—and without untoward incident.

In those days Harlem figured but little in the city's annals. The one "sensational" issue it had to face was the entrance of the first Negro child—daughter of a cook—into the school causing great consternation among the white parents. Otherwise Harlem still was a quiet country town shut off by a long ride or sail from its "ruling center." Finally, the immigrant Irish moved into the lower section, an area that came to be known as "Goatville," because of the domestic goats of the Irish squatters who lived in shacks in what is now the northern end of Central Park. The erection of the elevated railway in the nineties accelerated Harlem's development, and the area had a swift change in character.

Appropriately enough, it was the black aristocracy which first took up residence in Harlem—Bert Williams, the famous actor, and Harry T. Burleigh, the composer, were in that vanguard. An enterprising realtor, Philip A. Payton, induced the owners of town houses near Fifth Avenue to rent apartments long vacant to Negroes. Neither Payton nor the white property-owners envisioned the direct outcome. The little colony quickly expanded, spread west across Lenox Avenue and into the fashionable St. Nicholas Park area. The white residents became alarmed, mobilized their forces, and attempted to halt the advance.

A new type of racial warfare broke out with methods that were exceedingly subtle, even insidious. The whites formed the Harlem Property Owners' Improvement Association and brought pressure on financial institutions not to loan money to Negroes, and not to renew mortgages on properties which they occupied. Inflammatory handbills were surreptitiously circulated, which held that the Negro's presence depreciated real estate value. "This in itself," shouted the Indicator, a local real estate publication, "is an indication that their presence is undesirable among us. They should not only be disfranchised, but also segregated in some colony on the outskirts of the city, where their transportation and other problems will not inflict injustice and disgust on worthy citizens."

Massing much of their financial resources into a dummy corporation, the Hudson Realty Company, white people bought up properties that housed Negroes and evicted them. Enlisting the prestige and influence of the white community, the campaign to drive blacks from Harlem gained compelling momentum. The metropolitan press rose in all its "yellow" might and denounced the "black invasion." Even the liberal Old World came thundering down the stretch, editorially, and sought by tortuous logic to reconcile its ordinarily progressive policy with bigotry. The Negro was entitled to pitch his tent wherever he wished, it conceded, but wherever he did "calamitous depreciation" resulted.

"The assimilative ideal is premature," was the final judgment of that great organ.

Negroes stood alone. But with wonderful zeal they rapidly took counter steps. Dipping into their savings, in what assumed the proportions of a mass demonstration, they organized companies to buy and lease Harlem property. Negro press and pulpit launched blasting campaigns to stimulate (or to shame) black men into swift action, holding that it was a "race duty" to acquire property, dispossess whites, and rent to members of their own race. Inroads were made and a toehold secured as the profit motive (or avarice) operated to the Negro's advantage. But the largest of these crusading companies, the Afro-American Realty company—ambitiously capitalized at five hundred thousand dollars though never fully subscribed—was soon defunct. Extermination of the blacks seemed final, irrevocable.

No one figured—certainly not Negroes—on one of those curious ironies of capitalistic progress. About this time, the Pennsylvania Railroad Company was seeking a site for a new central terminal, and chose the area upon which one of the oldest Negro congregations in the city, Saint Philip's Protestant Episcopal Church, had its sprawling plant. An offer was made, but Negroes were reluctant to sell, as Harlem looked none too inviting. The company countered by jacking up the bid to the sufficiently persuasive figure of five hundred and forty thousand dollars in cash. This sum was immediately turned to strategic use: a row of thirteen large apartment houses was purchased in the very heart of Harlem—to be exact, 135th Street near Lenox Avenue. The area quickly became the most fashionable in the country for Negroes and was to become one of the most widely known streets in the world.

White people threw up their hands in despair and in panic fled as from a flood, leaving house after house, and block after block, in yawning vacancy. Properties were sold far below assessed values. The Equitable Life Assurance Society, trying desperately to unload its Harlem holdings quickly, sold some eighty brick houses designed by Stanford White, each of which contained fourteen large rooms, two baths, French doors, and hardwood floors, for an average price of eight thousand dollars apiece. Some were bought for as low as six thousand dollars—five hundred dollars down payment and the balance in small yearly installments. Negroes grabbed up these buys, situated in an area that later was to become fashionable as "Strivers' Row," or "Block Beautiful," the strong-hold of Negro society. The handwriting was clearly on the wall as to the future of Harlem.

Yet, with all the hue and cry, barely a thousand Negroes had moved into the neighborhood. They occupied but three or four blocks. Actually, Harlem did not begin to take shape and character as a Negro community until 1910. The growth thereafter was nothing short of phenomenal. The immediate reason was the mass movement from the South. The United States was preparing to enter the first World War and there was a considerable pressure for increased production. Large numbers of white men left industrial pursuits for military service both in the United States Army and in the armies of their native lands, thereby causing an unprecedented shortage of labor.

A mad race began to draw on the South's reservoir of black labor. Agents traveled to Southern cities and towns and, over the protests of whites, literally gathered up consignments of blacks and shipped them North. The Department of Labor aided and encouraged the migration through its employment service. Acting upon the urgent requests of industry, the Pennsylvania and Erie Railroads picked up trainloads of Negroes "on the promise of a long, free ride to the North." James Weldon Johnson saw two thousand persons snatched up in batches of a hundred, tagged, and packed tightly into day coaches, along with their cardboard baggages and lunch boxes. Like cattle, hundreds of others were stuffed into boxcars in the pell-mell journey North.

"Come North, where there is more humanity, some justice and fairness," cried Northern Negro newspapers. Chain letters repeating the same refrain were dispatched hither and yon. Negroes made the pilgrimage to Harlem on foot, by train, and by boat. Their travels were marked with joy and prayers of thanksgiving. Solemn ceremonies were held as they crossed the Mason-Dixon Line. Men stopped their watches to begin a New Day in the North. Amid tears, the migrants sang the old familiar songs of deliverance. They were glad, glad, glad, to escape a pattern of life in which competing groups of the white race wielded ruthless power to preserve racial inequalities. They were fed up with the abuses of the tenant farm system, lack of schooling, and miserable living conditions—legends of urban freedom were alluring.

This migration was in fact a flight from a feudal to a modern way of life—a surging mass movement that was to drive on unabated. Into this exodus to Harlem swept a largely unnoticed element—dark-skinned immigrants. So desperate was the demand for black labor that its pull had reached down into the islands of the Caribbean and even to a certain extent into faraway Africa. Actually, though, Negro immigrants had been settling in New York since the Civil War—no doubt attracted by the conspicuous liberality of the United States in freeing the slaves. Before the turn of the century more than fifty thousand had entered the country. But just prior to the first World War, they came in mighty droves. By 1920 New York's black population had jumped to one hundred and fifty thousand—and conservative estimates put the total Negro ownership of Harlem property at two hundred million dollars.

The developments of the period extended to sterner affairs. For back in the summer of 1908, the country was shocked by a race riot in Springfield, Illinois—the home of Lincoln—in which scores of Negroes were killed or wounded and thousands of others driven from the city. A white woman of wealth and influence, Mary White Ovington, was moved to approach other liberal white people to form "a large body of citizens" to revive the "spirit of (the) abolitionists." In a little room of a New York apartment in 1909, the National Association for the Advancement of Colored People was born, an organization which has ever since been in the struggle for the rights of the Negro.

Oswald Garrison Villard, grandson of William Lloyd Garrison, the abolitionist, and then publisher of the New York *Evening Post*, later issued a call which brought to the movement such white persons as Charles Edward Russell, Jane Addams, John Dewey, Lillian D. Wald, Rabbi Stephen S. Wise, the Reverend John Haynes Holmes, and William Dean Howells; and the Negroes Bishop Alexander Walters, Idea Barnett and the Reverend Francis J. Grimke. A prominent Boston lawyer, Moorfield Storey, was elected president, offices were established at 20 Vesy Street 9 (now at 69 Fifth Avenue), and W. E. B. Du Bois, already an outstanding figure, was called from his professorship at Atlanta University to become director of publicity and research, and later editor of the organization's official organ, *The Crisis*—considered the most effective and best-written propagandist periodical in the United States.

Du Bois, bearded, scholarly, and ornate, was born in Great Barrington, Massachusetts and educated at Harvard and Heidelberg, and had come to the fore in 1903 with his attack on Booker T. Washington's conciliatory philosophy. Du Bois held that "The Negro race, like all races, is going to be saved by exceptional men." This group he called the "Talented Tenth," or educated Negro elite. "The best and most capable of the [Negro] youth," he declared, "must be schooled in the colleges and universities of the land. . . . Not too many collegebred men, but enough to leaven the lump, to inspire the masses, to raise the talented tenth to leadership." He criticized Washington's speech at Atlanta, Georgia, later termed the "Atlanta compromise," because the Southern leader had distinctly asked colored people to give up, at least for the present, political rights, insistence on civil rights, and higher education for Negro youth. Under Du Bois's leadership a conference was held in 1903 at Buffalo, New York, and the Niagara Movement was launched to abolish all distinctions based on race, class, or color. Hampered as it was by a lack of funds, and by membership confined to one race, the movement died an early death.

The influence of Du Bois and his Negro colleagues in the program of the N.A.A.C.P. is evident, for that body adopted a platform essentially that of the Niagara Movement. Broadly, the aims of the association were—and are—to encourage the Negro's intellectual development, economic progress, and social advancement, and to protect his civil rights—a platform declared to be extremely radical at the time. By holding mass meetings, issuing educational pamphlets, and by frequent release of articles to the press, the association sought to bring the Negro's cases before the white public. More practically, it proposed to discover and by legal action redress individual and group injustices, and to make systematic studies of conditions affecting the race.

Much of the early success of the organization was due to Du Bois's almost fanatical belief in his cause and indefatigable work in advancing it. He became a towering figure in Negro life, reserved, removed, essentially the intellectual aesthete. A humorous story is told about Du Bois, concerning his aloofness. After living in New York for some years, he was scheduled to make an address at Harlem's Bethel African Methodist Episcopal Church. On the night of the affair, Du Bois failed to put in an appearance. With hundreds waiting, couriers were sent to find him—only to discover that the Negro leader was lost in Harlem, and couldn't find his way to the meeting place!

Besides Du Bois, the association's program was largely carried on by Dean William Pickens, Phi Beta Kappa Yale graduate and orator; Daisy E. Lampkin, copublisher of the Pittsburgh Courier; and James Weldon Johnson, writer and diplomat. When Du Bois retired in 1933, Roy Wilkins, former newspaperman, succeeded him as editor of *The Crisis*, which by then had gained a national circulation; and when Johnson resigned in 1931, Walter White, teacher and writer, took the helm as executive secretary. . . .

Stimulated by a racial upsurge, the post-war radical movement, and by race idealism, Negroes started to articulate their complaints in writings of protest. What happened in the decade following America's entry into the World War appeared to be a sudden awakening. Actually, it was marked by a renewed, country-wide struggle for the rights of the Negro. A typical development was the formation of the influential National Equal Rights League and the emergence as a national leader of William Monroe Trotter, the zealous editor of the Boston Guardian. He was perhaps one of the most fearless and unselfish public figures, with a consuming passion for the rights of his race. Unable to procure a passport, he went abroad as a ship's waiter to place the American Negro's case before the League of Nations. He later went to Paris and filed several petitions with the World Peace Conference. He was the first Negro elected to the Phi Beta Kappa Fraternity at Harvard University. He died a suicide in 1934.

Where a previous generation had all but given up in despair, the war generation found hope in the preachings of new and militant leaders. This was the beginning of a broad political, social, and eventually cultural development—often referred to as the "Negro Renaissance." It proved to be a movement that was national in sweep with Harlem as its conspicuous center.

Chapter 11

A Final View

To a great extent, immigration to North America reflects the expansion of Europe since 1400, the increase of national states up to the sixteenth century, and profound changes in European societies that caused immigration to increase steadily through the nineteenth century. The United States became the greatest receiver of immigrants because its own lands were relatively underpopulated and a hospitable reception was offered to newcomers of many types. This was not completely an altruistic acceptance because the industries and growers in America were eager to have the cheaper labor that immigrants provided. The uprooting and relocation of peoples that resulted from these movements had a very deep and lasting effect upon the countries the immigrants left and those where they settled.

Pushes and Pulls of Immigration

Among the early American immigrants were many people who wished to make more of their innate talents than their mother countries had permitted them. Immigration was the vehicle that enabled them to fulfill their potentialities in ways they could not have done at home. Also, America had a reputation of affording a place of refuge for the oppressed, especially those who found religious intolerance unbearable. In the nineteenth century, people who had fled religious persecution were joined by political refugees who no longer felt free to profess their political ideas. They sought greater political liberty in the New World.

The conquering of the Atlantic Ocean in the 1840s by steam-powered ships was another factor that encouraged people to move to other countries of their choice. In the seventeenth and eighteenth centuries, ships were constructed of wood and propelled by wind. On those ships the quarters of immigrants were cramped and uncomfortable. The journey was long and arduous, sometimes taking a great toll in lives. Further, it was difficult for most immigrants to get to European seaports from their inland homes. The roads held a certain danger and numerous tolls made travel by the rivers too expensive. Such conditions discouraged emigration through the first few years of the nineteenth century. However, after steam-powered ships were put into operation, a large number of the old wooden ships were converted and used to transport passengers. Concurrently, passenger fares dropped considerably. For example, in the 1850s an individual could get from Ireland to America for as little as ten dollars, and this of course was a contributing factor in the increased volume of Europeans who resettled in America. Steamers increased in size after 1865 and shortened the journey to a week or so and that allowed even more emigrants to make the journey to America. Finally, the expansion of the railroad network across Europe made it easier to travel to port cities, which in turn further stimulated emigration.

Adventurers were usually the first to undertake the journey, followed by artisans. Laborers and poor peasants were next to seek a new land, particularly if some disaster stimulated them to leave. Famines, plagues, and wars are examples of natural disasters that lent impetus for people to seek a new home. Millions of people left the European continent in the 1800s and 1900s, and that was to the mutual benefit of both the immigrants and the countries they left. Overpopulation was relieved; the labor market was eased; and a steady flow of money that comprised part of the earnings of the immigrants was sent to the original homelands to help support dependents left behind.

American history books acknowledge Great Britain's influence on the American heritage. Without a doubt, it is the foremost country that shaped the direction of the United States. But it was not the only country. Equally important is the fact that few books cite in detail the contributions of ethnic groups that do not belong to Anglo-Saxon groups. Although it is an undisputed fact that the United States grew out of the thirteen colonies that revolted against England, those colonies comprised only a small part of the territory that is the

United States. Furthermore, even the original colonies included Dutch and Swedish settlements.

Since becoming an independent nation, the United States has expanded by buying or taking land acknowledged as Indian, French, Spanish, and Mexican territories. Therefore if no additional immigrants had come to the United States since its formation, it still would have been a nation of immigrants. During the period from 1820 to 1930, more than thirty million immigrants came to the United States. This did not include more than twelve million African-American descendants of slaves. The American immigration process occurred in waves, with ethnic groups from various countries ebbing and flowing during certain periods of time. Additionally, the immigrants came from countries that were in different stages of social and industrial development. Thus the various groups had different social and personal aspirations as well as different socioeconomic skills. It is important to note that the early immigrants did not scatter randomly throughout America. To the contrary, they tended to settle in cultural enclaves that often survived for several generations. The immigrants' rate of assimilation into the larger American society through intermarriage, increased income, and residential relocation was in direct relationship to their racial and ethnic identities.

Ethnic group oppression has been debilitating to every ethnic group in America, but its effects on the various groups have been different. The process of immigration in America clearly illustrates how a slight shift in power can establish the dominance of immigrant groups over indigenous people. Once in power, the dominant immigrant group takes necessary steps to restrict the rewards and opportunities of the subordinated groups, thereby institutionalizing its own power (Shibutani & Kwan, 1965). Some groups, mainly Anglo-Christian Caucasians, have been able to culturally assimilate and thus be absorbed into the mainstream. Africans, Hispanics, Indians, Japanese, Chinese, and Jews have received the brunt of long-term individual and group discrimination. But this does not mean that Anglos were not oppressed. Catholics in general and Irish Catholics in particular were, like the other groups cited in earlier chapters, objects of *xenophobia* (hatred of foreigners) and *nativism* (the policy of keeping America pure).

Of all the groups, none changed the ethnic composition of the United States more than Europeans. Although the first wave of immigrants came for political, economic, and religious reasons, the European immigration that occurred between 1860 and 1914 was primarily due to the economic constraints that fettered people in their homelands. The competition of cheap grain from foreign countries during the 1860s and 1900s was especially significant in England, Germany, and Sweden. The introduction of trains and cargo steamers for transporting grain reduced the cost of exporting products and this allowed farmers in the United States and other developing nations to penetrate the northwestern and central European markets. That competition ultimately destroyed the old agrarian economy. Equally important were the crop failures in Europe between 1861 and 1869, which caused famine in many areas. Thousands of European agricultural laborers were forced to emigrate in order to earn their daily bread.

The nonagricultural reasons for emigration include the economic decline in the timber industry caused by the shift from wooden ships to iron ones, and the depression of sales in the European iron and steel industries. Also important was the dislike of the populace for involuntary military service that was instituted in many countries after 1866 when the North German Confederation was brought under Prussian control. There was a sharp decline in British, Irish, German, and Scandinavian immigration to the United States after 1890. The reason for the decline in immigrants from those countries was largely the industrialization there, a declining birthrate, and ample job opportunities in northern and western Europe. In addition, companies in the United States started recruiting most of their unskilled laborers from the southern and eastern areas of Europe where wages were lower. Prior to this time, most of the countries in those regions forbade their citizens to emigrate. However, citizens of Italy were allowed to leave after the unification movement that began in 1850. In 1867, the political reorganization in Austria and Hungary opened the national boundaries to thousands of previously entrapped people. Large areas of the Balkans gained the right to emigrate after the Russo-Turkish War in 1877 when many Slavic peoples—Bulgarians, Serbs, and others—were emancipated from Turkish rule.

In the last decades of the nineteenth century, the peoples of the sprawling empire of the Hapsburgs—Germans, Romanians, Slavs, and Magyars—benefited from the abolition of feudal dues. This allowed the transition of peasants into free proprietors. Along with this change came the right in the 1860s to divide family land. The subdivision of homesteads into tiny pieces resulted in even fewer persons being able to earn a livelihood as farmers. Consequently, large numbers of Czechs, Slovaks, Poles, Romanians, Croats, Serbs, Slovenes, and Magyars immigrated to the United States. It is important to note that not all the immigrants settled in North America. A substantial number of them relocated in South America.

By the latter half of the nineteenth century, Italy could not adequately accommodate its burgeoning population. Southern Italy, in particular, was economically depressed. Large estates were owned by absentee landlords who took almost everything out of the land and put little back to improve or replenish it. And to make matters worse, only a few landlords adopted modern agricultural methods. Therefore, unemployment and poverty became impetus for emigration movements. The final push came with the end of feudalism and the secularization of church land. The unstable Italian economy was not equipped to efficiently handle additional land.

Unlike the movement from Italian and Slavic communities, emigration from Russia was undertaken primarily for religious and political reasons. The first large group to leave Russia for the United States consisted of Russo-German Mennonites who had intentionally relocated in Russia by invitation of Catherine the Great. In 1870, the Mennonites' religious freedom and exemption from military service were revoked. But the largest number of Russian immigrants were Russian Jews, not Mennonites. In 1881, after the assassination of Czar Alexander II, there was a series of anti-Jewish riots. This led to strict enforcement of the regulation and requirement that all Jews must live within circumscribed settlement areas of Austria, Germany, and Romania. In 1882, laws were enacted that restricted Jewish worship, barred them from all civil service jobs, and excluded them from most agriculture and industry professions. Countless Jews were massacred in the pogroms of 1881, 1882, 1891, 1905, and 1906.

While most new immigrants came from Austria, Hungary, Italy, and Russia, substantial numbers also came from other European countries such as Greece, Portugal, Romania, Bulgaria, and Finland. Outside of Europe, they came from China, Japan, the Philippines, Mexico, and Canada. Although the reasons for emigration were basically the same, the immigrants themselves represented a broad spectrum of countries that were substantially different. It was this varied admixture that gave new shapes and colors to the American human mosaic. There were other positive results from the emigration of such large numbers of people. The immigrants formed a huge aggregate of willing laborers who were anxious to work at rates that were beneficial to entrepreneurs. Their willingness to work at reduced rates cut the risks for potential investors, thus making the immigrants an important stimulus to the development of new industries and to the mechanization of existing ones. For example, coal, iron, and copper industries and those that manufactured automobiles, steel, clothing, and shoes all depended on this increasing new supply of workers. Initially, that labor force was used without damaging the circumstances of old immigrant Americans.

The new immigrants worked for low wages but they did not compete with existing groups of farmers and laborers. Instead they pushed them upward on the ladder of job categories. By increasing both production and consumption, new immigrants created additional opportunities for old immigrants to advance to positions of foremen, clerks, executives, and owners. The new immigrant labor force was recruited voluntarily and thus did not depress the status of earlier workers, as had been the case in England and Germany, and it occurred without use of compulsion which had been the case in the Soviet Union.

Urban Conditions

Physical appearance was one of the most revealing characteristics of most low-income immigrant neighborhoods. Neglect and disorder were common. Buildings were in a state of deterioration, highlighting structural neglect and social decline. Slum neighborhoods were over-crowded with buildings, and buildings were overcrowded with people. The population consisted mainly of people who were not welcome in other areas or who could not afford to live elsewhere. The slums had unusually low standards of sanitation, and garbage-strewn streets and alleys were overrun by rats. Infant and maternal mortality rates were high as were unemployment and underemployment. Vice was rampant in the slums, although it was by no means confined to this area. Slums were the habitat of occupationally marginal men and women and the hiding place of fugitives. From the 1800s to about 1960, many urban neighborhoods in the United States underwent considerable population change as wave after wave of ethnic groups moved through them. Specifically, they were scenes of a large exodus of old immigrants concurrent with a larger influx of new ones. Robert Park described this phenomenon as an *ecological invasion*:

> An urban area may witness a series of invasions within a relatively short time. The near west side of Chicago, for example. . . was first settled by Czechs, but when the Jews began to crowd into the area after the Chicago fire in 1877 . . . [the Czechs] forsook the region for more desirable quarters . . . . The Jewish residents had hardly became firmly entrenched when the Italians came. Between 1910 and 1918 more than half the Jewish population . . . moved to other parts of the city. The coming of Negroes provided an added stimulus to the Jewish exodus. (Quoted in Gist & Halbert, 1956, p. 280)

Neighborhoods not only changed in ethnicity but also in socioeconomic characteristics. Generally, they changed from white to black
and from middle class to lower class.

Gifts from the Oppressed

When evaluating the effects of immigration upon American life, we
often consider its many diverse cultural strains. In the great influxes
to the New World were joined huge masses of unskilled laborers who
were exceptional men and women excited by opportunities in America. Other immigrants were skilled people compelled to leave their
homelands because of political or religious persecution. Each group
made significant, varied contributions to American society. In the
previous chapters, we list ways in which the Indians, African slaves,
old immigrants, and new immigrants contributed to the establishment and growth of the United States of America. Let's briefly review
some of their achievements.

Among the first wave of European immigrants, the Irish were probably the most oppressed. Their climb up the social ladder was slow,
laborious, and often painful. Working as unskilled laborers, most of
the early Irish immigrants performed the low-paying, strenuous
domestic construction required on canals, railroads, and factory jobs.
In a few cities, they managed to work up through the ranks and gain
status in skilled and professional jobs. For example, by the 1870s
Irish Americans in Boston accounted for the majority of policemen
and firefighters. In the 1880s, they comprised one-fourth of the
Boston and New York City public school teachers, and there was a
substantial number of Irish-American teachers in Buffalo, Chicago,
and San Francisco. By 1890, there were twice as many Irish Americans in the construction industry as any other ethnic group. James
McNichol and Edward Lafferty were two successful Philadelphia
Irish-American contractors. McNichol helped build the city sewers,
water filtration plant, and subways. Lafferty built the waterworks.

The most prestigious Irish occupations were in the Roman Catholic
Church and in politics. Beginning in the 1840s and continuing
through the 1960s, the Irish were the dominant ethnic group in the
American Catholic Church hierarchy. This tradition is reflected in
Archbishop John Hughes of New York and Frances Cardinal Spell-
man of New York. The Irish dominated local politics in the cities of
Albany, Boston, Buffalo, Chicago, Hoboken, Jersey City, Kansas City
(Missouri), New Orleans, New York, Omaha, Pittsburgh, St. Paul, St.
Louis, and San Francisco. John F. Kennedy was the first Catholic to
be president of the United States.

The Germans, the largest of all immigrant ethnic groups, achieved high social status more quickly than the Irish. There were two major reasons for this difference in acceptance. German immigrants usually were more affluent and more educated. In the 1860s, 1870s, and 1880s, German Americans comprised the bulk of America's skilled workers. They were highly represented as bookbinders, cabinet makers, and furniture makers. Most notable was their skill in making beer. By the early twentieth century, German Americans had achieved a monopoly in brewing beer. St. Louis and Milwaukee became the beer centers of America, largely because of the Anheuser-Busch, Miller, Pabst, and Schlitz families. In a related area, Paul Kruge developed vineyards in California. The inventiveness of German Americans can be seen in the success of George Westinghouse, Charles Steinmetz, and John Roebling. Westinghouse invented the air brakes for trains, and founded the Westinghouse Corporation. Steinmetz helped found the General Electric Company. Roebling, an expert on steel cables, died while supervising the construction of the Brooklyn Bridge. German Americans also excelled in music. In addition to gaining fame as singers and mastering musical instruments, they were well known as piano makers.

Like the Germans, the Swedes advanced quickly in America. Being successful farmers, they achieved rapid sociomobility in the New World. Beginning initially in rural areas in the upper Midwest, they branched out and became skilled workers in adjacent cities such as Chicago and Minneapolis. One of the foremost examples of twentieth-century success is Rudolph Peterson, who became president of the Bank of America in 1961. In the early twentieth century, only British Americans held more of America's skilled jobs than Swedish Americans. The Norwegian immigration patterns were similar to those of the Swedes, but in addition to being farmers and farm laborers, they were employed as sailors. They became successful in business, skilled trades, and the professions requiring special training or education. Both Norwegians and Swedes learned to excel in politics. In 1892, Knute Nelson, a Norwegian American, was elected governor of Minnesota. This was the beginning of hundreds of Norwegian-American top-level political successes in Minnesota, Wisconsin, and adjacent states.

Slavic ethnic immigrants began their American job experiences largely as unskilled industrial workers and the second and third generations did not improve their socioeconomic position as fast as western European immigrants. Nineteenth century U.S. working-class neighborhoods had a disproportionate number of Russians, Poles, and Hungarians. Like the Irish who preceded them, they were prudent spenders who invested in their homes, schools, and churches. It was not until the late twentieth century that most Slavs in the United States achieved a middle-income economic level. In 1968, Edmund Muskie of Maine became the first Polish American to run for vice president of the United States. Also in 1968, Spiro Agnew became the first Greek-American vice president of the United States.

Most early Italian immigrants were garment workers in New York City, laborers or miners in Pennsylvania, and other kinds of unskilled and semi-skilled workers in big cities. Upward social mobility was slow for them. Gradually they advanced up the socioeconomic ladder. While most nineteenth century Italian immigrants lived in cities, a few of them became successful truck farmers on the East Coast and West Coast. Of special note were the California Italian wineries, a prime example being the Gallo Brothers. A. P. Giannini, founder of the Bank of America, was but one of several Italian-American industrialists. It is in politics, however, that Italians have had the greatest impact on local, state, and national affairs. In 1946, for example, John Pastore of Rhode Island became the first Italian American elected to the U.S. Senate. Earlier, Fiorello LaGuardia had won elections to the U.S. House of Representatives; later he became mayor of New York City. In 1949, Carmine Desapio became leader of New York's Tammany Hall. In 1974, Meade Esposito and Joseph Margiata were two of the most powerful political leaders in New York. Italian-American leadership in private industry was exemplified in the early 1970s when Lee Iacocca was president of the Ford Motor Company and John Ricardo was president of the Chrysler Corporation. Iacocca later became president of Chrysler.

Of all the European immigrants who came to the United States in the nineteenth century, no group was subjected to as much discrimination and concurrently achieved as much economic success as the Jews. Most of the Sephardic Jews who came during the colonial period had achieved middle-class status by 1880. Years later, the Lehman family and the Seligman family were prominent in finance and banking, while Benjamin Altman and Adam Gimbel established large department stores. By the 1970s, the family income and educational levels of the American Jews were higher that any other ethnic group. Two Russian-born Jews, David Sarnoff and William Paley, founded the Radio Corporation of America (RCA) and Columbia Broadcasting System (CBS), respectively. In the long list of prominent Jews, there is Arthur Goldberg, former U.S. Supreme Court justice and ambassador to the United Nations; writers Saul Bellow and Norman Mailer; Jonas Salk, discoverer of the polio vaccine; violinist Yehudi Menuhin; musical conductor Leonard Bernstein; and Albert Einstein who developed the theory of relativity and contributed to the discipline of quantum physics.

None of the newcomers, except black Africans, were discriminated against as much as Asians. After Chinese were forced out of the mines and were no longer needed to build railroads and raise crops in California, they gravitated to cities in order to find jobs. Initially, they worked as domestics, especially in family-owned laundries, and as cooks and waiters in restaurants. In fact, Chinese restaurants were first established in mining camps along the railroads so the Chinese could prepare their own food. *Chop suey* and *chow mein*, two popular Chinese restaurant items, originated in the United States. It was not until after World War II that technical and professional jobs opened up to a large number of Chinese Americans. And it was in the areas of mathematics and science that Chinese Americans began to excel, including Chen Ning Yang and Tsung-dao Lee who won Nobel Prizes in physics in 1957.

We should not forget the horrendous treatment of Japanese Americans during World War II. They were incarcerated, not because of their deeds but instead because of their ethnic identity. No other group of Americans has been treated in this manner. Other groups can claim individual political prisoners, but the entire Japanese American population was considered a military risk. Yet the heroism of the *Nisei* combat troops is overshadowed only by the educational success of the *Sansei*, the third-generation Japanese Americans. Thus the United States owes much to the *Issei* who dared migrate to the New World.

There were striking similarities between Jewish and Japanese immigrants. They both had histories of enterprise and emphasis on intellectual achievement and, relatedly, they both were subjected to greater discrimination as they achieved economic and educational successes. For example, when Japanese immigrants acquired a large amount of land in California's San Joaquin Valley in 1913, white residents tried to restrict their landownership. Similar restrictions were aimed at Jewish businessmen. Also like the Jews, the Asian immigrants did not seek full assimilation into white American cultures. Instead, they perpetuated their own native customs and, to a lesser extent, their languages. Jews and Asian Americans were among the foremost spokespersons for cultural pluralism. The cultural pluralism concept was earlier developed by Horace Kallen, himself a Polish immigrant philosopher (Bennett, 1986).

African Americans are a cultural enigma. They have been subjected to the most abject conditions of racial segregation, achieved some of the most outstanding cultural feats, and yet have consistently lagged behind most ethnic groups in income, education, and social acceptance. African Americans helped build roads, canals, and railroads. They replaced Irish immigrants as America's largest group of unskilled workers and domestic servants. They worked in the factories and coal mines alongside the Slavs. Ecologically, they replaced other ethnic groups as slum dwellers when the neighborhood patterns of "white flight" and "black succession" became a recurrent housing pattern in the early twentieth century. As other ethnic groups climbed the social ladder, African Americans seemed frozen at the lower rungs. Only recently have American students been given an opportunity to become familiar with the cultural contributions of African Americans. In some schools, Crispus Attucks is becoming as well known as Paul Revere; and the writing of Langston Hughes, Gwendolyn Brooks, and Ralph Ellison stand beside those of Charles Dickens, Jane Austen, and Jack London. But not even the pistonlike fists of Joe Louis and the Olympic feats of Jessie Owens nor the profoundly moving speeches of Martin Luther King Jr. were able to lift the masses of African Americans from second-class citizenship.

Very little is reflected in textbooks or historical monuments that does justice to the cultures and histories of the diverse peoples called American Indians. Even less has been written about the suffering and degradation that the original occupants of the land endured. History books of the nineteenth and early twentieth centuries praised the heroism of white settlers in the development of the North American continent, and cheered without critical analysis the subduing of "hostile savages." Only recently has the creativity of Native Americans been acknowledged. In the arts, Nampeyo and Maria Montoya Martinez were "discovered" by early twentieth-century white art critics who praised the women as two of the world's greatest potters. There have been scores of other such discoveries since then. We can only speculate about what would have happened to Indians if in fact they had not been so unsuitable as slaves for the white colonists.

The differences among immigrant groups can be partially attributed to their work assignments and places of entry into the job market. Both the industry locations and the positions initially acquired by most members of an ethnic group strongly influence subsequent ethnic group employment trends. Groups that are most recent in industries with low-paying jobs requiring little education have the slowest rate of social advancement. Industries that facilitate workers' advancement also help them push up the social ladder more quickly than those that offer few opportunities for advancement. In the 1800s and early 1900s, several industries were dominated by single ethnic groups such as Chinese in laundries, Irish in construction, Slavs in steel, and Jews in garment manufacturing.

The long lists of immigrants who made important contributions to the development of America only tell part of the story. For every individual singled out for an outstanding contribution, there have been thousands of lesser-known persons who also made significant contributions. Many writers believe that the greatest contribution those people made was to survive and pass on to their children and friends a part of their own native cultural heritage. But it is not easy to maintain cultural identity. For example, the descendants of the English, Scots, Dutch, Scandinavian, and German immigrants who came to America in the eighteenth and nineteenth centuries have assimilated to such a degree that it is difficult, if not impossible, to make distinctions between group boundaries. But this fact does not diminish the importance of the early contributions of those groups.

The 103rd Congress is symbolic of the progress racial and ethnic minorities are making. Counting nonvoting delegates there were sixty-eight African Americans, Hispanics, Asians, and Native Americans— including Lucille Roybal-Allard, the first Mexican-American woman in Congress; Ben Nighthorse Campbell, the first Native American in the Senate since 1932; Jay Kim, the first Korean American in Congress; Carol Moseley Braun, the first African-American woman in the Senate; and Lydia Velasquez, the first Puerto Rican woman in the House of Representatives. Also, five southern states elected African-American representatives for the first time in the twentieth century.

Beyond the Melting Pot

Built on the foundation of the original immigrants' settlement or colonies, the typical immigrant ethnic group experience in America can be characterized as follows: Within each ethnic group there developed a network of formal organizations and informal social relationships that allowed and encouraged its members to remain within the ethnic group colony for most of their primary relationships. Eventually, the ethnic group enclave declined in scope and significance as succeeding generations learned English, attended public schools, intermarried, changed from extended families to nuclear families, and dispersed throughout the country. But this does not mean that the resulting outcome is ethnic-neutral people. The United States is an English-oriented country in which a small degree of non-Anglo-Saxon identity is allowed to be expressed and transmitted.

The kind of identity sought in the United States has varied from time to time, as in the case of the seventeenth-century Protestants who fled predominantly Catholic countries, or the Jews who departed nineteenth century Europe. It was the freedom to practice religion that they sought. Or as in the case of the ethnic minority immigrants from parts of Russia and the Austro-Hungarian empire of the Hapsburgs, it was the right to have one's language recognized as an official medium of expression, and the right to have it taught in parochial schools. Throughout the years, each ethnic minority group has sought majority group toleration of one or more of its cultural themes, and each has resisted coerced absorption by the dominant group. The first three generations of European and Asian ethnic groups who immigrated to the United States began their citizenship as pluralistic minorities. Almost all of those ethnic groups were absorbed into the English society, but now a growing number of their descendants are trying to recover and preserve their lost heritage.

Some attention should be given to Arab immigrants who comprise more than one million American immigrants. More than half of them are assimilated third- and fourth-generation descendants of Arabs who migrated to the United States between 1875 and 1948 (Mehdi, 1978). Almost all of the original Arab immigrants were Christians from the Ottoman Empire. Most of them called themselves Syrians, since the Republic of Lebanon was not established until 1946. The Arabs who experienced the most problems were Muslims, however. Muslims who lived and worked in non-Muslim communities had great difficulty exercising their religious rituals. For many of them, it was not possible to observe the Sabbath on Friday, pray five times a day, and fast during the sunlight hours during the holy month of Ramadan. Protestant and Catholic employers in particular would not accommodate the "heathen" customs. Despite being strangers in the New World, the literary contributions of Syrian writers Khalil Gibran, William Blatty, and Vance Bourjaily have been significant.

The situation is less fluid for the nation's most recent immigrants—comprised largely of Vietnamese, Cubans, and Haitians. As new groups of immigrants come to the United States and as available jobs decrease, tolerance tends to give way to intolerance; nonviolence frequently gives way to violence. And the newest immigrants, especially the non-European ones, increasingly become the objects of prejudice and discrimination. Furthermore, as the new immigrants concentrate in specific areas and form urban clusters or colonies, they become highly visible and in some cities very disliked by people of other ethnic groups with whom they compete for jobs, education, and social status. Each new immigrant group not only has its own language or dialect which tends to create a communication barrier, but it also has its own social and religious institutions which usually perpetuate innergroup solidarity and intergroup hostility.

Nations Within

When the waves of immigration reached full peak in the early 1900s, culminating in one million immigrants a year, some writers began to question whether the United States should or could be a melting pot. At that time, the newcomers came mainly from southern Europe and eastern Europe as well as the eastern Mediterranean area. The English, Germans, Irish, and Scandinavians who came before them had already assimilated and obviously for them the ethnic melting pot worked effectively. However, the later immigrants— Italians, Poles, Slavs, Portuguese, Greeks, and some others—did not assimilate rapidly because the melting pot had cooled. But not even the old immigrants were content to assimilate completely.

Many Germans and some Irish came to America with the intention of creating their own ethnic nation within the New World. For instance, in the 1830s, a large number of German liberals who aspired to create a new, free Germany in America settled in Missouri and southern Illinois. In the 1840s, German noblemen bought large tracts of land in Texas and sent thousands of German settlers to create a German nation there. A few years later, a large number of Germans immigrated to Wisconsin. They too conspired to create a German nation. By the third and fourth generation, however, most German Americans spoke English and their religious sermons were delivered in English. In 1818, Irish associations in New York and Philadelphia petitioned Congress for a large tract of land on which to relocate poverty-stricken Irish from the eastern cities. The denial by Congress of the petition settled once and for all the issue of European immigrants recreating of their homeland in the United States.

Though the Swedes and Norwegians showed little outward interest in setting up their own states, for a short while that is precisely what they did. They lived in isolated rural areas where they spoke their native language, established their own churches and schools, and published newspapers and books written in their native languages. German Americans established fewer homogeneous colonies because they were more widely distributed geographically and occupationally than were the Swedes and Norwegians. Irish Americans were concentrated in cities which made isolated ethnic group existence impossible. Indeed, they were even more dispersed occupationally than the Germans.

As long as ethnic groups lived in remote isolated areas, they could maintain some semblance of being ethnic nations within America. But the growth in cities brought about the decline of farming populations and ethnic colonies. For the immigrants who settled in cities, a shorter time was required to discard their native language and culture. But it is too simplistic to think of any ethnic group as melting away without leaving a trace of its cultural heritage. All ethnic groups have infused portions of their cultures into the tapestry of American history.

The early eastern European immigrants were a very disparate mixture of peoples. They came from nations that were trying to become states—Poland, Czechoslovakia, Lithuania, and Yugoslavia; and from states trying to become nations—Italy, Turkey, and Greece—as well as areas outside the Western concept of either state or nation. All of them included people such as Jews who did not easily fit into any of these categories. But the urbanization of the European immigrants created a common denominator of experience: competition for jobs. The situation becomes even more complicated when attempting to analyze the cultural identities of non-European ethnic minority groups.

The distinctive cultures of the various non-European minority groups were in stark contrast to European cultures. Being a minority had serious obstacles to assimilation and, more importantly, to achieving equal opportunities. Nonwhite immigrant groups in the United States occupied specific low-status niches in the economy which resulted in similarities among their members in such things as occupations, standard of living, level of education, place of residence, access to political power, and quality of health care. Likenesses *within* groups and differences *outside* of groups facilitated the formation of stereotypes and prejudices that inhibited the full appreciation of the many contributions all groups made to the development of the United States. Cognizant of this condition, Catholic, Jewish, and Protestant representatives issued in 1943 a Declaration of World Peace that set forth the rights of minorities. In essence, they stated that national governments and organizations must respect and guarantee the rights of ethnic, religious, and cultural minorities to economic and cultural development and political equality.

As noted earlier, immigrants who held highly esteemed occupations—such as lawyers, artists, engineers, scientists, and physicians—became Americanized much faster than those who held less esteemed positions such as unskilled laborers, farm workers, coal miners, and stock clerks. But even in this instance there were pro-European biases and stereotypes. For example, French chefs, Italian opera singers, Polish teachers, German conductors, and Russian scientists were more highly recruited than Africans, Haitians, or Mexicans having the same skills. Thus the opportunities to Americanize were not equal. Racial and quasi-racial groups—including American

Indians, Mexican Americans, African Americans, and Puerto Ricans—were not nearly as readily absorbed as various Caucasian ethnic groups.

More than two hundred thousand Vietnamese have immigrated to the United States since the defeat of the Saigon government in 1975. Beginning in 1979, thousands of boat people fled their Southeast Asian countries in decrepit boats and were denied asylum in neighboring countries and came to America. In the 1980s and early 1990s, large numbers of Cubans and Haitians joined the long list of people who came to the United States to gain political and economic relief. As the new immigrants find their way into American communities, incidents of immigrant-bashing tend to increase. While not as numerous or intense as the nativism and xenophobic bigotry of the 1890s and the period shortly after World War I, racial and ethnic group hatred claims heavy casualties. The majority of the new immigrants are nonwhite peoples from Asia, Latin America, and the Caribbean countries. Most of the abuses are verbal; some are physical attacks— a few of them are fatal. For example, two skinheads in Houston stomped to death a Vietnamese boy, Hung Truong, in 1990. The victim cried out before dying: "God forgive me for coming to this country. I'm so sorry."

For most people of color, the melting pot has been—and continues to be—an unreachable mirage. This does not in any way detract from the significance of any group's contributions to the United States. It merely highlights the necessity for placing more emphasis on equalizing opportunities. Throughout this book, ethnic group immigration histories and examples of cultural contributions support the contention that each group is an integral part of a whole nation. Although Americans of Indian, Mexican, Chinese, African, and other Third World ethnic groups have contributed to American life, they frequently are treated like second-class citizens. Yet, the peoples of the United States are bound together not as separate ethnic groups but as members of different ethnic groups united in spirit and behavior and locked into a common destiny.

Trapped in an egocentric society, many ethnic minority immigrants have adapted and typically become the people Erich Fromm (1956) called "marketers." Those who fit this category derive their self-esteem from their value as commodities or investments—their identity is found in their jobs ("I am what I do"). The responsibility of securing their freedom is too frightening for them, and they live by conforming to social pressures and seeking approval from majority group persons. Despite economic or educational success, there is an overwhelming sense of emptiness among them. Feeling impotent within bureaucratic organizations, they ultimately turn into passive consumers. For example, countless African Americans have become black Anglo-Saxons in values and lifestyles. In most instances, increased urbanization has meant a decline in ethnic group solidarity, a decline in a sense of ethnic community, and resignation to being second-class citizens. It was against these conditions that Martin Luther King Jr., Bayard Rustin, Ralph Abernathy, Roy Wilkins, Whitney Young Jr., Jesse Jackson, Floyd McKissick, Elijah Muhammad, Malcolm X, Shirley Chisholm, Stokely Carmichael, Dick Gregory, and James Meredith—to mention a few black American civil rights leaders—sought to rally the masses of black people to fight.

The situation of resignation and apathy was equally challenging for Wendell Chino, a member of the Mescalero Apache tribe of New Mexico, who was the first president of the National Congress of American Indians—the first all-Indian nationwide organization; Dan Kachongeva, a member of the Ponca tribe of Southern Arizona, who promoted reservation economic and social programs; and Clyde Warrior, a member of the Ponca tribe in Oklahoma, who was one of the most militant "young warriors." Similarly, the strategies of Mexican-American or Chicano leaders, like other ethnic minority leaders, has ranged from nonviolence to violence. Caésar Chávez organized the 1965 grape pickers strike and founded the United Farm Worker's Organizing Committee. Reies López Tijerina, "King Tiger," founder of the Alianza Federal de Mercedes (Federal Alliance of the Free City States), sought to reclaim millions of acres of communally owned land in northern New Mexico and southern Colorado allegedly taken from Spanish Americans by the U.S. government through trickery in violation of the Treaty of Guadalupe Hildalgo. Rudolfo "Corky" Gonzáles founded the Crusade for Justice to help Mexican Americans reclaim their communities.

All of the ethnic groups discussed in this book helped create the United States of America. It is evident from the data presented in earlier chapters that America has meant different things to the various peoples who came or were brought here. To some people America has been an *alien port* harboring alien people—culturally possessed and dispossessed, culturally advantaged and disadvantaged, culturally different. Many of these aliens still remain in their port of disembarkation trying to get enough money to move elsewhere. Unfortunately, most of them will earn just enough to migrate to communities that frequently are worse. To other immigrants America is a *plantation* administered by paternalistic—and often sadistic landowners. Discipline is strict and rebels are beaten and, in numerous instances, killed. To most immigrants the United States is a *safe haven*, the place of the most opportunities in the world.

To all immigrants, America has at some time been a *foreign country* in which established residents have viewed them as "uncivilized" or "lower-class heathens" doomed to a social hell as poor white trash, uppity blacks, drunken Indians, lazy Spanish-speaking people, and so forth. It is a miracle the nation has not been torn asunder. The fragile coalition of peoples has yet to create a society where all citizens can live in dignity, eat a wholesome diet, sleep in a safe shelter, live in economic and social freedom, and finally die a timely death unhurried by racism or bigotry. Fortunately, each generation tends to move closer to the American dream. And their stories must be told.

REFERENCES

Bennett, C. E. (1986). *Comprehensive multicultural education*. Boston: Allyn & Bacon.

Fromm, E. (1956). *The art of loving*. New York: Harper.

Gist, N. P., & Halbert, L. A. (1956). *Urban society*. New York: Thomas Y. Crowell.

Mehdi, B. T. (Ed.) (1978). *The Arabs in America, 1492–1977: A chronology and fact book*. Dobbs Ferry, NY: Oceana.

Shibutani, T., & Kwan, K. M. (1965). *Ethnic stratification: A comparative approach*. New York: Macmillan.

Index

Wounded Knee massacre, 32–33, 37
Wovoka (Paiute tribe member), 36–37
Wright, Frank Lloyd (architect), 56

Xenophobia, 179–80, 286

Yale, Elihu (colonist), 56
Yale University, 52, 56
Yankovic, Frank (musician), 124
Ysaye, Eugens (violinist), 100
Yugoslavia, 111, 112, 120–21, 139, 274, 285. *See also* Croats; Serbs; Slovenes

Zabriskie, Albert (colonist), 117
Zaharias, Mildred "Babe" Didrikson (athlete), 86
Zahrzewska, Maria (physician), 117
Zapata, Carmen (actress and producer), 216–17
Zavalishin, Dimitri, 114–15
Zivich, Fritzie (athlete), 123
Zoot suit riots, in Los Angeles, 214
Zorina, Vera (actress), 86
Zukor, Adolph (film producer), 142
Zwinglians, 89